W9-AAG-681

# Foundations of Generative Syntax

*Current Studies in Linguistics*
Samuel Jay Keyser, general editor

1. *A Reader on the Sanskrit Grammarians,* J. F. Staal, editor
2. *Semantic Interpretation in Generative Grammar,* Ray Jackendoff
3. *The Structure of the Japanese Language,* Susumu Kuno
4. *Speech Sounds and Features,* Gunnar Fant
5. *On Raising: One Rule of English Grammar and Its Theoretical Implications,* Paul M. Postal
6. *French Syntax: The Transformational Cycle,* Richard S. Kayne
7. *Pānini as a Variationist,* Paul Kiparsky, S. D. Joshi, editor
8. *Semantics and Cognition,* Ray Jackendoff
9. *Modularity in Syntax: A Study of Japanese and English,* Ann Kathleen Farmer
10. *Phonology and Syntax: The Relation between Sound and Structure,* Elisabeth O. Selkirk
11. *The Grammatical Basis of Linguistic Performance: Language Use and Acquisition,* Robert C. Berwick and Amy S. Weinberg
12. *Introduction to the Theory of Grammar,* Henk van Riemsdijk and Edwin Williams
13. *Word and Sentence Prosody in Serbocroation,* Ilse Lehiste and Pavle Ivic
14. *The Representation of (In)definiteness,* Eric J. Reuland and Alice G. B. ter Meulen, editors
15. *An Essay in Stress,* Morris Halle and Jean-Roger Vergnaud
16. *Language and Problems of Knowledge: The Managua Lectures,* Noam Chomsky
17. *A Course in CB Syntax: Lectures on Binding and Empty Catagories,* Howard Lasnik and Juan Uriagereka
18. *Semantic Structures,* Ray Jackendoff
19. *Events in the Semantics of English: A Study in Subatomic Semantics,* Terence Parsons
20. *Principles and Parameters in Comparative Grammar,* Robert Freidin, editor
21. *Foundations of Generative Syntax,* Robert Freidin

# Foundations of Generative Syntax

Robert Freidin

The MIT Press
Cambridge, Massachusetts
London, England

© 1992 Massachusetts Institute of Technology

All rights reserved. No part of this book may be reproduced in any form or by any electronic or mechanical means (including photocopying, recording, or information storage and retrieval) without permission in writing from the publisher.

This book was typeset by The MIT Press in New Baskerville using Aldus PageMaker 4.01. It was printed and bound in the United States of America

Library of Congress Cataloging-in-Publication Data

Freidin, Robert.
Foundations of generative syntax / Robert Freidin.
p. cm. — (Current studies in linguistics series ; 21)
Includes bibliographical references (p. ) and index.
ISBN 0-262-06144-9
1. Grammar, Comparative and general—Syntax. 2. Generative grammar. I. Title. II. Series.
p291.F74 1992
415—dc20 91-29723
CIP

If you have built castles in the air, your work need not be lost; that is where they should be. Now put foundations under them.

H. D. Thoreau, *Walden*

Concepts which have proved useful for ordinary things easily assume so great an authority over us, that we forget their terrestrial origin and accept them as unalterable facts. They then become labelled as "conceptual necessities, "*a priori* situations," etc. The road of scientific progress is frequently blocked for long periods by such errors. It is therefore not just an idle game to exercise our ability to analyze familiar concepts, and to demonstrate the conditions on which their justification and usefulness depend, and the way in which these developed, little by little, from the data of experience. In this way they are deprived of their excessive authority. Concepts which cannot be shown to be valid are removed. Those which had not been coordinated with the accepted order of things with sufficient care are corrected, or they are replaced by new concepts when a new system is produced which, for some reason or other, seems preferable.

A. Einstein, "Ernst Mach" [*cited in The Born-Einstein Letters*]

# Contents

# Acknowledgments

The idea for this text was conceived while I was teaching an introductory syntax class at Brown University in the fall of 1979, following three years of postdoctoral research at MIT. I am indebted to my students at Brown for their enthusiasm for the project in its initial stages and to my students at McGill, Cornell, and Princeton for their interest in and encouragement for the project as it evolved. In particular, I thank my former students Christopher Tancredi and Apoorva Muralidhara for their written commentary on some of the earlier drafts. I also thank my colleages Noam Chomsky, Lori J. Davis, Phil Johnson-Laird, James McCawley, Stephen Neale, Carlos Otero, Yael Ravin, Paul Roberge, Scott Soames, Rex Sprouse, and Edwin Williams for their comments on various portions of the manuscript at various stages. I am indebted to Howard Lasnik, Carlos Otero, Carlos Quicoli, Henk van Reimsdijk, Jean-Roger Vergnaud, and Edwin Williams for their strong support for this project.

To Howard Lasnik I am especially indebted for extensive commentary on the final drafts of the manuscript. This book has benefited immeasurably from his pedagogical wisdom as well as his keen analytical insight and broad knowledge of linguistic theory.

And finally, I would like to thank Anne Mark, whose thoughtful copyediting has enhanced the quality of this book, and also Lorrie LeJeune and Mike Beach, who transformed my computer files into the printed pages that follow.

# Foundations of Generative Syntax

# Introduction

The purpose of this text is to bridge the gap between introductory lectures and the frontiers of research in syntax. There are basically two solutions to this central problem in teaching syntax today. One is to take a historical approach. If we teach students the history of the field, then they begin at the beginning, which is supposedly simple and easy, and when they are done, they know the current theory as well as what led up to it. Alternatively, we can start at the other end—that is, from the frontiers of research. To solve the central problem from this perspective, we must provide a rational reconstruction of the current theory of grammar in terms of the basic concepts on which it is built. The historical sequence A to X that linguists have traveled as syntactic theory has evolved is not necessarily a logical sequence or even the shortest distance between the two theoretical points. But having arrived at our current perspective X, we can look back and reconstruct a logical, coherent, and economical path to this perspective that emphasizes both the connections between the steps along the way (often in a manner that had not been apparent during the actual historical development) and the basic concepts that underlie this reconstruction. It is this second approach that informs the following discussion of syntactic theory.

As a rational reconstruction of the theory of generative syntax, this book elucidates the basic concepts of syntax that serve as the foundations for current syntactic theory and shows how these concepts are used to address the fundamental questions of syntactic analysis (e.g., concerning the relationship between lexical and phrasal categories, the restricted distribution of certain types of lexical item, and levels of syntactic representation). As an explication of the "foundations" of generative syntactic theory, the book begins with relatively simple concepts concerning the phrase structure analysis of languages and progresses naturally to more complicated concepts such as those involved in binding theory and the analysis of empty categories.

The development of material in this book adheres to the rather standard assumption within generative grammar that the study of linguistic structure centrally involves the study of formal grammar. To put it in a slightly different form: formal grammar is a way of thinking about language. This view is forcefully expressed in the first paragraph of Chomsky's preface to *Syntactic Structures* (repeated here—excluding the last two sentences):

> This study deals with syntactic structure both in the broad sense (as opposed to semantics) and the narrow sense (as opposed to phonemics and morphology). It forms part of an attempt to construct a formalized general theory of linguistic structure and to explore the foundations of such a theory. The search for rigorous formulation in linguistics has a much more serious motivation than mere concern for logical niceties or the desire to purify well-established methods of linguistic analysis. Precisely constructed models for linguistic structure can play an important role, both negative and positive, in the process of discovery itself. By pushing a precise but inadequate formulation to an unacceptable conclusion, we can often expose the exact source of this inadequacy and, consequently, gain a deeper understanding of the linguistic data. More positively, a formalized theory may automatically provide solutions for many problems other than those for which it was explicitly designed. Obscure and intuition-bound notions can neither lead to absurd conclusions nor provide new and correct ones, and hence they fail to be useful in two important respects. I think that some of those linguists who have questioned the value of precise and technical development of linguistic theory may have failed to recognize the productive potential in the method of rigorously stating a proposed theory and applying it strictly to linguistic material with no attempt to avoid unacceptable conclusions by ad hoc adjustments or loose formulation.

In this book we will be concerned with rigorous formulations of both grammatical rules and the syntactic representations they generate.

In order to ground this rational reconstruction of generative syntactic theory in the most general terms, chapter 1 begins by considering how syntax constitutes in part the study of knowledge of language. This involves demonstrating how a speaker's knowledge can be modeled in terms of phrase structure rules and representations. A second section works out some of the ramifications of the psychological interpretation of grammar that is implicit in the first section. The remaining chapters explicate the model of grammar in detail. They explore the basic concepts of grammar that are incorporated in the mechanisms and principles of grammar and how these concepts apply to the formal analysis of natural language.

Chapters 2 through 8 are organized as follows. Chapter 2 begins with phrase structure analysis and the theory of phrase structure and concludes with a transformational analysis of noun phrases and some constraints on the output of transformational rules. The material covered is purposely limited to phrases with lexical heads (e.g., VP and NP), and thus excluding clauses. The phrase structure of clauses is covered in the remaining chapters. In chapter 3 some aspects of sentential structure are investigated in terms of *wh*-questions (sentences containing interrogative pronouns like *who*). The analysis of *wh*-questions is also used to introduce movement transformations and conditions on the boundedness of such movements. Chapter 4 extends the analysis of sentential structure in terms of the English auxiliary verb system. This chapter introduces several distinct transformations, thereby facilitating an investigation of the interaction of transformational rules. As in chapter 3, it is demonstrated that the behavior of transformational rules can be determined almost exclusively in terms of conditions on syntactic representations (filters), rather than conditions on the operation of the rules themselves. Chapter 5 expands the filtering approach to the analysis of infinitival sentential forms in which the notions of Case and government play a central role. The analyses of infinitivals in chapter 5 and of *wh*-questions in chapter 3 make crucial use of the notion empty category. Chapter 6 explores further conditions on constructions containing empty categories—involving the concept of government, predicate-argument relations, and the binding of empty categories to antecedents. Chapter 7 continues the investigation of binding phenomena. This chapter addresses the limited distribution of lexical anaphors (nouns that must be bound to an antecedent within the sentence in which they occur) in terms of conditions on proper binding. The binding relation, which is expressed as coindexing between an anaphor and its antecedent, also holds between a pronoun and an antecedent. Again there are principled limitations on the distribution of bound pronouns that can be handled by extending the binding theory to pronoun binding. Chapter 8 further extends the binding-theoretic analysis to cover coindexing between two nonanaphoric, nonpronominal noun phrases (referred to as "R-expressions") and shows how this analysis varies cross-linguistically. Having established a basic version of binding theory for three lexical NP-types (anaphors, pronouns, and R-expressions), this final chapter proceeds to more complicated issues—including the application of binding theory at various levels of syntactic representation and the extension of binding theory to empty categories.

These chapters develop a version of the Principles-and-Parameters theory of generative syntax (also called Government-Binding Theory (GB)), the most influential and most widely studied of the current syntactic theories under investigation (including Generalized Phrase Structure Grammar, Lexical-Functional Grammar, and Relational Grammar).*

Given the formal nature of much of the material presented here, the reader is assumed to have an interest in contemporary syntax. Under this assumption, the book is most appropriate for graduate and advanced undergraduate students—that is, those who have had some exposure to the formal analysis of natural languages and want to deepen their knowledge of syntactic theory. Because it is written as a step-by-step reconstruction of the system of generative grammar, it does not presuppose extensive familiarity with syntactic analysis or theory. Therefore, it should be accessible to any student with either some background in linguistic analysis or some familiarity with formal analysis in other disciplines (such as logic, mathematics, physics, or computer science).

A student who works through the material in this book should end up with a solid background in contemporary generative syntax—a basis for further reading and investigation (including Van Riemsdijk and Williams 1986, Chomsky 1981, 1986a,b, Lasnik and Uriagereka 1988, and Haegeman 1991). Having said this, let me point out that this book is not meant to be either a definitive or an exhaustive account of any of the topics covered. Instead, it is concerned with presenting some basic concepts of syntactic theory and explicating a way of thinking about the topics and phenomena that are discussed. In as vital a field as generative syntax, alternative proposals are continually being explored. And as usual in a vigorous enterprise, it is far from clear which of these proposals are correct. At best we can try to understand the strengths and weaknesses of each, and in particular, how they relate to one another. One important aspect of this evaluation is understanding the new ideas in relation to the basic concepts that have served as the foundations for the enterprise of generative syntax.

* See Sells 1985, Horrocks 1987 for an overview and comparison of these theories (excepting Relational Grammar). See Blake 1990 for an introduction to Relational Grammar.

# 1 The Study of Syntax

## 1.1 Introduction to the Study of Syntax

The study of syntax is concerned with the structural representation of sentences in human languages. It constitutes a part of the study of grammar, which also includes the study of sound (phonology) and meaning (semantics). The syntactic component of a grammar consists of mechanisms and principles that govern the construction of sentential representations and that provide a set of syntactic structures that are subject to interpretation by the semantic and phonological components. The model of grammar can therefore be represented as a group of three interconnecting components, as shown in figure 1.1. Both the phonological and the semantic components are considered to be **interpretive** in the sense that they assign phonetic and semantic representations to the syntactic representations that serve as their input. The syntactic component is considered to be **generative** in the sense that it provides the

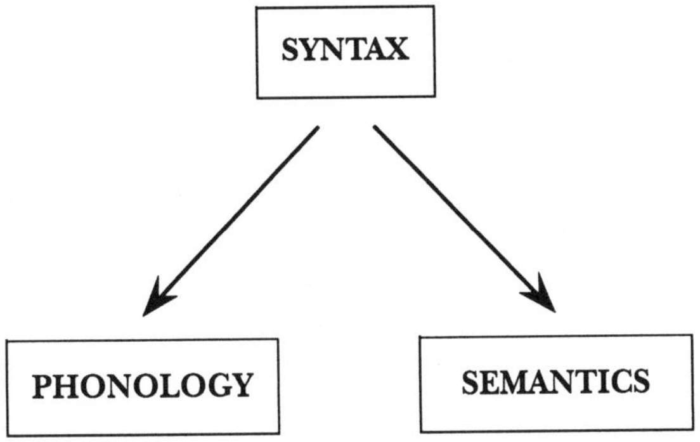


**Figure 1.1**
The major components of grammar

syntactic representations that are processed by the other two components. The syntactic component generates (in the mathematician's sense of "enumerate") a set of syntactic structures that are assigned sound by the phonological component and meaning by the semantic component. This is a model of what is called a **generative grammar**, where "generative" denotes nothing more than "explicit," though in linguistics the term is usually associated with a psychological interpretation of grammar (see section 1.2) and therefore connotes something more than just formal grammar for natural language.

Within the framework of generative grammar, a grammar is taken to be a model of a speaker's knowledge of his or her language. The analysis of ambiguous sentences provides one illustration of this perspective. Consider the following English sentence:

(1) the boy read the book in the study

A native speaker of English will be aware that (1) may be interpreted in two different ways, though none of the words in the sentence is ambiguous. (Compare the sentence *The boy wouldn't drink the orange juice,* where the word *orange* is lexically ambiguous—that is, it can be analyzed as either the adjective designating the color or the noun designating the fruit.)[1] Under one interpretation the book that the boy read is in the study, while under the other the place where the boy read the book was the study. The first entails that the book is located in the study, but not necessarily that the boy read it there. The second entails that the reading took place in the study, but not that the book is located there.

These two interpretations of (1) can be distinguished in terms of two distinct structural representations. They share a common basis: a string of words (*The boy read the book in the study*) analyzed in terms of **lexical categories** (or "parts of speech" in more traditional terminology). Thus, at this level of analysis both interpretations of (1) can be represented by (2), where N = noun, V = verb, Det = determiner ("article" in traditional grammar), and P = preposition.

(2)

| Det | N | V | Det | N | P | Det | N |
|---|---|---|---|---|---|---|---|
| \| | \| | \| | \| | \| | \| | \| | \| |
| the | boy | read | the | book | in | the | study |

Beyond this, the various lexical categories can be grouped into phrases of various sorts. For example, the determiner *the* and the noun *study* together constitute a **noun phrase** (NP), and this phrase in turn combines with the preposition *in* to form a **prepositional phrase** (PP). Thus, a PP can contain an NP as a **constituent**—where the term "constituent" is defined as a syntactic category (either lexical (e.g., N) or phrasal (e.g., PP)) that is contained as a part of another syntactic category.

A more precise definition of (phrasal) structural categories such as NP and PP and their relation to lexical categories such as N and P will be given in chapter 2. For now we can proceed with intuitive definitions: an NP is a phrase that bears a certain relation to a noun that it contains and a PP is a phrase that bears a certain relation to a preposition that it contains. By our definition, a lexical item (word) is not considered to be a constituent of a lexical category. Thus, the relation between a lexical category and the lexical item that instantiates it (e.g., P and *in* in (2)) is different from the relation between a lexical category and a phrasal category, as will be discussed in chapter 2.

The relationships between syntactic categories can be graphically represented in a labeled **tree diagram**, where the category labels constitute "nodes" of the tree and lines between nodes indicate "branches." The tree diagram in (3) gives the constituent structure of the PP in (1).

(3)
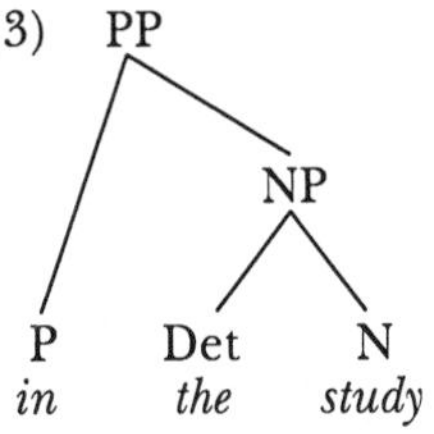


(3) shows that P, NP, Det, and N are constituents of PP. The relationship between P and PP is, however, quite different from the relationship between N and PP. P is an **immediate constituent** of PP, whereas N is not. The relation "immediate constituent" is defined as follows:

(4) A category B is an *immediate constituent* of a category C iff
  a. B is a constituent of C, *and*
  b. B is not a constituent of any constituent of C.

In terms of tree diagrams, B is an immediate constituent of C if they are connected by a single branch—in which case C is "immediately above" B in the diagram. Using this relation, we can sharpen our definition by saying that a PP is a phrase that contains a P as an immediate constituent and an NP is a phrase that contains an N as an immediate constituent.

The question that now arises is, What phrasal category in the structural analysis of (1) contains the PP in (3) as an immediate constituent? As we shall see, there is more than one answer to this question—which provides an account for the ambiguity of (1). To see how this works, let us continue the structural analysis of (1).

Given that (1) is a sentence, the categories that analyze (1) will all be constituents of a category S (for "sentential structure"). Following the traditional analysis of a sentence as consisting of two major parts (a subject and a predicate), we say that S contains two immediate constituents. The subject of (1), *the boy,* consists of a phrase of the form Det + N (just like the phrase *the study* that is the object of the preposition *in*) and hence is designated as an NP. The predicate, *read the book in the study,* is a phrase containing a V followed by the string Det + N + PP. In terms of syntactic categories, the predicate phrase can be identified as a **verb phrase** (VP)—under a definition of VP as a phrase containing a V as an immediate constituent (and thus parallel to NP and PP). S is therefore analyzed as a phrasal category containing two immediate constituents, NP + VP, as illustrated in (5).

(5)

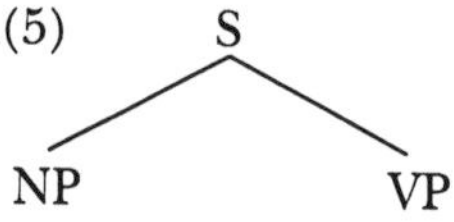


The VP of (1) can be assigned two different analyses. Note first that like S and PP, VP contains an NP (*the book*), the direct object of the verb *read.* The PP (*in the study*) can be analyzed as an immediate constituent of VP and therefore not a constituent of the direct object NP, as shown in (6a). Alternatively, the PP can be analyzed as an immediate constituent of the direct object NP, as shown in (6b).

(6)a

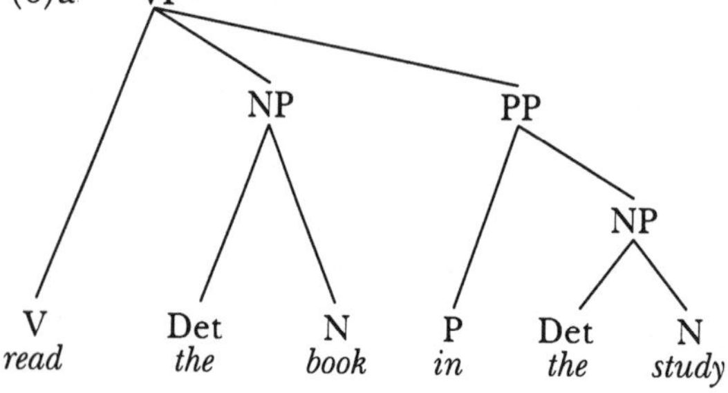

(6)b

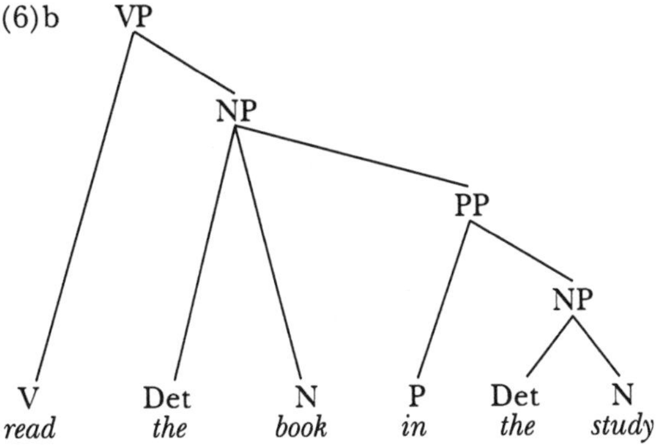


In the first analysis, VP has three immediate constituents (V, NP, and PP); in the second it has only two (V and NP). Under the hypothesis that the constituents of a phrase contribute to the meaning of the phrase, the PP as a constituent of NP in (6b) is construed as modifying the N b*ook*, and (6b) therefore corresponds to the interpretation in which the book is identified as being in the study. (6a), where *the book* and *in the study* are independent constituents of VP, corresponds to the interpretation in which the reading took place in the study. The difference in interpretation—and hence the ambiguity of (1)—correlates directly with a difference in the constituent structure of VP.

Our knowledge about the ambiguity of (1) follows in part from our knowledge that NPs may be of the form Det + N + PP or Det + N and VPs may be of the form V + NP + PP or V + NP. This knowledge can be represented explicitly in terms of formal rules of grammar that express the internal structure of phrases. For the examples under discussion, the rules would be given as in (7).

| | | | | | |
|---|---|---|---|---|---|
| (7) | a. NP | ⟶ | Det | N | PP |
| | b. NP | ⟶ | Det | N | |
| | c. VP | ⟶ | V | NP | PP |
| | d. VP | ⟶ | V | NP | |

The rules in (7) are called **phrase structure rules**, where the arrow expresses a relationship between a single category on the left and a string of categories on the right. The relationship from the category to the string is one of immediate constituency. Thus, Det, N, and PP are immediate constituents of NP in (7a) while V, NP, and PP are immediate constituents of VP in (7c). The relationship from the string to the category is an "is a" relationship. Thus, the string Det + N + PP is an NP, and so on.

Thus, a grammar containing the rules in (7) can assign two distinct structural analyses to sentences like (1), where each structural analysis correlates with a different semantic interpretation. Such a grammar constitutes a model of a native speaker's knowledge for such cases. Note, however, that though the ambiguity itself is part of a speaker's conscious knowledge, the grammatical basis for it is not, nor is it necessarily available via introspection. Rather, the grammatical basis is constructed in accordance with normal scientific procedures of hypothesis formation and testing.

---

**Exercise 1.1**
The phrase structure rules in (7) can be applied to further cases as in (i).

(i) a. Mary hit the man with a stick
 b. the boy remembered the snake on the boulder

State how each sentence is ambiguous, by giving its two interpretations. Show how the rules of phrase structure provide a basis for the ambiguity by giving two distinct structural analyses for each example and identifying which structure goes with which interpretation.

---

**Exercise 1.2**
The sentence *the boy read a report about that proposal by three senators* is two ways ambiguous. Under one interpretation the PP *by three senators* modifies *proposal*; under the other it modifies *report*. Show how this ambiguity may be expressed via phrase structure representation by providing two distinct phrase structure representations (tree diagrams) for the NP *a report about that proposal by three senators*, and indicate which interpretation goes with each tree diagram.

---

**Exercise 1.3**
The ambiguity of *Mary writes books on trains* concerns the interpretation of the preposition *on*. *On* can be interpreted as either 'aboard' or 'about'. This lexical ambiguity involves phrase structure differences as well. Give the two phrase structure trees that correlate with the two interpretations of this sentence.

---

We have seen how a grammar provides a model for a speaker's knowledge regarding ambiguous sentences in terms of a small number of statements about syntactic structure. The range of cases this model covers is infinite because the number of sentences for which a grammar will provide structural analyses is infinite. This is based on the empirical fact that no real limit on the length of sentences has ever been observed. What follows is a demonstration of how a finite number of rules of grammar can determine an infinite number of sentences.

This demonstration concerns sentences that contain sentential structures as constituents. Consider the structural analysis of a sentence like (8).

(8) John knew Einstein discovered relativity theory

Under the analysis of sentences discussed above, (8) is an S consisting of an NP *John* and a VP *knew Einstein discovered relativity theory*. This VP can be further analyzed as containing two constituents, a V *knew* and an S *Einstein discovered relativity theory*. The embedded S can also be analyzed as an NP + VP sequence where the VP consists of a V *discovered* and an NP *relativity theory*. (For the purposes of exposition it will be assumed that *relativity theory* is a compound noun.) Thus, the phrase structure of (8) would be represented as (9).

(9)

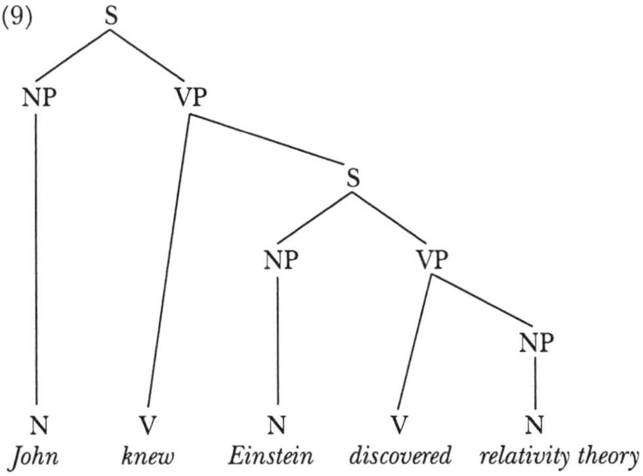


The phrase structure of (8) can therefore be defined in terms of a finite number of statements about constituency.

These statements can also be formulated as phrase structure rules that give the internal phrasal structure of sentences.

| | | | | |
|---|---|---|---|---|
| (10) a. | S | ⟶ | NP | VP |
| b. | VP | ⟶ | V | S |
| c. | VP | ⟶ | V | NP |
| d. | NP | ⟶ | N | |

Rule (10a) states that a string NP + VP is an S, where both the NP and VP are immediate constituents of S. Rule (10d) states that a single N can be an NP, demonstrating that the "is a" relationship may hold between a single category on the left and a string on the right consisting of a single category.

The phrase structure rule in (10a) is instantiated twice in (9), reflecting that fact that one S (*Einstein discovered relativity theory*) is contained (embedded) within the VP of another S (*John knew Einstein discovered relativity theory*). It is instantiated a third time in the longer S (11), where the sentential structure (9) has been embedded in another VP.

(11) Martha said John knew Einstein discovered relativity theory

This sort of embedding can be extended without limit. No matter how long the resulting sentence becomes, it is still analyzable in terms of the same finite set of rules (10). This follows from the recursive property of phrase structure, which allows any category to recur as a constituent of another instance of the same category. In (10a–b), for example, the "expansion" of the category S to the string NP + VP ultimately results in another instance of S, which is then subject to the original rule.

By interpreting the phrase structure rules in (10) as formation rules for English sentences, we can construct an unlimited number of sentences. Consider a derivation of a sentential structure using only these rules. The derivation could proceed as follows. Beginning with an initial symbol S, we apply rule (10a) to generate the constituents NP and VP (a subject and a predicate). At this point we have two choices for expanding VP: either by rule (10b) or by rule (10c). If we choose to apply (10c), then the derivation will terminate after the expansion of NP as N. The resulting structure will be that of a simple sentence where the VP contains a V and an NP object (for example, *The philosopher pondered the problem*). If, instead, we choose to apply rule (10b), then another S is generated that will serve as input for the reapplication of rule (10a). Such a derivation is illustrated in (12).

(12) a. S (initial symbol)
b. NP VP (by rule (10a))
c. NP V S (by rule (10b))

This derivation results in a complex sentence form whose main clause predicate contains an embedded sentence. Again there are two options for the form of the embedded predicate (i.e., the VP of the embedded S in (12c)): (10b) or (10c). If (10b) is chosen, then we must reapply (10a).

The derivation will terminate only when (10c) applies at some point. Schematically, the set of possible derivations in the grammar containing rules (10a–d) can be represented as (13).

(13)

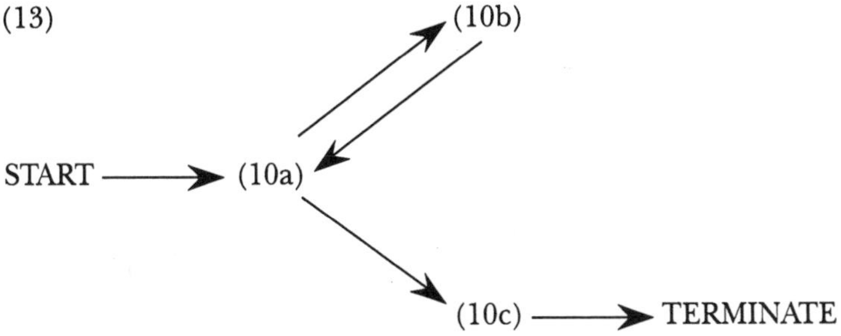


The connection between rules (10a) and (10b) forms a loop. Since there is no limit to the number of times a derivation may involve this loop, there can be no grammatical limit to the length of a sentence, and hence no limit on the number of possible well-formed sentences formed in this manner. Once rules allow the embedding of any phrase XP as a constituent of an XP—the recursive property—then automatically there will be no limit on the length of sentences generated by these rules.

---

**Exercise 1.4**

Give the phrase structure analysis of (11) in terms of a tree diagram. Using the rules in (10), give the derivation of (11) along the lines of (12).

---

As part of our model of speakers' knowledge of their language, rules like (10) provide the basis for an account of speakers' ability to recognize arbitrarily long sentences as sentences of the language they speak—including sentences they have never encountered before. Given a system of grammatical rules with this recursive property, we have a model of how finite human knowledge can be extended indefinitely. Given that an individual's knowledge is finite, speakers of a language cannot directly know an infinite number of sentences—rather, they know a finite number of grammatical rules that extend over an infinite set of sentences. In short, speakers know a grammar, and not a set of sentences.

In the remaining chapters of this book we will investigate in detail the rules and principles that determine syntactic representations in human languages. As noted above, this system of rules and principles is taken to be a model of a speaker's knowledge of language. From this perspective, certain consequences follow that should be made explicit before we proceed to more technical discussions of the form and function of the syntactic component.

## 1.2 The Psychological Interpretation of Grammar

From the point of view developed in section 1.1, the study of generative grammar falls within the framework of individual psychology. A grammar is therefore a model of a psychological capacity. This was implicit when we were considering some aspects of what native speakers know about their language and the grammatical basis of that knowledge. Note further that a grammar is a model of a speaker's knowledge only (sometimes called linguistic **competence**). It is not a model of how that knowledge is put to use (linguistic **performance**)—that is, a grammar is not a model of language production or language comprehension. For example, a model of linguistic competence will account for the possibility of grammatical sentences of 500 words. The fact that no speaker uses sentences anywhere near this long is to be explained by a model of linguistic performance. The theory of linguistic competence underlies the theory of linguistic performance in essential ways that remain to be determined by the construction of a model of linguistic performance. It is clear, however, that the rules of grammar should not be interpreted as actual sentence production/comprehension procedures.

The psychological interpretation of grammar raises the important epistemological issue of acquisition: *How does a child acquire the grammar of his or her language?*

The situation of every child acquiring the grammar of a first language can be characterized as follows. On the basis of a limited set of primary data (the utterances the child hears), the child must come up with a grammar that generates the language he or she will eventually speak.[2] Since the primary linguistic data may be compatible with any number of extensions (as shown in figure 1.2) and since only one extension, $L_x$, is the language the child acquires, the problem for the language acquisition mechanism is projecting the primary data onto the correct language (the **projection problem**). Two other facts serve to intensify this problem: we cannot suppose that all children are exposed to exactly the same primary linguistic data, and the primary data a child hears probably does not consist of only grammatically well-formed sentences. Spoken language often contains sentence fragments and utterances that native speakers would, if asked, reject as not being sentences of their language. It appears

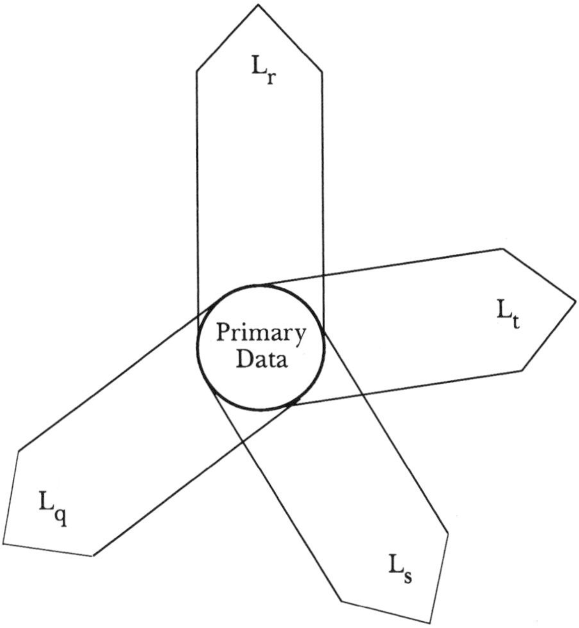


**Figure 1.2**
Projection of primary data to language

that a child acquiring a language is able to filter the primary data so that ill-formed utterances have no effect on the acquisition of a grammar.

A solution to the projection problem can be formulated in terms of a theory of grammar that delimits the notion "possible grammar" for natural language. The theory of grammar is also subject to a psychological interpretation as part of the human cognitive capacity to acquire language. If the theory of grammar allows only a limited range of grammars, then we might assume that only a very limited number of grammars will be compatible with the primary data. If the theory of grammar is restrictive enough, then ideally only one grammar will be compatible with the primary data: the actual grammar of the language. If, however, the theory allows more than one grammar that is compatible with the primary data, then a choice must be made among them in terms of some further condition(s)—referred to as an "evaluation metric"—which will also be a part of the theory of grammar.

Under this view, language learners begin in some initial state and on exposure to linguistic data proceed to a steady state (i.e., a grammar of the language to which they have been exposed).

(14) $S_{initial}$ + Data ⟶ $S_{steady}$

$S_{initial}$ constitutes a cognitive capacity that makes it possible for the language learner to acquire a grammar on exposure to limited primary data. It incorporates the theory of grammar and therefore also determines what is a possible $S_{steady}$.

From this perspective, $S_{initial}$ is subject to two boundary conditions: it must be rich enough to account for the fact that children can acquire the grammar of any natural (i.e., human) language to which they are exposed and it must be restricted enough to account for the fact that only grammars of natural languages are acquired. For example, given that unrestricted sentential embedding is a property of English grammar (in fact, a property of the grammar of every human language as far as we know), no child would acquire a grammar of English that arbitrarily limits the number of sentential embeddings in sentences—even though the primary linguistic data the child is exposed to contains only instances where sentential embedding is arbitrarily limited. For example, presumably no child hears a sentence with fifteen sentential embeddings; nonetheless, adult speakers will recognize such sentences as part of their language.

If $S_{initial}$ is universal across the species, then it provides the basis for the acquisition of the grammar of any natural language. The theory of grammar, which belongs to $S_{initial}$, therefore constitutes a **Universal Grammar** (henceforth UG). UG consists of a set of categories and primitive operations from which grammatical rules are constructed, conditions on the form of grammatical rules, and conditions on rule application and output. UG will be rich enough to allow the grammar of any natural language, depending on the richness of the primitive operations available for grammar construction. It will be restrictive enough to allow only grammars of natural languages, depending on the nature of the constraints it imposes on possible grammars.[3]

Under the psychological interpretation of grammar, UG accounts for the human cognitive capacity for language acquisition. That is, UG provides an important part of the explanation of *how it is possible* to acquire a grammar—not how the acquisition of grammar is actually carried out. The theory of UG that is developed in the remaining chapters of this book indicates that this cognitive capacity is specific to language and so constitutes part of a faculty of language distinct from other cognitive capacities. This view of UG as a species specific and species universal (and hence genetically determined) cognitive capacity can be characterized as the **Innateness Hypothesis for the language faculty** (see Chomsky 1972a, 1975a, 1980a for further discussion).

This hypothesis for an innate language faculty is also supported by the fact that the linguistic environment is too impoverished to determine the full extent of what native speakers come to know about their language. As a concrete instance, consider some basic facts about English sentences containing interrogative pronouns (e.g., *who, what*).

(15) a. who does John like
b. who did Mary say [$_S$ John likes]
c. who does Sam believe [$_S$ Mary said [$_S$ John likes]]

(16) a. who did John hear stories about
b. *who did stories about annoy John

In each example in (15) the interrogative pronoun *who* functions as the direct object of the verb *like.* (15b) shows how the interrogative pronoun at the front of a sentence can function as the object of a verb of an embedded sentence. (15c) shows how this is possible with two sentential embeddings. As can be easily verified, there is no grammatical limit to the depth of embedding for such structures. In (16a) the interrogative pronoun *who* functions as the object of the preposition *about.* In (16b), however, where the interrogative pronoun that is interpreted as a constituent of the subject NP ([$_{NP}$ stories about who(m)]) occurs at the front of the sentence, the result is deviant (indicated by the "*"). A sentence is deviant (or **ungrammatical**) when it does not conform to the rules and principles of the grammar of the language—otherwise it is considered **grammatical**. The phenomena in (15) can be accounted for by a rule that moves an interrogative pronoun (from the object position of *likes* in each example) to sentence-initial position. Given the data in (15) and the recursive nature of sentential embedding, this rule appears to be unconstrained in how far it can move the pronoun. In contrast, (16b) shows that this movement rule is indeed subject to some constraint.

Native speakers of English know that (16b) is not a sentence of English without having been told that this is a fact. But how can this be, since sentences like (16b) are precisely what a child acquiring English does not hear? If children do not glean this knowledge from the primary language data, then we might assume that it comes from the innate schematism that constitutes the theory of grammar. The theory of grammar must be so constructed that rules of grammar may generate sentences like (15a–c) and (16a), but not (16b). This hypothesis explains how a native speaker of a language knows more about the language than is provided by the linguistic environment. This type of argument for the Innateness Hypothesis goes under the general heading of **argument from poverty of the stimulus** (see Chomsky 1980a for further discussion). Additional arguments from poverty of the stimulus are given in subsequent chapters where ungrammaticality is determined on the basis of general principles of grammar.

One might object that arguments from poverty of the stimulus do not reveal anything about innately specified cognitive structure on the grounds that native speakers gain evidence about the ungrammaticality of sentences from their absence in the environment. Thus, one might suppose that children who are acquiring English will know that (16b) is ungrammatical because they never hear such sentences.

The problem with this objection is that the linguistic data a child is exposed to prior to acquiring a grammar is extremely limited compared to the number of sentences an individual produces over a lifetime (or more significantly, the infinite set of sentences a grammar can generate). Speakers of a language regularly produce novel utterances—that is, sentences they have not previously heard or read. Chomsky has discussed this ability as one component of what he calls **the creative aspect of language use**.

> But the normal use of language is not only innovative and potentially infinite in scope, but also free from the control of detectable stimuli, either external or internal. It is because of this freedom from stimulus control that language can serve as an instrument of thought and self-expression, as it does not only for the exceptionally gifted and talented, but also, in fact, for every normal human.
>
> Still, the properties of being unbounded and free from stimulus control do not, in themselves, exceed the bounds of mechanical explanation. And Cartesian discussion of the limits of mechanical explanation therefore took note of a third property of the normal use of language, namely its coherence and its "appropriateness to the situation"—which of course is an entirely different matter from control by external stimuli. Just what "appropriateness" and "coherence" may consist in we cannot say in any clear or definite way, but there is no doubt that these are meaningful concepts. We can distinguish normal use of language from the ravings of a maniac or the output of a computer with a random element.
>
> Honesty forces us to admit that we are as far today as Descartes was three centuries ago from understanding just what enables a human to speak in a way that is innovative, free from stimulus control, and also appropriate and coherent. This is a serious problem that the psychologist and biologist must ultimately face and that cannot be talked out of existence by invoking "habit" or "conditioning" or "natural selection." (Chomsky 1972a:12-13)

(See Chomsky 1966 for further discussion of the creative aspect of language use.)

We must assume that native speakers can distinguish between ill-formed sentences and novel well-formed sentences. Since neither of these is part of the initial data that children use to acquire a grammar of their language, the ability to make this distinction cannot rest on considerations of the linguistic environment alone. To explain how a speaker of a language comes to know certain facts about that language without overt evidence, we must instead turn to specific hypotheses about an innate UG. As we shall see in the remaining chapters, hypotheses about the character of UG can be formulated on the basis of a study of generative grammar.

It is important to note here that "grammatical" and "ungrammatical" are technical terms, referring to sentences that do or do not conform to the formal rules and principles of a grammar. A "*" indicates that the example to which it is prefixed fails to conform to a generative grammar of the language in question, either the example cannot be assigned an appropriate phrase structure representation or the phrase structure that can be assigned violates some condition on rule application or on syntactic representation. Thus, the * is assigned in terms of a formal model of grammar. However, when speakers judge that some particular example is or is not a part of their language, they are using not only a grammar ($S_{steady}$, which falls under a model of linguistic competence) but also sentence-processing mechanisms (which fall under a model of linguistic performance) and other cognitive systems that interact with the language faculty. The point to keep in mind is that speakers do not have direct access (via introspection) to the grammar of their language. When a speaker judges that a sentence is not part of his or her language, we cannot know for sure whether the sentence is judged unacceptable because it is ungrammatical (in the technical sense) or because it causes problems with some other cognitive system. We can designate an unacceptable sentence as ungrammatical only when we can produce a formal grammar to which the sentence does not conform.

Given this discussion, it should be apparent that sentences that a speaker judges to be unacceptable may in fact be grammatical. Consider (17) and (18).

(17) a. Mary threw out [$_{NP}$ the notebook]
b. Mary threw [$_{NP}$ the notebook] out

(18) a. Mary threw out [$_{NP}$ the notebook which John had told her he wanted back]
b. Mary threw [$_{NP}$ the notebook which John had told her he wanted back] out

Suppose there is a rule of English that accounts for the inversion of an object NP and what is called a "particle" (or intransitive preposition—e.g., *out*), as indicated by the two permissible orderings in (17). Suppose further that this rule has the effect of moving the particle to the right of the object NP.[4] Nonetheless, native speakers of English usually find examples like (18b) unacceptable. If the rule of grammar that accounts for (17b) also generates (18b) without violating any conditions on rules or syntactic representations, then (18b) is grammatical, although unacceptable (for a reason yet to be specified).

Though it is clear that unacceptable examples may be either grammatical or ungrammatical and that acceptable examples may be grammatical, we might ask whether acceptable examples can be ungrammatical. Given the little that we know about the interaction between linguistic competence and linguistic performance, nothing forces us to the conclusion that all acceptable examples are grammatical. It is logically possible that some sentence that speakers judge to be acceptable violates some rule or principle of the grammar. Consider the following examples (due to Anthony Kroch, personal communication):

(19) a. that's the only thing they do is fight
b. the problem is is that I can never get that screw in right

Though both examples seem acceptable, they would cause serious problems if they had to be incorporated in a generative grammar of English. (19a) could be a blend of two grammatical sentences: *That's the only thing they do* and *The only thing they do is fight.* (19b) seems to have an extra *is*—in contrast to *The problem is that I can never get that screw in right,* which is easily accounted for in terms of generative grammar.

These considerations show that speaker judgments (intuitions) must be used with some caution. Such judgments do not come tagged with respect to the grammar and therefore are open to some interpretation. The interpretation of speaker judgments must, in the final analysis, be supported by a formal grammar from which they follow. The formal grammar itself will be subject to various criteria like empirical coverage, simplicity, and depth of explanation. The main point to keep in mind is that with respect to grammaticality, formal analysis is always necessary because (speaker) intuitions are based on more than just grammar.

## Bibliographical Comments

The issues surrounding knowledge of language have been debated by philosophers and psychologists, as well as linguists. On the historical roots of the debate, see Chomsky 1966, 1972a. On the more recent controversy, see in addition Chomsky 1975a, 1980a, 1986b—and the works cited there. The initial (and still important) discussion of the competence/performance distinction occurs in the first chapter of Chomsky 1965. For further discussion, see Chomsky 1975a and the works cited there. The Innateness Hypothesis, Universal Grammar, and poverty of the stimulus are considered in some detail in Chomsky 1972a, 1975a, 1986b.

The issues surrounding the theory of generative grammar and language acquisition were first discussed in Chomsky 1965. For further discussion see Baker and McCarthy 1981. The term "projection problem" is due to Peters 1972b. The relation between syntactic theory and the projection problem is explored in some detail in Baker 1979.

For a general overview of the issues concerning grammatical theory and the study of language, see Lightfoot 1982 and Newmeyer 1983 as well as the works by Chomsky cited above.

# 2
# Introduction to Formal Grammar

This chapter lays the groundwork for syntactic analysis within generative grammar. It deals with the three major grammatical devices touched on in chapter 1: phrase structure rules, transformations, and principles that limit the form and function of rules of grammar. The basic notions of phrase structure analysis of natural languages are presented in section 2.1. Section 2.2 takes up the issue of lexical insertion—that is, how words of a language are introduced into the phrase structure analysis of sentences. Lexical insertion cannot be handled satisfactorily in terms of phrase structure rules; rather, it requires a transformational solution, which depends in part on a feature analysis of lexical categories. This feature analysis is extended to phrasal categories in section 2.3, where a theory of phrase structure is developed that provides a more principled account of the relationship between lexical and phrasal categories, and of the internal constituent structure of phrasal categories. This approach is brought to bear on the analysis of noun phrases in section 2.4, where a transformational approach to the distribution of certain grammatical formatives (e.g., the *'s* in *the king of England's hat*) in complex noun phrases is explored. It is then demonstrated that the simplest formulation of the required transformations will in some instances result in the generation of the wrong syntactic structures, and that these problems can be solved by formulating general principles of grammar that determine the well-formedness of linguistic representations. The chapter concludes with an appendix that gives a more formal account of the mechanism of phrase structure rules and the relationship between the formal mechanism and the kinds of syntactic representations it generates.

The chapter serves as a microcosm of the whole enterprise in that it is concerned with the three central topics that are developed in the rest of the book: (i) the question of syntactic representation for natural languages, (ii) the question of how to account for the limited syntactic distribution of certain types of lexical items and grammatical formatives, and (iii) the relation of the first two topics to a principled general theory of syntactic representations in terms of a theory of generative grammar.

## 2.1 Phrase Structure Analysis

As illustrated in chapter 1, the basic idea of phrase structure analysis is that sentences of a language can be divided into constituent parts such that each word in a sentence is a constituent of some phrase that, in turn, is ultimately a constituent of the sentence. The constituent structure of sentences is determined in part by the phrase structure rules of the grammar (henceforth PS rules).

To see how PS rules generate constituent structure representations for sentences, consider the following set of PS rules needed to generate sentences like *The boy likes the book.*

(1) a. S ⟶ NP VP
    b. VP ⟶ V NP
    c. NP ⟶ Det N

PS rules are a subclass of **rewrite** rules (see appendix for details) where a single syntactic category is "rewritten" or "expanded" as a string of categories (including the string consisting of a single category, as in (10d) of chapter 1). Thus, rule (1a) should be read as "the category S rewrites as the string consisting of an NP followed by a VP." The rules apply as follows. Beginning with an **initial symbol** S, the rules apply one at a time until each phrasal category (e.g., S, NP, and VP) has been rewritten as a string of lexical categories (e.g., Det, N, and V).

The rules in (1) allow several distinct but equivalent derivations—two of which are given in (2).

(2)

| a. S | | b. S | |
|---|---|---|---|
| NP VP | (by (1a)) | NP VP | (by (1a)) |
| NP V NP | (by (1b)) | Det N VP | (by (1c)) |
| Det N V NP | (by (1c)) | Det N V NP | (by (1b)) |
| Det N V Det N | (by (1c)) | Det N V Det N | (by (1c)) |

The derivations (2a) and (2b) are equivalent in that the same phrase structure rules are applied to the same categories in each case. They differ in the order in which the rules are applied: rule (1b) precedes rule (1c) in (2a), whereas rule (1c) precedes rule (1b) in (2b). As a result, derivation (2a) contains a string NP–V–NP that is not contained in derivation (2b); and conversely, (2b) contains a string Det–N–VP that is not contained in derivation (2a). The set of strings from all equivalent derivations is called a **phrase marker**. The phrase marker is a set of strings that assigns a phrase structure interpretation to a **terminal string** (the string of lexical categories that terminates the phrase structure derivation). The phrase marker of the terminal string Det–N–V–Det–N is the set of strings given in (3).

(3) {S, NP–VP, NP–V–NP, Det–N–VP, Det–N–V–NP, NP–V–Det–N, Det–N–V–Det–N}

---

**Exercise 2.1**
Which string in (3) is not in either derivation (2a) or (2b)? Construct a third equivalent derivation that contains this string.

---

This phrase marker can be represented as either a tree diagram (4) or a labeled bracketing (5)

(4)

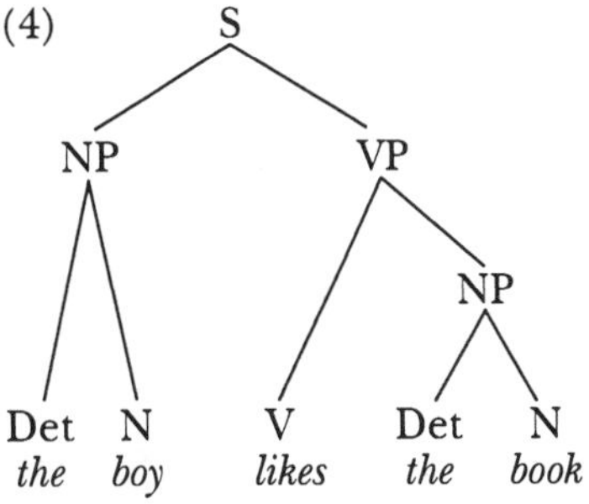


(5) $[_S\ [_{NP}\ [_{Det}$ the] $[_N$ boy]] $[_{VP}\ [_V$ likes] $[_{NP}\ [_{Det}$ the] $[_N$ book]]]]

For expository purposes, we will use tree diagrams or labeled bracket representations to represent phrase markers, instead of sets of strings.[1]

Before we consider how lexical items are introduced into phrase markers, it will be useful to discuss the relations between the elements in phrase markers. The relation between a category and its constituents is called **dominance**. That is, a category **dominates** all of its constituents. For example, the category VP in (4) dominates the categories V, NP, Det, and N. However, the relation between VP and NP is different from the relation between VP and N. VP **immediately dominates** NP, but it does not immediately dominate N since another category, NP, intervenes between VP and N. We say that a category X immediately dominates a category Y when X dominates Y and every other category dominating Y dominates X. When X immediately dominates Y, then Y is an immediate constituent of X. In the example under discussion, both NP and N are constituents of VP, but only NP is an immediate constituent of VP. Dominance relations between categories in a structural description determine the **hierarchical structure** of sentences. If two categories in a phrase marker are not in a dominance relation, then they are in a **precedence** relation—for example, the subject NP in (4) precedes VP. Precedence relations determine the linear (left-to-right) ordering of elements in the phrase marker and hence determine the **linear structure** of sentences.

In terms of tree diagrams, two kinds of branching are possible: **unary branching** (where a category immediately dominates only one constituent) and **n-ary branching** (where a category has two or more immediate constituents). When a category has just two immediate constituents, it constitutes an instance of **binary branching**. As we will see in section 2.3, the branching property of structural descriptions plays an important role in defining principles of syntactic theory.[2]

As noted in chapter 1, some phrasal categories are defined in terms of the lexical categories they contain (e.g., VP in terms of V). The lexical category stands as the **head** of its phrasal category, and the phrasal category is designated as the **phrasal projection** of the lexical category. Whether or not every lexical category projects its own phrasal category is open to discussion. We will assume, however, that it is not the case. For example, Det in (4) does not project its own phrasal category. Rather, it is a lexical constituent of the phrasal projection of N (= NP). A similar relationship holds between the adverb *very* and the adjective *happy* in the adjective phrase (henceforth AP) *very happy about the results of the experiment* as analyzed in (6).[3]

(6)

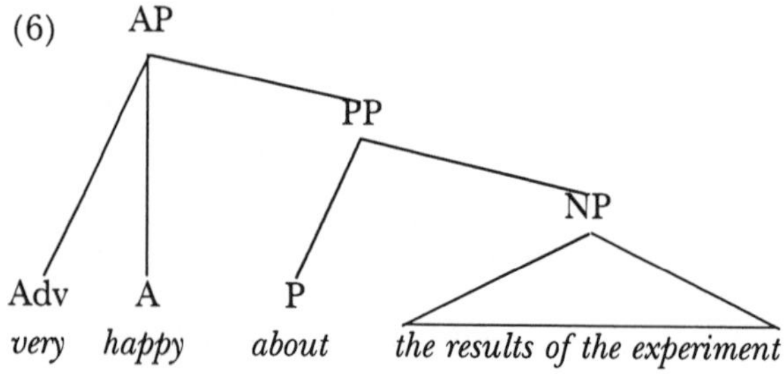

Lexical constituents of phrasal projections like Det and Adv act as modifiers of the lexical head of the projection. Each can be referred to as a **specifier** of the lexical head it modifies. Phrasal constituents of phrasal projections are designated as **complements** of the phrasal head. Thus, in (4) the object NP is a complement of V; in (6) the PP is a complement of A, and the NP is a complement of P. (These notions will be sharpened in section 2.3 within a richer and more finely tuned theory of phrase structure that will account for a wider range of cases.)

The one phrasal category that is not defined in terms of a lexical head is S. Consequently, its immediate phrasal constituents NP and VP cannot be designated as complements.

In general, the nonhead constituents of phrasal projections are optional. For example, NPs can lack determiners, as in *John admires Mary.* Parentheses are used to express the optionality of constituents; for example, the notation in (7) indicates that Det is an optional constituent of NP.

(7) NP ⟶ (Det) N

Rule (7) as formulated is an abbreviation for two distinct rules, given in (8).

(8) a. NP ⟶ Det N
b. NP ⟶ N

Similarly, rule (1b) above can be reformulated as (9) to express the fact that some verbs occur without NP objects (e.g., *sleep*).

(9) VP ⟶ V (NP)

(9) too is an abbreviation of two rules.

Braces are used to collapse rules where a disjunctive choice of constituents is involved. For example, English VPs may be of the form V–NP–NP (*told Bill a story*) or of the form V–NP–S (*told Bill Mary was leaving*). Since English does not have VPs of the form V–NP–NP–S (or V–NP–S–NP), it appears that the occurrence of a second NP complement in a VP precludes the occurrence of an S complement, and conversely. This disjunction can be represented by placing NP and S in braces to indicate that only one can be chosen in the expansion of VP, as illustrated in (10).

(10) $\text{VP} \longrightarrow \text{V} \; (\text{NP}) \; \left(\begin{Bmatrix} \text{NP} \\ \text{S} \end{Bmatrix}\right)$

**Exercise 2.2**
(10) abbreviates five distinct phrase structure rules. List them, and give a sentence illustrating each.

In order to complete the description of how phrase structure rules participate in the assignment of structural descriptions to sentences, it is necessary to introduce rules that associate lexical categories with actual lexical items (or words)–what are called **lexical insertion rules**. The problem of lexical insertion is the subject of the next section. It has been generally assumed that lexical insertion is not handled by phrase structure rules, for reasons that will become apparent.

## 2.2 Lexical Insertion

So far we have developed a formalism for rules that generate constituent structures for sentences. We must now relate constituent structures to sentences—that is, strings of words in a language. This relationship is established at the level of lexical categories and therefore crucially concerns the relationship between lexical categories and lexical items. In what follows, we will see that a lexical item is just an *instantiation* of a lexical category—from which it follows that a lexical item is not a constituent of a lexical category.

A lexical item is in some sense like the grammar in miniature. It consists of three separate parts that concern sound, meaning, and structure. Consider for example the kinds of information that would be contained in a lexical entry for *man*.

(11) *man*

$$\begin{bmatrix} \text{/mæn/} \\ +\text{N} \\ +\text{animate} \\ -\text{plural} \\ +\text{human} \\ +\text{masculine} \\ \vdots \end{bmatrix}$$

The phonemic transcription (/mæn/) gives a representation of the lexical item *man* in terms of its sound. The [+N] is a **categorial feature** indicating that *man* belongs to the class of nouns. Categorial features provide syntactic information about lexical items. Finally there is a group of features that relate to the semantic interpretation of *man*. Thus, *man* is [–plural] as opposed to *men*, which is [+plural]; [+masculine] as opposed to *woman*, which is [–masculine]; [+animate] as opposed to *plant*, which is [–animate]; and [+human] as opposed to *bull*, which is [–human]. Representations like (11) are not meant to indicate that the semantic representation of lexical items can be given exhaustively in terms of binary (+/–) features. Nonetheless, lexical items can be represented at least partially in terms of sets of features that relate to their phonological, syntactic, and semantic form.

Given representations for lexical items like (11), the relation between lexical items and lexical categories turns on the relation between categorial features and lexical categories ([+N] and N in the example under discussion). Since we can simply construe categorial features as an equivalent notation for lexical categories (thus, [+N] ≡ N), the distinction between features and categories here becomes rather artificial. Under this equivalence, lexical insertion can be formulated as an operation that *substitutes* a fully specified lexical feature matrix (the lexical item) for a partially specified matrix (the categorial feature alone). So the derivation of a sentence containing the lexical item *man* would include an operation that substitutes (11) for a [+N] in the phrase marker.

As formulated, lexical insertion maps a phrase marker containing an element [+N] onto another phrase marker containing the lexical item *man* (i.e., the feature matrix (11)) in its place, as illustrated in (12).

(12) {. . . ,+N, . . . } ⇒ {. . . ,*man*, . . . }

An operation that maps a phrase marker onto another phrase marker is called a **transformation**. In the case of lexical insertion, we are dealing with a substitution transformation. The substitution operation can be given in its most general form as (13), where $\alpha$ and $\beta$ are feature matrices.

(13) Substitute $\alpha$ for $\beta$.

As it stands, (13) could substitute the lexical entry for a verb [+V] for a matrix containing [+N]. To block this possibility, substitutions must be constrained by a nondistinctness condition, (14).

(14) $\alpha$ must be nondistinct from $\beta$.

The relation **nondistinct** is defined as follows:

(15) $\alpha$ is *nondistinct* from $\beta$ if $\alpha$ contains all the features of $\beta$.

In the case of lexical insertion, the features of β will be a subset of the features of α. Thus, in a phrase marker where a head N is designated only [+N], we could substitute the lexical entry (11) for the categorial feature since (11) is nondistinct from [+N].[4]

Ensuring that lexical insertion by substitution involves the same categorial feature in both the phrase marker and the lexical item is necessary but not sufficient, as the following examples illustrate.

(16) a. David slept
b. *David slept the book

(17) a. David mentioned the book
b. *David mentioned

(18) a. David put the receipt in the book
b. *David put in the book
c. *David put the receipt
d. *David put

The examples in (16)–(18) show that the lexical insertion of verbs is sensitive to syntactic context. Thus, a verb like *sleep* cannot be inserted into a phrase marker where V is followed by an object NP, as in (16b); nor can a verb like *mention* be inserted into a phrase marker where V is not followed by an object NP, as in (17b). In the case of *put*, V must be followed by both an object NP and a PP.

To account for this context-sensitivity of lexical insertion, the grammar must be able to distinguish among three distinct subcategories of verbs: (i) verbs that may not occur with an NP object (*sleep*), (ii) verbs that must occur with an NP object (*mention*), and (iii) verbs that must occur with both an NP object and a PP (*put*). These three subcategories can be specified in terms of the syntactic contexts "before #" (where the symbol "#" indicates the end of the phrase containing V—e.g., VP), "before NP#," and "before NP PP#." These contexts can be represented as follows, where the underline bar indicates the position of V: ___#, ___NP#, and ___NP PP#. Note, however, that grammatical sentences like *John slept soundly, John slept on the couch, John slept for three hours,* and *John slept because he was exhausted* show that the interpretation of the context ___# should be limited to a subphrase containing V—in fact, the same one that contains the NP object—and does not apply to all syntactic constituents to the right of V. (We will return to this issue briefly in the next section.)

Since the syntactic context in which a verb may occur determines its subcategory, we can translate the contexts for verbs as features.

(19) a. *sleep*: [+___#]
b. *put*: [+___NP PP#]
c. *mention*: [+___NP#]

In this way, we derive a set of **contextual features** for verbs. Given that verbs are subcategorized in terms of which phrasal categories occur with them in a subphrase, these contextual features are designated as **subcategorization features**.

Under this analysis, lexical entries for verbs will contain both non-contextual features like the categorial feature [+V] and subcategorization features, as illustrated in (20).

(20) *sleep* *mention* *put*

$$\begin{bmatrix} +\mathrm{V} \\ +\_\_\_\# \end{bmatrix} \quad \begin{bmatrix} +\mathrm{V} \\ +\_\_\_\mathrm{NP}\# \end{bmatrix} \quad \begin{bmatrix} +\mathrm{V} \\ +\_\_\_\mathrm{NP\ \ PP}\# \end{bmatrix}$$

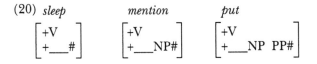

The contextual features in (19)–(20) require further interpretation. For example, the feature [+___#] in the lexical entry for *sleep* must entail [–___NP#] and [–___NP PP#] to account for examples like (16b). Similarly, the feature [+___NP PP#] must be interpreted as [–___#], [–___NP#], and [–___PP#] to account for examples like (18b–d). Let us suppose that only proper contexts need be stated in terms of contextual features. If positive subcategorization features are interpreted as a full specification of exactly what constituents may occur in the subcategorization domain, then it will follow that each positive subcategorization feature given above is distinct from the others and that no negative features need be mentioned. Thus, if "#" is taken as the right boundary of the subcategorization domain, then [+___#] entails that no constituents occur in it—in contrast to [+___NP PP#], which contains an NP and a PP in that order. This still leaves open the possibility that a verb may be specified with two distinct positive contextual features—for example, the verb *believe* as in (21).

(21) a. Mary believed [$_{NP}$ the story]
b. Mary believed [$_{S}$ Bill was lying]

Under the assumption that the verb *believe* is the same lexical item in both sentences, its contextual feature is given as a disjunction of the two features [+___NP] and [+___S].

Let us designate the constituents that are involved in the subcategorization of a verb as its **complements**. Thus, *believe* takes an NP or S complement. *Sleep* takes no complements, *mention* takes an NP (or S, as in *John mentioned* *he had been invited too*) complement, and *put* takes both an NP and a PP complement. In terms of syntactic configuration, a verb and its complements will be immediate constituents of the same phrasal category. Given the examples cited, complements share another property that is less easily characterized. They are all arguments of the verb (viewed as an *n*-place predicate along the lines of logical analysis) that are also constituents of the verb phrase. For example, we can analyze *believe* as a 2-place predicate (BELIEVE $(x,y)$), where $x$ and $y$ are argument variables representing the arguments corresponding to the syntactic subject and object of *believe* as in (21a). In (21b) $y$ is instantiated as a proposition (S). Under this analysis, *put* is a 3-place predicate (PUT $(x,y,z)$), where $x$ corresponds to the syntactic subject, $y$ corresponds to the object complement, and $z$ corresponds to the PP complement. Thus, in (18a) the predicate *put* links three arguments: *David, the receipt,* and *the book.*[5] Finally, a verb like *sleep* that takes a subject but no complements is a 1-place predicate.

In the examples cited so far, the complements of the verbs are obligatory. This is not always the case, as the following paradigms illustrate.

(22) Object + PP complement
- a. Mary bought a book for Bill
- b. Mary bought a book
- c. *Mary bought for Bill
- d. *Mary bought

(23) Double object construction
- a. Mary bought Bill a book
- a. *Mary bought Bill
- a. Mary bought a book
- a. *Mary bought

With a verb like *buy*, which takes both an indirect object NP and a direct object NP (as in (23a)), the indirect object (*Bill*) can occur either in a PP after the direct object *book* (as in (22a)) or as an NP between the verb and the direct object (as in (23a)). Both paradigms (22) and (23) show that the direct object is obligatory (see the (d)-examples) and that the indirect object is optional (see (22b) and (23c)). Since the object NP must be a constituent of the subcategorization domain, it follows from the basic conditions on phrase structure representations (see the appendix) that the indirect object NP in (23b) must also. Given that the indirect object in a double object construction must be a complement of the verb and that the indirect object constitutes an argument of the predicate *buy* in both constructions, it seems inescapable that the PP containing the indirect object is also a complement of *buy*. Therefore, the subcategorization feature for *buy* with respect to paradigm (23) will be [+___NP (PP)#]. Because the optionality of the indirect object in these constructions is now accounted for via the optionality of the PP complement, it is possible to give the subcategorization feature for the double object paradigm (23) as [+___NP NP#] (in other words, it is not necessary to indicate optionality of the indirect object in this subcategorization feature). This assumes that (23c) is not part of the paradigm for double object constructions.

Paradigms (21), (22), and (23) illustrate that a single lexical item may take more than one subcategorization feature. As long as we refrain from equating differences in subcategorization features with differences in semantic interpretation, this analysis is unproblematic.

Exactly how subcategorization features account for the context-sensitivity of lexical insertion requires further interpretation. As formulated, the rule of lexical insertion will **misgenerate** the starred examples in (16)–(18) given that subcategorization features are not part of the phrase marker to which the substitution operation applies. This is not a problem if we can motivate some other mechanism in the grammar which accounts for the ungrammaticality of such examples.

Let us assume that lexical insertion does misgenerate subcategorization violations (i.e., cases where there is a mismatch between the subcategorization feature of a lexical item and its actual syntactic context). A subcategorization feature constitutes a lexical property of a specific lexical item. When the subcategorization feature and actual syntactic context of the lexical item match, we can say that this lexical property is **satisfied**. When they do not match, the lexical property is not satisfied. We will assume that there is a principle of grammar that requires lexical properties to be satisfied.

(24) **Principle of Lexical Satisfaction**
Lexical properties must be satisfied.

The effect of (24) is to designate a sentence as ungrammatical if it contains a lexical item whose lexical properties are not satisfied in that sentence. Thus, (24), in conjunction with subcategorization features of lexical items, will account for the ungrammaticality of the starred examples in (16)–(18). That is, the grammar consisting of phrase structure rules, a lexical insertion transformation, and the Principle of Lexical Satisfaction will designate as ungrammatical any sentence containing a lexical item whose subcategorization feature does not match its actual context in a phrase marker.

**Exercise 2.3**
Predicate adjectives also exhibit context-sensitivity with respect to lexical insertion. Consider the following examples:

(i) a. John is happy
b. John is happy about his work
c. John is happy Mary is arriving soon
d. *John is happy about his work it is going well

Formulate the subcategorization features for *happy*. In terms of subcategorization features, what is the difference between the predicate adjective *happy* and the predicate adjective *red*?

In addition to subcategorization violations, the lexical insertion transformation will generate ill-formed examples like (24a). The problem here is not subcategorization, since *annoy* takes an NP object as illustrated in (24b).

(25) a. *John annoyed the book
b. John annoyed the woman

(25a) is ill formed because the verb *annoy* requires an animate object, whereas *book* is inanimate. The distinction between (25a) and (25b) turns on a difference in the value of a feature ([±animate]) of the head of the object NP. To account for restrictions on the occurrence of a verb with respect to the features of its object, we need to introduce another type of contextual feature. Thus, the lexical item *annoy* will contain a feature [+___. . .[+animate]] that defines a connection between the verb and an inherent feature of the noun that heads its object NP. That this connection holds between the verb and the lexical head of the object NP (and not just any lexical noun contained in the object—e.g., *author* in (26b)) is illustrated in the following paradigm, where the head of the object NP is [+animate] in (26a) but [–animate] in (26b).

(26) a. the actors annoyed [$_{NP}$ the play's author]
b. *the actors annoyed [$_{NP}$ the author's play]

Note that we are assuming that *author* (in contrast to *play*) is the lexical head of NP in (26a) and that *play* (in contrast to *author*) is the lexical head of NP in (26b). The relation between the verb *annoy* and the head of its object NP is called **selection** (in the sense that *annoy* selects an animate object); hence, these particular contextual features are designated as

**selectional features** (or **selectional restrictions**). Selection is a head-to-head relation.

---

**Exercise 2.4**
A similar relation holds between some verbs and their subjects. Consider the following examples:

(i) a. *the book admires John
b. the woman admires John

(ii) a. [$_{NP}$ the inventor of these microcircuits] admired Einstein
b. *[$_{NP}$ these microcircuits of the inventor] admired Einstein

Formulate the selectional feature of the verb *admire* and discuss how (ii) demonstrates that selectional restrictions on subjects also involve only the lexical head of the subject NP.

---

Like subcategorization features, selectional features constitute lexical properties of particular lexical items. Thus, selectional violations fall under the Principle of Lexical Satisfaction (24). A selectional feature is satisfied only when there is a match between the inherent feature it mentions and the inherent feature of the lexical head of the appropriate NP in the actual phrase marker. When there is a mismatch, the Principle of Lexical Satisfaction is violated—in exactly the same way that subcategorization violations arise.

This completes our discussion of lexical insertion. Having established how lexical items instantiate lexical categories, we can turn to the relationship between lexical and phrasal categories.

## 2.3 A Theory of Phrase Structure

The analysis of phrase structure addresses two fundamental questions:

A. What is the class of possible syntactic categories?
B. What determines the internal organization of these categories?

In this section we will explore a theory that attempts to provide principled answers to these basic questions.

Up to this point we have been assuming the lexical categories of noun, verb, adjective, and preposition. In what follows, we will take these lexical categories as primitives—and therefore will not attempt to justify choosing them as distinct word classes.[6]

In addition to N, V, A, and P, we can distinguish the following lexical categories:

(27) Adverb (Adv) *quickly, soon, . . .*
Conjunction (Conj) *and, but, or, . . .*
Determiner (Det) *a, the, this, these, . . .*
Auxiliary verb (Aux) *have, be, will, should, . . .*
Quantifier (Q) *all, every, some, . . .*

One reason for distinguishing quantifiers from determiners is the existence of phrases like *all the men*—assuming of course that this phrase is an NP with a lexical head *men.* (Note that under this analysis we would have to explain **some the men* and **every the men*—so the syntax of quantified NPs (NPs containing a quantifier) becomes a complicated issue.)

As noted in section 2.1, whether every lexical category projects its own phrasal category (in the way that N projects NP, for example) is an open question. It appears that Adv projects an AdvP since an adverb and a modifying degree word like *very* seem to form a phrasal unit, as in *very quickly.* For the other categories listed in (27), the issue is not so clear. Therefore, the following discussion of the relation between lexical and phrasal categories will be limited to the clear cases, those involving N, V, A, and P. It should be obvious at this point that the answer to question A above depends significantly on the specification of the full class of lexical categories.

To distinguish between lexical categories and their phrasal projections, we will utilize a star notation in which phrasal categories are represented by a lexical category symbol that is marked with a star to the right, in contrast to lexical categories, which bear no star.[7]

(28) [+N]*
|
[+N]

In this way, the set of lexical categories (or a subset of them) determines in part the class of phrasal categories. That is, a lexical category X (where X represents a category variable) projects a phrasal category XP (or X* in our notation), where X is the lexical head of XP.

As noted in section 2.2, lexical categories and categorial features are equivalent notations (e.g., N = [+N]). This equivalence between categories and features can be extended to phrasal categories as well. For example, a phrasal category NP constitutes a phrasal projection of the feature [+N]. Given the equivalence between category notation and feature notation,

(28) can also be represented as (29) where N is the lexical head of the phrasal projection N*.

(29) N*
|
N

Let us further assume that only categorial features can be used to define phrasal categories. This limits the class of phrasal categories. For example, it is not possible to use a feature such as [±plural] to define two phrasal categories [+N, +plural]* ($NP_{plural}$) and [+N, –plural]* ($NP_{singular}$). These would be distinct phrasal categories, just like NP and VP, even though they share the feature [+N]. The problem with such analyses is that they increase the class of possible syntactic categories in ways that fail to capture generalizations. If the [±plural] distinction is used to define phrasal projections of nouns, then for transitive verbs taking a single NP object we will have to state two distinct subcategorization features, [+___[+N, +plural]] and [+___[+N, –plural]], instead of one. This misses the point that the [±plural] distinction is generally not relevant for determining the syntactic distribution of NPs (e.g., direct objects, indirect objects, and objects of prepositions). Similar objections can be raised against employing contextual features to define phrasal categories. To exclude noncategorial features from the definition of phrasal categories and thereby further restrict the class of possible syntactic categories, let us adopt (30) as a principle of the theory of grammar.

(30) **Principle of Category Composition**
Syntactic categories are determined solely on the basis of categorial features.

A theory of categories that includes (30) excludes *in principle* phrase structure grammars that miss the above-mentioned kinds of generalizations about the distribution of phrasal categories. Thus, $NP_{[-plural]}$, for example, is not a possible syntactic category under this theory. In delimiting the class of possible syntactic categories, the Principle of Category Composition provides part of the answer to question A, as well as clarifying the nature of phrasal projection in phrase structure theory. (Having utilized the equivalence of categories and features in this way, we will, however, continue to use category notation for the purpose of exposition.)

Another issue related to both question A and question B concerns the phrasal projections of lexical heads. Can there be more than one phrasal projection per lexical head? If so, what is the categorial relation between these phrasal projections? The idea that a lexical head can project multiple levels of phrasal projection is the central postulate of the **X-bar theory** of phrase structure. All of these questions are explored in the explication of X-bar theory that follows.

We begin with the evidence for postulating more than one level of phrasal projection for certain lexical categories. The evidence concerns (i) the analysis of subcategorization and (ii) an apparent structural parallelism between S and NP with respect to verbs and their corresponding nominalizations (e.g., the verb *criticize* and its nominalization as *criticism*). The following discussion illustrates how empirical arguments for multiple phrasal projections from a single lexical head might be formulated. It is to be hoped that as the study of phrase structure deepens, further (and perhaps stronger) arguments may come to light.

We begin with an analysis of verbal subcategorization. Recall that "#" in the subcategorization feature of intransitive verbs ([+___#]) cannot be interpreted as 'end of sentence' because these verbs can be followed by syntactic material.

(31) a. John slept soundly
b. John slept on the couch
c. John slept for three hours
d. John slept because he was tired

For "#" to be interpreted as 'end of VP', we would have to establish that the syntactic material to the right of *slept* in each example was not a constituent of VP. One diagnostic that has been used (though it is not without problems) involves the ability of a phrase to the right of a verb to be moved to the front of the sentence. It is assumed that if a phrase can be preposed to the front of a sentence, then it is a constituent of S; whereas if it cannot be preposed, then it is a constituent of VP. Of the examples in (31), only (31c–d) seem to allow such preposing—hence the distinction between (32a–b) and (32c–d).

(32) a. *soundly, John slept
b. *on the couch, John slept
c. for three hours, John slept
d. because he was tired, John slept

If the adverb in (31a) and the PP in (31b) are constituents of VP as this diagnostic indicates, then "#" in the subcategorization feature of *sleep* cannot be construed as 'end of VP'. Within X-bar theory, there is another possibility—namely, that an intermediate level of phrasal projection exists between the lexical head V and the phrasal projection we have been calling VP. Thus, there will be two levels of phrasal projection for V. If we designate the phrasal projection that immediately dominates the lexical head to be the domain of subcategorization for verbs, then "#" will designate 'end of the subcategorization domain'. Thus, the VP of (31a) will have the internal phrase structure given in (33), where the category symbol V stands for the feature [+V] and the "*" indicates phrasal projection.

(33)

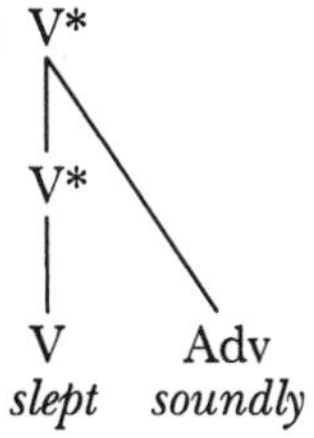


(Having established that lexical items are simply instantiations of lexical categories, we now have a rationale for tree diagrams in which lexical items (here, *slept* and *soundly*) are set in italic type directly below their respective lexical categories (rather than by joining them with a tree branch).)

Granting that there is more than one level of phrasal projection for V, we can distinguish the two phrasal categories in (33) by designating the V* that dominates Adv as the "maximal phrasal projection" of V. Thus, a **maximal phrasal projection** of a lexical head X is the X* that dominates all the other X* projections of X (and consequently is not dominated by any phrasal projection of X). In this way, "maximal phrasal projection" is a relational notion. For the sentence *The boy slept*, the following phrase structure representation is possible.

(34)

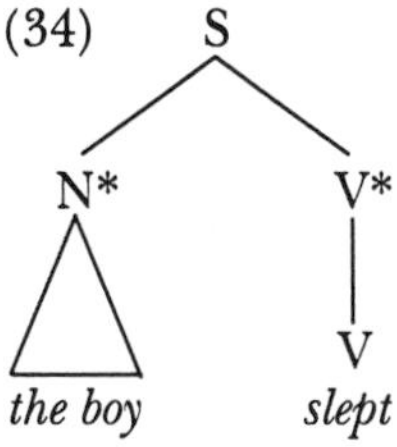


In (34) V* is the maximal phrasal projection of V. It is also the subcategorization domain of V as discussed above. The phrase marker for (34), {S, N* V*, N* *slept*, . . .}, will not change if we introduce a second level of phrasal projection for V in the tree diagram (34). In fact, there is no way to represent V* dominating only V* in a phrase marker—which is one way that phrase markers are different from and also more restrictive than tree diagrams. This provides some motivation for the relational interpretation of the notion "maximal phrasal projection."[8]

If subcategorization for verbs is limited to immediate constituents of the phrasal category that immediately dominates the head, then it must follow that other constituents of VP that do not determine the subcategorization of verbs must be constituents of further phrasal projections of V. Let us designate the subcategorization domain as the **strictly local domain** of V. As discussed earlier, the constituents in the strictly local domain of V are designated as complements of V. Constituents of V* that are outside the strictly local domain are designated as **adjuncts**. Adjuncts are generally phrases (e.g., AP, PP, S) or lexical constituents (e.g., Det for NP) that modify a phrase or the head of a phrase. Assuming that the complement versus adjunct distinction applies across categories, we have the following general schema for phrase structure.

(35)

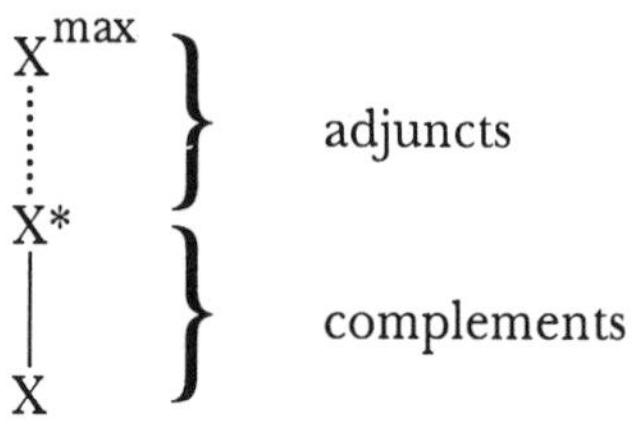


The maximal phrasal projection of X is designated $X^{max}$. The dotted line between X* and $X^{max}$ indicates the possibility of other levels of phrasal projection of X, whereas the straight line between X and X* indicates that X* immediately dominates X.

---

**Exercise 2.5**

Identify the phrases in brackets in (i.a–e) as complements or adjuncts and discuss the motivation for your analysis.

(i) a. Sam left [the party] [early] [because he was tired]
b. Jill destroyed [the letter] [when she realized [who had sent it]]
c. Tom persuaded [the committee] [that Mary should be appointed]
d. George praised [the committee] [for their dedication]
e. John ate [too quickly] [without chewing [each mouthful] [carefully]]

Note that in (i.b) and (i.e) the bracketed phrases themselves contain bracketed phrases that are to be identified.

---

The distinction between complement and adjunct applies to the internal structure of NP as well as VP. (Note that here and in what follows the designation "XP" (here "NP") is being used as an abbreviation for "a maximal phrasal projection of [+X]" (here [+N]).) This is illustrated by the parallelism in structure between NP and VP—for example in (36), where α in (36b) represents a phrasal category to be identified below.

(36) a. Blanche [$_{VP}$ studies physics at MIT]
b. [$_{NP}$ the [$_{\alpha}$ student of physics at MIT]]

The lexical head of the VP in (36a) is the verb *studies.* The direct object *physics* in (36a) is a complement of *studies,* whereas *at MIT* is taken to be an adjunct on the grounds that the act of studying involves *Blanche* and *physics,* but not *MIT* (cf. the role of *couch* in (31b)). Therefore, *physics* is a constituent of the subcategorization domain, whereas *at MIT* is not. The lexical head of the NP in (36b) is the noun *student* (which corresponds to the verb *studies* in (36a)). The NP in (36b) is related to the VP in (36a) in the sense that someone who is a student of physics at MIT is someone who studies physics at MIT. If *physics* and *MIT* bear the same relationships to the noun *student* as they do to the verb *studies,* then *of physics* is a complement of the noun *student* (on a par with the related verb *study*), and *at MIT* functions as an adjunct with respect to *student.* Thus, *of physics* must be a constituent of the subcategorization domain, and *at MIT* (which cannot be a constituent of the subcategorization domain, given the analysis developed above), must be a constituent of a higher level of phrasal projection. The internal structure of (36b) will then be (37).

(37)

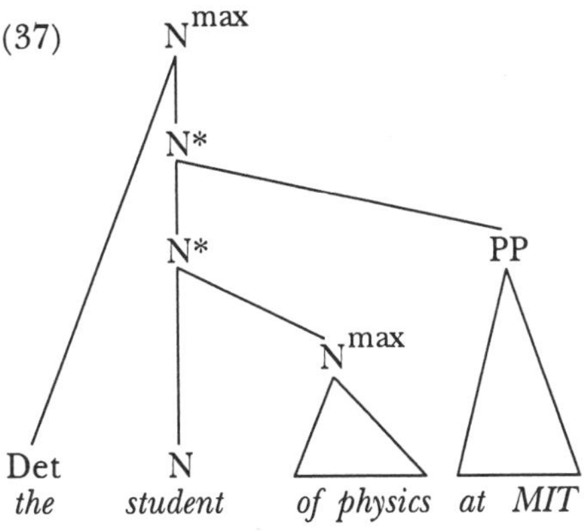


(The analysis of the phrase *of physics* as NP rather than PP will be justified in section 2.4.)[9]

Under the analysis that distinguishes *physics* and *MIT* as complement and adjunct, the ungrammaticality of (38) follows.

(38) *a student at MIT of physics

The phrase *at MIT* could not precede the phrase *of physics* unless either *at MIT* could occur as a constituent of the subcategorization domain, or the complement *physics* could occur as a constituent outside the subcategorization domain. If neither is possible, as we are assuming, then (38) is excluded. In this way, the linear order of complements and adjuncts follows from the hierarchical order of constituents.

---

**Exercise 2.6**

A similar case can be made for the noun *student* using a second adjunct phrase *with red hair.* Discuss the the ordering of phrases in the following examples:

(i) a. a student of physics with red hair
 b. *a student with red hair of physics
 c. a student of physics with red hair from MIT
 d. a student of physics from MIT with red hair

Be sure to distinguish complements and adjuncts in your answer.

---

In this analysis, the NP *physics* subcategorizes the noun *student* in the same way that this NP subcategorizes the verb *study*—both are [+___NP]. The noun *student* therefore contrasts with nouns like *boy*, which takes no complements (as indicated by the ill-formedness of **a boy of physics*) and is therefore [+___#].

There is, however, a distinction to be made between subcategorization in VPs and subcategorization in NPs. In VP the elements that subcategorize a verb generally fill some grammatical function—such as direct or indirect object—with respect to the verbal head. In NP this is not always the case. Although an argument can be made that *physics* functions as the object of the noun *student* in *student of physics*, this does not hold for *physics* and *book* in the following phrases:

(39) a. a book of physics in German
 b. *a book in German of physics

The ordering facts parallel those of (36b) and (38). If the ordering facts in (39) also follow from hierarchical structure, then subcategorization for nouns has a wider basis than the notion "grammatical function." We will assume this to be the case in what follows, having noted that the issues raised are far from settled.

In the case of true adjuncts, ordering appears to be free. Consider (40).

(40) a. a book about physics in German
b. a book in German about physics

Comparing (40) with the analysis of (38), we would say that the PPs *about physics* and *in German* are both adjuncts rather than complements of *book* and therefore are constituents of a second level of phrasal projection. If both PPs are constituents of the same level of phrasal projection, then their linear order need not be fixed, as (40) illustrates. It should also be noted that differences in hierarchical structure between (39a) and (40a) do not necessarily result in a difference in interpretation, since both NPs appear to have roughly the same interpretation. That is, the distinction is exclusively a syntactic one based on facts about linear order.

The hierarchical distinction between adjunct and complement also accounts for the linear ordering of sentential forms in NPs. Consider the following paradigm, where the relative clause *which had been misplaced* is interpreted as modifying *report* in both examples.

(41) a. the report that they had defected which had been misplaced
b. *the report which had been misplaced that they had defected

(41) contains two sentential forms, *that they had defected* and *which had been misplaced.* The former is a sentential complement (cf. *I reported that they had defected*); the latter, a relative clause. We will assume that the sentential complement is a constituent of the subcategorization domain of *report,* since not all nouns can occur with a sentential complement (e.g., **The boy that they had defected*). In contrast, virtually any common noun can be modified by a relative clause (e.g., *the boy who they had found*). If relative clauses are analyzed as adjuncts, (41a) has a structural analysis that conforms to our assumptions about the hierarchical ordering of complements and adjuncts in NP, whereas (41b) does not.

To summarize: We assume that the phrasal projection that immediately dominates its lexical head is the level of subcategorization for all lexical heads. The notion "subcategorization" involves the notion "grammatical relation" (specifically "object") with respect to verbs and their corresponding nouns, but requires further clarification as it extends to nouns in general, to adjectives, and to prepositions. It follows from this analysis of subcategorization that the internal structure of phrases containing either specifiers or adjuncts must involve more than one level of phrasal projection.

Independent of this analysis of subcategorization, the existence of intermediate phrasal structure between the head of a phrase and its maximal phrasal projection draws further support from a parallelism between S and NP with respect to structures containing bound anaphors like the reciprocal *each other.*[10] Consider the sentence (42a) and the corresponding NP structure (42b).

(42) a. they criticized each other
b. their criticisms of each other

(Assume that *their* is a pronoun form for the third person plural and hence an N that projects an N* (corresponding to the N* *the men's* in the NP *the men's criticisms of each other*).) In each case the third person plural pronoun is interpreted as the antecedent of the anaphor. Furthermore, the anaphor must occur in a particular structural relationship with its antecedent, as the contrast between (42) and (43) shows.

(43) a. *each other criticized them
b. *each other's criticisms of them

This relationship can be characterized in terms of hierarchical structure, as discussed below.

In the sentential structure (44), there is an asymmetry in the hierarchical relation between $NP_1$ and $NP_2$.

(44)

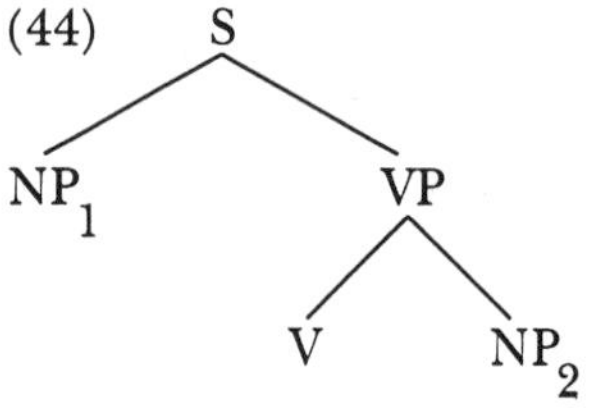


The node that immediately dominates $NP_1$ (i.e., S) also dominates $NP_2$; but the node that immediately dominates $NP_2$ (i.e., VP) does not dominate $NP_1$. The asymmetry is formalized in the relation of **constituent command** (henceforth c-command) which is based on the branching property of phrase markers.

(45) A category $\alpha$ *c-commands* a category $\beta$ if and only if the category that immediately dominates $\alpha$ also dominates $\beta$, and neither $\alpha$ nor $\beta$ dominates the other.[11]

It is assumed that c-command is a relation that holds only between pairs of constituents in a linear relation (thus the stipulation lack of dominance). Given (45), the following c-command relations hold in (44):

(46) a. $NP_1$ c-commands $NP_2$
b. $NP_2$ does not c-command $NP_1$
c. $NP_2$ c-commands V
d. V c-commands $NP_2$
e. V does not c-command $NP_1$

The category that immediately dominates a is the c-command domain of a. Thus, S is the c-command domain of $NP_1$ and VP is the c-command domain of V and $NP_2$.

The difference between (42a) and (43a) can be stated in terms of c-command. In the ill-formed example (43a), the anaphor c-commands its antecedent. Let us assume that this ill-formedness follows from a principle of grammar, specifically (47).

(47) **C-command Condition on Anaphors**
An anaphor may not c-command its antecedent.

Since the subject position in a sentence c-commands the object position of the sentence, (43a) violates the C-command Condition on Anaphors.

Principle (47) bears on the analysis of the internal structure of the NPs. Consider the options (48a) and (48b) for the internal structure of the NPs (42b) and (43b).

(48) a.

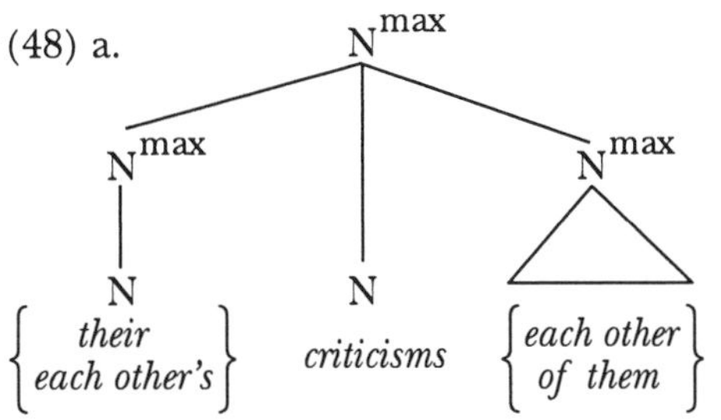


(48) b.

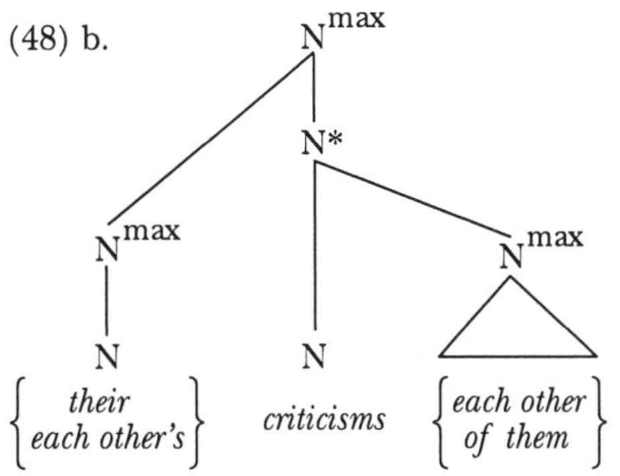

If we analyze these NPs as having the so-called flat structure in (48a), where both embedded NPs are immediate constituents of the NP that dominates them, then principle (47) incorrectly predicts (42b) to be ill formed. If, however, the analysis of these NPs is as in (48b), then principle (47) correctly distinguishes the well-formed (42b) from the ill-formed (43b) and thereby generalizes to NPs. In this way, the most general account of anaphor-antecedent relations provides empirical evidence regarding the internal phrase structure of NPs.

This completes our discussion of the empirical evidence for postulating more than one level of phrasal projection for a given lexical head. Given that for all lexical heads X, there is only one corresponding phrasal category X*, we can formulate a general set of phrase structure rules as follows, where "..." indicates other lexical or phrasal categories.

(49) a. X* ⟶ . . . X* . . .
b. X* ⟶ . . . X . . .

In any given derivation, the highest level of phrasal projection will be designated as the maximal phrasal projection. The phrasal projection that immediately dominates the lexical head will constitute the subcategorization domain.

---

**Exercise 2.7**

Considering the following examples, how many levels of phrasal projection for N can you motivate using the principles and analyses discussed above?

(i) a. their books about each other
b. *each other's books about them

Assume that the phrase *about N** is an adjunct. Discuss the motivation for your analysis in as much detail as you can.

---

**Exercise 2.8**

The idea that all levels of phrasal projection of a particular lexical head are categorially nondistinct seems to be supported for N* by a phenomenon called *One*-Substitution. Thus, in sentences containing identical NPs it is often possible to replace a portion of the second NP with the anaphoric expression *one*. Consider the following examples:

(i) a. Mary has a beautiful cup and John has an ugly cup
b. Mary has a beautiful cup and John has an ugly one

(ii) a. the student from Princeton was wiser than the student from Harvard
b. the student from Princeton was wiser than the one from Harvard

Give an analysis of the NPs affected by *One*-Substitution and identify the structure(s) *one* substitutes for.

Now consider the following pair:

(iii) a. the student of philosophy was wiser than the student of physics
b. *the student of philosophy was wiser than the one of physics

Why is (iii.b) ungrammatical?

How do the following examples fit into the analysis of *One*-Substitution?

(iv) a. John has a green cup and I want one too
b. the report that John was lying which I revised was more convinc ing than the one which I tore up

State what *one* stands for in each example.

Now test your general hypothesis by providing another example (distinct from the structures above) and showing whether it supports your analysis.

---

From the Principle of Lexical Satisfaction (24), it will follow that every lexical head projects at least one phrasal category if every lexical head is linked to a subcategorization feature via the lexicon. Given our functional interpretation of maximal phrasal projection, every lexical head projects a maximal phrasal projection. Thus, phrase structure representations like (50a) will be allowed under this theory of grammar, but ones like (50b) will not.

(50) a.

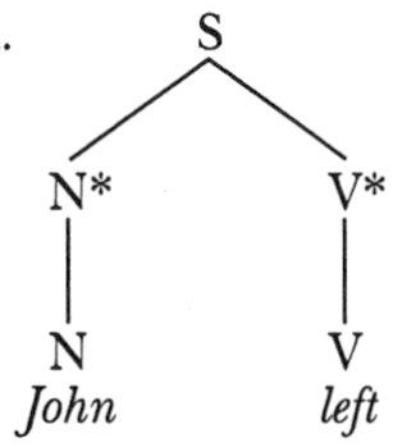


b.

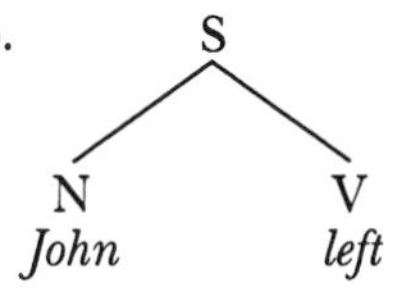


Thus far it has been established that a lexical head projects at least a maximal phrasal projection, and in some cases an intermediate phrasal level between the head and the maximal phrasal projection. Whether there is evidence for postulating more than one intermediate phrasal level remains to be determined. Presumably, it would be possible to distinguish between the intermediate levels configurationally in terms of constituency. Thus, the intermediate phrasal level that contains the head as an immediate constituent would be the subcategorization domain, given that subcategorization is strictly local. A phrasal level that directly dominates another phrasal level would therefore contain adjuncts or modifiers (if such a distinction is motivated) rather than complements.

## 2.4 The Transformational Structure of NP

In this section we will take up a more detailed analysis of the phrase structure of NPs, based on the X-bar theory presented in the previous section. In particular, we will be considering the phrase structure analysis of NPs that contain NPs as constituents, as in (51)—under the assumption that *student, physics, Max,* and *Princeton* in these examples are Ns.

(51) a. the student's criticism
b. the study of physics
c. Max's study of physics at Princeton

Under this assumption, it follows from the X-bar theory that each of these Ns projects a phrasal category. What, then, is the relation between *'s* and *of* and their respective NPs? We will see that *'s* in (51a) and (51c) and *of* in (51b) (51c) can be designated as constituents of NP and as such are predictable via a rule of grammar—in each case, a transformation that inserts *'s* or *of* into a phrase marker. The introduction of these transformations leads to a preliminary discussion on the form and operation of transformations.

One rationale for treating the phrase *of physics* in (51b-c) as an NP rather than a PP concerns the definition of the grammatical relation "object of" within X-bar theory.[12] Given that NP objects occur within the subcategorization domains of V and P, we can define an "object" configurationally as an NP that is a **sister node** to the lexical head (V or P). The sisterhood relation is defined as follows:

(52) A category $\alpha$ is a *sister* of a category $\beta$ iff the category that immediately dominates $\alpha$ immediately dominates $\beta$.

In this way, the notion "object" generalizes across categories, so an NP object can be designated as [NP;X] (where ";" indicates 'sister of' and X stands for any lexical head (e.g., V, P, N, or A) which takes a sister NP).

In the case of N, this analysis seems desirable because it allows us to capture a parallelism between verbs and their corresponding nominals, as illustrated by a comparison of (51c) and (53).

(53) Max studies physics at Princeton

In each example, the NP *physics* is interpreted as the logical object—of the verb *study* in (53) and of its corresponding noun *study* in (51c).[13]

Under this analysis, *of* is a grammatical formative attached to NP (rather than being a lexical item, such as a preposition, which, as a lexical head, projects its own phrasal category). Unlike a preposition, the grammatical formative *of* appears to contribute nothing to the semantic interpretation of the construction in which it occurs. The distribution of this *of* is limited to a particular context in NP and is therefore predictable via a rule of grammar that is formulated in terms of this context—given in (54), where "___" indicates the linear position of *of* and $N^{max}$ stands for an N* that is the maximal phrasal projection of some lexical head N.

(54) $[_{N^{max}}$ N ___ $N^{max}]$

We are assuming that *of* is not generated by a phrase structure rule so as to avoid having NPs containing this grammatical formative occurring in any NP position (e.g., (**of*) *the boy read the book, the book terrified* (**of*) *the boy, John read about* (**of*) *the disaster*). Instead, we will assume that *of* is inserted in a phrase marker by a transformational operation that maps (54) onto (55).

(55) $[_{N^{max}}$ N $[_{\wedge N^{max}}$ of $N^{max}]]$

($\wedge N^{max}$ is just a copy of the $N^{max}$ it directly dominates; therefore, it is also an instance of N* categorially.) This insertion cannot take place by substitution since there is no category in (54) to which the substitution operation could apply. In this instance the insertion is achieved by adjoining *of* to N*.

The adjunction operation is a transformation, like substitution, which maps a phrase marker onto another phrase marker. Consider the underlying phrase marker for the phrase *criticisms of Freud*, given in tree representation as (56). (To avoid confusion over which N* is a projection of which N, maximal phrasal projections will be identified with a superscript "max" in the following representations. Bear in mind, though, that a maximal phrasal projection is just like any other phrasal projection; that is, $X^{max}$ is just another instance of X*.)

(56)

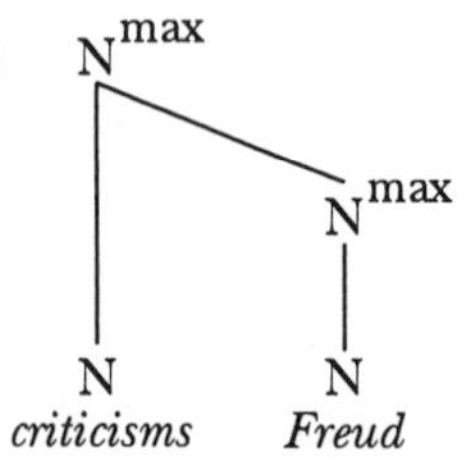


Because *criticisms* is specified with a subcategorization feature [+___NP], it follows from the Principle of Lexical Satisfaction that the topmost $N^{max}$ (= N*) in (56) must be a projection of *criticisms* and not *Freud*. Thus, our analysis of subcategorization excludes an interpretation of (56) where the highest $N^{max}$ is the maximal phrasal projection of the N *Freud*.

The actual phrase marker for (56) is given in (57), where the lexical items represent the lexical category N and the phrasal projections are given as N*.

(57) {N*, *criticisms* N*, *criticisms Freud*}

The phrase marker expresses the "is a" relation, spelled out in (58), that holds between the various strings of categories and single categories.

(58) a. *criticisms N** is an N*
b. *criticisms Freud* is an N*
c. *Freud* is an N*

When *of* is inserted by adjunction, we obtain a new terminal string *criticisms of Freud*. To create a **derived phrase marker** for this new string, we must establish how adjunction affects the set of "is a" relations in the phrase marker. In the case of *of*-insertion,[14] let us assume that the grammatical formative *of* adjoins to $N^{max}$—that is, adjunction has the effect of making *of* an immediate constituent of $N^{max}$. There are two options to consider, shown in (59). (From this point on tree diagrams will distinguish lexical items (in italic type) from grammatical formatives—e.g., *of* in (59a) and (59b)—(in Roman type). In (59a) *of N** is an $N^{max}$. On the one hand, this is a struc-tural relation that did not exist before the transformation applied; the adjunction operation has built new structure into the phrase marker and is therefore designated a **structure-building** operation. On the other hand, structural information has been lost in

(59a), because *Freud* by itself is no longer an $N^{max}$ (i.e., N*). The kind of adjunction that maps (55) onto (59a) is therefore **structure-destroying** in a sense.

(59) a.

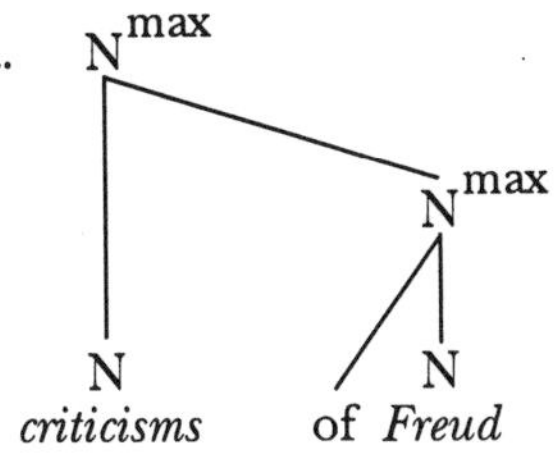


b.

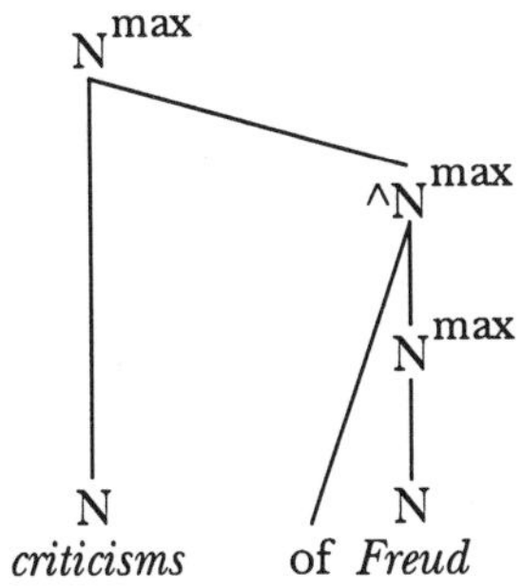


In contrast, the kind of adjunction represented in (59b) is only structure-building. The derived phrase marker is minimally changed. To see this, it is necessary to interpret $^\wedge N^{max}$ properly. In the initial phrase marker (57) the N* dominating only *Freud* is a maximal phrasal projection. To retain this relationship and at the same time accommodate the insertion of *of* as a constituent of the NP, we must construct a copy of this $N^{max}$ that takes *of* and the entire projection of *Freud* as immediate constituents. Thus, *Freud* by itself is still an $N^{max}$ and *of Freud* is also an $N^{max}$. Given as a set of strings, the phrase marker (57) is changed by changing the terminal string to *criticisms of Freud* and adding a single new string *of* $N^{max}$. Compare (57) with (60), where the N*s have been replaced with their interpretations as $N^{max}$.

(60) {$N^{max}$, *criticisms* $N^{max}$, *of* $N^{max}$, *criticisms of Freud*}

Under this interpretation, N* immediately dominated by $^\wedge N^{max}$ designates a maximal phrasal projection of N that is immediately dominated by a copy of itself. This distinguishes N*, which is a true phrasal projection of N, from $^\wedge N^{max}$ which is not projected from N in the same sense. In what follows we will represent the adjunction site as $^\wedge N^{max}$ immediately dominating $N^{max}$.

From here on we will assume that all adjunctions behave like the rule of *Of*-Insertion. Schematically, the adjunction of a category α to a category β can have only two possible outcomes, shown in (61a) and (61b).

(61) a.
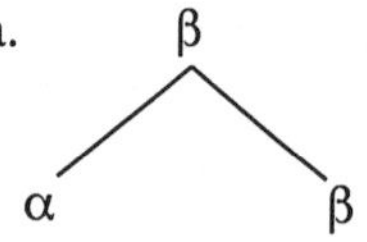


b.
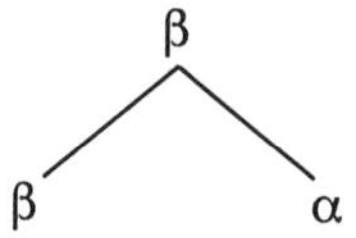

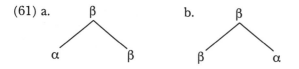

(61a) is an instance of "left adjunction," (α is adjoined to the left of β); (61b) is an instance of "right-adjunction."

Having determined the effect of the elementary transformational operation that inserts a grammatical formative *of* in NP, let us consider how this operation is incorporated into a formal rule of grammar. A **transformation** is a rule that consists of two parts: (i) a **structural description** (SD), which identifies those phrase markers that are subject to the transformation by virtue of their structural properties, and (ii) a **structural change** (SC), which indicates how the phrase marker is to be reorganized. *Of*-Insertion is formulated as in (62).

(62) *Of*-Insertion

| | | | | | | | |
|---|---|---|---|---|---|---|---|
| | X | – | N | – | $N^{max}$ | – | Y |
| SD: | 1 | | 2 | | 3 | | 4 |
| SC: | 1 | | 2 | | *of* + 3 | | 4 |

In (62) N and $N^{max}$ are **constant terms** (or "constants") and X and Y are **variables**, which range over strings of constants or the null string. The SD is given as a string of terms (constants and variables), each with a unique structural index (1–4 in (62)). The SC indicates how this string is affected by the transformation. In (62) "+" indicates the elementary operation of adjunction. Thus, the linear order of the terms in the SD of (62) is unaffected by the SC, with the exception of adjacency between terms 2 and 3. Note that the term $N^{max}$ in (62) is an interpretation of some N* adjacent to an N, and not an actual category designation in the phrase marker.

*Of*-Insertion applies only when a phrase marker meets the SD of (62). Consider (63) (where V* and A* are obviously maximal phrasal projections of their respective heads and hence are not identified as such).

(63)

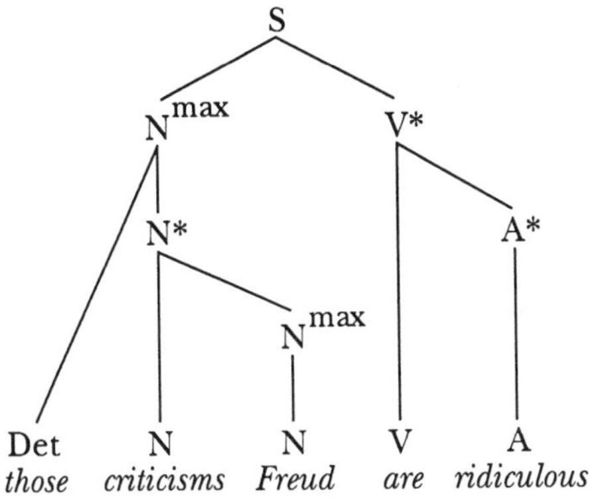


The phrase marker (63) can be analyzed by (62) since it contains a string *N* $N^{max}$–namely, *Det N* $N^{max}$ *VP*. This can be represented by parsing the phrase structure tree as shown in (64).

(64)

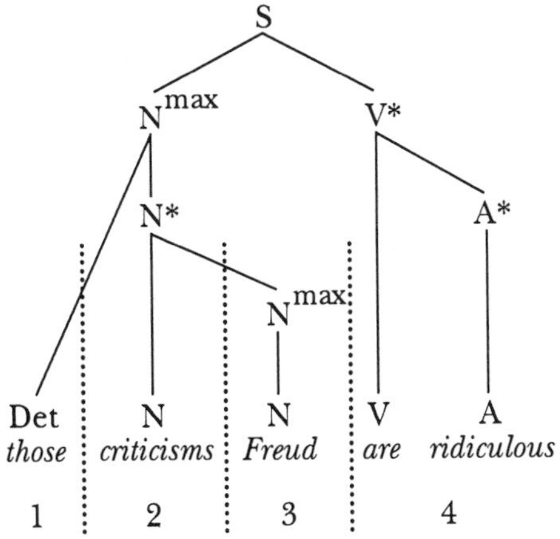


The variable X in the SD in (62) (term 1) covers the determiner *those*, the variable Y (term 4) covers VP. The constant terms are as given in (64). (If we were instead considering the phrase marker for *Criticisms of Freud are often amusing*, then the variable X (term 1) would cover the null string.) The output of (62) as applied to (63) is (65):

(65)

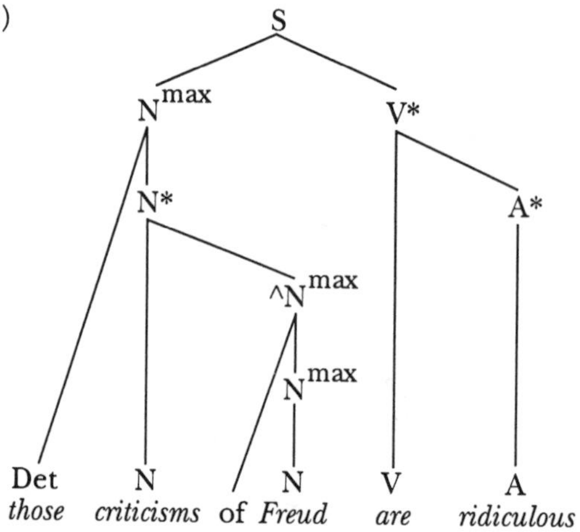


Note that (62) *must* apply to (63) in order to generate a grammatical English sentence. Thus, (62) should be considered an **obligatory** rule—one that must apply when a phrase marker meets its SD—and must be designated as such. (Obligatory rules contrast with **optional** rules, which may apply when a phrase marker meets their SD, but need not apply at all.)

Designating *Of*-Insertion as obligatory creates an immediate problem—namely, the output of the rule also fits the SD of the rule. Thus, the $N^{max}$ *of Freud* in (65) can be analyzed by (62) as an instance of term 3. If the rule must apply when its SD is met (which is after all the definition of an obligatory rule), then (62) must reapply to (65), producing the ill-formed sentence **Those criticisms of of Freud were ridiculous.* As formulated in (62), the rule will continue to reapply to its own output indefinitely—in which case the derivation will never terminate. To prevent this possibility, the rule of *Of*-Insertion cannot be designated as obligatory; rather, it must be an optional rule. Hence, it will be necessary to account for the obligatoriness of (62) in some other way. Specifying (62) as optional allows for the possibility that *Of*-Insertion will apply once and once only to a given NP. It does not account either for the fact that the rule *must* apply once to an NP that meets its SD or for the fact that it *cannot* apply more than once (i.e., that it cannot apply iteratively to its own output). A solution to these problems will be deferred until the transformational analysis of the distribution of *'s* is presented below—where the identical problems arise.

As formulated, (62) is a language-specific rule for inserting the English grammatical formative *of* by adjunction. The adjunction operation itself, however, is not language-specific; rather, it is part of the theory of grammar—specifically, the subtheory of transformations. We expect that the adjunction operation figures in transformational rules of other languages besides English. For example, the distribution of French *de* in NPs might also result from an adjunction operation similar to that of English grammar, as suggested by the following parallelism.

(66) a. the enemy destroyed the city
b. l'ennemi a détruit la ville

(67) a. the destruction of the city by the enemy
b. la destruction de la ville par l'ennemi

Presumably the same argument for the transformational insertion of *of* based on the correspondence between the sentence (66a) and the NP (67a) carries over to French *de* in the NP (67b). What is language-specific to (62) is the element that is adjoined (*of* for English and *de* for French) and the structural condition under which the adjunction applies (i.e., the fact that N must be adjacent to an $N^{max}$ to the right). These factors determine the behavior of the adjunction operation, as does the obligatoriness of the rule. At this point the behavior of the adjunction operation that inserts *of* is stipulated in the formulation of the rule. Later we will see that some of this behavior follows from more general considerations in the theory of grammar and therefore need not be stipulated in the formulation of the rule itself.

We turn now to the distribution of NPs like *Mary's*, which occur in specific contexts (as shown in (68)), but not generally (as shown in (69)).

(68) a. Mary's son likes green olives
b. John told Mary's son a joke
c. John told a joke to Mary's son

(69) a. *Mary's likes green olives
b. *John told Mary's a joke
c. *John told a joke to Mary's

Because the distribution of *'s* forms is limited to certain contexts, it is unlikely that they are generated by context-free lexical insertion.[15] Given this fact, and the fact that the occurrence of *'s* is predictable from syntactic context, we might consider a transformational account. We will therefore consider *'s* as a grammatical formative (analogous to *of* in the constructions discussed earlier) that is transformationally inserted via adjunction.

Although *'s* is joined to the noun in standard orthographic practice, there is evidence that *'s* is actually adjoined to $N^{max}$. One function of *'s* is to indicate possession; thus, *'s* forms are often referred to as "possessives." In (70), for example, *friend* is the possessor and *hat* is the possessed object.

(70) a friend's hat

In (71) these relations remain unchanged, although orthographically *'s* is attached to the noun *Bill* and not *friend.*

(71) a friend of Bill's hat

Thus, (71) would have the partial syntactic representation (72), indicating that *'s* is adjoined to the maximal projection of *friend* and not to either the noun *Bill* or the maximal projection of that noun.

(72) $[_{N^{max}}$ $[_{\wedge N^{max}}$ $[_{N^{max}}$ a friend of Bill] 's] hat]

This analysis extends to nouns modified by relative clauses and PPs, as in (73).

(73) a. a mathematician who is from Göttingen's proof
b. a mathematician from Göttingen's proof

Although (73b) may be stylistically preferable to (73a), (73a)—which is awkward at worst—will be generated by the most general account of the rules of English grammar, as will be demonstrated below.[16]

Like *Of*-Insertion, the rule for inserting *'s* involves adjunction of a grammatical formative to an $N^{max}$ constituent of NP. Unlike the SD of *Of*-Insertion, however, the SD of *'s*-Insertion cannot be given in terms of an $N^{max}$ adjacent to N because of examples like (74).

(74) Wolfe's incredibly ingenious deduction

In (74) the AP *incredibly ingenious* intervenes between the $N^{max}$ *Wolfe* and the N *deduction.* Thus, the adjunction of *'s* to $N^{max}$ is not conditioned by the adjacency of $N^{max}$ to N—as seems to be the case for *Of*-Insertion. Instead, the SD of *'s*-Insertion must be given as in (75) where $N^{max}$ is adjacent to N*, which can include an AP as a constituent.

(75) *'s*-Insertion

| | | | | |
|---|---|---|---|---|
| | X – | $N^{max}$ – | N* – | Y |
| SD: | 1 | 2 | 3 | 4 |
| SC: | 1 | 2 + *'s* | 3 | 4 |

(75) would analyze the underlying phrase marker of (73b) as indicated in (76a) and map it onto the phrase marker given in (76b).

(76) a.

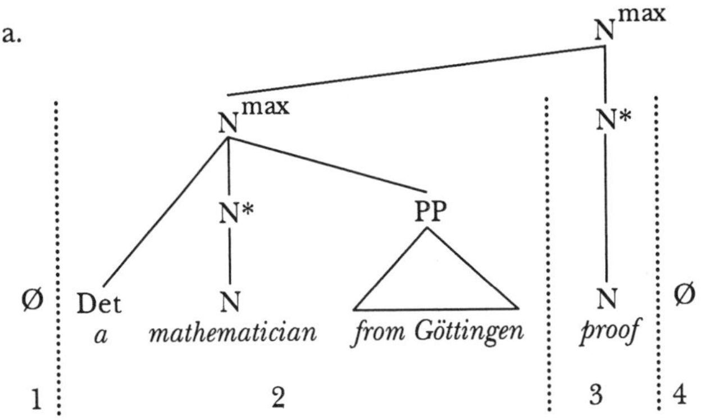


b.

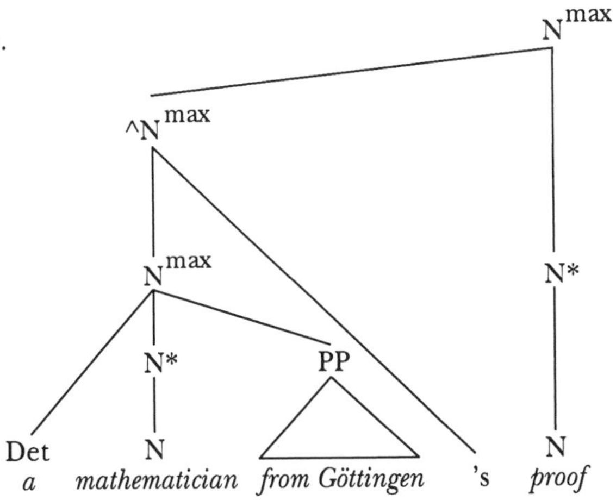


In a grammar, an underlying phrase marker is generated by phrase structure rules and the rule of lexical insertion that instantiates lexical categories as lexical items via substitution. Following current terminology, we will designate the initial underlying phrase marker in a derivation as a **D-structure** (also "deep structure" in earlier work on transformational grammar) and the phrase structure rules plus the rule of lexical insertion that generates D-structures as the **base component** of the grammar. A D-structure may be mapped onto a derived phrase marker via the application of a transformation, as in the case of (76a–b). If no other transformation applies to the derived phrase marker, then it constitutes the output of the transformational component which is called an **S-structure**.[17] If more than one transformation applies, only the final derived phrase marker constitutes the S-structure of the sentence in question. If no transformations apply to a particular D-structure, then we say that the D-structure and the S-structure of the sentence are identical. These relations among the base component, D-structure, transformations, and S-structure give the model of the syntactic component of a grammar shown in figure 2.1.

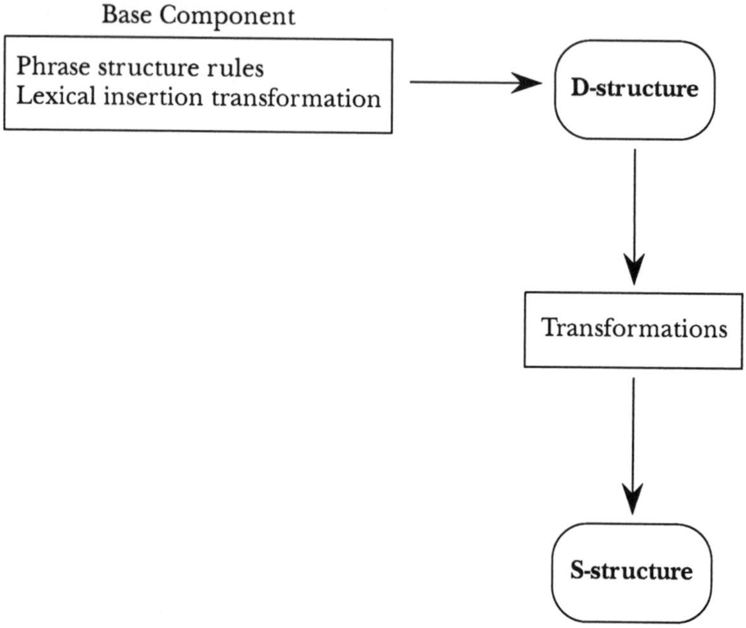


**Figure 2.1**
The syntactic component

Transformational derivations proceed stepwise. A D-structure will be analyzed by a transformation and mapped onto a derived phrase marker, which in turn may be analyzed by a transformation (the same one or another) and mapped onto another derived phrase marker—and so on until the last transformation in the derivation has applied.

---

**Exercise 2.9**
Using the rules of *Of*-Insertion (62) and *'s*-Insertion (75), give the transformational derivation for each of the following examples:

(i) a. John's brother's hat
b. Russell's account of Frege's theory
c. Kripke's criticisms of Russell's account of Frege's theory

That is, give the underlying phrase marker for each example and show how it is mapped onto its S-structure representation by applying one transformation at a time.

---

Rule (75) allows for the insertion of the affix *'s* in NPs generally. This does not account for NPs containing personal pronouns, as illustrated in (77).

(77) a. my copy of *Syntactic Structures*
b. her past achievements
c. their attempts at sarcasm

(77) shows that when a personal pronoun occurs in the position where a nonpronominal NP+*'s* occurs, the *'s* is suppressed; hence, we find *my* instead of the ill-formed *my's* in (77a). The problem is how to prevent *'s*-Insertion from applying to an $N^{max}$ when the lexical head N is a personal pronoun. If the rule is optional, we will be able to generate the grammatical examples in (77) from the nonapplication of the rule. But something more is needed to prevent the rule from applying to the NP projected by the pronoun. Since the theory of transformations does not allow rules that are formulated in terms of the lexical structure of phrase markers (e.g., it does not allow rules of the form "*'s*-Insertion applies only when the lexical head of term 2 is not a personal pronoun"), the ungrammaticality of NPs like **my's* must be accounted for in some other way.

An analysis of personal pronoun forms suggests that the solution concerns the notion of Case.[18] Consider the first person singular pronoun. This pronoun occurs in a variety of morphological forms (*I, me, my*), where choice of form depends on the syntactic context. The differences between the forms are characterized as differences in Case: *my* is the genitive Case of the first person singular pronoun, *I* is the nominative Case, and *me* is the objective Case.

Suppose that personal pronouns do not occur with the *'s* affix because they are inherently Case-marked in the lexicon (whereas nonpronominal nouns are not); that is, each personal pronoun has the Case specification in its lexical entry (e.g., *my* is marked [GENITIVE]). This suggests that the *'s* affix functions as a Case marker. Under this analysis, the question to be answered is why the *'s* affix and the feature [GENITIVE] cannot cooccur in the same NP. Since both are analyzed as Case markers, the straightforward solution is to prohibit NPs that are multiply marked for Case. The prohibition can be stated as a general principle concerning the uniqueness of Case assignment.

(78) **Case Uniqueness Principle**
A lexical NP may have only one Case marking.

This principle belongs to a subpart of the theory of grammar that concerns Case called Case theory.

The Case Uniqueness Principle constitutes a condition on syntactic representations. Such conditions function as **filters** to exclude ill-formed structures that would otherwise be generated by the rules of a grammar. Thus, the Case Uniqueness Principle filters out pronominal NPs like **my's* that are marked for Case twice: once by the grammatical formative *'s* and again by the inherent lexical feature [GENITIVE].

The Case Uniqueness Principle solves another problem that arises with the *'s*-Insertion rule. Like *Of*-Insertion, *'s*-Insertion as formulated in (75) can apply iteratively to its own output. In (76b), for example, the transformation can analyze the $N^{max}$ *a mathematician from Göttingen's* as term 2 and then reapply to yield the ill-formed (79).

(79) *a mathematician from Göttingen *'s's* proof

The Case Uniqueness Principle accounts for the ungrammaticality of (79) under our analysis of *'s* as a Case marker. (79) shows that the principle applies to multiple tokens of the same Case marker, as well as to different types of Case marker (assuming that *'s* and [GENITIVE] are not different types).

So far, the Case Uniqueness Principle explains (i) why *'s*-Insertion does not apply when the lexical head of NP is a personal pronoun, and (ii) why the rule does not iterate on its own output.

The Case Uniqueness Principle also solves another potential problem that arises from the formulation of *'s*-Insertion. The phrase marker of (73b), for example, contains more than one $N^{max}$ which is adjacent to an N* and hence can be analyzed as term 2 of (75). If the NP object of the PP *from Göttingen* is analyzed as term 2 of rule (75), then the derived phrase marker will show the Case marker *'s* adjoined to the $N^{max}$ *Göttingen*. Under the assumption that a preposition Case-marks its object as [OBJECTIVE] (see chapter 5 for details), the $N^{max}$ *Göttingen* will be multiply Case-marked in violation of the Case Uniqueness Principle.

**Exercise 2.10**
This shows that the NP *a mathematician from Göttingen's proof* can be assigned two different structural representations by the rules of grammar. One representation will be well formed and the other, ill formed. Give the underlying phrase marker for (73b). Show how *'s*-Insertion applies to yield a well-formed structure. Now show how the rule can misapply to yield an ill-formed structure—in other words, discuss how this structure violates the Case Uniqueness Principle.

This Case-theoretic approach to *'s*-Insertion unifies three otherwise unrelated problems concerning (i) application to NPs with personal pronoun heads, (ii) reapplication to the output of the rule, and (iii) misapplication to the wrong NP. Given the Case Uniqueness Principle, it follows that *'s*-Insertion can apply only once to a particular NP. A complete account of the rule's behavior now requires an explanation for why the rule *must* apply once. If the effect of *'s*-Insertion is to Case-mark an NP, then we might assume that it is Case marking itself that is obligatory. This follows if (80) is a principle of grammar.

(80) **Case Filter**
Every NP must be marked for Case.[19]

In English, Case marking is generally nonovert, so that when we talk about an NP being marked for Case, we are talking about an abstract notion rather than the concrete realization that does show up on the personal pronouns (e.g., nominative *I* vs. accusative (or objective) *me* vs. genitive *my* vs. absolute genitive *mine*). However, in other languages with extensive morphological Case systems (e.g., Russian, and standard German), NPs must be marked overtly with the appropriate Case.

The Case Filter accounts for the ungrammaticality of examples like (81), where *'s*-Insertion has not applied.

(81) *[$_{NP}$ [$_{NP}$ the boy] book] is on the shelf

Thus, the obligatoriness of *'s*-Insertion follows from a principle of grammar, another part of Case theory, and need not be stipulated as part of the rule. If so, then *'s*-Insertion can be designated as optional, like *Of*-Insertion. The fact that the rule must apply once and only once now follows from the Case Filter in conjunction with the Case Uniqueness Principle.

At this point we can consider whether a Case-theoretic analysis of *Of*-Insertion would solve analogous problems for the formulation in (62). Under the assumption that the grammatical formative *of* is involved in assigning Case to the NP to which it is adjoined, then the fact that *Of*-Insertion must apply when its SD is met will follow from the Case Filter and the fact that it cannot apply iteratively to the same NP will follow from the Case Uniqueness Principle.[20]

---

**Exercise 2.11**
Show how the Case Uniqueness Principle prohibits the iterative application of *Of*-Insertion. First demonstrate how *Of*-Insertion as formulated in (62) could reapply to its own output, thereby producing the ill-formed (i).

(i) *a rational reconstruction of of the theory

Then state how (i) would be designated as ungrammatical under the Case theory presented here.

---

The Case Uniqueness Principle does not, however, solve all problems concerning the misapplication of *Of*-Insertion. Consider for example the under-lying phrase marker for the NP *criticisms of Freud's writings*, given in (82).

(82)

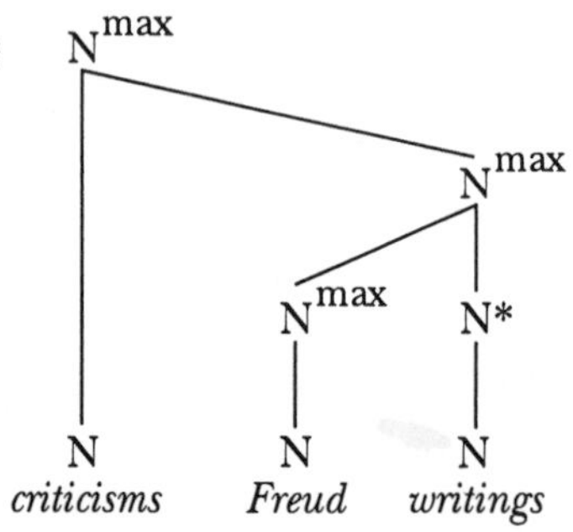


Recall that the designation $N^{max}$ in (82) is simply an interpretation of the phrasal category N* projected from N. The phrase marker (82) can satisfy the SD of (62) in either of two ways so that *of* can be adjoined to the maximal phrasal projection of either *Freud* or *writings*. In fact, *of* could be adjoined to both NPs without violating the Case Filter or the Case Uniqueness Principle.

**Exercise 2.12**
Give the transformational derivation of (82) in which *Of*-Insertion applies to both NPs. Show that the ordering of the two applications of the rule is of no consequence. Explain how the resulting phrase marker violates neither the Case Filter (assuming that the maximal phrasal projection of *criticisms* is going to be Case-marked in some way) nor the Case Uniqueness Principle.

Since the result will be ill formed, we need to find another way to exclude this possibility.

Let us begin by examining the configurational relation between the N *criticisms* and the maximal phrasal projection of *Freud* versus the maximal phrasal projection of *writings*. The N *criticisms* and the maximal phrasal projection of *writings* are sister nodes (see (52)); whereas *criticisms* and the maximal phrasal projection of *Freud* are not. Therefore, we could exclude the adjunction of *of* to the maximal phrasal projection of *Freud* by placing a condition on the *Of*-Insertion rule such that the two constants mentioned in the SD (terms 2 and 3) must be sisters.

Although this will solve the problem for *Of*-Insertion, it will fail for *'s*-Insertion with respect to double object constructions. The phrase marker for a double object construction will meet the SD of *'s*-Insertion even if a sisterhood condition holds between the two constant terms. Thus, the phrase marker (83) will yield the ill-formed (84).

(83)

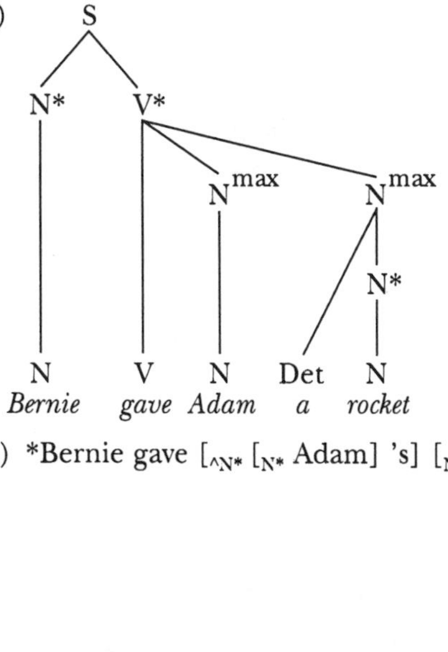


(84) *Bernie gave $[_{^{\wedge}N*}$ $[_{N*}$ Adam] 's] $[_{N*}$ a rocket]

The ungrammaticality of (84) follows from the Case Uniqueness Principle *if* it is assumed that the NP *Adam* is Case-marked by *gave* as well as via *'s*-Insertion. However, since the obligatory behavior of Case marking already follows from the Case Filter, there is no reason to stipulate that any Case-assignment rules are obligatory. If all Case-assignment rules are optional, then *Adam* might be assigned Case by *gave*, or by *'s*-Insertion, or by both, or by neither. Thus, it might happened that *Adam* was assigned only genitive Case, in which case (84) could not be ruled out by the Case Uniqueness Principle after all. We must therefore find another means of ruling it out.

Since genitive Case can only occur on an NP that is a constituent of an NP, we could prohibit (84) on the grounds that the occurrence of genitive Case on the NP *Adam* is not "licensed." Let us say that genitive Case is licensed when it occurs on an NP that is in the proper configurational relation with a lexical head N–namely, when the NP is a constituent of the maximal projection of an N (to its right—that is what the SD of *'s*-Insertion stipulates). Thus, the problem of double object constructions as exemplified in (84) is eliminated if (85) is a principle of grammar.

(85) **Principle of Case Licensing**
Each instance of Case must be properly licensed.

Presumably, N cannot license genitive Case outside of its maximal phrasal projection. In other words, a maximal phrasal projection is a "barrier" with respect to Case licensing. Note that this holds as well for maximal phrasal projections that are constituents of a phrasal projection of N. Thus, genitive Case cannot be licensed for the NP *Göttingen* in *a mathematician from Göttingen's proof* (see (76a)) because the maximal phrasal projection P* intervenes between the NP and the licensing category N (*proof*).

We are now ready to formulate Case licensing more precisely. Since this crucially concerns a lexical head N and its maximal phrasal projection, we can define a relation **m-command** between the lexical head N and the constituents of its maximal phrasal projection as (86).

(86) A category $\alpha$ *m-commands* $\alpha$ category $\beta$ if and only if the first maximal projection dominating $\alpha$ dominates $\beta$, and neither $\alpha$ nor $\beta$ dominates the other.

A lexical head m-commands all the constituents of its maximal phrasal projection.

**Exercise 2.13**
Compare the definitions of m-command (86) and c-command (45). Construct a tree diagram for the sentence *Mary refuted John's criticisms of the Case Filter.* Using this structure, show that it is possible for a node X to (i) c-command a node Y but not m-command Y; (ii) m-command Y but not c-command Y; and (iii) c-command and m-command Y.

Therefore, a lexical head N must m-command an NP in order to license Case on that NP. This accounts for the barrier effect with respect to the maximal phrasal projection of that N.

To capture the barrier effect for maximal phrasal projections that N m-commands, we need to define another relationship between a lexical head N and the constituents of its maximal phrasal projection that is narrower than m-command. This relationship, called **government**, is defined as (87).

(87) A lexical head α *governs* a category β iff α m-commands β *and* β m-commands α.

Under this definition, the N *proof* in (76a) governs the maximal phrasal projection of *mathematician.* It does not govern the NP *Göttingen,* which is governed instead by the P *from.* Thus, Case licensing involves government. A particular Case will be properly licensed if it is attached to an NP that is governed by an appropriate lexical head—under the assumption that different lexical heads are associated with distinct Case values. (For more on this, see chapter 5).

**Exercise 2.14**
Construct an underlying phrase marker for *The student's remarks about his professor's proof of the theorem shocked the class.* Identify the government relations that hold for each lexical head. Explain why it is not possible for a constituent to be governed by more than one lexical category.

Given the addition of the Principle of Case Licensing to Case theory, it is no longer necessary to constrain the application of *'s*-Insertion. If an ill-formed structure results, it will violate some principle of Case theory. That is, if we assume that the *'s*-Insertion transformation applies freely (that is, without any constraint on when it may apply), then the result of any misapplication of the rule (including failure to apply at all) can be excluded on the grounds that the phrase marker at S-structure will be ill formed according to some principle of grammar. Rather than being constrained by conditions stated on each individual rule, then, the application of transformations is taken to be constrained by general principles belonging to the theory of grammar (UG). A similar account is possible for *Of*-Insertion.[21]

---

**Exercise 2.15**

The Principle of Case Licensing is also necessary to account for the misapplication of lexical insertion with respect to personal pronouns. Consider the following examples:

(i) a. {my/*me/*I} picture just appeared in the newspaper
    b. {I/*me/*my} read the report with great interest

State the problem that the ungrammatical forms in (i) pose. Show how they conform to the Case Filter and the Case Uniqueness Principle, but violate the Principle of Case Licensing.

Now consider the following example:

(ii) *[$_{NP}$ that criticism me] was painfully accurate

Which Case principle is violated in (ii)? How does this example show that the obligatory character of *Of*-Insertion is different from that of *'s*-Insertion?

---

**Exercise 2.16**

Given the Case-theoretic account of *'s*-Insertion and *Of*-Insertion, it may no longer be necessary to formulate the rules in terms of the designation $N^{max}$ (as opposed to N*). Consider what would happen if the rule of *'s*-Insertion analyzed a nonmaximal projection of N as term 2. Show how such a derivation would result in a violation of the Case Filter (using *the student of physics from MIT's grades* as an example). If all such applications of the rules result in violations of general principles of grammar, then the rules can be stated in purely structural terms (e.g., N*) without reference to an interpretation of the categorial structure (e.g., as $N^{max}$).

---

A Case-theoretic analysis of *Of*-Insertion might also explain why predicate adjectives in English that seem to take an NP complement require the presence of a semantically empty *of*, as illustrated in the contrast between (88a) and (88b).

(88) a. *Mary is proud John
b. Mary is proud of John

Suppose that an adjective cannot assign Case to an NP object, and therefore (88a) violates the Case Filter. (88b) then satisfies the Case Filter under the assumption that *of* in this construction functions like *of* in the nominal constructions discussed earlier. Under this analysis (88b) is transformationally derived from the structure underlying (88a). If this analysis is correct, then the formulation of *Of*-Insertion should be generalized to constructions containing N or A heads. This suggests that the categories N and A are related in a linguistically significant way (they cannot assign Case, in contrast to V and P).

One way to express this relation and at the same time capture the generalization about *Of*-Insertion is to define lexical categories in terms of more than one categorial feature. Thus, we might assume, following Chomsky 1981, that lexical categories are composed of feature complexes of at least [±N, ±V].[22] Using this feature complex, we can define the basic lexical categories as follows.

(89) a. N = [+N, –V]
b. V = [–N, +V]
c. A = [+N, +V]
d. P = [–N, –V]

From this analysis we derive the following classes.

(90) a. [+N] = {N, A}
b. [–N] = {V, P}
c. [+V] = {V, A}
d. [–V] = {N, P}

Given (90a) the rule of *Of*-Insertion (62) can be generalized to predicate adjective constructions like those in (88) simply by changing term 2 from N to [+N]. This provides some evidence for the multiple feature analysis of categories in (89). This kind of analysis will be extended in chapters 4 and 5.[23]

---

**Exercise 2.17**

Consider the following paradigm from the Case-theoretic point of view developed above:

(i) a. John's friend vs. *John friend
b. *my's friend vs. my friend

c. a friend of John's vs. *a friend John's
d. a friend of mine vs. *a friend mine

How does the pronoun *mine* differ in syntactic behavior from the pronoun *my*? Propose an analysis that accounts for this difference. What evidence is there that the *'s*-marking on the name *John* in prenominal position (i.a) should be analyzed as different from the *'s*-marking on the name *John* in postnominal position (i.c)?

---

**Exercise 2.18**
Given the discussion of the phrase structure of NPs so far, what would rule out the ill-formed NP **the the boy's hat*? Discuss what sort of phrase structure a grammar might assign to such a construction. Also discuss how the *'s*-Insertion rule would reapply to such a structure. What would we have to assume about the grammar of English to exclude such ill-formed examples?

---

In this section we have seen how the behavior of certain syntactic rules can be determined on the basis of general principles that are assumed to be part of the theory of grammar. In the next chapter we will extend this kind of account to other syntactic phenomena that are subject to a transformational analysis.

## Appendix: Phrase Structure Grammar—A Formal Characterization

The purpose of this appendix is to show how constraints on the rewrite rule mechanism correlate with constraints on constituent structure representations in relation to tree diagrams.

In Phrase Structure Grammar (PSG), a well-formed structural description of a sentence must meet the following three conditions (where V(L) stands for 'vocabulary of L, a language'—that is, the set of category symbols):

(I) No element of V(L) may be an immediate constituent of two different phrases.
(II) Every element of V(L) must be an immediate constituent of some phrase, with the exception of root S.
(III) Only a string of adjacent elements of V(L) may constitute a phrase.

(I) rules out representations like (91), where *y* is an immediate constituent of both *C* and *D*.

(91)

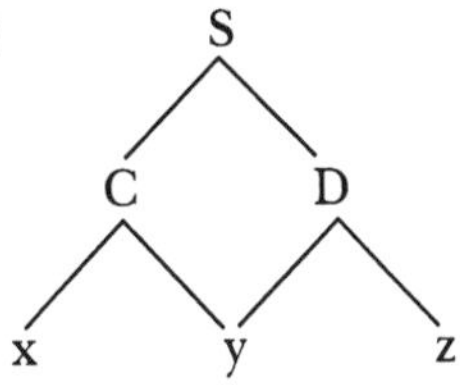


(II) rules out representations like (92), where the parsing of the sentence is incomplete.

(92)

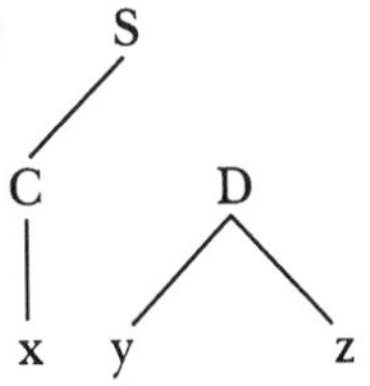


(III) rules out representations like (93), where immediate constituents of a phrase are separated by an element that is not a constituent of that phrase.

(93)

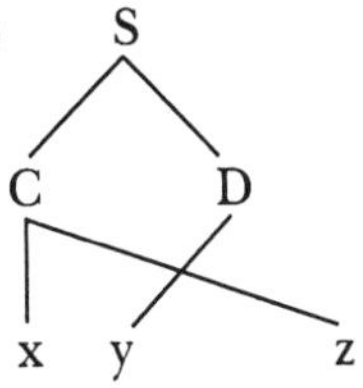


By (III), constituents of a phrase must form a continuous string.

The PSGs discussed in the previous sections meet conditions (I)–(III) because the rules of these grammars are constructed in a way that conforms to the conditions. Phrase structure (PS) rules constitute a subclass of the class of **rewrite rules**. To illustrate how PS rules meet conditions (I)–(III) by construction, we will consider the special characteristics of these rules as opposed to rewrite rules in general.

The general form of a rewrite rule is (94).

(94) $\Phi A \Psi \longrightarrow \Phi B \Psi$

The Greek letters Φ and Υ and the Roman letters *A* and *B* stand for strings of V(L) or the null string *e*. The frame [Φ ___ Υ] in (94) specifies the context in which *A* rewrites as *B*. Thus, we can write (94) equivalently as (95a) or (95b).

(95) a. A ⟶ B in the context: Φ ___ Υ

b. A ⟶ B / Φ ___ Υ

(95) gives the general schema for **context-sensitive** (CS) rewrite rules. Where both Φ and Υ stand for the null string, the rewrite rule is said to be **context-free** (CF). The general schema for CF rules is given in (96).

(96) A ⟶ B

Note that CF rules are a subclass of CS rules: the subclass for which both Φ and Υ are null and thus A in any context rewrites as B. In the following discussion we will consider only the subclass of CF rules; however, the analysis holds for the wider class of CS rules as well.

Under the interpretation of the variables *A* and *B* given above, the rule schema (96) permits the following sorts of rewrite rules.

(97) a. *e* ⟶ rst
b. Q ⟶ *e*
c. CDG ⟶ W
d. GHI ⟶ mnop

In (97a) the null string is rewritten as the string *rst*. Such rules would create problems with respect to condition (II) since the null string cannot be legitimately considered a constituent of any particular category or a member of $V_N$. Given that the null string is not a category (i.e., not a member of V(L)), rule (97b) would be interpreted as a deletion (erasure) of the category *Q*. Thus, without any restrictions the rewrite rule schema (96) allows for contracting derivations—that is, derivations whose last line is shorter than the longest line in the derivation. Rule (97c) allows for contracting derivations of a different sort, where a string of symbols rewrites as a shorter string of symbols. Such rules create problems with respect to phrase structure representation. By condition (I), *W* cannot be interpreted as an immediate constituent of the three categories *C*, *D*, and *G*; therefore, it must be an immediate constituent of one of them (by condition (II)), though the rule is nonspecific as to which one. The same problem arises with (97d) where the rule does not produce a contraction in the derivation.

Grammars containing at least one unrestricted rewrite rule are called **unrestricted rewriting systems** (URS). The difference between URS and PSG is that all the rules of the latter are constrained by the following two conditions.

(98) a. A must be a single symbol of $V_N$.
b. B must be nonnull.

(98a) eliminates the possibilities of (i) rewriting the null string as a string from V(L), and (ii) having derivations which do not uniquely specify the immediate constituency of the elements of V(L). (98b) eliminates deletions from the phrase structure rules; and (98a) and (98b) in conjunction eliminate contracting derivations where the null string is not involved. Thus, rewrite rules meeting both conditions in (98) will be designated as phrase structure rules (PS rules). PS rules may be either context-sensitive or context-free. A PSG containing at least one CS rule is designated a CS-PSG; a PSG containing no CS rules is designated a CF-PSG.

Under the assumption that PSG provides a natural way to characterize human languages, we were led to investigate the "rewrite rule" device, which is the sole grammatical mechanism in a PSG. Because the descriptive power of this device goes far beyond what seems necessary for the description of natural languages, we were able to place restrictions on rewrite rules—thereby reducing the descriptive power of such rules and hence of the grammars available for describing languages. In limiting descriptive options by restricting the descriptive power of grammars, we make stronger empirical claims about the properties of human languages and the grammars that account for them. Clearly, a theory of grammar that allows unrestricted rewriting rules can account for any language described in terms of PSG, since PSG constitutes a subclass of the rewriting systems available given unrestricted rewrite rules. However, the point to be explained is that grammars of human languages do not require the wider descriptive options. Viewed in this light, one goal in linguistic research is to narrow descriptive options in the hope of discovering the general properties of grammars of human languages.

## Bibliographical Comments

The original discussion of phrase structure analysis in generative grammar occurs in chapters 7 and 8 of Chomsky 1975b. Prior to 1964 it was assumed that lexical insertion was done via phrase structure rule. The transformational analysis of lexical insertion was first discussed in Chomsky 1965, which contains the original proposal for syntactic features—including subcategorization and selectional features. Chomsky 1970 proposes the analysis of categories as features, thereby eliminating the distinction between features and categories. The X-bar formalism for phrase structure is also introduced in this paper. The multiple feature analysis of lexical categories is suggested in footnote 32 of Chomsky 1972b; the analysis of categories in terms of the features [±N, ±V] occurs in Chomsky's unpublished Amherst lectures (1974), though it does not appear in the published literature until Chomsky and Lasnik 1977. Jackendoff 1977 presents an extensive analysis of phrase structure using an extended version of X-bar theory, one that allows contextual features to define lexical categories. Such extensions are explicitly prohibited by the Principle of Category Composition, which was proposed in Freidin 1983. The Principle of Lexical Satisfaction originates in Freidin and Babby 1984. The relative interpretation of phrasal projections presented in this chapter entails that phrasal projections of a head will not be categorially distinct. The idea that there is only one phrasal category per lexical head has been proposed independently as "the single projection-type hypothesis" in Stuurman 1985, which is devoted to a detailed investigation of this analysis compared with previous proposals. For further proposals concerning the feature analysis of categories and their phrasal projections, see Emonds 1985 and Muysken and Van Riemsdijk 1986. Baltin and Kroch 1989 provides a broad variety of current views on the nature of phrase structure.

A transformational analysis of NPs—including the rules of *'s*-Insertion and *Of*-Insertion—was first proposed in Chomsky 1970. The Case-theoretic interpretation of *Of*-Insertion first occurs in Chomsky 1980b:fn. 33 (see Chomsky 1981:49f.). The original impetus for Case theory came from Jean-Roger Vergnaud (see the bibliographical comments for chapter 5). The first published proposal for a general Case Filter as such occurs in Chomsky 1980b. The concept of "government" as it relates to Case is also due to Vergnaud. The analysis is developed in detail in Chomsky 1980b and Rouveret and Vergnaud 1980. The relation "c-command" is first proposed and developed in Reinhart 1976. This relation is essentially the same as the relation "in construction with" of Klima 1964 (see Culicover 1976 for discussion). The concept "m-command" results from the integration of c-command within the X-bar framework where maximal phrasal projections constitute natural syntactic domains. The definition of "government" in terms of m-command is explored in Aoun and Sportiche 1982.

The concept of filtering in grammar begins with the discussion of the filtering function of transformations in Chomsky 1965. Perlmutter 1971 (based on Perlmutter's unpublished doctoral dissertation (MIT, 1968)) contains the first systematic proposals for filters (which are not transformations) that apply to D-structure or S-structure. Chomsky and Lasnik 1977 develops the notion of "surface filter" as a means of restricting the descriptive power of transformations—that is, placing limitations on the kinds of transformations that can occur in the grammar of a natural language.

The concept of structure preservation in generative grammar is introduced in Emonds 1970, 1976. For a review of this work and its relation to later developments in the theory of transformations, see Freidin 1978a.

For discussion of formal grammars and formal languages, see Chomsky 1963. Wall 1972 provides an excellent introduction to the basic concepts involved. See also Partee, Ter Meulen, and Wall 1990 for a more recent and more extensive treatment.

3

# Recursion, Movement, and Bounding

NPs that contain other NPs as constituents provide examples of **recursion** in phrase structure, where a phrasal category recurs as a constituent of a category of the same type. NP recursion occurs when a complement or modifier in NP contains another instance of NP. Consider, for example, the NPs in (1).

(1) a. $[_{NP}$ $[_{NP}$ the mathematician's] proof]
  b. $[_{NP}$ one $[_{N*}$ criticism of $[_{NP}$ the proof]]]
  c. $[_{NP}$ an $[_{N*}$ anecdote $[_{PP}$ about $[_{NP}$ Hilbert]]]]

Recursion may involve immediate constituents, as in (1a), or nonimmediate constituents, as in (1b–c). Given such recursion in NP, a phrase structure grammar of English will allow for arbitrarily long NPs along the lines of (2).

(2) John's brother's teacher's interpretation of Dr. Seuss's story about Bartholomew's problem with King Derwin of Didd's obsession concerning the sameness of the seasons

---

**Exercise 3.1**
Give the phrase structure analysis of (2). Identify the head of the entire NP. How many NPs is the noun *seasons* a constituent of? Construct an even longer NP that contains (2) as a constituent.

---

Furthermore, NPs may contain sentential constituents (designated with the category label "S") that themselves will contain one or more NP constituents. Thus, the recursion of NP may also result from sentential embedding in NP, as illustrated in (3).

(3) a. $[_{NP}$ Bill's belief $[_{S}$ that $[_{NP}$ John] is lying]]
  b. $[_{NP}$ the story $[_{S}$ (which) $[_{NP}$ John] told to $[_{NP}$ Bill]]]

In (3a) *that John is lying* is a sentential complement of the noun *belief* (compare the corresponding sentence *Bill believes that John is lying*, where *that John is lying* is a sentential complement of the verb *believe*). The embedded sentential structure in (3b) is a relative clause that modifies the noun *story*. (The parentheses around the relative pronoun *which* indicate that it is optional, so that *the story John told to Bill* is also a well-formed NP.)

Embedding the NPs in (3) in a sentence produces instances of S recursion (e.g., [$_{S}$ Mary belittled [$_{NP}$ Bill's belief [$_{S}$ that [$_{NP}$ John] is lying]]]). Recursion of S also occurs in sentences containing sentential complements of verbs and adjectives, as in (4).

(4) a. [$_{S}$ Bill [$_{VP}$ believes [$_{S}$ John admires Mary]]]
 b. [$_{S}$ Bill [$_{VP}$ persuaded us [$_{S}$ that John admires Mary]]]
 c. [$_{S}$ Bill [$_{VP}$ is [$_{AP}$ happy [$_{S}$ John admires Mary]]]]

A full analysis of these examples would also reveal recursion of VP (which follows as a consequence of S recursion in the examples cited in (4)).

---

**Exercise 3.2**
Construct examples involving recursion of PP and AP and indicate how they might be extended indefinitely. (Hint: For the AP examples, consider how you could extend (4c).)

---

As noted in section 1.1, it is possible to construct arbitrarily long sentences by embedding sentential complements within other sentential complements an indefinite number of times. The examples in (5) illustrate how this might be done for one to three sentential embeddings.

(5) a. [$_{S}$ Mary said [$_{S}$ John likes persimmons]]
 b. [$_{S}$ Sam knows [$_{S}$ Mary said [$_{S}$ John likes persimmons]]]
 c. [$_{S}$ Joan told me [$_{S}$ Sam knows [$_{S}$ Mary said [$_{S}$ John likes persimmons]]]]

As can easily be verified, even longer sentences with additional sentential embeddings can be constructed in this fashion.

In such constructions, an embedded S is directly linked to the "adjacent" S that contains it by virtue of being the sentential complement of the main (as opposed to auxiliary (or "helping")) verb of that S. An embedded S is only indirectly linked to a "nonadjacent" S that contains it. For example, in (5b) the embedded S *John likes persimmons* is directly linked to the S whose main verb is *said* as a sentential complement of *said*, but it is only indirectly linked to the main clause (henceforth root S) as a complement to the main verb of the sentential complement of the root S main verb. A similar analysis holds for (5c).

In contrast to declarative sentences like those in (5a–b) where there is no direct syntactic link between the most deeply embedded S and the root S, interrogative sentences involving an interrogative pronoun (e.g., *who/whom* and *what*) can establish a direct syntactic link between such "nonadjacent" Ss, as illustrated in (6a–c) corresponding to (5a–c).

(6) a. [$_S$ *what* did Mary say [$_S$ John likes __]]
b. [$_S$ *what* does Sam know [$_S$ Mary said [$_S$ John likes __]]]
c. [$_S$ *what* did Joan tell me [$_S$ Sam knows [$_S$ Mary said [$_S$ John likes __]]]]

For each example, the interrogative pronoun *what* is interpreted as grammatical object of *likes.* In other words, there is a direct syntactic link between the interrogative pronoun that is attached to the root S (in a way that remains to be determined) and an NP position in the most deeply embedded S. This direct syntactic link between the interrogative pronoun and this NP position of the embedded sentence can extend over an indefinite number of embedded clauses (abstracting away from considerations of style and memory limitations for sentence processing). Thus, this link is essentially **unbounded** in scope—there are no syntactic boundaries that prevent the formation of these links in such constructions and therefore the interrogative pronoun and the NP position to which it is linked may be arbitrarily far apart.

Whereas the examples in (6) and their extensions illustrate the unbounded character of the link between a sentence-initial interrogative pronoun and an NP position in a deeply embedded S, the examples in (7) demonstrate that this link is actually **bounded** in certain constructions.

(7) a. *whom did [$_{NP}$ John's enthusiasm for __] please Mary
(cf. John's enthusiasm for whom pleased Mary)
b. *whose did you dislike [$_{NP}$ __ criticism] the least
(cf. whose criticism did you dislike the least)

From these examples it appears that NP forms a boundary that the interrogative/NP-position link may not cross. Note that the factor that determines bounding is not a measure of the distance (say, in terms of the number of words) between the interrogative pronoun in S-initial position and some NP position since this distance is clearly greater in the grammatical (6c) than in the ungrammatical examples in (7). Thus, we are faced with an apparent paradox: the link between an interrogative pronoun in sentence-initial position and an embedded NP position must be bounded (as illustrated by (7)) and may be unbounded (as indicated in our discussion of (6)).

In the remainder of this chapter we will look at a formal account of interrogative pronoun phenomena that explains this apparent paradox and we will see how this account can generalize to other syntactic phenomena. To provide this account, we will develop a transformational movement analysis of interrogative sentences in which the empirical constraints on these constructions follow from some general conditions on the transformational analysis itself.

### 3.1 *Wh*-movement and the Structure of Sentential Constructions

Following standard practice, we will henceforth refer to interrogative pronouns as ***wh*-forms** (noting that this designation can be extended to relative pronouns (e.g., *the woman who Fred wants to marry*) as will be demonstrated). This section will deal with interrogative sentences where the *wh*-form occurs in sentence-initial position, as in (8).

(8) a. who has Bernie invited
    b. who did Adam send a card to on Valentine's Day

Two questions immediately arise: How are we to characterize the sentence-initial position occupied by the *wh*-form, and How is the *wh*-form linked to the appropriate grammatical function position given the interpretation of the question? That is, *who* is interpreted as the grammatical object of the verb *invited* in (8a) and as the grammatical object of the preposition *to* in (8b). In fact, we can construct interrogative sentences of a slightly different sort by placing the *wh*-form in its proper grammatical function position, as illustrated in (9a–b).

(9) a. Bernie has invited who
    b. Adam sent a card to who on Valentine's Day

In these so-called **echo questions** the *wh*-form is uttered with a rising intonation, unlike the *wh*-form in (8), and the sense is that the questioner is asking for information to be repeated.[1]

Given the grammaticality of constructions like (9), a grammar of English must be able to generate *wh*-form in grammatical function positions. Assuming that an interrogative pronoun is just another instance of a pronoun, and thus of a noun, a *wh*-form will be subject to lexical insertion in any grammatical function position that an ordinary noun can occupy.

The ungrammaticality of examples like (10) shows that when a *wh*-form occurs in sentence-initial position, one grammatical function position in S must remain empty.

(10) a. *who has Bernie invited Jill
b. *who did Adam send a card to Gail on Valentine's Day

In (10a) *who* can no longer be linked to the grammatical object position of *invited* since that position is now filled by a distinct lexical N, *Jill*, and similarly for (10b).

The ungrammaticality of (10) poses a problem if we assume that a *wh*-form in sentence-initial position arises via lexical insertion of the *wh*-form in that position. That is, there would be nothing to prevent lexical insertion from inserting lexical items in all N positions in a phrase marker when a *wh*-form occurs in sentence-initial position. An alternative analysis that does not confront this problem is the standard movement (by transformation) analysis of *wh*-questions where (i) it is assumed that no interrogative pronoun can be lexically inserted in sentence-initial position, (ii) the *wh*-form is lexically inserted in a grammatical function position, and (iii) the *wh*-form is then moved to sentence-initial position by a movement operation. The transformational analysis assumes that *wh*-questions like (8) have an "underlying" structure like the corresponding examples in (9) and are "derived" from structures like (9) via a movement operation (a transformation) that shifts the *wh*-form to sentence-initial position.

In this informal transformational movement analysis for deriving regular *wh*-questions, the rule under consideration moves a phrase from one position in a phrase marker to another. With respect to all such movement operations, we will call the position from which an element is moved the **movement site**, and the position to which it is moved the **landing site**.[2] To state this *Wh*-Movement rule, more formally, we must answer three basic questions:

(I) How do we characterize the landing site?
(II) What is the nature of the transformational operation that performs the movement?
(III) How is the relation between movement site and landing site to be characterized?

As will become apparent, the answers to (I) and (II) are interdependent.

In our informal account of *wh*-questions, the position of the *wh*-form was characterized as sentence-initial position. If we continue to assume that the landing site for *wh*-movement is this sentence-initial position, then the answer to (I) is obtained by formally characterizing sentence-initial position. One way to do this is to identify the leftmost element possible in a sentence. As the examples in (11) illustrate, the subject NP is not the leftmost position possible in S.

(11) a. John arrived in Princeton yesterday
b. yesterday John arrived in Princeton

In (11b) the time adverb *yesterday* can occur to the left of the subject NP. Let us assume that the adverb's sentence-initial position in (11b) is the result of a transformation that adjoins the adverb to S, as illustrated in (12).

(12)

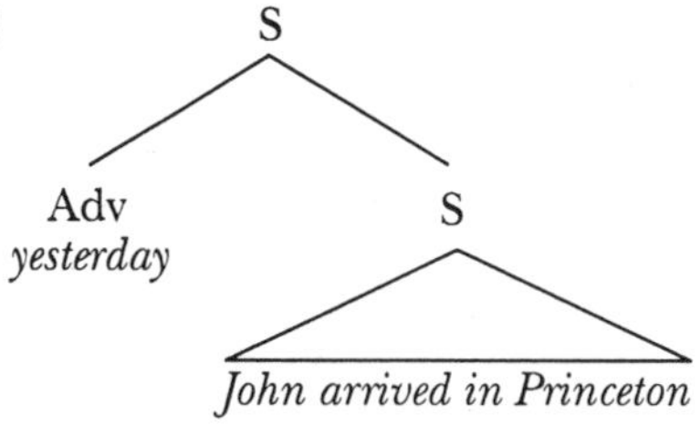


Under this analysis the adjunction site of the adverb marks sentence-initial position. However, the position of the adverb is still not the leftmost possible position in a sentential construction as demonstrated in the complex sentences of (13).

(13) a. Mary knows [that John arrived in Princeton yesterday]
b. Mary knows [that yesterday John arrived in Princeton]

In both (13a) and (13b) *that* is a **complementizer** that marks the beginning of an embedded finite clause. Note that the time adverb *yesterday* that modifies the embedded S cannot be positioned to the left of the complementizer *that* and still modify the embedded S.

(14) a. %Mary knows yesterday that John arrived in Princeton
b. Mary knew yesterday that John arrived in Princeton

To the left of the complementizer, the adverb must be interpreted as modifying the main clause. This results in an interpretive anomaly in (14a) because the main clause verb is in the present tense. (Interpretive anomalies are indicated with a "%" rather than with the "*" that marks a syntactically ill-formed structure.) In (14b) *yesterday* can only be interpreted as modifying the main clause—hence, (14b) has the interpretation 'it was yesterday when Mary knew that John arrived in Princeton'. In this way, the complementizer appears to mark the leftmost boundary between the embedded S and the main clause.

The syntax of complementizers provides some evidence for the analysis of sentential constructions. The following paradigm suggests that a complementizer is the head of a sentential complement in accordance with the X-bar theory of phrase structure developed in chapter 2.

(15) a. *believe*
   i. I believe that John talked to Mary
   ii. *I believe whether John talked to Mary
   iii. *I believe if John talked to Mary

  b. *wonder*
   i. *I wonder that John talked to Mary
   ii. I wonder whether John talked to Mary
   iii. I wonder if John talked to Mary

(15) shows that although both *believe* and *wonder* take a finite clause complement, *believe* but not *wonder* allows the complementizer *that* (cf. (15a.i) and (15b.i)). If we take the complementizer C to be a lexical category—the lexical head of a projected complementizer phrase CP—then the constraint that holds between the matrix verb and the form of the complementizer follows straightforwardly from the head-to-head relation of selection discussed in section 2.2: the verb selects the complementizer. This analysis presupposes that *whether* and *if* are both complementizers and that they share a feature whose value is the opposite of the value taken by *that.*

Given that *wonder* also allows an indirect question as sentential complement, as illustrated in (16), we might assume that the feature that distinguishes *whether* and *if* from *that* also involves an interrogative property so that the former are [+Q] and the latter is [–Q].

(16) a. I wonder $[_{CP}$ who John talked to]
  b. I wonder $[_{CP}$ who talked to Mary]

Under this analysis, *wonder* has a selectional restriction [+___ [+Q]]. In (16) this lexical property of *wonder* is satisfied indirectly through the presence of the interrogative pronoun *who,* which presumably instantiates the feature [+Q]. This sharing of features between a lexical head of a projection and some other constituent of the projection occurs in NP as well, as illustrated in (17).

(17) a. this book
  b. these books
  c. *this books
  d. *these book

The demonstrative article must agree in number with the noun it modifies. Under the X-bar analysis of NP, the demonstrative article is a specifier of the noun (designated SPEC-N, or alternatively SPEC-NP). The agreement between a specifier and the head it modifies is called **SPEC-head agreement**. It is assumed in X-bar theory that SPEC-head agreement holds generally for all phrasal projections. The SPEC-head agreement analysis of CP explains how the selectional feature of *wonder* is satisfied in (16a–b) where the complement CPs contain null (nonovert) complementizers. If the *wh*-form occupies the SPEC position in CP (henceforth SPEC-CP), then an agreement relation holds between the interrogative pronoun and the null complementizer—both are [+Q]. The feature [+Q] selected by *wonder* is lexically instantiated as the interrogative pronoun. Thus, lexical satisfaction of the selectional restriction is achieved via SPEC-head agreement. Given that the *wh*-form is itself a phrase (e.g., NP in the examples cited above), the complement CPs in (16) have the structure given in (18).

(18)

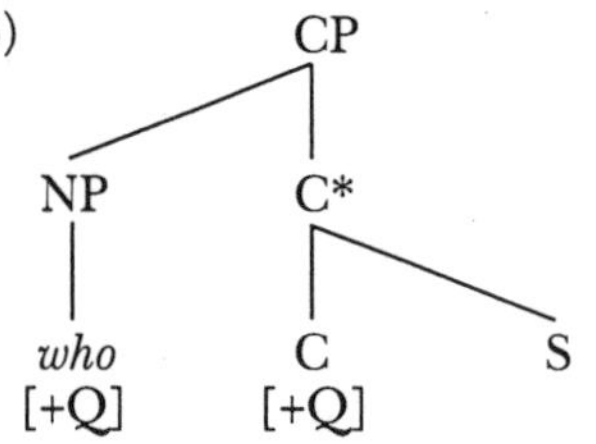


In (18) S is limited to an NP–VP structure that is structurally a complement of C.[3] As illustrated in (19), the SPEC-CP must accommodate NP, AP, or PP—all of which can be moved as wh-phrases.

(19) a. $[_{\text{NP}}$ who] did Mary insult
b. $[_{\text{AP}}$ how angry] was John
c. $[_{\text{PP}}$ about whom] were John and Mary complaining

Thus, SPEC-CP can be realized as either NP, AP, or PP, and for this reason is designated as XP, where X is a category variable that can be realized as N, A, or P.

---

**Exercise 3.3**

Given this analysis of clause structure, provide phrase structure trees for the examples in (19), and for the following examples:

(i) a. John believes that Mary is clever

b. Susan wonders whether Bill reads Dickens
c. Sam asked me if we liked the movie

---

In addition to the selectional relation between a verb and the head of its CP complement, there is a relation between the form of the complementizer and the form of its sentential complement. The complementizer *that* can only occur with finite clause complements, and when infinitival complements occur with a complementizer, they take *for*.

(20) a. *That*-complementizer
i. it was odd [$_{CP}$ that [$_S$ the meeting had finished in half an hour]]
ii. *it was odd [$_{CP}$ that [$_S$ the meeting to have finished in half an hour]]

b. *For*-complementizer
i. *it was odd [$_{CP}$ for [$_S$ the meeting had finished in half an hour]]
ii. it was odd [$_{CP}$ for [$_S$ the meeting to have finished in half an hour]]

Let us refer to the finiteness of a sentential form as its **inflection**, related but not identical to the notion of "inflectional morpheme" in morphology (e.g., the past tense marker "ed" in the sentence *We walk<u>ed</u> to the movies after dinner*). The inflection of a sentence can be instantiated as an independent lexical item, as with the modal auxiliary verb *will* in (21).

(21) the meeting will finish in half an hour

Let us further suppose that the modal auxiliary in (21) acts as a lexical head of S—thus S is a phrasal projection of a category Inflection (henceforth I, alternatively Infl).[4] Applying X-bar theory, we now identify S as IP. Thus, IP takes NP and I* as immediate constituents, where I* immediately dominates I and its complement, VP. IP itself is a complement of C. (See (23) for a tree diagram of these relationships.)

Under the assumption that a complementizer and the head features of its complement IP are generated independently, we can explain the dependency between a complementizer and the inflection of its complement as illustrated in (20) in terms of selection.

---

**Exercise 3.4**
Discuss each example in paradigm (20) in terms of selection.

---

Following this line of analysis, consider the following paradigm in (22).

(22) a. i. John wants *(for) Bill to leave*
ii. *John wants *(that) Bill should leave*
b. i. *John thinks *(for) Bill to leave*
ii. John thinks *(that) Bill should leave*

In terms of subcategorization, both *want* and *think* are verbs that take a CP complement. They differ, however, in terms of selectional features. *Want* is specified for the feature [+___ [–finite]] and *think* is specified [+___ [+finite]]. The complementizers in turn select the features of Infl (as either [+finite] or [–finite]). When a verb or adjective specifies no selectional restriction for its sentential complement CP, then C may be either [+finite] or [–finite] and thus IP may be either finite or nonfinite as well, as in the case of predicate adjectives like *odd* as in (20). The CP/IP analysis of clauses (where IP is a complement of C) establishes the chain of selectional relations among V, C, and Infl illustrated in (23).

(23)
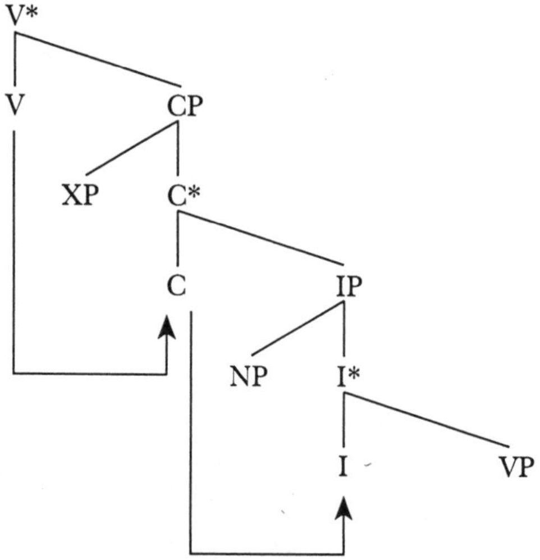


In this way, the matrix V (indirectly) determines the form of its complement Infl.

---

**Exercise 3.5**
Using this SPEC-head agreement analysis, discuss the following paradigm:

(i) a. I didn't say that John will talk to Mary
b. I didn't say whether/if John will talk to Mary
c. I didn't say who John will talk to

d. *I didn't say who that John will talk to
e. *I didn't say who whether/if John will talk to

Give the CP/IP analysis of the embedded sentential complement. Discuss the selectional properties of *say* as illustrated in these examples. Explain how the SPEC-head agreement analysis accounts for (i.c–d) and why it does not account for (i.e).

---

The CP/IP analysis of clauses developed above suggests a precise characterization of the landing site for *Wh*-Movement. It must be SPEC-CP; otherwise, we cannot explain how a *wh*-phrase in CP would satisfy the selectional properties of a verb like *wonder.*

The CP/IP analysis also requires that *wh*-movement occur via a substitution operation into SPEC-CP rather than an adjunction operation (e.g., to CP). The theory of grammar allows for both substitution and adjunction as **elementary transformational operations**—the basic operations from which transformational rules are formulated and which cannot be further defined in terms of more basic transformational operations. Adjunction is **structure-building** in that it creates new hierarchical structure with respect to the category to which something is adjoined. In contrast, substitution is **structure-preserving** in that the hierarchical relationships between the category affected by the substitution and those categories that dominate it remain unchanged (see appendix B for further discussion). If *wh*-movement occurred via adjunction to CP, then the SPEC-head agreement relation that we have used to explain constructions like (16) would not hold between the *wh*-phrase and C. Under a substitution analysis of *Wh*-Movement, a *wh*-phrase is moved via substitution into the SPEC-CP.

Having characterized the landing site for *Wh*-Movement as the SPEC position of CP and the transformational operation that effects the movement as substitution, let us now consider how the relation between the movement and landing sites is to be characterized. This concerns the effect of movement on the movement site itself. Given a question like *Which journals do you recommend to students?*, with an underlying structure where the *wh*-phrase is in the grammatical function position of object, there are two possibilities: either the object position is eliminated from the sentential representation as a result of *wh*-movement, or some remnant of the position remains.

Starting with the first possibility, suppose that *Wh*-Movement changes the underlying structure of the VP of our example, (24a), into its derived structure (24b).

(24) a.

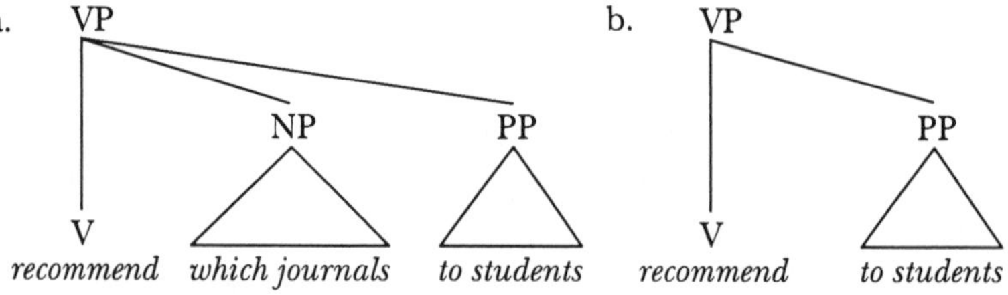


That is, the NP *which journals* has been deleted from VP. Under this analysis, the movement effected by substitution is not entirely structure-preserving since it results in the destruction of structure at the movement site. Suppose, however, that the elimination of structure results from the operation of another elementary transformational operation, **deletion**, which is structure-destroying in the sense that it eliminates structure in a phrase marker. If (24b) is the correct way to represent the derived structure of the VP, then the *Wh*-Movement transformation will involve two distinct elementary operations: substitution and deletion. Note that the deletion of the object NP eliminates from the derived phrase marker the information that the phrase *which journals* functions as the object of the verb *recommend.*

An alternative to (24b) is a derived structure like (25), where the *wh*-phrase that moves into CP leaves behind an empty maximal phrasal projection that is coindexed with the moved *wh*-phrase.

(25)

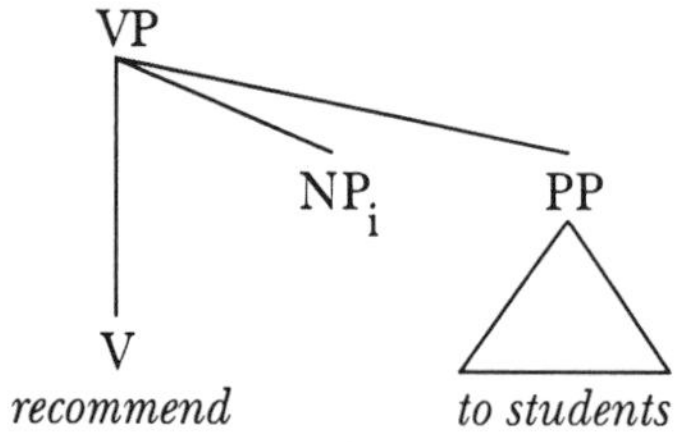


In this way, substitution will be structure-preserving with respect to the subcategorization domain of V. The fact that *recommend* takes an object NP is retained in the transformational derivation of the *wh*-question *Which journals do you recommend to students?*[5] The empty NP that bears the index of the moved phrase is designated as a **trace** of the *wh*-phrase in CP. A *wh*-phrase in CP that bears the same index as a trace in a grammatical function position in IP is said to **bind** the trace. Thus, the relation between the movement site and the landing site for *Wh*-Movement is characterized as the relation of trace binding, as illustrated in (26).

(26)

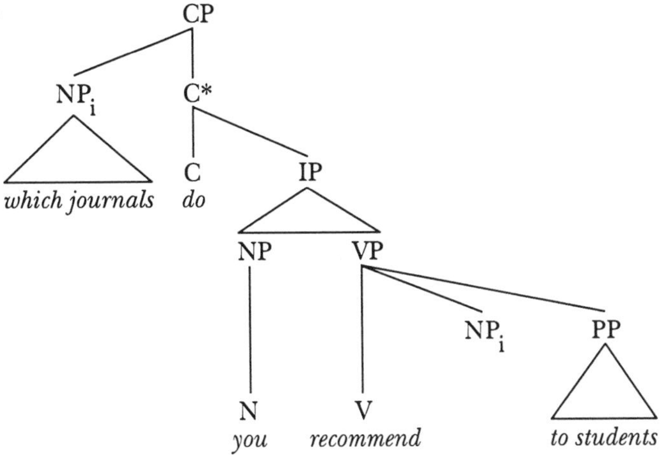


(The syntax of the auxiliary verb *do* (its categorial designation and its constituency in CP) and the internal structure of the Infl projection are discussed in detail in chapter 4.) Through trace binding, the information regarding the grammatical function of a *wh*-phrase in CP is preserved in derived structure.

The trace-theoretic analysis of *Wh*-Movement illustrated in (25) and (26) is preferable to the structure-destroying alternative illustrated in (24) because it preserves subcategorization properties throughout a derivation. Adopting the trace analysis will allow us to say that the Principle of Lexical Satisfaction holds for derived structure as well as underlying structure. This in turn will make our theory of grammar more restrictive than it would be if it required only that lexical satisfaction be met in underlying structure. If the Principle of Lexical Satisfaction holds for both underlying and derived structure, then grammatical transformations may not allow deletion operations to be compounded with movement operations where the deletion will affect the structural representation of lexical properties (e.g., subcategorization frames).[6]

The *Wh*-Movement rule can be given informally as (27).

(27) Move *wh*-phrase into CP.

More formally the rule would be stated as a substitution operation, where term 5 would be a *wh*-phrase and term 2 would be SPEC-CP.

(28) ***Wh*-Movement**

| | | | | | |
|---|---|---|---|---|---|
| | X - | XP - | Y - | XP - | Z |
| SD: | 1 | 2 | 3 | 4 | 5 |
| SC: | 1 | 4/2 | 3 | | 5 |

The slash "/" in the SC of (28) stands for the relation "substitutes for," where in this instance term 4 substitutes for term 2.[7]

---

**Exercise 3.6**

Consider the following examples of *wh*-movement:

(i) a. Mary can't remember what she ate for dinner
 b. John wonders how angry his roommate will be when he gets the news
 c. Joan won't say to whom she gave the information
 d. Fred has forgotten which picture (of Mary) he sent to his publisher
 e. Fred has forgotten whose picture (of Mary) he sent to his publisher

Identify the *wh*-phrase in each example. Compare and contrast the syntactic structures of the various *wh*-phrases. What is the problem that arises in trying to give a single syntactic characterization of the notion "*wh*-phrase"?

---

A methodological aside is in order at this point. So far we have considered one particular analysis for clause structure and *wh*-movement in detail, noting points where variation or even a rather different analysis would be possible. It should be readily apparent that data alone fail to uniquely determine the correct analysis or theory. Therefore, it is necessary, while pursuing a particular analysis, to keep in mind alternative analyses and theories that may account equally well for the same phenomena. In general, the only way to determine the strengths and weaknesses of a particular analysis or theory is to work it out in detail. The physicist Richard Feynman expresses this important methodological rule of thumb this way:

> Suppose you have two theories, A and B, which look completely different psychologically, with different ideas in them and so on, but that all the consequences that are computed from each are exactly the same, and both agree with experiment. The two theories, although they sound different at the beginning, have all consequences the same, which is usually easy to prove mathematically by showing that the logic from A and B will always give corresponding consequences. Suppose we have two such theories, how are we going to decide which one is right? There is no way by science, because they both agree with experiment to the same extent. So two theories, although they may have deeply different ideas behind them, may be mathematically identical, and then there is no scientific way to distinguish them.

However, for psychological reasons, in order to guess new theories, these two things may be very far from equivalent, because one gives a man different ideas from the other. By putting the theory in a certain kind of framework you get an idea of what to change. There will be something, for instance, in theory A that talks about something, and you will say, 'I'll change that idea in here'. But to find out what the corresponding thing is that you are going to change in B may be very complicated - it may not be a simple idea at all. In other words, although they are identical before they are changed, there are certain ways of changing one which look natural which will not look natural in the other. Therefore psychologically we must keep all the theories in our heads, and every theoretical physicist who is any good knows six or seven different theoretical representations for exactly the same physics. He knows that they are all equivalent, and that nobody is ever going to be able to decide which one is right at that level, but he keeps them in his head, hoping that they will give him different ideas for guessing. (1965:168)

There is perhaps even greater necessity to follow this practice in linguistics since, unlike physical theories, linguistic theories are not yet at a stage where we have precise mathematical formulations to work with.

Returning to our analysis of *wh*-movement, the *Wh*-Movement rule, as formulated in (28), would analyze the phrase marker underlying (29a) as (29b).

(29) a. which journals do you recommend to students

b.

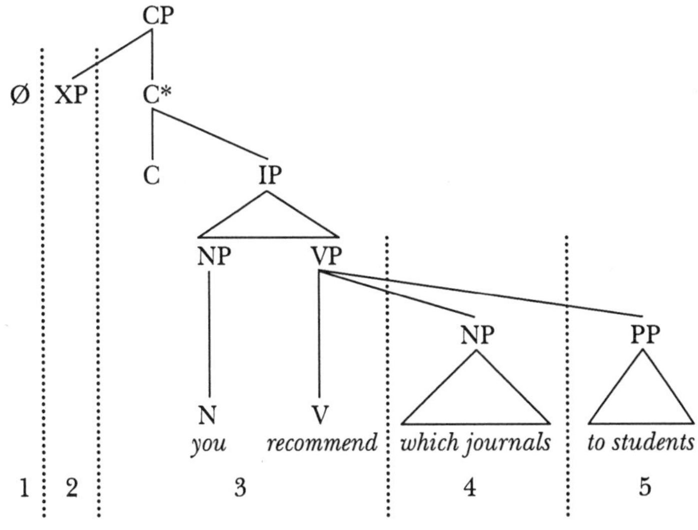


The SC would yield a phrase marker similar to (26)—minus the auxiliary verb *do*.

So far we have dealt only with *wh*-movement in simple sentences. As the following examples show, *wh*-movement also occurs within embedded sentences.

(30) a. John knows who Mary admires
b. Jill forgot which books her neighbor had borrowed
c. Max told Fred how angry Celia had become

Under the trace-theoretic analysis of *wh*-movement, the examples in (30) would be analyzed as in (31), where $e_i$ indicates the trace of the moved *wh*-phrase. (A subscripted indexed category label will be given as the category followed by a colon and the index, as in (31b–c).)

(31) a. John knows [$_{CP}$ who$_i$ [$_{IP}$ Mary admires e$_i$]]
b. Jill forgot [$_{CP}$ [$_{NP:i}$ which books] [$_{IP}$ her neighbor had borrowed e$_i$]]
c. Max told Fred [$_{CP}$ [$_{AP:i}$ how angry] [$_{IP}$ Celia had become e$_i$]]

The embedded CPs in (31) with the *wh*-phrase in SPEC-CP are called **indirect questions** (in contrast to the **direct questions** discussed above, where the *wh*-phrase occurs in the SPEC-CP of the main clause). Note that indirect questions may have direct question variants. (32a–c) are the direct questions corresponding to the indirect questions (30a–c).

(32) a. who does John know Mary admires
b. which books did Jill forget her neighbor had borrowed
c. how angry did Max tell Fred Celia had become

In both (30) and (32) the *wh*-phrase is interpreted as the grammatical object of the embedded verb. Under the trace theory of movement rules we are assuming, the *wh*-phrase in both (30) and (32) originates as the grammatical object of the verb of the embedded IP. For this reason, (30) and (32) have the same underlying phrase marker.

Given the formulation (28) of the *Wh*-Movement rule, the direct questions in (32) can be derived in two different ways. Under the first derivation, the *wh*-phrase is moved from the object position in the sentential complement directly to the SPEC position of the **matrix CP** (or main clause). Under the second, the *wh*-phrase is moved from the object position in the sentential complement to the SPEC position of the embedded CP, and then from that SPEC position to the SPEC position of the matrix CP. The difference is that the multiple-step derivation involves moving the *wh*-phrase from CP to CP, whereas the single-step derivation does not. Schematically, the two options can be represented as (33a–b), where the Roman numerals indicate the order of steps.

(33) a. $[_{CP}$ XP $[_{IP} \ldots [_{CP}$ XP $[_{IP} \ldots$ [*wh*-phrase]]]]]

I

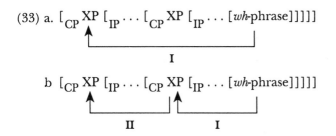

b $[_{CP}$ XP $[_{IP} \ldots [_{CP}$ XP $[_{IP} \ldots$ [*wh*-phrase]]]]]

II I

Note that the formulation of *Wh*-Movement in (28) makes no distinction between the "long-distance" movement option of (33a) and the stepwise CP-to-CP movement option of (33b).

---

**Exercise 3.7**
Show how the formulation of *Wh*-Movement in (28) allows for two distinct derivations of (32b)—that is, via CP-to-CP movement and via long-distance movement. Show how the resulting phrase markers differ under an analysis that assumes traces.

---

There is evidence that a *wh*-phrase may move to the SPEC position of any CP that dominates its underlying grammatical function position. Such evidence is provided by the examples in (34), where in each example *what* functions as the object of *want.* ((34a) is an echo question, where the *wh*-phrase is not moved from its underlying grammatical function position.)

(34) a. Martha told Ben Barbie said Bernie knows Adam wants *what*
b. Martha told Ben Barbie said Bernie knows *what* Adam wants
c. Martha told Ben Barbie said *what* Bernie knows Adam wants
d. Martha told Ben *what* Barbie said Bernie knows Adam wants
e. *what* did Martha tell Ben Barbie said Bernie knows Adam wants

However, such examples do not motivate a choice between the long-distance movement option and the CP-to-CP movement option with respect to our *Wh*-Movement rule. For example, given the formulation of *Wh*-Movement as (28), (34c) can be derived either by a single movement from the object position of *wants* to the SPEC-CP of the clause *Bernie knows . . .*, or by one movement to the SPEC-CP of the clause *Adam wants . . .* and another to the closest c-commanding SPEC-CP.

Under a CP-to-CP analysis, the derivation of (34e) would be represented as (35), where the Roman numerals again indicate the ordered steps in the derivation.

(35)

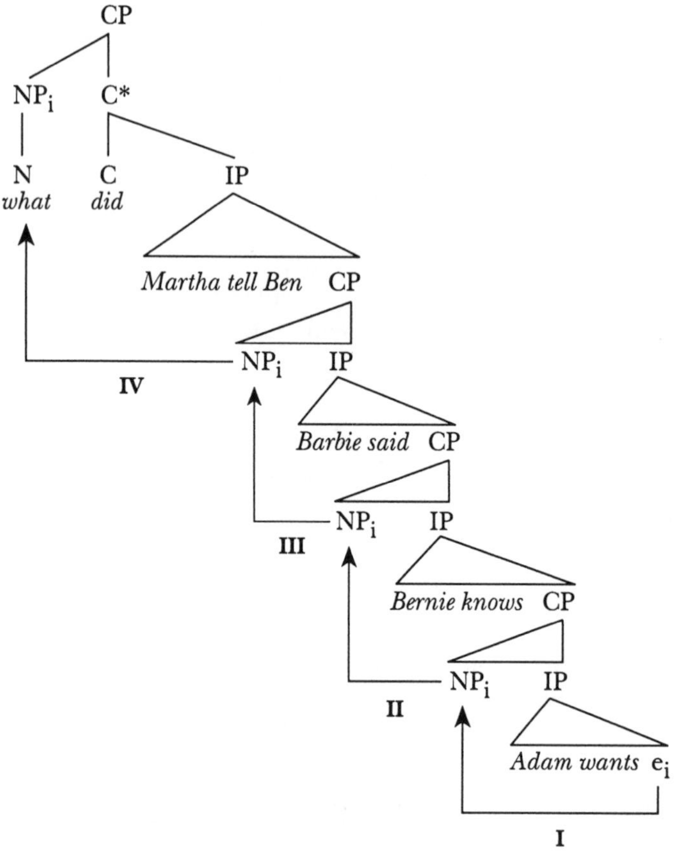


Under this characterization, each CP constitutes a domain of application for the rule of *Wh*-Movement. As a consequence, *Wh*-Movement can apply in a CP domain $D_i$ and then reapply in another CP domain $D_j$ that contains $D_i$ as a constituent. In this way, *Wh*-Movement may apply "cyclically" through successively larger CP domains so that each c-commanding SPEC-CP in the phrase marker is affected by the rule. A rule that may reapply to its own output in a way that affects successively larger domains is called a **cyclic rule**. The smallest domain in which it applies is called its **cyclic domain**.[8] Thus, CP is the cyclic domain for *Wh*-Movement. (35) gives a cyclic derivation for (34a), where each cyclic domain constitutes a **cycle** of a derivation and where the *wh*-phrase *what* moves **successive cyclically** through each c-commanding SPEC-CP to the matrix SPEC-CP. Each movement into CP is upward bounded within a cyclic domain since a *wh*-phrase (in a grammatical function position or in SPEC-CP) and the nearest c-commanding SPEC-CP can never be indefinitely far apart. Thus, each movement of a *wh*-phrase into SPEC-CP is limited within certain fixed boundaries. A series of such movements, however, gives the effect of unbounded movement.

---

**Exercise 3.8**
This discussion assumes that *Wh*-Movement actually applies on each cycle. If, however, the transformation is optional (as indicated by the existence of echo questions where the *wh*-phrase remains in its original grammatical function position), then it is possible that *Wh*-Movement would not apply on one cycle but then apply on the next. Show how (34a,c,d) could be generated in this way and that therefore something more is needed to distinguish the CP-to-CP movement option and the long-distance movement option.

---

Under the single movement analysis for *wh*-questions, there is only one type of *wh*-movement: from a position in IP into SPEC-CP. This position in IP may be a grammatical function position (e.g., subject or object) or not (i.e., an adverbial position containing a *wh*-phrase, such as *where, when, why*).

So far, neither the principles of grammar we have discussed nor the formulation of *Wh*-Movement in (28) distinguishes between an analysis of *wh*-movement which allows CP-to-CP movement and one that does not. In the next section we will see how an analysis of the boundedness of *wh*-movement provides a basis on which to choose between the two options.

## 3.2 Syntactic Islands

Although *wh*-phrases can be moved indefinitely far away from their underlying grammatical function positions in some constructions, there are other constructions out of which wh-phrases cannot be moved at all. That is, there are empirical limitations on what the variable *Y* in (28) can range over. In this section we will examine these limitations and how they are to be formulated within the theory of grammar. It turns out that the most general formulation induces the bounded movement analysis involving CP-to-CP movement.

Let us begin by considering two distinct constructions from which a *wh*-phrase may not be moved into a c-commanding SPEC-CP.

(36) a. *whose$_i$ did you read [$_{NP}$ e$_i$ book]
(cf. whose book did you read)
b. *which books$_j$ did she say [$_{CP}$ who$_i$ [$_{IP}$ e$_i$ read e$_j$]]
(cf. she said who read which books)

In (36a) the *wh*-phrase *whose* has been moved out of the object NP into SPEC-CP. In (36b) the *wh*-phrase *which books* has been moved out of a sentential complement that contains another *wh*-phrase in SPEC-CP. For the purposes of this discussion, we will call a CP that contains a *wh*-phrase in SPEC-CP a ***wh*-clause**. As we will see in detail below, a *wh*-phrase contained in a *wh*-phrase or certain NPs may not be moved into a SPEC-CP that c-commands the construction.

A construction from which a constituent may not be moved by a transformation is designated as an **island** (following Ross 1967). The conditions that prohibit movement out of islands are called **island constraints** (see appendix A for a brief historical comment). With respect to *wh*-movement, there appear to be at least two island types: NPs and *wh*-clauses. What follows is a detailed investigation of NPs and *wh*-clauses that constitute islands for *wh*-movement and the constraints on rules and representations that account for these island phenomena.

### 3.2.1 NP Islands

Recall that an NP may occur in three distinct positions in IP: (i) subject of IP, (ii) complement of V—either as an object of V or as the object of a P (where the PP is a complement of V), or (iii) an adjunct position. These positions are illustrated in (37).

(37) a. NP annoyed Bill [subject]
b. Bill recommended NP to NP [complement]
c. Sally teaches philosophy at NP [adjunct]

By substituting an appropriate wh-phrase for NP in (37), we can obtain the following *wh*-questions in (38).

(38) a. which film annoyed Bill
b. i. which film did Bill recommend to his students
ii. which students did Bill recommend the film to
iii. to which students did Bill recommend the film
c. i. *which university does Sally teach philosophy at
ii. at which university does Sally teach philosophy

(38b.iii) and (38c.ii) both show that the designation *wh*-phrase may extend to a PP containing a *wh*-NP. The phenomenon where *wh*-movement involves more than just the *wh*-word has been dubbed **"pied piping"** in the literature. Thus, the non–*wh*-words that move with the *wh*-word as part of the *wh*-phrase are said to be pied-piped along. (38b) suggests that for complements moving the entire PP is just an option, whereas (38c) suggests that for adjuncts it is a requirement.

---

**Exercise 3.9**

The preceding statement suggests that a test for complement versus adjunct status can be formulated on the basis of *wh*-movement possibilities. A complement PP in V* that contains a *wh*-NP will allow the extraction of just the NP, leaving the P behind in V*; whereas an adjunct PP requires the movement of the entire PP to form a *wh*-question. Does this heuristic work for the clear cases covered previously (e.g., *put*)? Construct further examples that test the distinction.

---

Any of the three NP positions in IP (subject, complement, adjunct) could contain an NP that properly contains a *wh*-phrase. Furthermore, a *wh*-phrase properly contained in an NP could itself occur in any of three distinct positions corresponding to the NP positions in IP: (i) an immediate constituent of $N^{max}$ (e.g., *whose books*) (henceforth "the subject of NP"),[9] (ii) a complement of a head N (e.g., *reviews of which books*), or (iii) a constituent of an adjunct to a head N (e.g., *a student of mathematics at which university*, where the NP is contained in the PP adjunct). Since (38c) shows that movement of a *wh*-NP out of an adjunct is itself problematic, independently of the question concerning the islandhood of NPs in adjunct positions, the following discussion of NP islands will be limited to subject and complement positions in IP.

Consider NPs in subject position that properly contain a *wh*-phrase. (39a) and (40a) give the underlying structures.

(39) a. $[_{CP}$ $[_{IP}$ $[_{NP}$ whose comment] $[_{VP}$ has annoyed you]]]

b. *$[_{CP}$ whose$_i$ $[_{IP}$ has $[_{NP}$ e$_i$ comment] $[_{VP}$ annoy you]]]

(40) a. $[_{CP}$ $[_{IP}$ $[_{NP}$ a comment about whom] $[_{VP}$ has annoyed you]]]

b. *$[_{CP}$ who(m)$_i$ $[_{IP}$ has $[_{NP}$ a comment about e$_i$] $[_{VP}$ annoyed you]]]

c. *$[_{CP}$ $[_{PP:i}$ about whom] $[_{IP}$ has $[_{NP}$ a comment e$_i$] $[_{VP}$ annoyed you]]]

In (39) the *wh*-phrase *whose* (which is an NP—the *wh*-form corresponding to a non–*wh*-NP like *the boy's*) is moved out of the subject position of the subject NP, whereas in (40) the *wh*-phrase *(about) who(m)* is moved out of complement position. The corresponding facts hold for indirect questions as well—though note that the subject and tensed auxiliary do not invert in embedded sentences.

(41) a. *we wondered $[_{CP}$ whose$_i$ $[_{IP}$ $[_{NP}$ e$_i$ comment] has annoyed you]]
b. *we wondered $[_{CP}$ whom$_i$ $[_{IP}$ $[_{NP}$ a comment about e$_i$] has annoyed you]]
c. *we wondered $[_{CP}$ $[_{PP:i}$ about whom] $[_{IP}$ $[_{NP}$ a comment e$_i$] has annoyed you]]

We are assuming that the structural representation given in (41a) is ill formed, on a par with (39b), where the *wh*-NP *whose* is separated from its NP source by the auxiliary verb *has*. However, unlike the string of words in (39b), the string *We wondered whose comment has annoyed you* in (41a) can be assigned an alternative structural description that is well formed.

(42) we wondered $[_{CP}$ $[_{NP:i}$ whose comment] $[_{IP}$ e$_i$ has annoyed you]]

In (42) the *wh*-phrase in CP has not been moved out of an NP that properly contained it. Given that NPs in subject position are always islands with respect to *wh*-movement, (41a) (but not (42)) constitutes an island violation. The contrast between (41a) and (42) shows how rules in a grammar (in this instance, *Wh*-Movement) can assign two distinct structural descriptions to an unambiguous sentence, only one of which is well-formed. If *Wh*-Movement analyzes the NP *whose* as the *wh*-phrase to be moved, then (41a) is derived. If it analyzes the NP *whose comment* as the *wh*-phrase, then (42) is derived. These examples show that NPs in the subject position of IP are always islands for *wh*-movement.

Before discussing NPs in other positions, let us try to formulate a condition that will account for the fact that subject NP is an island for *wh*-movement. Aiming at maximal generality, we might propose something along the lines of (43), which would prohibit any kind of movement out of a subject NP.

(43) **Subject Island Condition**
A subject (NP) is an island.

Though (43) covers all the ill-formed cases in (39)–(41), it does not generalize to other kinds of movement out of subject NP, as we will see. Thus, our account of the island status of subject NP requires a more fine-grained analysis.

Although *wh*-movement may not affect a *wh*-phrase properly contained in subject NP, there appear to be rules of English grammar that can extract other constituents properly contained in a subject NP. Consider the following pair of sentences.

(44) a. a man who I want to meet is coming to dinner
b. a man is coming to dinner who I want to meet

*Who I want to meet* is a relative clause that modifies the head of the subject *man*. In (44a) the relative clause is a constituent of the subject NP, whereas in (44b) it has been moved out of the subject to the end of the sentence. Assuming that the movement results from the adjunction of the relative clause (CP) to VP via a rule called Extraposition, we would analyze the structure of (44b) as (45).

(45)

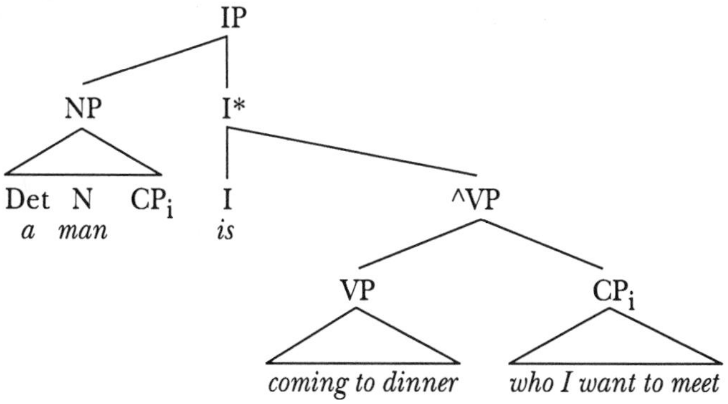


The empty CP in the subject NP represents the trace of the extraposed relative clause in VP. This case could be covered by invoking an asymmetry between leftward movement and rightward movement. That is, the difference between the ungrammatical (41b–c) and the grammatical (44b) could be handled by claiming that a subject NP is an island with respect to leftward movement, but not rightward movement.

It would be false, however, to claim that rightward movement (as opposed to leftward movement) is unbounded. As the following examples illustrate, extraposition, like *wh*-movement, is bounded.

(46) a. $[_{NP}$ a picture of $[_{NP}$ a man $[_{CP:i}$ who I admire tremendously]]] is on the wall
b. *$[_{NP}$ a picture of $[_{NP}$ a man $e_i$]] is on the wall $[_{CP:i}$ who I admire tremendously]

(47) a. $[_{NP}$ a picture of $[_{NP}$ a man] $[_{CP:i}$ which I admire tremendously]] is on the wall
b. $[_{NP}$ a picture of $[_{NP}$ a man] $e_i$] is on the wall $[_{CP:i}$ which I admire tremendously]

In (46a) the relative clause modifies the noun *man* and is therefore a constituent of two distinct NPs, the maximal phrasal projection of *man* and the maximal phrasal projection of *picture*. (46b) shows that in this instance the relative clause may not extrapose to the end of the sentence. In contrast, the relative clause in (47a), which modifies the noun *picture* and is a constituent of only one NP, may extrapose, as illustrated in (47b).

This shows that the relative clause out of subject NP is bounded just as the leftward movement of a *wh*-phrase is bounded. If the constraint on bounding can be stated so that it covers (46b), as well as the ill-formed examples in (39)–(45), then we will have eliminated this apparent asymmetry between leftward and rightward movement. Given that the island constraints involve the hierarchical properties of phrase markers, it is reasonable to try to avoid stating conditions in terms of the linear direction of movements. If island phenomena are determined solely in terms of hierarchical structure, then what sort of phrase is being extracted should not be significant in and of itself.

What (46b) shows is that the relative clause cannot move rightward too far from the movement site. The question is how to formalize the notion "too far." Since (46)–(47) together indicate that a relative clause may move over one NP boundary, but not two NP boundaries, we might consider characterizing "too far" for Extraposition in terms of NP boundaries. This analysis takes NP to be relevant to the boundedness of movement. Let us designate NP as a **bounding category** (or node) and say that two categories (or positions) that are in a linear precedence relation in a phrase marker are **subjacent** if they are separated by no more than one bounding category.

(48) A category α is *subjacent* to a category β if neither dominates the other and the set of bounding nodes that contain one category as a constituent is identical to the set that contains the other or differs from it by no more than one bounding node.

The relation "subjacent to" is symmetric: if α is subjacent to β, then β is also subjacent to α. A bounding condition can be formulated in terms of this relation as follows:

(49) **Subjacency Condition**
No rule may move a constituent to a nonsubjacent position.

As formulated, this condition accounts for the boundedness of Extraposition as illustrated in (46b), where Extraposition has moved the relative clause out of two bounding categories (i.e., the two NPs that dominate the relative clause in (46a)). To extend the Subjacency analysis to account for the examples (36) and (39)–(41) that initiated our discussion of syntactic islands, other bounding categories in addition to NP must be specified. In this way, Subjacency can provide a general account for the boundedness of movement.

Evidence that there is another bounding category in addition to NP comes from yet another case of the boundedness of extraposition. Consider the examples in (50), where the CP *that a man . . . is coming to dinner* functions as the subject of the matrix IP.

(50) a. that a man who I want to meet is coming to dinner is unusual
b. that a man is coming to dinner who I want to meet is unusual
c. *that a man is coming to dinner is unusual who I want to meet

The contrast between (50b) and (50c) shows again that an extraposed relative clause may move only so far and no farther.

Suppose for the purposes of discussion that the structure of (50a) is (51), with some details aside.

(51)

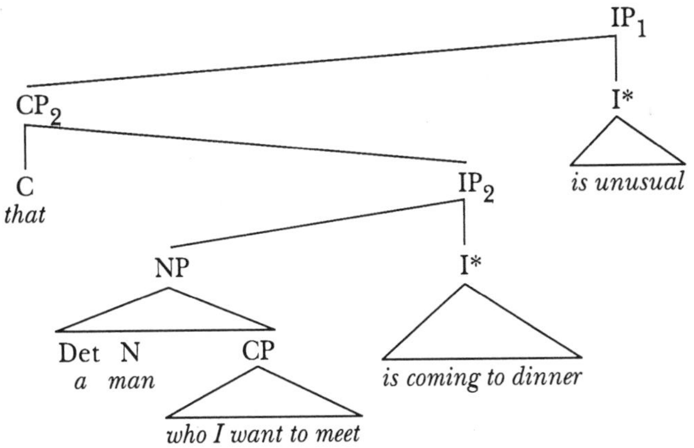


Let us assume further that the rule of CP-Extraposition that moves the relative clause to the end of VP involves an adjunction operation as formulated in (52).

(52) **CP-Extraposition**

| | | | | | |
|---|---|---|---|---|---|
| | X– | CP – | Y – | VP – | Z |
| SD: | 1 | 2 | 3 | 4 | 5 |
| SC: | 1 | | 3 | 4+2 | 5 |

Since the extraposition rule moves a CP across a variable, it can analyze (51) in two different ways. It can choose the VP in $I^*_2$ ($VP_2$ = *is coming to dinner*) as term 4 of the rule, or it can choose the VP in $I^*_1$ ($VP_1$ = *is unusual*). If $VP_2$ is analyzed as term 4, then the grammatical (50b) is derived, with a structure as given in (53).

(53) $[_{IP}$ $[_{CP}$ that $[_{IP}$ $[_{NP}$ a man $e_i]$ $[_{VP}$ $[_{VP}$ is coming to dinner] $[_{CP:i}$ who I want to meet]]]] $[_{VP}$ is unusual]]

If $VP_1$ is analyzed as term 4, however, then the ill-formed (50c) results, with the derived structure given in (54).

(54) *$[_{IP}$ $[_{CP}$ that $[_{IP}$ $[_{NP}$ a man $e_i]$ $[_{VP}$ is coming to dinner]]] $[_{VP}$ $[_{VP}$ is unusual] $[_{CP:i}$ who I want to meet]]]

Although the movement of the relative clause CP to $VP_2$ is allowed, movement of $CP_3$ to $VP_1$ is not. (We will deal with the impossibility of using (53) as an intermediate step in the derivation of (54) in section 3.3.)

If the ungrammaticality of (54) follows from Subjacency, then the extraposition of $CP_3$ to $VP_1$ must have crossed more than one bounding category. Since the movement crosses only three categories (NP, IP, and CP), either IP or CP must count (in addition to NP) as a bounding category.[10] If we take IP to be the other bounding category, then Subjacency accounts not only for all cases of the boundedness of CP-extraposition but also for all cases of the boundedness of *wh*-movement discussed above (e.g., (41a)) (because the movement of a *wh*-phrase properly contained in a subject NP into a c-commanding SPEC-CP will always cross an NP and an IP boundary). (Verification is left as an exercise.)

This analysis of Subjacency now eliminates the asymmetry noted earlier between leftward and rightward movement out of subject NP.[11] In this way, it provides a general account of island phenomena involving subject NPs.

---

**Exercise 3.10**

The examples under discussion involve extraposition of a relative clause out of a subject NP. It is also possible to extrapose a relative clause from an NP that is in SPEC-CP. Consider the following examples:

(i) a. how many people that John really likes did you meet
  b. how many people did you meet that John really likes

Give the underlying phrase marker for the examples in (i). Show how the rules of *Wh*-Movement and CP-Extraposition apply in deriving the two examples. Note that (i.b) can be derived in two different ways, depending on the order in which the two transformations are applied. Demonstrate that the ordering is inconsequential by showing how the two different derivations yield the same result.

---

Taking NP and IP as bounding categories, the Subjacency Condition as formulated in (49) covers the following eight possibilities:

(55) a. Leftward movement

| | α | β | $(X \longleftarrow Y)$ |
|---|---|---|---|
| i. | NP | NP | $X \ldots [_{NP} \ldots [_{NP} \ldots Y$ |
| ii. | NP | IP | $X \ldots [_{NP} \ldots [_{IP} \ldots Y$ |
| iii. | IP | NP | $X \ldots [_{IP} \ldots [_{NP} \ldots Y$ |
| iv. | IP | IP | $X \ldots [_{IP} \ldots [_{IP} \ldots Y$ |

b. Rightward movement:

| | β | α | $(Y \longrightarrow X)$ |
|---|---|---|---|
| i. | NP | NP | $Y \ldots {}_{NP}] \ldots {}_{NP}] \ldots X$ |
| ii. | NP | IP | $Y \ldots {}_{NP}] \ldots {}_{IP}] \ldots X$ |
| iii. | IP | NP | $Y \ldots {}_{IP}] \ldots {}_{NP}] \ldots X$ |
| iv. | IP | IP | $Y \ldots {}_{IP}] \ldots {}_{IP}] \ldots X$ |

Because *Wh*-Movement always involves movement over an IP-boundary, (55a.i–ii) cannot be illustrated with the rule of *Wh*-Movement. That is, *wh*-movement out of NP will always be a case of (55a.iii). We can of course construct examples of illicit *wh*-movement which illustrate these configurations, but an IP-boundary at the left will also be involved. Some examples are provided in (56).

(56) a. *John wondered $[_{CP}$ who(m)$_i$ $[_{IP}$ $[_{NP}$ stories about $[_{NP}$ pictures of e$_i$]] would annoy Susan]]

b. i. *John asked us $[_{CP}$ what$_j$ $[_{IP}$ $[_{NP}$ the boy $[_{CP}$ who$_i$ $[_{IP}$ e$_i$ gave e$_j$ to Mary]]] had talked to Susan]][12]

ii. *John asked us $[_{CP}$ who(m)$_i$ $[_{IP}$ $[_{NP}$ the report $[_{CP}$ that the committee had recommended e$_i$]] had been circulated]][13]

(56a) involves *wh*-movement across two NP boundaries (⇝ (55a.i)). The examples in (56b) involve movement out of an IP properly contained in an NP (⇝ (55a.ii)): out of a relative clause in (56b.i), and out of a sentential complement in (56b.ii). In the literature of generative grammar, these are often called **complex NP** cases (where a complex NP is any NP that contains an embedded CP—just as a complex sentence is any IP which contains an embedded subordinate CP). It appears to be a fact about the languages of the world that no phrase may be moved out of a CP in a complex NP. This prohibition is called the **Complex NP Constraint** (henceforth CNPC; see appendix A for further discussion).

The Subjacency Condition (49) provides a reasonably accurate characterization of the island status of subject NP with respect to both leftward and rightward movements. In what follows we will see how this analysis extends to NPs in nonsubject positions and to the behavior of *wh*-clauses as islands.

In nonsubject positions, NP is also an island for *wh*-movement from the three possible positions within NP (subject, complement, and adjunct). The subject position case is given in (57); the complement position case, in (58); and the adjunct position case, in (59).

(57) a. $[_{CP}$ $[_{IP}$ you criticized $[_{NP}$ whose story]]]
b. *$[_{CP}$ whose$_i$ $[_{IP}$ did you criticize $[_{NP}$ $e_i$ story]]]

(58) a. $[_{CP}$ $[_{IP}$ you criticized $[_{NP}$ a story about who(m)]]]
b. *$[_{CP}$ who(m)$_i$ $[_{IP}$ did you criticize $[_{NP}$ a story about $e_i$]]]
c. *$[_{CP}$ $[_{PP}$ about whom$_i$ $[_{IP}$ did you criticize $[_{NP}$ a story $e_i$]]]]

(59) a. $[_{CP}$ $[_{IP}$ you talked to $[_{NP}$ a student of physics from which university]]]
b. *$[_{CP}$ which university$_i$ $[_{IP}$ did you talk to $[_{NP}$ a student of physics from $e_i$]]]
c. *$[_{CP}$ from which university$_i$ $[_{IP}$ did you talk to $[_{NP}$ a student of physics $e_i$]]]

As before, the (a)-examples in (57)–(59) give the underlying structures of the corresponding ill-formed (b)- and (c)-examples. All the starred examples fall under the Subjacency Condition since the *wh*-phrase is moved over two bounding categories: the NP that properly contains it in underlying structure and the IP that is a sister of the C into whose SPEC it moves. These examples are also instances of (55a.iii).

The Subjacency Condition also blocks *wh*-movement out of the CP of a relative clause—which always yields an ungrammatical sentence. Consider, for example, (60), where the head of the direct object *boy* is modified by a relative clause.

(60) $[_{CP}$ $[_{IP}$ Alice saw $[_{NP}$ the boy $[_{CP}$ who$_i$ $[_{IP}$ Mary likes $e_i$]]]]]

If the *wh*-phrase in the SPEC-CP of the relative clause were to be analyzed by the *Wh*-Movement transformation, then the rule could apply by moving the *wh*-phrase *who* from the CP of the relative clause to the CP of the matrix IP, yielding the ill-formed (61).

(61) *[$_{CP}$ who$_i$ [$_{IP}$ did Alice see [$_{NP}$ the boy [$_{CP}$ e$_i$ (that) [$_{IP}$ Mary likes e$_i$]]]]]

Because the *wh*-phrase would have moved across two bounding categories, NP and IP, in order to move from the relative clause CP to the matrix CP, examples like (61) are excluded by the Subjacency Condition.[14]

Although *wh*-extraction out of NP appears to be generally prohibited, there are instances where it is possible.

(62) a. [$_{CP}$ who$_i$ [$_{IP}$ did you take [$_{NP}$ a picture of e$_i$]]]
b. [$_{CP}$ who$_i$ [$_{IP}$ did you see [$_{NP}$ a picture of e$_i$]]]

The acceptability of such constructions seems to depend in part on the matrix verb, as illustrated by comparing (62) with (63).[15]

(63) ?*[$_{CP}$ who$_i$ [$_{IP}$ did you ridicule [$_{NP}$ a picture of e$_i$]]]

("?*" indicates that speakers find the example slightly more acceptable than an outright deviant construction, though not completely acceptable.) Furthermore, the acceptability of constructions like those in (62) is strictly limited to the particular construction and does not extend to other NP constructions—even with the same matrix verb.

(64) a. *who$_i$ did you {see, take} [$_{NP}$ Bernie's picture of e$_i$]
b. *whose$_i$ did you {see, take} [$_{NP}$ e$_i$ picture of Adam]

In (64) *wh*-extraction is blocked when the NP contains a lexical subject. In (64a) the lexical subject is independent of the *wh*-phrase, whereas in (64b) *wh*-phrase is the lexical subject.

---

**Exercise 3.11**

Relative clause extraposition is also blocked when an NP contains a lexical subject:

(i) a. the claim that all languages are context-free was refuted
b. the claim was refuted that all languages are context-free

(ii) a. John's claim that all languages are context-free was refuted
b. *John's claim was refuted that all languages are context-free

Analyze (i)–(ii) in terms of the relevant labeled bracketing and traces. A condition against the binding of a trace across a subject could account for (ii.b). Discuss how this condition extends to some of the wh-movement cases considered so far.

---

Constructions like (64) therefore reinforce the conclusion that NPs constitute islands for *wh*-movement generally, as predicted by the

Subjacency Condition, and suggest that examples like (62) are exceptions that require some further analysis to explain their acceptability. For example, verbs like *take* and *see* may neutralize the bounding category status of their object NP (when that NP lacks a syntactic subject; compare (64), in contrast contrast to verbs like *ridicule.* Why this is possible remains to be determined.

This completes our discussion of leftward movements out of NP. We return now to rightward movements out of NP (i.e., (55b.i–iii)).

As noted in the discussion of examples (44), (47), and (50), the rightward movement of a relative clause out of subject NP is permissible under certain circumstances. There is, however, a limitation on such rightward movements that is identical to the limitation on leftward *wh*-movement: a single movement cannot cross more than one bounding category. The examples cited concerned rightward movement across two NPs and also out of NP and IP that immediately dominates it—instances of (55b.i-ii). Since the rule of Extraposition under discussion always involves movement out of NP, we have no pure case of (55b.iv).

---

**Exercise 3.12**

As an illustration of (55b.iii), consider the following examples:

(i) a. a report that John had lied has been published
    b. a report has been published that John had lied
(ii) a. a report that Mary said that John had lied has been published
    b. a report has been published that Mary said that John had lied
    c. *a report that Mary said has been published that John had lied

In (i.b) the sentential complement of the noun *report* has been extraposed. Discuss the analysis of these examples and show how Subjacency accounts for the ungrammatical (ii.c).

---

**Exercise 3.13**

In addition to relative clauses, PPs may be extraposed out of NP and adjoined to VP. In (i.b) extraposition moves a PP out of the subject NP and in (ii.b) the PP moves out of CP. The (a)-examples give the nonextraposed variants.

(i) a. a new book about Hilbert has just appeared
    b. a new book has just appeared about Hilbert
(ii) a. how many new books about Hilbert did John review
    b. how many new books did John review about Hilbert

As illustrated in (iii) and (iv), PP-extraposition is bounded in the same way as CP-extraposition.

(iii) a. a review of a new book about Hilbert has just appeared
b. *a review of a new book has just appeared about Hilbert

(iv) a. how many reviews of a new book about Hilbert has John read
b. *how many reviews of a new book has John read about Hilbert

Demonstrate this by giving a detailed analysis of (i)–(iv) and showing how Subjacency rules out the ill-formed examples.

As in the case of CP-extraposition, PP-extraposition is also blocked when the NP from which the PP is to be moved contains a lexical subject (see exercise 3.11). Construct an example that demonstrates this.

---

So far we have seen that NP-island phenomena can be subsumed under a general constraint, Subjacency, which need not distinguish the directionality of movement operations. We turn now to the analysis of wh-clauses, which, like NPs, appear to be islands with respect to certain movement phenomena.

### 3.2.2 *Wh*-Islands

Under the definition of a *wh*-clause as a CP that contains a *wh*-phrase in SPEC-CP, the bracketed CPs in (65) are examples of *wh*-clauses.

(65) a. Calvin remembers [$_{CP}$ who$_i$ [$_{IP}$ e$_i$ mentioned sushi]]
b. Calvin remembers [$_{CP}$ what$_i$ [$_{IP}$ Bill mentioned e$_i$]]

As (66) illustrates, it is possible for a *wh*-clause to contain more than one *wh*-phrase.

(66) Calvin remembers [$_{CP}$ who$_i$ [$_{IP}$ e$_i$ mentioned what]]

A clause with more than one interrogative *wh*-phrase is called a **multiple *wh*-question**. As we will see, the behavior of *Wh*-Movement with respect to multiple *wh*-questions is determined in part by the Subjacency Condition.

Though it is possible for *Wh*-Movement to move a *wh*-phrase from the SPEC-CP of a *wh*-clause to another SPEC-CP, *wh*-movement out of IP in a *wh*-clause produces a deviant sentence. For example, suppose that the *wh*-phrase subject of *mentioned* in (66) were moved directly into the SPEC-CP of the main clause by *Wh*-Movement. The resulting ill-formed (67) provides another example of the boundedness of *wh*-movement.

(67) a. *who does Calvin remember what mentioned
b. *$[_{CP}$ who$_i$ $[_{IP}$ does Calvin remember $[_{CP}$ what$_j$ $[_{IP}$ $e_i$ mentioned $e_j$]]]]

(67) shows that IP in a *wh*-clause is an island with respect to *wh*-movement. We will call such an IP a ***wh*-island**. Because *wh*-movement out of a *wh*-island involves movement across two IP boundaries (as in (67b)), *wh*-island violations, which are instances of (55a.iv), follow from Subjacency.

Given the Subjacency Condition, in order for a *wh*-phrase to move indefinitely far away from its original grammatical function position in underlying structure, *wh*-movement must be a bounded movement that applies successive cyclically. If any SPEC-CP is filled with a *wh*-phrase, then movement over it to the next subjacent SPEC-CP will result in a Subjacency violation—regardless of whether movement of the *wh*-phrase ($wh_j$ below) is from a grammatical function position to SPEC-CP (as in (68a)) or SPEC-CP-to-SPEC-CP (as in (68b)).

(68) a. $[_{CP}$ $[_{IP}$ . . . $[_{CP}$ $wh_i$ $[_{IP}$ $wh_j$ . . . ]]]]
b. $[_{CP}$ $[_{IP}$ . . . $[_{CP}$ $wh_i$ $[_{IP}$ . . . $[_{CP}$ $wh_j$ . . . ]]]]]

The single movement of $wh_j$ to the empty matrix SPEC-CP necessarily involves two IP boundaries, in violation of Subjacency. Thus, the island phenomena that empirically motivate the Subjacency Condition also provide an empirical foundation for the bounded analysis of *wh*-movement.

As formulated in (49), Subjacency is interpreted as a condition on the application of rules. Given this interpretation, it is possible to construct derivations of *wh*-island violations that do not violate Subjacency. Consider again the case of a sentential complement containing multiple *wh*-phrases, as in the underlying structure (69).

(69) $[_{CP}$ $[_{IP}$ Calvin remembers $[_{CP}$ $[_{IP}$ who mentioned what]]]]

Suppose that each *wh*-phrase is moved into a CP: one into the complement CP and the other into the matrix CP. There are two possible outcomes, both deviant, (though it has been reported that some speakers find (70a) worse than (70b)).

(70) a. *who does Calvin remember what mentioned
b. *what does Calvin remember who mentioned

If (70a–b) are derived by extracting a *wh*-phrase out of the embedded IP and moving it into the matrix CP directly, then Subjacency is violated. If, however, the *wh*-phrase in the matrix CP has moved through the CP of the sentential complement, followed by the movement of the other *wh*-phrase into this vacated CP, then Subjacency is not violated. This derivation for (70a) is given in (71), where (71a) represents the underlying phrase marker and the arrows indicate what movement has taken place.

(71) a. $[_{CP:1}$ XP $[_{IP:1}$ Calvin remembers $[_{CP:2}$ XP $[_{IP:2}$ who mentioned what]]]]

b $[_{CP:1}$ XP $[_{IP:1}$ Calvin remembers $[_{CP:2}$ $who_i$ $[_{IP:2}$ $e_i$ mentioned what]]]]

c. $[_{CP:1}$ $who_i$ $[_{IP:1}$ Calvin remembers $[_{CP:2}$ $e_i$ $[_{IP:2}$ $e_i$ mentioned what]]]]

d. $[_{CP:1}$ $who_i$ $[_{IP:1}$ Calvin remembers $[_{CP:2}$ $what_j$ $[_{IP:2}$ $e_i$ mentioned $e_j$ ]]]]

Each of the indicated movements obeys the Subjacency Condition, yet the result is ill formed just as if Subjacency had been violated.

---

**Exercise 3.14**
Construct the analogous derivation for (70b).

---

One way to eliminate the derivation is to prohibit the third movement, from (71c) to (71d). This can be done by placing a condition on the cyclic application of rules. Recall that CP is a cyclic domain for the application of *Wh*-Movement. $CP_2$ is therefore a cyclic subdomain of $CP_1$. Given this, the movement of *who* into the SPEC-CP of the sentential complement applies on the $CP_2$ cycle, and the movement of *who* into the SPEC-CP of the matrix CP applies on the $CP_1$ cycle. But then the derivation is at the $CP_1$ cycle when *what* moves into the SPEC-CP of the sentential complement. This application affects only a cyclic subdomain of the current cycle ($CP_1$). If we prohibit this derivational possibility, the ungrammaticality of (70a) may result from the violation of another condition on rule application, (72).

(72) **Strict Cycle Condition**
No rule may apply solely within a cyclic subdomain of the current cycle.

The Strict Cycle Condition (SCC) ensures that once a cycle has been passed in a derivation, it is inaccessible to any rule that does not analyze it as a subdomain—that is, by making crucial reference to some constant term in the matrix domain. For example, suppose that, given a complex structure (73), a rule $R_i$ applying on the $IP_1$ cycle transformed the structure of $IP_2$ in such a way that a rule $R_j$ could then apply solely within $IP_2$, where the structural description of $R_j$ was not met before the application of $R_i$.

(73)

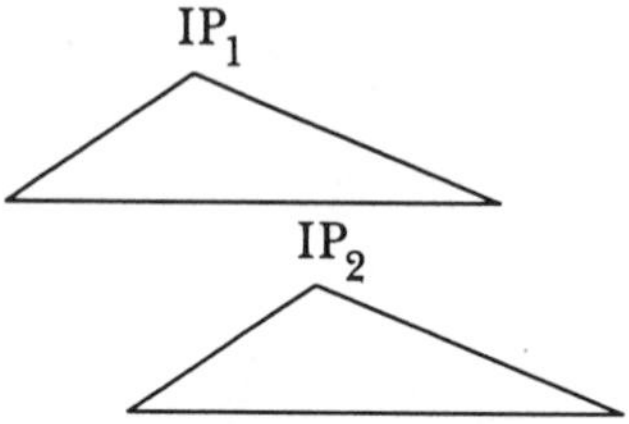


In this derivation $R_i$ "feeds" $R_j$ (i.e., the output of $R_i$ serves as the input for $R_j$), and the feeding relationship holds between a cyclic domain and its cyclic subdomain. The SCC prohibits such feeding relationships, as is required to rule out certain derivations of (70).

Both derivations of (70a)—the one that violates Subjacency and the one that violates the SCC—yield the same representation, (74).

(74) $[_{CP:1}$ who$_i$ $[_{IP:1}$ Calvin remembers $[_{CP:2}$ what$_j$ $[_{IP:2}$ $e_i$ mentioned $e_j$ ]]]]

---

**Exercise 3.15**

Construct a third possible derivation of (74) that violates both Subjacency and the SCC.

---

If Subjacency is interpreted as a condition on the application of rules (i.e., on derivations), then the SCC is necessary to rule out the one derivation of (74) that does not violate Subjacency. The SCC can only be construed as a condition on derivations. This is not true for Subjacency. Subjacency may be interpreted as a *condition on representations* by reformulating it as applying to the binding of traces after the application of movement transformations. Thus, no matter how (74) is derived, the resulting representation contains a trace $e_i$ that is not subjacent to its antecedent *who*$_i$. Because the effect of the SCC is subsumed under this latter interpretation of Subjacency, and the Subjacency Condition is independently motivated by island phenomena that are unrelated to the issue of strict cyclicity, the SCC is unnecessary for the analysis of (70a). This holds generally for all the *wh*-island violations whose derivation violates the SCC.[16]

**Exercise 3.16**
Show how this works for (70b).

The formulation of Subjacency as a condition on representations concerns the way in which traces left by movement operations are bound. This could be done by reformulating (49) as a **filter**, (75), which assigns a "*" to any sentence meeting its structural description.

(75) **Subjacency (II)**
$* \ldots A_i \ldots [_\alpha \ldots [_\beta \ldots e_i \ldots ] \ldots ] \ldots A_i \ldots$
where α, β are bounding categories (NP or IP) and α contains no other $A_i$.

In (75) ". . ." stands for a string variable, $A_i$ represents a category (i.e., a constant) coindexed with a trace. The qualification that a contains no other $A_i$ is necessary for preventing (75) from analyzing an $A_i$ that is not subjacent to $e_i$, when there is an intervening $A_i$ that is subjacent to it.

**Exercise 3.17**
Show how the structural analysis of (34d) could meet the structural description of (75) if we ignore the qualification.

Alternatively, we can eliminate direct reference to an $A_i$ in a by reformulating Subjacency in terms of trace binding. Let us say that a trace is **bound** if and only if it is coindexed to an antecedent (that is, another constituent of the same category). A trace is bound in a specific syntactic domain (e.g., CP) if and only if the trace and its coindexed antecedent occur as constituents of that domain. When the antecedent of the trace does not occur in the same domain as the trace, the trace is **free** in that domain. In (74), for example, $e_j$ is bound in $CP_2$ but is free in $IP_2$; that is, it has no binder in $IP_2$. Using this terminology, Subjacency can be reformulated as (76).

(76) **Subjacency (Filter)**
$*[_\alpha \ldots [_\beta \ldots e_i \ldots ] \ldots ]$
where α, β are bounding categories (NP, IP) and $e_i$ is free in α.

With (76) the boundedness of movement operations is translated as a restriction on unbound traces within certain domains.

The formulation of the Subjacency Condition in (76) is preferable to the formulation in (75) because the linear relation between a trace and its binder is not crucial for bounding. With leftward movements (e.g., *wh*-movement), the binder usually c-commands its trace; but this does not seem to generalize to the structural relation between antecedent-trace pairs created by rightward movement. Given our analysis of the examples of licit rightward movement discussed earlier (such as (45)), a trace resulting from a rightward movement is not c-commanded by its antecedent. In generalizing Subjacency for leftward and rightward movement in terms of a condition on representations, the c-command relation of the trace-binder pair does not seem to be relevant. What is important is that a trace have an antecedent within a subjacent domain. In (76) a marks the boundary of the domain in which an antecedent could be subjacent to $e_i$.

### 3.2.3 Parametric Variation across Languages

So far we have been investigating the boundedness of movement operations in a grammar of English. If the Subjacency Condition is a general condition on bounding, it must in some sense be part of the innate mechanism a child brings to the task of grammar acquisition. If so, we might expect Subjacency to hold for movement rules in other languages. It turns out, however, that boundedness properties for movement rules are not identical in all languages. In Italian, for example, sentences corresponding to a certain class of *wh*-island violations in English are well formed; and in Russian, CP-to-CP movement is not possible. Such facts can be incorporated naturally into an extension of the Subjacency analysis. As we will see, these differences show us how bounding categories may vary within a limited range across languages.

In Italian, indirect questions do not constitute *wh*-islands for *wh*-movement of relative pronouns. As illustrated in (77a), with its S-structure (77b), a relative pronoun may be extracted out of an indirect question.[17]

(77) a. tuo fratello, a cui mi domando che storie
your brother to whom I wonder which stories

abbiano raccontato, era molto preoccupato
(they) told was very troubled

(77) b.

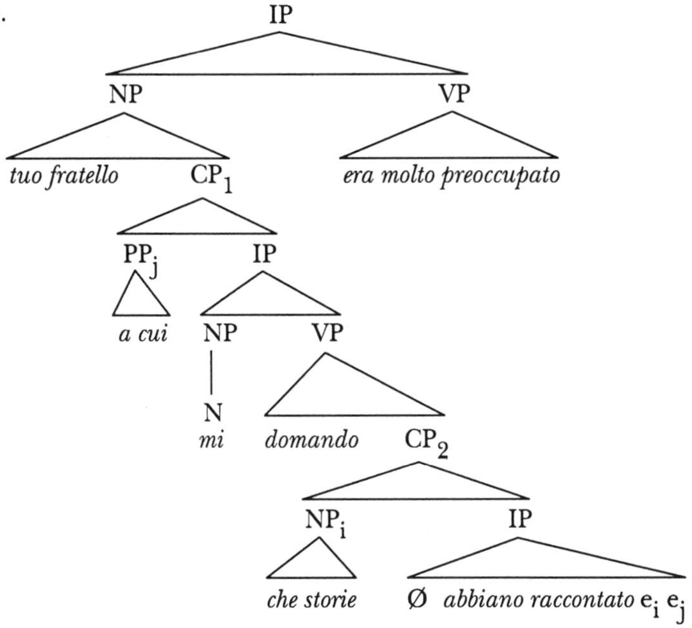


(The "Ø" in this and the following representations indicates a null subject position.) In (77) the relative pronoun *a cui* can be extracted out of $CP_2$ across the internal CP, which contains a *wh*-phrase. Since the corresponding English sentence is ill formed, English and Italian have different properties with respect to boundedness. The question now is, How do we formulate this difference and how does this formulation relate to the Subjacency Condition?

If w*h*-movement in Italian showed no island effects, then the whole Subjacency analysis would be largely irrelevant. This is not the case, however. Italian does manifest island effects for *wh*-movement—in particular, Complex NP Constraint effects (henceforth CNPC effects) and certain *wh*-island effects. (In other words, not all *wh*-island violations in Italian yield well-formed sentences.) (78a) constitutes a CNPC violation resulting from *wh*-movement of a relative pronoun.

(78) a. *tuo fratello, a cui temo la possibilità
your brother to whom (I) fear the possibility

che abbiano raccontato tutto . . .
that they told everything

(78) b.

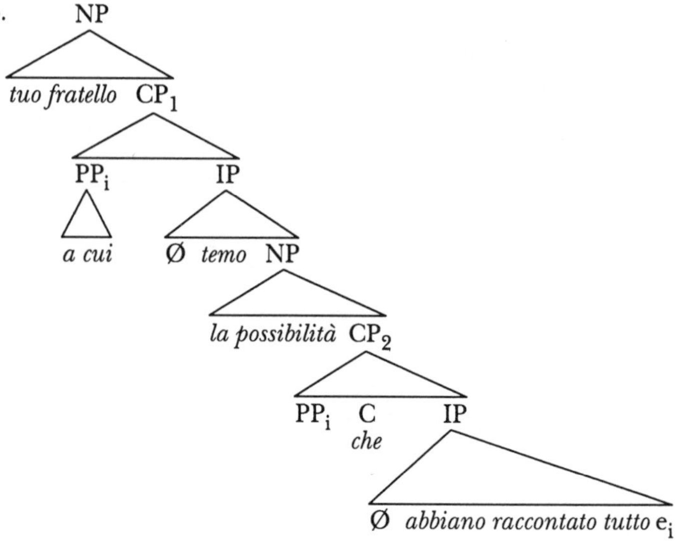


Note that we are assuming here that wh-movement of *a cui* takes place via the SPEC-CP of $CP_2$ since this option is open. *Che* in the SPEC-CP of $CP_2$ is the complementizer equivalent to *that* in English. Under this analysis it is the relation of the trace in $CP_2$ to its antecedent in the SPEC of $CP_1$ that is relevant for determining the boundedness of movement in Italian. Whatever accounts for boundedness in this case will of course extend to the case where *a cui* moves directly into the SPEC of $CP_1$. If the bounding categories for Italian are NP and CP, then Subjacency will account for both cases.

In English, CNPC effects follow from Subjacency since *wh*-movement out of a complex NP involves the NP boundary and an IP boundary that dominates that NP, as shown schematically in (79).

(79) $[_{CP}\ wh_i\ [_{IP} \ldots [_{NP}\ [_{CP}\ e_i\ [_{IP} \ldots e_i \ldots ]]]]]$

This account is not possible in Italian because of constructions like (77), which show that IP does not function as a bounding node in Italian. That is, *a cui* in the grammatical (77) binds its trace across two IPs. If the general idea underlying the Subjacency Condition is the appropriate one for explaining boundedness of movement operations and the CNPC effects in particular, then the antecedent-trace relation (or alternatively movement between the two positions) in (79) must cross two bounding categories for Italian too. Suppose that instead of IP, CP is a bounding category in Italian. Then the CNPC in Italian also follows from the Subjacency Condition as modified for Italian.

The choice of CP as a bounding category is empirically supported for Italian by the ill-formedness of constructions like (80), as well as (78).

(80) a. *questo incarico, che non so proprio chi
this task that (I) really don't know who

possa avere indovinato a chi affiderò,
might have guessed to whom (I) will entrust

mi sta creando un sacco di grattacapi
is getting me into trouble

b.

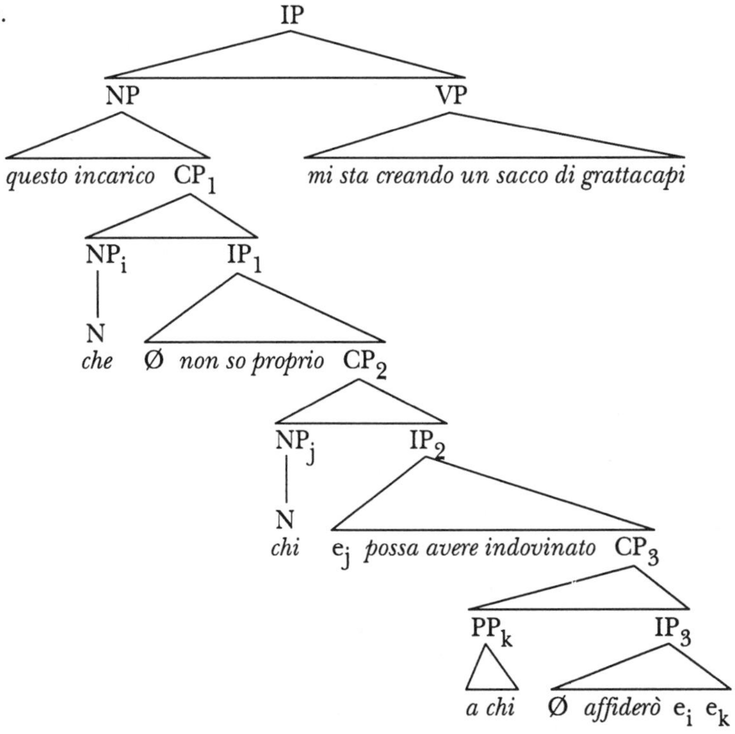

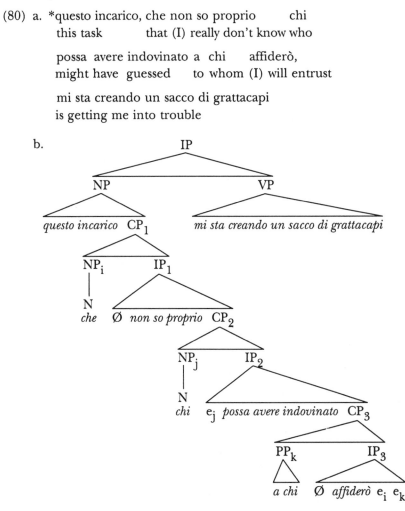

The relative pronoun *che*$_i$ binds its trace across $CP_2$ and $CP_3$. If CP is a bounding category in Italian, then these constructions fall under the modified Subjacency Condition. Although extraction out of a *wh*-island is permissible in Italian, such extractions are nonetheless limited to a single *wh*-island. When a *wh*-island is embedded in another *wh*-island, as in (80), extraction out of this "double" *wh*-island is prohibited.

**Exercise 3.18**

The same analysis applies to French. Consider the following examples (from Sportiche 1981):

(i) voilà $[_{NP}$ quelqu'un
here is someone

$[_{CP}$ à qui je crois que je sais lequel j'offrirais]]
to whom I think that I know which one I will offer

(ii) *voilà $[_{NP}$ quelqu'un
here is someone

$[_{CP}$ à qui je sais lequel je crois que j'offrirais]]
to whom I know which one I think that I will offer

Provide the relevant analysis with traces for the bracketed relative clause in each example and discuss how this pair of examples shows that French has bounding properties identical to those of Italian.

In Spanish there is also evidence that CP not IP is a bounding category for Subjacency. This evidence concerns the fact that *wh*-movment in Spanish involves an obligatory reordering of the subject and the verbal string, as illustrated by the contrast between (iii.a) and (iii.b—c) (data adapted from Torrego 1984).

(iii) a. $[_{CP}$ qué $[_{IP}$ ha organizada la gente ]]
what have organized (the) people
'what have people organized'
b. *qué ha *la gente* organizada
c. *qué *la gente* ha organizada

The data in (iv) show that this reordering occurs successive cyclically and that certain long distance wh-movements can occur whereas others may not.

(iv) a. $[_{CP}$ con quién $[_{IP}$ creías *tú* $[_{CP}$ que $[_{IP}$ quería *Juan* $[_{CP}$ que $[_{IP}$ hablara María]]]]]]
with whom think you that wanted John that will-speak Mary
'who do you think that John wanted Mary to speak with'
b. con quién creías *tú* que quería *Juan* que *María* hablara
c. ???*con quién creías *tú* que *Juan* quería que *María* hablara
d. ???con quién creías *tú* que *Juan* quería que hablara *María*

Provide the relevant analysis with traces for each example in (iv). Discuss how the analysis of (iv.b) shows that IP is not a bounding category for Spanish and how the status of (iv.c—d) follows if CP is a bounding category.

It follows from this formulation of Subjacency that a relative pronoun may be extracted out of an indirect question, unless the pronoun is in SPEC-CP. That is, (81a) is permissible, whereas (81b) is not. (82) provides a concrete instance of (81a); (83) exemplifies (81b).

(81) a.

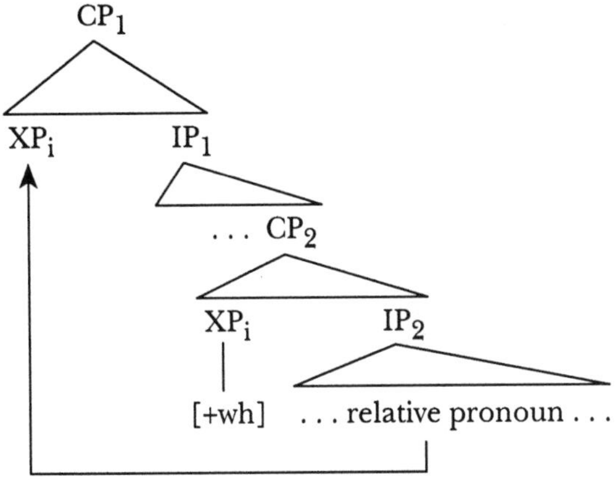


b.

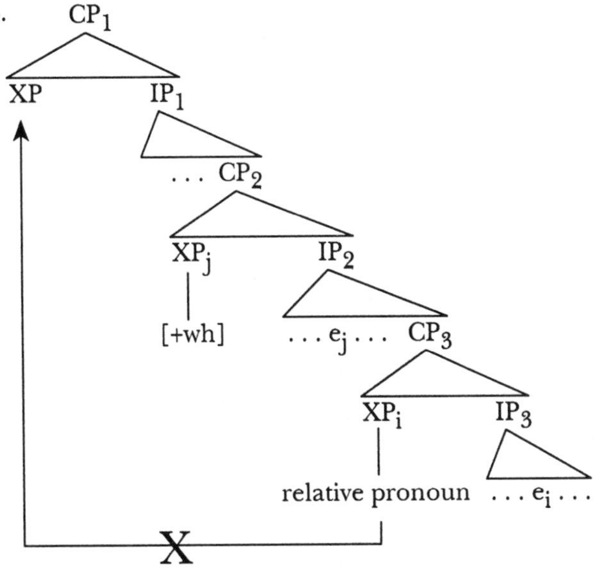

(82) a. il mio primo libro, che credo che tu sappia
my first book which (I) believe that you know

a chi ho dedicato, mi è sempre stato molto caro
to whom (I) dedicated has always been very dear to me

(82) b.

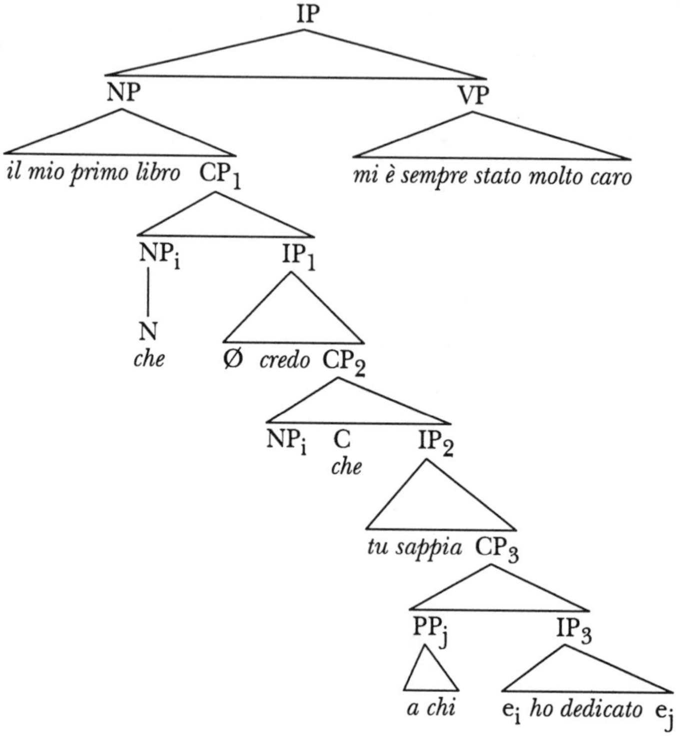


(83) a. *il mio primo libro che so a chi credi che
my first book which (I) know to whom you believe that

abbia dedicato, mi è sempre stato molto caro
(I) dedicated has always been very dear to me

(83) b.

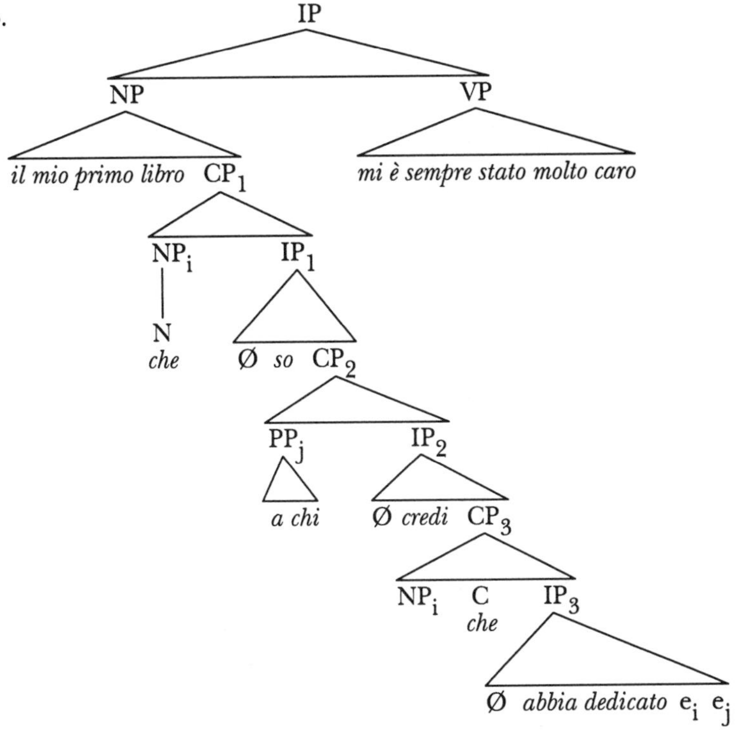


Note that the *che* of $CP_2$ in (82) and of $CP_3$ in (83) is a complementizer; the *che* in NP is a relative pronoun. In (82) the relative pronoun *che* moves directly into the SPEC of $CP_2$ over $CP_3$, which is filled with the *wh*-phrase *a chi*—as is allowed by the modified version of Subjacency under discussion. *Che* then moves from the SPEC of $CP_2$ to the SPEC of $CP_1$ in the usual way. In (83) we will assume that the relative pronoun moves into the SPEC of $CP_3$ on the $CP_3$ cycle, followed by the movement of the *wh*-phrase *a chi* directly from $IP_3$ to the SPEC of $CP_2$ on the $CP_2$ cycle. Thus, for the relative pronoun *che* to move into the SPEC of $CP_1$, it must cross the $CP_3$ and $CP_2$ boundaries, thereby violating Subjacency.

The formulation of the Subjacency Condition in which CP rather than IP is a bounding category predicts that a *wh*-phrase may be extracted out of a subject NP that properly contains it, as represented schematically in (84).

(84) $[_{CP}$ XP $[_{IP}$ $[_{NP}$ . . . *wh*-phrase . . . ] . . . ]]

Again, this appears to be possible with respect to relative pronouns, as in (85).

(85) a. questo autore, di cui so che il primo libro
this author by whom (I) know that the first book

è stato pubblicato recentemente, . . .
has been published recently

b.

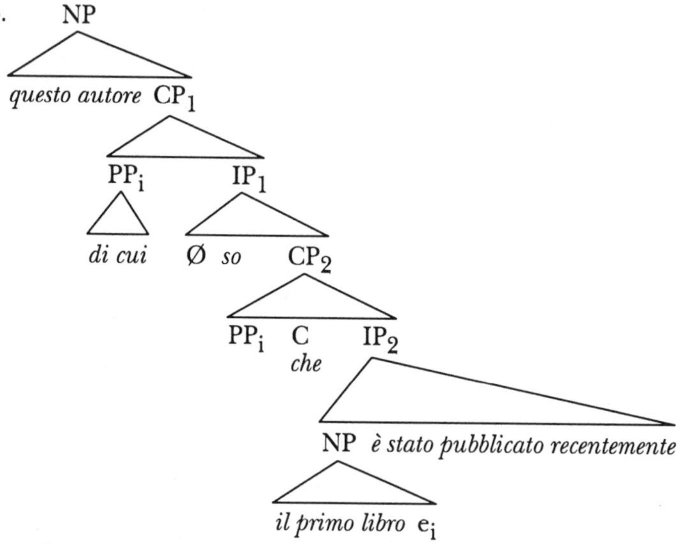


The relative pronoun *cui* moves through the SPEC of $CP_2$ without violating Subjacency.[18]

This discussion shows that the boundedness of movement in Italian is susceptible to the same sort of analysis provided earlier for English. Movements may not cross more than one bounding category at a time. English and Italian differ only in terms of what constitutes a bounding category. More precisely, the choice of IP or CP as a bounding category for Subjacency constitutes a **parameter** for bounding. Thus, we have a principle of grammar, Subjacency, associated with a parameter which can be fixed in one of two different ways in the grammar of a particular language. One setting of the parameter results in languages with the bounding properties of English, whereas the other setting results in languages with the bounding properties of Italian.[19]

Suppose that parts of UG are associated with certain open parameters that when fixed determine the grammar of particular language. The bounding category parameter of Subjacency is one instance. Another concerns word order of heads and complements in phrase structure. In English complements are to the right of their head; whereas in Japanese complements are to the left of their head. Thus UG might contain a head-initial versus head-final parameter associated with the principles of phrase structure. From this perspective, the task of language acquisition involves fixing the parameters in UG on the basis of the primary language data to which the child is exposed. If the differences in the structural properties among languages can be explained as differences in parameter settings, then we will have linked linguistic variation among languages to properties of UG.

The model for parameter setting presented above involves adjusting the value of a part of a condition from one category to another. There is an alternative model to be considered: one in which parameters are set by eliminating inappropriate values. Suppose that a language selects both IP and CP as bounding categories for Subjacency. It then follows that Subjacency prohibits CP-to-CP movement in that language as indicated in (86), where a *wh*-phrase in SPEC-CP binds a trace in SPEC-CP across CP and the IP that dominates it.

(86) $[_{CP}\ wh_i\ [_{IP} \ldots [_{CP}\ e_i\ [_{IP} \ldots\ e_i\ \ldots ]]]]$

Both Russian and German are languages that do not allow CP-to-CP movement and therefore, according to this analysis, select both IP and CP as bounding categories for Subjacency. In terms of the bounding categories IP and CP, then, we have three distinct language types:

(87) a. IP and CP: Russian, German
b. CP only: Italian, Spanish, French
c. IP only: English

The difference between the first type of language and the latter two is that the latter allow CP-to-CP movement. Presumably, exposure to CP-to-CP movement cases allows a child's "language acquisition device" to determine that both IP and CP cannot be bounding categories for Subjacency in the language that the child is learning—though this leaves open which one to eliminate. A child acquiring English will not be exposed to the relevant sentences that determine that IP rather than CP is the correct parameter for English; in other words, the child will not hear sentences like those in (88) or know that they are ill-formed (because they involve trace binding over more than one bounding category).

(88) a. $*[_{CP}$ who$_i$ $[_{IP}$ did John say $[_{CP}$ what$_j$ $[_{IP}$ $e_i$ saw $e_j]]]]$
b. $*[_{CP}$who$_i$ $[_{IP}$did $[_{NP}$Eliot's lack of interest in $e_i]$ surprise Virginia$]]$

If the language learner has no evidence that examples like these are illformed for English, then this has implications for the theory of how parameters are fixed in language acquisition: namely, it suggests the notion that parameters in UG are fixed along a scale of restrictiveness. That is, the child's "language acquisition device" will choose the most restrictive setting of the parameter unless there is evidence to the contrary. If the evidence to the contrary does not distinguish between alternatives, then the next most restrictive parameter setting will be assumed. For Subjacency, {NP, CP, IP} is assumed at the outset. In languages where there is positive evidence for CP-to-CP movement, the parameter for Subjacency will then be set at {NP, IP}. Only in Italian (and other languages of the same type), where there will be positive evidence against {NP, IP}, will the {NP, CP} option be chosen.

## 3.3 Successive Cyclic Movement and Conditions on Rules and Representations

In this section we will examine successive cyclic movement and consider why it is required in the operation of *Wh*-Movement, but blocked in the application of CP- and PP-Extraposition. Although the *wh*-movement analysis follows from the Subjacency Condition, the impossibility of successive cyclic extraposition requires the introduction of another condition on representations involving the notion of government. Government is also involved in yet another constraint on *wh*-movement, as we shall see. The discussion leads to a consideration of overlapping conditions—the situation that arises when two or more conditions apply to the same ungrammatical sentence.

Given the formulation of the Subjacency Condition in (76) (repeated here), it follows that seemingly unbounded *wh*-movement must be derived via successive cyclic bounded movement.

(76) **Subjacency (Filter)**

$*[_{\alpha} \ldots [_{\beta} \ldots ei \ldots ] \ldots ]$

where $\alpha$, $\beta$ are bounding categories (NP, IP) and $e_i$ is free in $\alpha$.

That is, each movement of a *wh*-phrase must be to the closest c-commanding SPEC-CP. To see how this works, consider the two representations in (90) for the derivation of the grammatical *wh*-question (89).

(89) what did Adam say Bernie wants

(90) a.

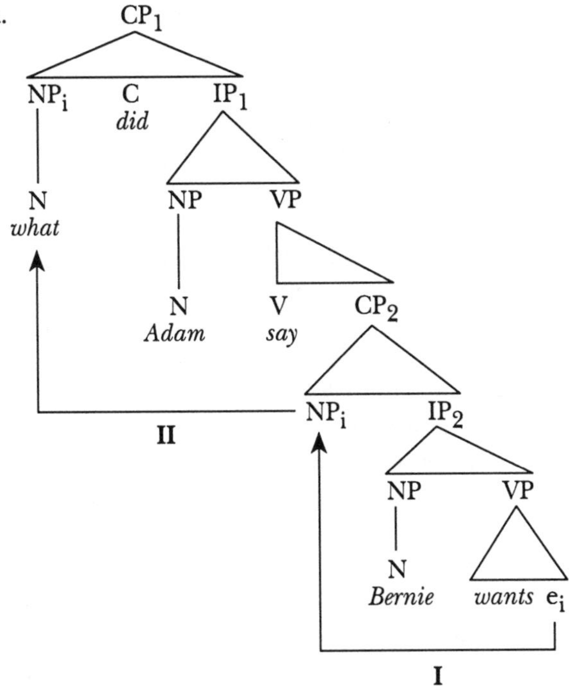
CP1
NPi
C
did
IP1
N
what
NP
VP
N
Adam
V
say
CP2
NPi
IP2
II
NP
VP
N
Bernie
wants ei
I

b.

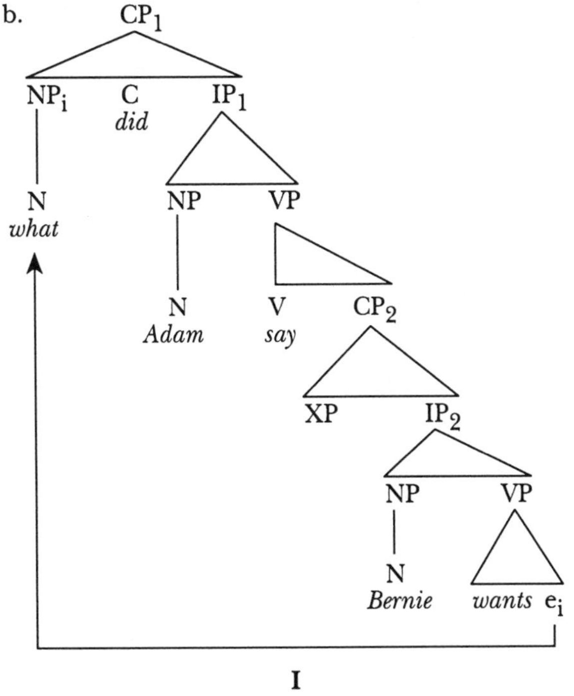
CP1
NPi
C
did
IP1
N
what
NP
VP
N
Adam
V
say
CP2
XP
IP2
NP
VP
N
Bernie
wants ei
I

In (90a) the *wh*-phrase moves through the CP of the sentential complement and leaves a trace in SPEC-CP. Each trace ($e_i$) satisfies the Subjacency Condition (76). The trace in the object position of the sentential complement is bound by the trace in SPEC-CP of the complement, and this binding relation crosses only one bounding category ($IP_2$). The trace in SPEC-CP is bound by the *wh*-phrase in the matrix CP, and the binding again crosses only one bounding category ($IP_1$).[20]

(90b), in contrast to (90a), violates the Subjacency Condition. The trace in complement object position is bound only by the *wh*-phrase in the matrix CP. Because this binding occurs across two bounding categories ($IP_1$ and $IP_2$), the trace fails to satisfy the Subjacency Condition. This shows that *Wh*-Movement must move a *wh*-phrase through a c-commanding SPEC-CP. In order to move long distance across an intervening c-commanding SPEC-CP, a *wh*-phrase must always move CP-to-CP on each cycle. Thus, it follows from the Subjacency Condition that successive cyclic movement into CP is obligatory for any well-formed instance of long-distance *wh*-movement.

In contrast, long-distance extraposition is never allowed—even if movement is achieved in a series of bounded steps. That is, successive cyclic extraposition (or more accurately, the analog to CP-to-CP movement) must be blocked. Because this will not be prevented by the Subjacency Condition (as illustrated below), another condition is needed. Consider the successive cyclic application of CP-Extraposition in the derivation (91) of the ill-formed (50c), **That a man is coming to dinner is unusual who I want to meet.*

(91) a. [$_{IP:1}$ [$_{CP:2}$ that [$_{IP:2}$ [$_{NP}$ a man [$_{CP:3}$ who I want to meet]] [$_{VP:2}$ is coming to dinner]]] [$_{VP:1}$ is unusual]]

b. [$_{IP:1}$ [$_{CP:2}$ that [$_{IP:2}$ [$_{NP}$ a man [$_{CP:3}$ e ]] [$_{\wedge VP:2}$ [$_{VP:2}$ is coming to dinner] [$_{CP:3}$ who I want to meet]]]]] [$_{VP:1}$ is unusual]]

c. [$_{IP:1}$ [$_{CP:2}$ that [$_{IP:2}$ [$_{NP}$ a man [$_{CP:3}$ e ]] [$_{\wedge VP:2}$ [$_{VP:2}$ is coming to dinner] [$_{CP:3}$ e ]]]] [$_{\wedge VP:1}$ [$_{VP:1}$ is unusual] [$_{CP:3}$ who I want to meet]]]

In terms of the derived phrase marker (91c), the successive cyclic movements occur as illustrated in (92) (some details omitted).

(92)

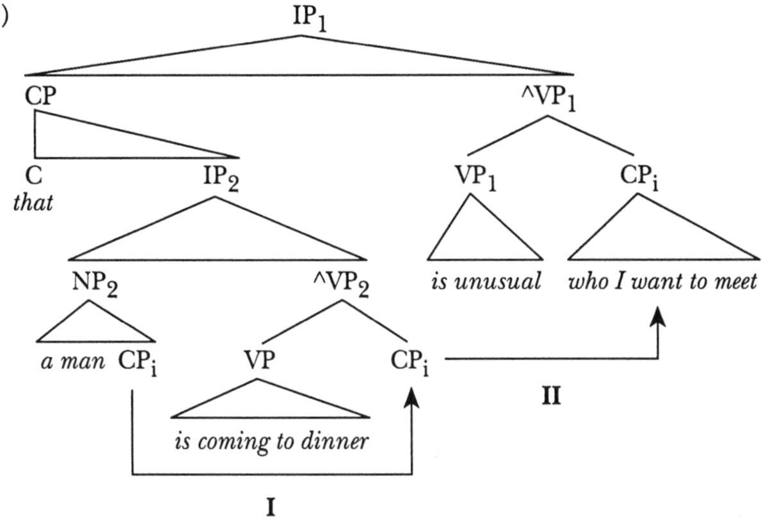


Neither the first movement, which adjoins $CP_3$ to $VP_2$, nor the second movement, which adjoins $CP_3$ to $VP_1$, violates the Subjacency Condition. In each instance only one bounding category is crossed: NP in the first instance and $IP_2$ in the second.

Although Subjacency eliminates the apparent asymmetry between leftward and rightward movements with respect to the statement of bounding domains, something more is needed to explain why rightward movement is strictly bounded within the subjacent domain of the original position in underlying structure. Given the possibility of a derivation like (91), the deviance of (50c) suggests that adjunctions may not iterate irrespective of Subjacency violations.

The noniterativity of adjunctions could simply be stipulated as part of a theory of elementary operations. Alternatively, we might consider why the resulting representations are grammatically ill formed.

If adjunctions cannot iterate, then under trace theory traces may not occur in adjunction constructions like (93), which schematizes the relevant portion of the ill-formed (91c).

(93)

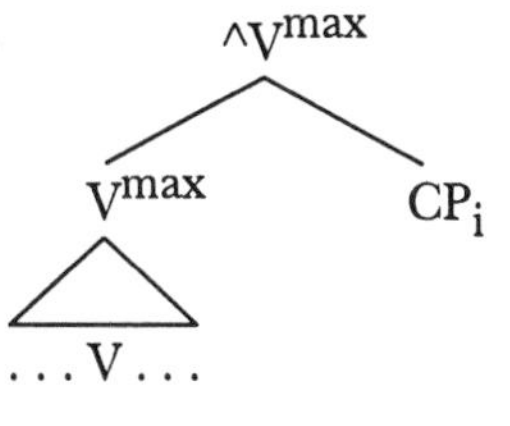

The question of why adjunctions cannot iterate can now be approached in terms of the salient characteristics of the configuration (93). More precisely, what is it about the position of the trace (of CP) that differentiates it from other configurations?

An answer can be given in terms of the notion of government defined in (86) of chapter 2 (repeated here for convenience).

(94) A lexical head α *governs* a category β iff α m-commands β and β m-commands α.

Recall that it follows from this definition that a maximal projection of a lexical head is a barrier to government. Thus, a lexical head cannot govern a category that is not a constituent of its maximal projection; nor can it govern a constituent of its maximal projection that is also the constituent of another maximal projection. Assuming that adjunctions are always to maximal projections, it follows that the adjunction elementary will always create a configuration in which the adjoined category is not governed. In (93) CP cannot be governed by V since $V^{max}$ is a barrier to government. Furthermore, $^{\wedge}V^{max}$, as a maximal projection, is also a barrier to government; and so CP cannot be governed by a lexical head that governs $^{\wedge}V^{max}$. To prohibit (93), and hence iterative adjunctions, we need only formulate a principle that prohibits the occurrence of trace in ungoverned positions.

(95) **Empty Category Principle**
A trace must be governed.[21]

(Recall that a trace is an empty category created by a movement operation. Further applications of the Empty Category Principle (henceforth ECP) are discussed in chapters 5 and 6.) As formulated, the ECP does not rule out "short-distance" extraposition (e.g., (91b)) since the resulting trace is governed by the lexical head of the NP containing it.[22] Under our analysis, the ungrammaticality of (50c) has two different explanations: the Subjacency Condition accounts for the impossibility of long-distance extraposition and the ECP accounts for the impossibility of successive cyclic (bounded) extraposition. Which applies depends on what structural description is assigned to (50c).

There is a further potential problem with successive cyclic *wh*-movement that the Subjacency Condition together with the ECP cannot solve. This concerns the analysis of PP containing a *wh*-NP object. As (96) illustrates, *Wh*-Movement may place the entire PP in SPEC-CP, or just the NP object.

(96) a. to whom did Adam give his drawing
b. who(m) did Adam give his drawing to

The problem arises when the *wh*-phrase analyzed by the transformation is in SPEC-CP. Suppose that the examples in (96) were embedded as complements of the verb *say* as in (97).

(97) a. Bernie said [$_{CP}$ [$_{PP:i}$ to whom] [$_{IP}$ Adam gave his drawing $e_i$]]
b. Bernie said [$_{CP}$ who$_i$ [$_{IP}$ Adam gave his drawing to $e_i$]]

Note further that the examples in (97) could represent intermediate stages in the derivation of the sentences in (98), where the *wh*-phrases in SPEC-CP of the sentential complement have been moved to the matrix CP.

(98) a. to whom did Bernie say Adam gave his drawing
b. who did Bernie say Adam gave his drawing to

Then, when *Wh*-Movement analyzes (97a), there will be two options with respect to the WH-PP in SPEC-CP: either move the entire PP CP-to-CP (in which instance (98a) is derived, or move only the *wh*-NP (in which instance the ill-formed (99) results).

(99) *who(m) did Bernie say to Adam gave his drawing

The analysis of (99) is given in (100).

(100) [$_{CP}$ who(m)$_i$ did [$_{IP}$ Bernie say [$_{CP}$ [$_{PP:j}$ to $e_i$]]] [$_{IP}$ Adam gave his drawing $e_j$]]]]

Neither the Subjacency Condition nor the ECP excludes (100). The trace in the CP of the sentential complement is bound across only one bounding category (IP), so that the Subjacency Condition is satisfied.[23] And since this trace is governed by P, it satisfies the ECP.

The problem is how to account for the ungrammaticality of (99). Given the Subjacency analysis, it follows that *wh*-PPs that move long distance must do so via successive cyclic CP-to-CP movement. The contrast between the well-formed (98a) and the ill-formed (99) suggests that once a PP containing a *wh*-NP is analyzed as a *wh*-phrase by the rule of *Wh*-Movement, it must continue to be analyzed as a *wh*-phrase on further applications of *Wh*-Movement. As it stands, this does not follow from the formulation of the *Wh*-Movement rule or from any condition on rules or representations that we have seen so far.

Rather than attempt a detailed solution to the problem, let us consider some general approaches. If we retain the *Wh*-Movement rule in its most general form, then there are two avenues to explore: general conditions on the application of transformations, and general conditions on the syntactic representations created by the rules of grammar. With respect to conditions on rule application, we might investigate the hypothesis that once a transformation analyzes a phrase as a constant term, it cannot analyze a constituent of that phrase as a constant term (or in the case of *Wh*-Movement, as the same constant term). If this prohibition holds in general, then we have an interesting solution to the problem. Alternatively, we might try to characterize some aspect of the representation (100) as ill formed. Along the lines of the ECP, we might try to show that at least one of the two traces is in a structural position that violates some general prohibition on the distribution of traces. Or we might try to show that some further requirement on trace binding (beyond the Subjacency Condition) is violated.

As an illustration of this last-mentioned approach, we might begin by noting the characteristics of trace binding for *wh*-movement. A chain created by Wh-Movement (see note 21) will contain a lexical *wh*-phrase in SPEC-CP and one or more traces with at least one trace in a grammatical function position. (100) involves two distinct chains:

(101) a. [*who*$_i$, $e_i$]
b. [$PP_j$, $e_j$]

(101a) meets the conditions for a chain derived via *wh*-movement. Presumably the chain (101b) does not because it no longer contains the *wh*-NP *whom* that would give it the status of a *wh*-phrase. Suppose there is a general prohibition against a trace in a grammatical function position being bound by an element in CP that is not a *wh*-phrase or the trace of a *wh*-phrase. Then (100) can be excluded on the grounds that (101b) is an ill-formed chain. If there is a principled explanation for this, then it need not be stipulated redundantly as part of the formulation of the rule of *Wh*-Movement. That is, the rule need not distinguish between *wh*- and non–*wh*-phrases. Following this line of reasoning, we should consider "*Wh*-Movement" to be one instantiation of a movement operation that substitutes one phrasal category in a phrase marker for another. From this perspective the rule that effects *wh*-movement can be given in its most general form as (102).

(102) Substitute $\alpha$ (for $\beta$).

Given that $\alpha$ and $\beta$ must be nondistinct (as in section 2.2), it will follow that they are instances of the same syntactic category; and therefore, mentioning $\beta$ may be unnecessary. When (102) moves a phrasal category which is a *wh*-phrase into SPEC-CP, then we have a legitimate instance of *wh*-movement. Given this formulation, the behavior of the rule must be determined by the phrase structure rules of the grammar (which indicate where landing sites for substitution might occur) and the general principles of grammar (which determine the manner in which rules apply and the well-formedness of the representations they generate).[24]

Thus far we have seen that the proper behavior of *Wh*-Movement can be accounted for in terms of general constraints on the distribution of traces in syntactic representations (e.g., the ECP and the Subjacency Condition). Whether the proper behavior of rules can be reduced to conditions on syntactic representations in all cases is not clear. Consider for example one possibility that arises with *wh*-questions containing multiple *wh*-phrases.

(103) a. who said what
b. *what did who say

(104) a. I know who said what
b. *I know what who said

Under the simplest formulation of Wh-Movement, it is possible to move the object *what* into SPEC-CP over the subject *who.* (103) illustrates the direct question construction and (104), the indirect question construction. In both constructions this possibility yields an ill-formed sentence. Yet the ill-formed sentences involve syntactic representations that violate neither Subjacency nor the ECP, as shown in (105).

(105) a. $[_{IP}$ what$_i$ $[_{IP}$ did who say e$_i$]] (= 103b)
b. I know $[_{CP}$ what$_i$ $[_{IP}$ who said e$_i$]] (= 104b)

In each instance the trace is both governed and bound by an antecedent in a subjacent domain.

One way to eliminate the ill-formed examples in (103) and (104) is to postulate a general constraint on the application of rules as follows:

(106) **Superiority Condition**
No rule may analyze a constant Y when there is another constant X analyzable by the rule and superior to Y.

(107) A category $\alpha$ is *superior* to a category $\beta$ where $\alpha$ asymmetrically c-commands $\beta$.

Given (107), in a sentence containing a subject and an object, the subject will be superior to an object. Thus, in multiple *wh*-questions, a *wh*-object that moves into SPEC-CP over a *wh*-subject violates the Superiority

Condition. The relation "superior to" is defined as asymmetric, therefore when $\alpha$ c-commands $\beta$, and $\beta$ c-commands $\alpha$, neither is superior to the other.[25]

---

**Exercise 3.19**

Consider the following paradigm for double object verbs. Give the phrase markers for these sentences with traces, and consider how the Superiority Condition applies to each one.

(i) a. *I wonder who(m) John gave which presents to
 b. I wonder to who(m) John gave which presents
 c. I wonder which presents John gave to whom
 d. I wonder which presents John gave whom

(Remember that double object verbs like give involve two distinct subcategorization frames: [+__NP NP] and [+__NP PP].)

Note that the Superiority Condition as formulated does not apply to (ii).

(ii) *I wonder whom John gave which presents

There is no need to reformulate the condition to account for (ii) since wh-movement of the indirect object is prohibited generally as illustrated in (iiia–b), where there is only a single *wh*-phrase.

(iii) a. *I wonder whom John gave a present
 b. *whom did John give a present?

---

The Superiority Condition as formulated in (106) extends to other cases: for example, extraction out of a WH-island involving long-distance *wh*-movement. Consider the syntactic representation (108b) of the ill-formed (108a) (compare (78a)).

(108) a. *who did John say what read
 b. $[_{CP}$ who$_i$ did John say $[_{CP}$ what$_j$ $[_{IP}$ e$_i$ read e$_j$]]]]

In (108), the long-distance movement of *who* from the complement subject position into the matrix CP violates both Subjacency and Superiority.

---

**Exercise 3.20**

There are two distinct ways to derive (108b). One will violate the Strict Cycle Condition but not the Superiority Condition. The other will violate the Superiority Condition (twice), but not the Strict Cycle Condition. Give both derivations for (108b).

---

Thus, (108) constitutes a case of overlapping conditions. In this instance each condition is independently motivated by phenomena that do not concern the other. Superiority and not Subjacency accounts for (103b); Subjacency (interpreted as a condition on representations) and not Superiority can account for WH-island violations whose derivations violate the Strict Cycle Condition. Note that Superiority as formulated can only be interpreted as a condition on the application of rules. Given these interconnections, it is worth trying to subsume the effects of one condition under the other, dealing with the leftover effects (i.e., the independent motivation) in terms of some other independently motivated condition.

Alternatively, overlapping conditions may be desirable—especially if speaker judgments can be fine-tuned in a way that distinguishes instances of overlap from those where no overlap occurs. That is, suppose an example that violates both Superiority and Subjacency is judged more deviant than examples that violate only one or the other condition. Then we would have empirical motivation for a theory with overlapping conditions. Note, however, that in the absence of empirical evidence, we are not warranted in assuming that overlapping conditions should yield a greater degree of ungrammaticality. It could turn out that sentences that violate more than one condition are not judged more deviant than those which violate only one. These are empirical issues that require careful investigation.

(108) represents one case of a WH-island violation where two independent conditions are violated (not including the Strict Cycle Condition). In contrast, (109) represents a case where, depending on what derivation has been assigned, either Superiority alone is violated or both Subjacency and Superiority are violated.

(109) *what did John say who read

If *who* remains in situ (i.e., in its original place in D-structure), then (109) is assigned a representation (110), where the derivation (specifically, movement I) violates only the Superiority Condition.

(110) $[_{CP}$ what$_i$ did $[_{IP}$ John say $[_{CP}$ e$_i$ $[_{IP}$ who read e$_i$ $]]]]$

II I

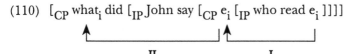

Subjacency is satisfied since $e_i$ in $IP_2$ is bound by $e_i$ in $CP_2$, which in turn is bound by *what* in $CP_1$. If, however, *who* is subsequently moved into the SPEC-CP of the sentential complement, as in (111), then Subjacency is violated as well because $e_i$ is free in its subjacent domain ($IP_1$).

(111) [$_{CP}$ what$_i$ did [$_{IP}$ John say [$_{CP}$ who$_j$ [$_{IP}$ e$_j$ read e$_i$ ]]]]

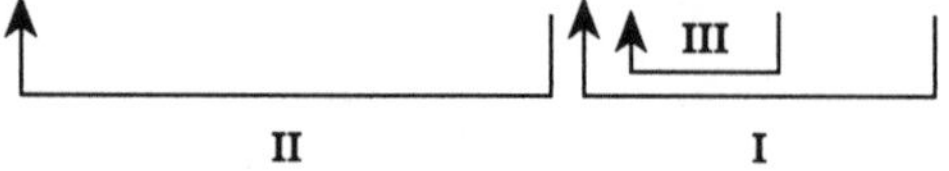

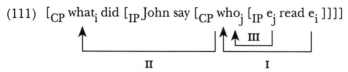

Thus, there are two possible explanations for the ungrammaticality of (109), depending on what representation the grammar assigns it. Note that in this case the difference in derivation results in a difference in representation—unlike the long-distance movement versus strict cycle violation derivations discussed earlier.

---

**Exercise 3.21**

Given this discussion of the Superiority Condition, it is possible to construct examples that look at first glance like *wh*-island violations, but are not. (i) is such an example.

(i) which books did you say which students read

Give a derivation for (i) that does not violate Subjacency (assume that Superiority has been appropriately modified to allow the (b)-examples in note 25.

Now compare (i) with (ii) in terms of relative grammaticality.

(ii) what did you say who read

As long as a sentence can be assigned a representation that conforms to the rules and principles of grammar, the fact that it may also be possible to assign it a representation that violates some principle appears to have no effect on acceptability judgments. If the representations assigned to sentences by the grammar play a role in mental computation, what does this observation suggest about how we process sentences? Show how this issue extends to the analysis of grammatical examples of long-distance *wh*-movement (where a representation violating Subjacency can also be derived).

---

Up to this point we have been considering how conditions like Subjacency block long-distance movements which yield ill-formed sentences. Subjacency also accounts for restrictions on the interpretation of sentences. Consider an example like (112) which involves an ambiguity in the interpretation of the subject NP.

(112) a report by three senators in favor of that proposal has just appeared

The ambiguity concerns whether the phrase *in favor of that proposal* modifies the noun *report* or the noun *senators*. The ambiguity disappears if the PP *in favor of that proposal* is extraposed to VP as in (113).

(113) a report by three senators has just appeared in favor of that proposal

In (113) the PP *in favor of that proposal* can only be interpreted as modifying the noun *report*. This follows from the Subjacency Condition, as can be easily verified.

---

**Exercise 3.22**

Construct the two phrase markers for (112) that account for the two possible interpretations. Then show how PP-extraposition is allowed in one case, but violates the Subjacency Condition in the other. Consider the following:

(i) a report has just appeared by three senators in favor of that proposal

Is (i) ambiguous? If you judge (i) to be ambiguous, state the ambiguity. Show how the two phrase markers you assign to (i) are derived via PP-Extraposition, indicating the underlying phrase markers in each instance. If you judge (i) to be unambiguous, state which reading you get for (i) and consider whether the conditions we have discussed will block the reading you do not get.

---

## Appendix A: A Brief Historical Comment on Island Constraints

The concept of "syntactic island" with respect to the operation of transformations was first proposed by John Ross (1967). Ross's dissertation took as its point of departure a critical discussion of Chomsky's A-over-A Principle (circa 1962), which was the first proposal in the literature attempting to deal with some of the constructions that came to be known as syntactic islands. In place of the A-over-A Principle, Ross proposed a set of constraints which block transformations from extracting constituents out of syntactic islands. In "Conditions on Transformations" (1973) Chomsky gave the first formulation of the Subjacency Condition, which in its current incarnation subsumes much of the phenomena covered by Ross's constraints.[26]

The A-over-A Principle has received several different formulations over the years. The following is from Chomsky 1973:235:

(114) If a transformation applies to a structure of the form
$[_{\alpha} \ldots [_{A} \ldots ] \ldots ]$
where $\alpha$ is a cyclic node, then it must be so interpreted as to apply to the maximal phrase of type A.

For this formulation, IP and NP are considered to be the cyclic nodes. Thus, if a transformation analyzes some constituent A as a constant term, then it cannot analyze an instance of A that is a constituent of some larger A in the phrase marker. This prohibits the extraction of an NP out of an NP that dominates it. However it does not prohibit the extraction of a PP out of an NP that contains it. Hence the A-over-A Principle as formulated will not account for NP-islands in general.[27]

In place of the A-over-A Principle Ross proposed the following constraints among others: the Complex NP Constraint (CNPC), the Coordinate Structure Constraint (CSC), and the Left Branch Condition (LBC). (The formulations in (115) are from Ross 1986, as are the reference numbers in parentheses.)

(115) a. **The Complex NP Constraint** (4.20)
No element contained in a sentence dominated by a noun phrase with a lexical head noun may be moved out of that noun phrase by a transformation.

b. **The Coordinate Structure Constraint** (4.84)
In a coordinate structure, no conjunct may be moved, nor many any element contained in a conjunct be moved out of that conjunct.

c. **The Left Branch Condition** (4.181)
No NP which is the leftmost constituent of a larger NP can be reordered out of this NP by a transformational rule.

Although the empirical effects of the CNPC are completely subsumed under the Subjacency Condition, the CSC covers some cases that Subjacency does not.

---

**Exercise 3.23**

The Subjacency Condition will also account for the impossibility of extracting a *wh*-phrase out of a conjoined NP structure, as illustrated in (i) below.

(i) *[$_{CP}$ who$_i$ [$_{IP}$ did John see [$_{NP}$ Mary and e$_i$]]]

It can be demonstrated that movement of a single conjunct from any conjoined structure yields an ill-formed sentence. If we assume that any maximal phrasal projection of a lexical head may occur in a conjoined structure (e.g., $X^{max}$ *and* $X^{max}$), then the extraction of a phrase out of certain conjoined $X^{max}$s (henceforth coordinate structures) will not fall under the Subjacency Condition. Construct coordinate structures involving PP, AP, and VP. Discuss whether Subjacency accounts for the impossibility of extracting a phrase out of a conjunct of these constructions.

---

The LBC effects are also subsumed under Subjacency with respect to *wh*-movement.

Current work on island phenomena is concerned with various attempts to integrate the formulations of Subjacency and the ECP in terms of the notion of government. This work is extremely technical (and at present speculative) in nature. See in particular Huang 1982, Kayne 1983, Lasnik and Saito 1984, and Chomsky 1986a for details.

## Appendix B: A Comment on the Theory of Transformations

Under the theory of transformations discussed in this chapter there are only three elementary operations: deletion, adjunction, and substitution. Each opertation affects structure in a different way. Deletion destroys structure, adjunction builds new structure, and substitution preserves structure. This theory of elementary operations is summarized in (116).

(116)

| | Operation | Character | Constrained by |
|---|---|---|---|
| a. | Deletion | Structure-destroying | Recoverability |
| b. | Adjunction | Structure-building | ? |
| c. | Substitution | Structure-preserving | Nondistinctness |

Exactly how the recoverability condition on deletions is to be stated remains to be determined. It is clear, however, that deletion operations must be constrained so that the material deleted from the phrase marker is recoverable in some sense from the resulting phrase marker itself or from the grammar. For example, in the case of gapping, where a verb in a conjunct is deleted, the deleted verb is recoverable from the phrase marker. Given the example in (117), the deleted verb in the second conjunct (indicated by "Ø") must be identical to the verb in the first conjunct.

(117) Barbie collects fossils, and Ed Ø old mysteries

(117) has only one interpretation (where Ø stands for *collects*). Without a recoverability condition on deletions, Ø could stand for any verb and hence the grammar would incorrectly predict (117) to be multiply ambiguous. In addition to deletion under identity, an element may be deleted even if no copy of it is left behind in the phrase marker, provided the deleted element is somehow predictable given the grammar. We might consider the deletion of the complementizer *that* to be in this category. Thus, deletion would account for the alternation given in (118).

(118) a. Alice believes that the mind is modular
b. Alice believes Ø the mind is modular

This assumes that there is an account of the notion "predictable given the grammar" according to which the complementizer *that* is in fact predictable.

In their most general form, elementary operations can be formulated as follows,

(119) a. Deletion: Delete $\alpha$
b. Adjunction: Adjoin $\alpha$ to $\beta$
c. Substitution: Substitute $\alpha$ for $\beta$

where $\alpha$ and $\beta$ are categories—constants in the structural description of a transformation. The theory of transformations can be further restricted by placing limitations on the choice of $\alpha$ and $\beta$.

In the examples of adjunction operations discussed earlier, $\alpha$ is adjoined is to a maximal projection. Therefore, we might conjecture that for adjunctions, $\beta$ is always a maximal projection. This conjecture has some intuitive appeal from the point of view of what it prohibits. If adjunctions are only to $X^{max}$, then the internal structure of a maximal projection can never be changed by a movement operation. Once the internal structure of a phrasal projection is fixed by the base rules, it remains a rigid unit.[28] Suppose we state the conjecture as the following postulate:

(120) **Postulate I**
Only maximal projections can be adjunction sites.

Whether this is the correct restriction for all adjunction operations remains to be determined.

Under a theory of transformations that includes only these three elementary operations and the further restriction that each grammatical transformation consists of a single elementary (i.e., compounding of elementary operations is not allowed), the particular structural description (SD) and structural change (SC) of a rule function as local (language-particular) conditions on the behavior of the elementary operation. Constants in the SD restrict the application of the elementary operation to particular categories with respect to both movement and landing sites. To further restrict the theory of transformations, we might consider whether any further conditions might be placed on SDs in terms of the possible relationships between constants.

Given that a phrase marker encodes both linear and hierarchical relationships, it is possible that two constants mentioned in the SD of a rule might be in either of two structural relationships: (i) one constant precedes the other (linear), or (ii) one constant dominates the other (hierarchical). In the case of *'s*-insertion, for example, where the two constant terms are adjacent in the SD of the rule, we assumed that the constants were in a linear relation. Whether there is a general constraint on the form of transformations stating that adjacent constants can only be in a linear relation is worth considering. For example, under the Case-theoretic analysis of *'s*-insertion presented in chapter 2, this would follow so that no stipulation about how to interpret the relation between constant terms is necessary.

Let us consider this issue from a more general perspective. Suppose we have a transformation with two constant terms. Now consider three theories:

A. No relation may be specified between the two terms.
B. It is assumed as part of the general theory that constant terms of a SD must be in a linear relation (see Lasnik and Kupin 1977).
C. For each SD of a transformation it is possible to specify the relation between the two terms as either precedence or dominance.

C yields a larger class of possible rules than A or B and therefore is less restrictive than the others. It is not clear that A and B can be compared in this way. B will yield a smaller class of derived structures, but beyond that there may be no difference. In fact, B may be the wrong theory for empirical reasons.

Theory A allows the possibility that for some transformation the two constants in the SD will be in a precedence relation in some cases and a dominance relation in others. Extraposition of CP from NP may be an example of this, where in (121a) CP initially precedes VP whereas in (121b) it is initially dominated by VP.

(121) a. $[_{NP}$ a man $e_i]$ $[_{\wedge VP}$ $[_{VP}$ is coming to dinner] $[_{CP:i}$ who I want to meet]]

b. John expects $[_{IP}$ Bill to $[_{\wedge VP}$ $[_{VP}$ call $[_{NP}$ people $e_i]$ up] $[_{CP:i}$ who he doesn't know]]]

Assuming that the extraposition of CP involves adjunction to VP, the transformation could be formulated as (122) (cf. (52)), where "+" indicates the adjunction operation.

(122) **CP-Extraposition** (revised)

| | X | – | N* | – | CP | – | Y | – | VP | – | Z |
|---|---|---|---|---|---|---|---|---|---|---|---|
| SD: | 1 | | 2 | | 3 | | 4 | | 5 | | 6 |
| SC: | 1 | | | | 3 | | 4 | | 5+3 | | 6 |

Given the underlying structure of (121a), terms 3 and 5 are in a linear relationship. In the underlying structure of (121b), however, these two constant terms of the transformation appear to be in a hierarchical relationship—assuming that the dislocation of the relative clause to the right of the particle *up* is the result of CP-Extraposition. Under theory A above, (122) could analyze the underlying phrase marker for (121b) as indicated in (123) (some details omitted).

(123)

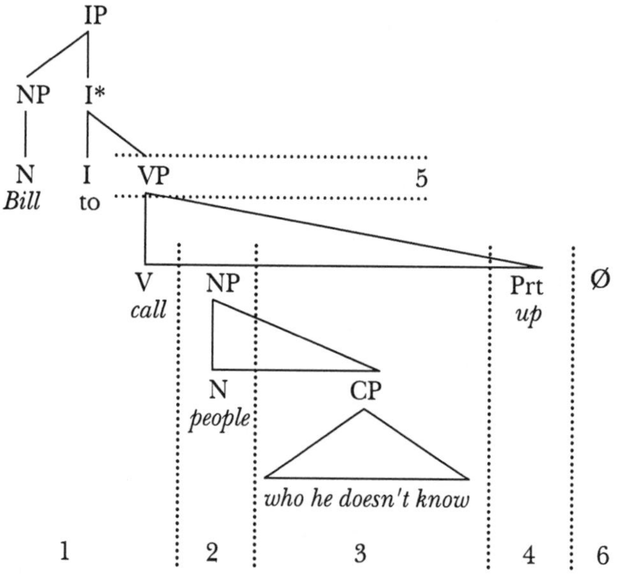


In this way, the analysis of CP-extraposition suggests that we may want to leave the relation between two constants in the SD of a transformation unspecified.

## Bibliographical Comments

The Subjacency Condition was first proposed in Chomsky 1973, which also contains the first proposals of the Superiority and Strict Cycle Conditions. The Subjacency analysis presented here is based on Chomsky's modifications in Chomsky 1977a, where he extends the analysis to additional construction types, including clefts and comparatives. The first discussion of extraposition in terms of Subjacency occurs in Akmajian 1975. The analysis of Subjacency as a filter was proposed in Freidin 1978b, where it is demonstrated that the empirical effects of the Strict Cycle Condition are derived from independently motivated principles of grammar. This result provided the first demonstration of how conditions on representations (filters) might eliminate the need for conditions on derivations (e.g., the SCC). The parametric analysis of Subjacency was proposed for Italian in Rizzi 1980. Similar analyses for French and Spanish are given in Sportiche 1981 and Torrego 1984 respectively. For further discussion of parameters in the theory of grammar, see Roeper and Williams 1987, Jaeggli and Safir 1989, and Freidin 1991. See Freidin and Quicoli 1989 for a discussion of the learnability issue concerning parameters in the theory of grammar.

The successive cyclic analysis of *wh*-movement originates in Chomsky 1973. The cyclic analysis of *wh*-movement begins with Bresnan 1971, where the rule scans each IP successive cyclically but moves a *wh*-phrase only once. Evidence for successive cyclic *wh*-movement is discussed in Kayne and Pollock 1978) (for French) and Torrego 1984 (for Spanish).

For further discussion of extraposition and bounding, see Baltin 1981, Taraldsen 1981, and Kroch and Joshi 1986.

# 4 The English Verbal Auxiliary System

In this chapter we will examine the interaction of transformational rules—in particular, the transformations that account for the form and distribution of verbal elements in English sentences, including auxiliary verbs (henceforth **auxiliaries**) like aspectual *have* and *be*, and modal auxiliaries like *can* and *would*. We will see that these interactions depend to a large extent on the exact form of the rules.[1] Moreover, we will find that the apparently complex interactions between these rules need not be stipulated as statements about the order in which transformations must apply. Instead this order of application follows from a rather natural condition on syntactic representations. Given this condition and others that have been discussed in the preceding chapters, these transformational rules can have relatively simple formulations.

The following material covers three related topics: (i) the general properties of the English auxiliary system, (ii) the phrase structure and transformational rules that account for these properties, and (iii) how much of the necessary interaction of these transformational rules follows from general conditions on syntactic representations, and what part of it remains to be accounted for.

## 4.1 General Properties of the Verbal Auxiliary System

In English there are three distinct and syntactically independent types of auxiliaries: the **modals** (e.g., *will*), **perfective aspect** (*have*), and **progressive aspect** (*be*), as illustrated in (1), where the auxiliary elements are italicized.

(1) a. One auxiliary
 i. Bernie *will* work on his Yugoslavia project
 ii. Bernie *is* working on his Yugoslavia project
 iii. Bernie *has* worked on his Yugoslavia project

b. Two auxiliaries
   i. Bernie *will be* working on his Yugoslavia project
   ii. Bernie *will have* worked on his Yugoslavia project
   iii. Bernie *has been* working on his Yugoslavia project

c. Three auxiliaries
   i. Bernie *will have been* working on his Yugoslavia project

As illustrated in (1a), each auxiliary is syntactically independent in that it may occur in a sentence without the others. Furthermore, any combination of auxiliaries is permissible, as illustrated in (1b–c). Finally, since none need occur in a sentence at all, as illustrated by (2), auxiliaries are optional.

(2) Bernie works on his Yugoslavia project every evening

In addition to being syntactically independent and optional, auxiliaries occur in a fixed linear order. A modal is the leftmost auxiliary when it occurs; and progressive aspect is the rightmost auxiliary when it occurs. Perfective aspect occurs to the right of a modal and to the left of progressive aspect when either occurs in a sentence.

(3) Modal > Perfective > Progressive > Verb

This order can be specified via phrase structure rule, as we will see. The exact constituency of the auxiliaries will be discussed in the next section since it is closely related to assumptions about the function of transformational rules.

Before considering the range of variation for the various verbal elements, we should note that English, unlike other languages (e.g., French), distinguishes only two morphological tenses: present and past. That is, main verbs in English may indicate past or present tense by their morphological form. Future tense, however, is indicated by the use of a modal like *will* or *shall*. (In contrast, the future tense in French is indicated by a set of morphological endings that are affixed to a main verb stem, as in *écrira* (écrir+a) 'he/she will write' and *écrirons* (écrir+ons) 'we will write'.) In English, the present/past tense distinction is morphologically realized on auxiliaries as well as the main verb. In fact, a main verb will be morphologically marked for tense (either present or past) only when it occurs with no auxiliaries. If a verb occurs with one or more auxiliaries, then the leftmost auxiliary will bear the morphological tense. In (1), for example, the first auxiliary in each sentence is morphologically marked for present tense. In (4), however, the corresponding auxiliaries are morphologically marked for past tense.

(4) a. One auxiliary
   i. Bernie *would* work on his Yugoslavia project for hours
   ii. Bernie *was* working on his Yugoslavia project
   iii. Bernie *had* worked on his Yugoslavia project

 b. Two auxiliaries
   i. Bernie *would be* working on his Yugoslavia project
   ii. Bernie *would have* worked on his Yugoslavia project
   iii. Bernie *had been* working on his Yugoslavia project

 c. Three auxiliaries
   i. Bernie *would have been* working on his Yugoslavia project

Under this analysis, the distinctions between *will/ would, has/ had, is/ was,* and *works/ worked* (when no auxiliaries are present) are considered to be a single morphological distinction between past and present tense.[2]

Though modal auxiliaries occur only in tensed forms, the other auxiliaries and the main verb may take other morphological forms. The range of variation is given in (5).[3]

(5)

| | | | |
|---|---|---|---|
| a. Modal auxiliary: | | | |
| | i. Present tense | will | (1a.i; 1b.iⅈ 1c.i) |
| | ii. Past tense | would | (4a.i; 4b.iⅈ 4c.i) |
| b. Perfective auxiliary | | | |
| | i. Present tense | has | (1a.iii; 1b.iii) |
| | ii. Past tense | had | (4a.iii; 4b.iii) |
| | iii. infinitive | have | (1b.ii; 1c.i; 4b.ii; 4c.i) |
| c. Progressive auxiliary | | | |
| | i. Present tense | is | (1a.ii) |
| | ii. Past tense | was | (4a.ii) |
| | iii. Infinitive | be | (1b.i; 4b.i) |
| | iv. Past participle | been | (1b.iii; 1c.i; 4b.iii; 4c.i) |
| d. Verb | | | |
| | i. Present tense | works | (2) |
| | ii. Past tense | worked | |
| | iii. Infinitive | work | (1a.i; 4a.i) |
| | iv. Past participle | worked | (1a.iii; 1b.ii; 4a.iii; 4b.ii) |
| | v. Progressive participle | working | (1a.ii; 1b.i&iii; 1c.i; 4a.ii; 4b.i&iii; 4c.i) |

(5) illustrates that modals are the most restricted forms, occurring only as tensed forms. The perfective auxiliary also allows the infinitive form;

and the progressive auxiliary allows the past participial form in addition to the infinitive. Verbs allow the widest range of morphological variation in that they occur in all the possible morphological forms.

The same information can be stated negatively as follows. Modals can never occur in the infinitive, past participial, or progressive forms. The perfective auxiliary can never occur in the past participial or progressive forms. And the progressive auxiliary can never occur in the progressive form. As we will see in section 4.2, these restrictions can be accommodated naturally within a transformational analysis of the auxiliary system.

The distribution of these forms is conditioned by syntactic context. The infinitive form occurs only after a modal; the past participial form occurs only after the perfective auxiliary; and the progressive form occurs only after the progressive auxiliary. Thus, the auxiliary system is based on a set of syntactic dependencies that can be described in terms of stems and affixes.

Let us begin our analysis with the progressive form of the verb, which is analyzed as a verbal stem plus the affix *ing*. Under this analysis, there is a dependency between the progressive auxiliary (whatever its morphological form) and the affix *ing* that is discontinuous because the verbal stem intervenes between the progressive auxiliary and *ing*. This is represented in (6a) by the arrow joining *ing* to the progressive auxiliary. The well-formed (6a) contrasts with the ill-formed (6b) where the affix on the verb form to the right of the progressive auxiliary is other than *ing*, and the ill-formed (6c), where the auxiliary preceding the progressive form of the verb is not a form of *be*.

(6) a. Bernie **is** work+**ing** on his Yugoslavia project

b. Incorrect affix
   i. *Bernie **is** work+**s** on his Yugoslavia project <present tense>
   ii. *Bernie **is** work+**ed** on his Yugoslavia project <past tense/past participial>
   iii. *Bernie **is** work+ ___ on his Yugoslavia project <infinitive>

c. Incorrect auxiliary
   i. *Bernie **will** work+**ing** on his Yugoslavia project <modal>
   ii. *Bernie **has** work+**ing** on his Yugoslavia project <perfective>
   iii. *Bernie ___ work+**ing** on his Yugoslavia project <no auxiliary>

("___" in (6a.iii) indicates the absence of an affix and in (6c.iii) it indicates the absence of an auxiliary.)

This analysis extends naturally to the past participial form, where there is a discontinuous dependency between the perfective auxiliary and the past participial affix (which has two overt morphological forms: *en*, as in *been* (be+en) and *stolen* (steal+en); and *ed*, as in *worked* (work+ed) and *finished* (finish+ed)). Therefore, in a sentence containing both perfective and progressive auxiliaries, there will be two overlapping discontinuous dependencies, as represented by the arrows in (7).

(7) Bernie **has** *be*+**en** work+*ing* on his Yugoslavia project

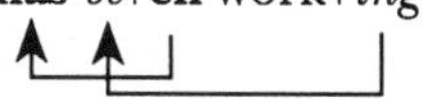

The overlapping of these discontinuous dependencies between affixes and auxiliaries constitutes yet another property of the English auxiliary system that needs to be accounted for.

The final property is that at most only one morphological form of each type may occur in a string of auxiliaries plus verb. For example, although each auxiliary may occur as a tensed form, it is not possible for all the auxiliaries in a string to occur as tensed forms.

(8) *Bernie will has was working on his Yugoslavia project.

Nor is it possible for more than one auxiliary to occur in the infinitive form, even though each auxiliary may occur in that form.

(9) *Bernie will have be working on his Yugoslavia project.

This shows that the discontinuous dependency between stems and affixes holds both ways. That is, when the *ing* affix appears on a stem, the preceding auxiliary must be progressive *be* and when the progressive auxiliary occurs, the verb must take the *ing* affix.

The following list summarizes the properties of the English auxiliary system that must be accommodated in any formal analysis:

1. There are three auxiliary elements with a fixed linear order: modal > perfective > progressive.
2. These auxiliaries are syntactically independent to the extent that there are no restrictions on their occurrence or cooccurrence.
3. The leftmost verbal element in a finite clause must be tensed.
4. Within each clause, there may be at most one morphological form of each type (tensed, infinitive, past participial, and progressive).
5. There are discontinuous dependencies between stems and affixes (e.g., between the perfective auxiliary and the *en* affix on the adjacent auxiliary or verb to the right) and also syntactic dependencies

between auxiliaries and the morphological form of the adjacent verbal element to the right (e.g., between modals and the infinitive form).
6. A main verb may occur with any verbal affix in a surface form.

We will see that all dependencies can be treated as continuous dependencies under a transformational analysis, and that properties 3, 4, and 6 will follow from this analysis as well.

## 4.2 A Transformational Account of the Verbal Auxiliary System (I)

The transformational analysis of the English auxiliary system is based on the idea that the discontinuous dependencies between stems and affixes in actual sentences can be analyzed as continuous dependencies by postulating another level of syntactic representation in which these stems and affixes are contiguous. At this abstract level of representation a stem and its corresponding affix will form a syntactic unit—a single constituent that expresses their relatedness as a continuous dependency. Given this phrase structure analysis, it is then necessary to separate these units via transformations that map an abstract underlying form onto a more concrete surface form.

Consider for example the progressive auxiliary and the affix *ing* bearing in mind that all the following remarks also apply to the perfective auxiliary and the affix *en/ed*). Under this analysis, in the sentence *Max was studying physics* the progressive auxiliary would have the underlying representation (10).

(10) $[_{PROG}$ BE + ING]

(The progressive auxiliary stem is represented abstractly in small capitals to indicate that its actual morphological form has yet to be determined.) The transformational mapping of the underlying structure of this sentence onto its surface form would therefore involve the following operations:

(11) a. Separating ING from BE and affixing it to the main verb, and
b. Changing BE to the past tense form that agrees in number and person with the subject of the sentence.

Since the progressive affix ING is associated with BE in underlying structure, we assume that ING cannot simultaneously occur as an affix on V in underlying structure. Therefore, when a verb occurs with the progressive auxiliary, it has no affix in underlying structure. But since the verb takes the ING affix in its surface realization, we assume that it is associated underlyingly with an affix *position.* In underlying structure, this position is empty. It is then filled with the ING affix in the course of a derivation. A corollary to these remarks is that the auxiliary stem BE, which is already associated with the affix ING in underlying structure, cannot simultaneously be associated with the tense affix. The tense affix is therefore assumed to be represented separately. Thus, in underlying structure the verbal string *was studying* will have the syntactic representation given in (12).

(12) [+past] [$_{PROG}$ BE + ING] [$_{V}$ STUDY + [e]]

The tense affix is given as a feature [±past], and [e] represents the empty affix position of the verb STUDY.

The transformational mapping of (12) onto the surface form (14) involves two instances of affix movement (the movement of an affix over a stem into another affix position). First, the ING affix moves out of the progressive auxiliary into V, leaving behind an empty affix position—that is, (12) maps directly onto (13)

(13) [+past] [$_{PROG}$ BE + [e]] [$_{V}$ STUDY + [ING]]

Second, the empty affix position after BE is filled by the tense affix. Thus, (13) maps directly onto (14).

(14) [e] [$_{PROG}$ BE + [+past]] [$_{V}$ STUDY + [ING]]

This is only one instance of an analysis that generalizes across the rest of the English verbal auxiliary system.

---

**Exercise 4.1**

Give a similar analysis for the following examples:

(i) a. Max has studied physics at Princeton
 b. Max has been studying physics at Princeton

Now consider (ii).

(ii) Max studied physics at Princeton

Show how the analysis of the tense affix in (i) generalizes to the analysis of the tense affix in (ii).

---

This analysis provides a straightforward account of certain properties of the auxiliary system noted earlier. By postulating that all verbs have empty affix positions underlyingly, we account for the fact that a verb may occur with any verbal affix as a surface form (property 6), depending on which auxiliary element is adjacent. By postulating that the tense affix is morphologically independent of any verbal stem in underlying structure (i.e., there is only one tense affix per string), we account for the fact that there is only one tensed form in a verbal string. This explanation naturally extends to all the other auxiliary forms—thus there is at most one affix per form per verbal string, and property 4 follows automatically. If derivation of the surface form of the verbal string always involves the movement of each affix from its underlying position to the next affix position to the right (henceforth **Affix Hopping**, as this operation is traditionally called), and if we assume that the tense affix is leftmost in underlying structure, then property 3 above follows as well.

To account for the infinitive forms of auxiliaries or verbs adjacent to modals under this Affix Hopping analysis, it would be reasonable to assume that modals too have an underlying affix position that contains a morphologically realized (though phonetically null) affix. Let us call this the **zero affix** and represent it as ø. Thus, the affixing of the zero affix to a form will result in a surface form that seems identical to the bare stem. Given this analysis, there will be a discontinuous dependency in surface structure between a modal stem and the zero affix of the adjacent form.

Assuming the Affix Hopping analysis, the underlying form of the verbal string *would have been studying* will be as in (15).

(15) [+past] [$\mathrm{M_{ODAL}}$ WILL + [ø]] [$_{\mathrm{PERF}}$ HAVE + [EN]] [$_{\mathrm{PROG}}$ BE + [ING]] [$_{\mathrm{V}}$ STUDY + [e]]

(15) contains four morphologically realized affixes. Therefore, the derivation of the surface string (16) will involve four applications of the Affix Hopping rule.

(16) [e] [$\mathrm{M_{ODAL}}$ WILL + [+past]] [$_{\mathrm{PERF}}$ HAVE + [ø]] [$_{\mathrm{PROG}}$ BE + [EN]] [$_{\mathrm{V}}$ STUDY + [ING]]

Morphological rules (whose exact form and function we will not explore here) will then map each auxiliary and the main verb onto its proper morphological form, as indicated in (17).

(17) a. [$_{\mathrm{MODAL}}$ WILL + [+past] ⇒ *would*
b. [$_{\mathrm{PERF}}$ HAVE + [ø]] ⇒ *have*

c. $[_{PROG}$ BE + [EN]] ⇒ *been*
d. $[_{V}$ STUDY + [ING]] ⇒ *studying*

Given the theory of elementary operations sketched in chapter 3, Affix Hopping could be formulated in two distinct ways: as an adjunction operation or as a substitution operation. The substitution analysis is the more natural one under our assumptions about the underlying lexical entries for verbs, and will be the analysis adopted here. If, at the point of lexical insertion, all verbs in a derivation contain an empty affix position (like *study* in (12)), then the assignment of a verbal affix to a verb will naturally involve filling the empty affix position with that affix (as ING fills the affix position of *study* in (13)). The general theory of substitution operations, which is part of the theory of grammar, predicts that when an affix moves to fill an empty affix position, it leaves an empty affix at the movement site ([e] in (13)). That is, when an affix moves via substitution, it leaves behind an empty category—just as the movement of an NP leaves behind an empty NP. If this empty affix position is part of an auxiliary, it is filled by a further application of the Affix Hopping rule.

Thus, the syntactic behavior of Affix Hopping is determined in part by the theory of grammar. The elements of its behavior that are not determined in this way must be stipulated in terms of the structural description (SD) and structural change (SC) of the rule. As an illustration, consider the following formulation of Affix Hopping.

(18) **Affix Hopping** [obligatory]

| | | | | | |
|---|---|---|---|---|---|
| | X – | [+af] – | [+v] – | [+af] – | Y |
| SD: | 1 | 2 | 3 | 4 | 5 |
| SC: | 1 | | 3 | 2/4 | 5 |

It will be assumed that each affix is marked with a feature [+af] to distinguish it from the verbal stem (marked [+v]) to which it may be attached.[4] As formulated in (18), Affix Hopping stipulates (i) that the substitution elementary (indicated by "/" in the SC) applies when an affix is to the left of another affix position and both affix positions are adjacent to the same verbal stem, (ii) that the movement is rightward, and (iii) that it is obligatory (when the SD of the rule is met, it must apply). Since it follows from the Nondistinctness Condition on substitutions discussed in section 2.2 that terms 2 and 4 must be nondistinct for the rule to apply (and therefore that term 4 must be empty), no further stipulation regarding term 4 is needed.

**Exercise 4.2**
Assume that Affix Hopping is an adjunction transformation. What would be different about the analysis of the underlying structure of the verbal string *would have been studying* given in (15)? (Hint: Remember that an affix position is created by the adjunction operation and does not exist underlyingly.) Give the derived structure of this string (i.e., the counterpart to (16), in which you have indicated the adjunction structures). Show how this formulation of Affix Hopping could apply to the same affix more than once (with unwanted consequences).

Could the directionality of the movement also follow from general principles and therefore not have to be stipulated in the statement of the rules? In the simplest case of a tense affix plus a verb (with its empty affix position), the only possible direction of movement via substitution is rightward, since the empty affix position starts out to the right of the affix to be moved. Thus, stipulating in the rule that movement is rightward will be redundant for this case, given our assumptions about the underlying form of the verbal string and the theory of elementary operations. However, this redundancy will be unavoidable as long as we formulate the transformation in terms of a linear string of elements. It would be eliminated if we could reformulate (18) without reference to a landing site at all, as in (19).

(19) Substitute [+af].

Here the transformation has been reduced to the bare essentials—stipulating which elementary operation is involved and what constant (i.e., category) it affects. The fact that the rule will only move a morphological affix into an empty affix position follows from the Nondistinctness Condition on substitutions, as noted above. The fact that this movement is rightward for the simple case of *tense affix* + *verb* follows from the fact that initially in underlying structure the empty affix position is the rightmost affix position.

To demonstrate that rightward movement of the affix need not be stipulated in the rule for all cases, we must show that leftward movement of an affix to an empty affix position is prohibited by independent considerations. Consider the following underlying structure:

(20) [+past] [$_{\text{MODAL}}$ WILL + ø] [$_{\text{PERF}}$ HAVE + EN] [$_{\text{PROG}}$ BE + ING] [$_{\text{V}}$ STUDY + [e]]

If the rule of Affix Hopping does not stipulate the direction of movement, then it should be possible to move an affix to the left. Suppose the following operations take place:

(21) a. EN substitutes for [e] in V.
b. ING moves leftward into PERF.
c. ø moves rightward into PROG.
d. [+past] moves rightward into MODAL.

(21) will generate the ill-formed (22), **would having be studied.*

(22) [$_{\text{MODAL}}$ WILL + [+past]] [$_{\text{PERF}}$ HAVE + ING] [$_{\text{PROG}}$ BE + ø] [$_{\text{V}}$STUDY + EN]

(Note that all of the affixes have been moved in this derivation.) The problem here is to find some general explanation for why a verbal affix may not concatenate with a verbal stem to its left. Otherwise, the formulation of Affix Hopping in (19) must be accompanied by a set of stipulations to the effect that (i) modals may not occur with aspectual affixes (i.e., ING and EN) and (ii) the perfective auxiliary may not occur with the progressive affix (ING)—stipulations that follow from Affix Hopping as formulated in (18).

What remains to be explained given the formulation in (19) is why the two affix positions affected by the rule must be adjacent to the same verbal stem (a requirement that is stipulated in the formulation in (18)). For example, we might consider what rules out a derivation in which the tense affix hops over the adjacent auxiliary and the main verb, as illustrated in (23).

(23) John [+past] [$_{\text{PROG}}$ BE + [ING]] [$_{\text{V}}$ STUDY + [ ]]

Since the form [$_{\text{V}}$ STUDY+ [[+past]]] will be properly generated for other derivations, the movement cannot be excluded on the grounds that it produces an impossible morphological form. On the other hand, the progressive auxiliary in an actual sentence cannot occur with an ING affix. Thus, whatever prohibition excludes the form [$_{\text{PROG}}$ BE + [ING]] will automatically account for the impossibility of (23). A similar explanation should be available for the other auxiliaries with respect to the affixes they are generated with in underlying structure. Thus, in S-structure no modal can occur with a ø affix, nor can HAVE occur with the EN affix. Again the formulation of Affix Hopping as (19) must be augmented with these additional stipulations.

Having noted the problems with the simpler formulation of Affix Hopping in (19), we will henceforth assume the more complicated formulation in (18).

One feature of (18), however, can be eliminated: the designation that the rule is "obligatory." Suppose for the simplest derivation (the tense affix + a verb) that Affix Hopping failed to apply. The resulting representation (e.g., (24)) would contain an affix that is not attached to any morphological stem.

(24) [+past] [$_V$ STUDY + [e]]

Although the reasons for generating the tense affix as an independent grammatical formative in underlying structure are straightforward, it is also clear that affixes should not remain independent in S-structure. Let us assume that this prohibition against independent affixes in S-structure is a general (rather than language-particular) constraint on linguistic form. The prohibition can be stated as in (25).

(25) **Dependent Affix Condition**
A morphologically realized affix must be a constituent of a morphologically realized lexical category at S-structure.[5]

A morphologically realized lexical category will be any category whose feature composition involves [±n, ±v] and that contains morphologically realized elements. Thus, an NP-trace, though a lexical category, is not a *morphologically realized* lexical category. This formulation is based on the assumption that the category which immediately dominates the tense affix in S-structure is not a lexical category.

Given the Dependent Affix Condition (henceforth DAC), no transformational derivation can allow the tense affix to remain in its base generated position (and hence unattached to some morphologically realized category). It follows from the DAC that Affix Hopping must apply to the tense affix. Since this cannot occur until all the other affixes have shifted to their appropriate surface positions (given rule (18)), it follows from the DAC and rule (18) that all applications of Affix Hopping will be obligatory. Thus, there is no need to stipulate as part of the Affix Hopping rule that it is obligatory.[6]

## 4.3 The Constituent Structure of the Verbal String

The DAC as formulated in (25) requires that the tense affix, which is generated as a morphologically independent element in underlying structure, must become a constituent of a morphologically realized lexical category. Suppose that the tense affix is underlyingly a constituent of a nonlexical category—for example, IP rather than VP. We can further assume that the tense affix constitutes the "inflection" of the sentence and therefore is a realization of a category I (henceforth "Infl" to avoid confusion with either the Roman numeral or the first person singular pronoun). Given our formulation of the DAC, Infl cannot be a lexical category—either in the narrow sense of "lexical head" or the extended sense of "projection of a lexical head."

Following the analysis of clauses given in chapter 3, we assume that Infl projects a phrase IP. Under this analysis, the phrase structure of IP and Infl could be specified as in (26).

(26)

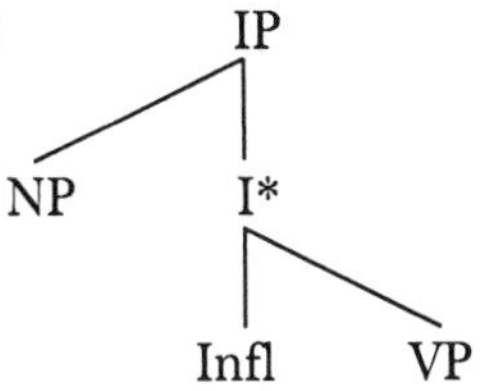


Infl itself can be realized as some set of features. If it is [+finite], then it will also be specified in terms of past versus present tense ([±past], what we might call "tense affix"). If it is [–finite], then Infl will be realized as the infinitival particle *to*.[7]

Let us now consider the constituency of the verbal auxiliaries themselves and how they are generated in terms of a set of base structures and lexical insertion. The analysis of yes/no questions involving auxiliary verbs provides some evidence concerning auxiliaries as constituents of Infl and VP, as the following paradigm illustrates. (Yes/no questions are, quite simply, questions that can be answered "yes" or "no.")

(27) a. i. will Adam be sleeping when I get home
ii. *will be Adam sleeping when I get home
b. i. has Adam been sleeping since you put him to bed
ii. *has been Adam sleeping since you put him to bed
c. i. is Adam sleeping
ii. *is sleeping Adam

In each well-formed question in (27) the auxiliary bearing the tense affix has been moved to the left of the subject NP. Assuming that this movement is the result of a transformational operation, and that transformations move only constituents (and not strings that do not form constituents), we can further delineate the constituency of the auxiliaries as follows. The tense affix and the auxiliary it attaches to must form a unique constituent at the point in the derivation where the inversion of the subject NP and the auxiliary occurs (henceforth, the rule of Subject-Auxiliary Inversion (or SAI)). If SAI operates on Infl, then the phrase structure rules must allow the option of base-generating, as a constituent of Infl, one auxiliary position that incorporates the tense affix.

However, since the ill-formed examples in (27) indicate that SAI does not move more than the tensed auxiliary, it follows that phrase structure rules may base-generate *only* one auxiliary position as a constituent of Infl. When a modal is base-generated in the auxiliary position in Infl, the other two auxiliaries must be base-generated (in a fixed order) as constituents of VP, as shown in (28).

(28) VP ⟶ (Perfective) (Progressive) V* . . .

The grammatical examples in (27), however, show that each of the three auxiliaries (modal, perfective, and progressive) may undergo SAI. Given an auxiliary construction containing a modal auxiliary, we will assume that a modal can be lexically inserted in Infl (or more precisely, that Infl can be lexicalized as a modal). (27a) shows that modals can occur in this position. Yet with respect to the grammatical examples in (27b–c), Infl must be realizable as the perfective or progressive auxiliary under the appropriate circumstances. Therefore, the auxiliary position in Infl must be specified in a way that does not distinguish among the various auxiliary forms.

These possibilities for the lexicalization of Infl can be realized if we consider Infl to have two parts: a tense feature and an optional auxiliary position. (Recall that the tense feature is motivated by the attempt to explain why a verbal string contains only one finite form, via an analysis where only one tense affix is available.) In terms of a feature analysis, the auxiliary position is specified as [+v, –n] (like verbs) and also [+aux] (in contrast to verbs, which are [–aux]).[8] Thus, the underlying structure of Infl is (29).

(29)

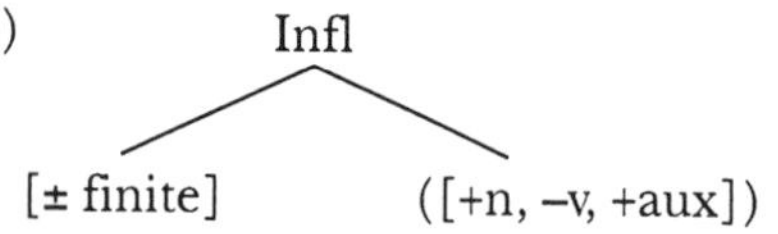


The optional auxiliary position in Infl can be utilized for lexical insertion of a modal, or for the insertion of one of the aspectual auxiliaries in VP (perfective *have* and progressive *be*) via substitution (that is, via a movement operation). Note that the auxiliary position in Infl must be optional in order to account for simple declarative sentences containing no verbal auxiliaries, such as *The dog barked.*

## 4.4 A Transformational Analysis of the Verbal Auxiliary System (II): Interrogative and Negative Sentences

In this section we will consider a group of transformational rules that interact with Affix Hopping. We will first explore that part of the transformational system that generates yes/no questions and then analyze the distribution of the negative *not*, since interrogative and negative sentences share common properties with respect to the auxiliary system.

### 4.4.1 Yes/No Questions

Given the theory of elementary operations developed in chapter 3, there are two options for deriving the inversion of the subject and the tensed auxiliary in yes/no questions: substitution or adjunction. If the movement is accomplished by substitution, then the most natural position for the substitution would be the complementizer position in CP, since it too would be marked as [+finite] in finite clauses. Under this analysis, the transformation that inverts the tensed auxiliary and the subject can be formulated as (30).

(30) **Subject-Auxiliary Inversion**

$$\begin{array}{llllll} & X\ - & C\ - & Y\ - & \begin{bmatrix} +\text{v} \\ +\text{aux} \\ \pm\text{past} \end{bmatrix} & -\ Z \\ \text{SD:} & 1 & 2 & 3 & 4 & 5 \\ \text{SC:} & 1 & 4/2 & 3 & & 5 \end{array}$$

This formulation presupposes that the features of C and the finite verbal form are nondistinct in the appropriate manner—and hence that C has not undergone lexical insertion. It follows that lexical insertion of complementizers is optional.[9]

Germanic languages such as German and Dutch provide some evidence for a similar verb movement known generally as **verb-second phenomena.** In these languages, the word order of subordinate clauses differs from that of main clauses. In subordinate clauses, the tensed form of the verb (V) follows the subject (S) and object (O), giving SOV order; whereas in main clauses it must occur after the first phrasal constituent (referred to as "second-position"), giving, for example, SVO order, where the subject is the first phrasal constituent of the sentence. This is illustrated by the German examples in (31) and (32).

(31) Main clauses (SVO, VSO)
  a. Max wird heute einen Roman lesen
     Max will today a novel read
  b. heute wird Max einen Roman lesen

(32) Subordinate clauses (SOV)
  a. ich weiß daß Max heute einen Roman lesen wird
     I know that Max today a novel read will
  b. ich weiß daß heute Max einen Roman lesen wird

To account for this variation, it has been assumed that the surface verb-second position results via a movement of the finite verb from an underlying clause-final position. Thus, the underlying word order in both main and subordinate clauses in German is SOV, and the SVO order of (31a) and the VSO order of (31b) are derived via a transformational operation that moves the finite verb into "second-position." As the movement of a verbal element to "second position" can involve the main verb as well as auxiliaries, this phenomenon can be called **head movement.**

Evidence that verb movement involves the complementizer position (henceforth C-position) comes from Dutch and concerns the position of weak subject pronouns with respect to the complementizer. (The following discussion is adapted from Den Besten 1983, which is also the source of the examples (34)–(37)). Subject pronouns in Dutch take two forms, designated weak and strong.

| (33) | Weak pronouns | Strong pronouns | |
|---|---|---|---|
| | je | jij | 'you' |
| | ze | zij | 'she' |
| | we | wij | 'we' |

In embedded clauses the weak forms must occur adjacent to the complementizer, as illustrated in (34).

(34) a. . . . dat je/ze gisteren ziek was
        that you/she yesterday ill were/was
  b. *. . . dat gisteren je/ze ziek was

In contrast, strong subject pronouns may occur in either position.

(35) a. . . .dat jij/zij gisteren ziek was
        that you/she yesterday ill were/was
  b.. . . dat gisteren jij/zij ziek was

The distribution of weak subject pronouns in root clauses is similar to their distribution in embedded clauses. In a root clause, however, a weak subject pronoun must be adjacent to the finite verb, where the complementizer does not occur. The paradigm for root clauses is given in (36)–(37).

(36) a. i. was ze gisteren ziek
was she yesterday ill
ii. *was gisteren ze ziek
b. i. waarom was ze gisteren ziek
why was she yesterday ill
ii. *waarom was gisteren ze ziek

(37) a. i. was zij gisteren ziek
was she yesterday ill
ii. was gisteren zij ziek
b. i. waarom was zij gisteren ziek
why was she yesterday ill
ii. waarom was gisteren zij ziek

The paradigms for embedded clauses (34)–(35) fall together with those for root clauses (36)–(37) under the assumption that the verb in the root clauses occupies the C-position and that the weak subject pronouns must occur adjacent to C for reasons yet to be determined.

Under the assumption that the clause-initial position is occupied by some moved phrase (as in the case of *wh*-movement), the German and Dutch facts provide suggestive (if not conclusive) evidence that the C-position is the canonical second position in a clause. We can indicate the clause-initial position as XP since the value of X appears to be relatively free (e.g., NP, PP, or AP for *wh*-movement in English, as noted in chapter 3). Thus, the first two constituents of CP are XP and C in that order. Presumably XP is optional and therefore C may in some constructions occur as the sentence-initial position.

If we grant that verb-second phenomena in German (and other languages such as Dutch) result from a substitution operation that moves a finite verb into C-position, it seems plausible to consider SAI in English as a similar substitution operation that moves a finite auxiliary verb into C. Thus, question formation in English generally could be treated as a verb-second phenomenon, although English yes/no questions are not, strictly speaking, verb-second constructions.

As formulated in (30), the SAI transformation interacts with the Affix Hopping transformation as follows. Consider for example the derivation of (38) which has the underlying structure given in (39).

(38) will Bernie study at the library

(39)

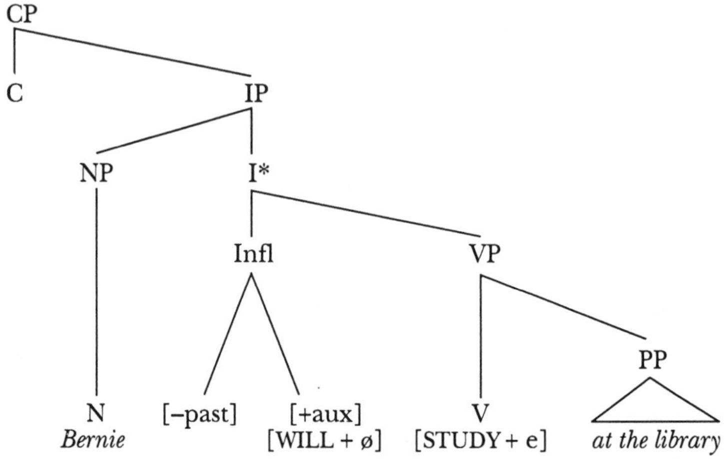


Affix hopping (as formulated in (18)) analyzes (39) as indicated in (40a), mapping (39) onto (40b). It then analyzes (40b) as indicated, mapping (40b) onto (40c).

(40) a.

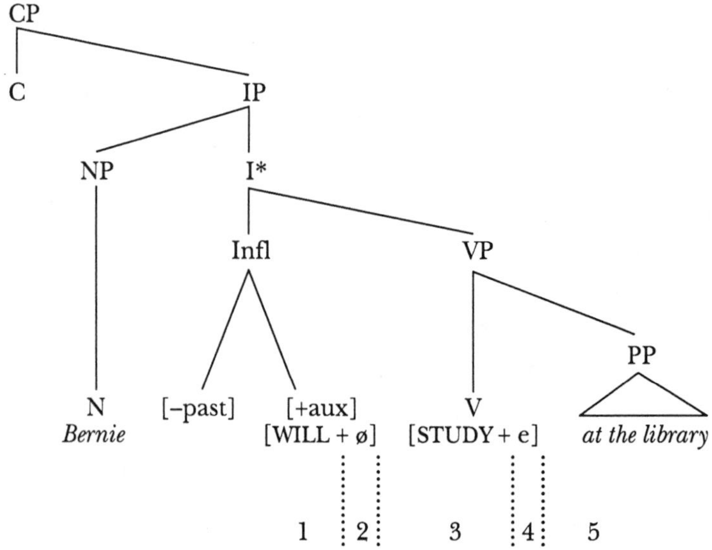

(40) b.

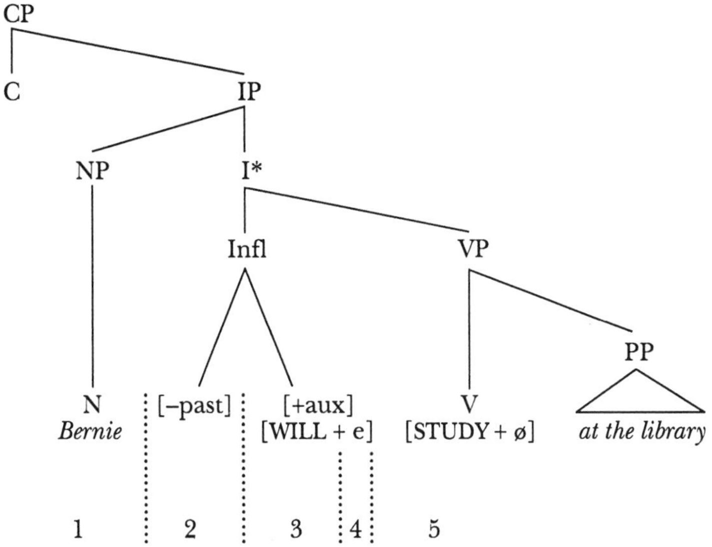


c.

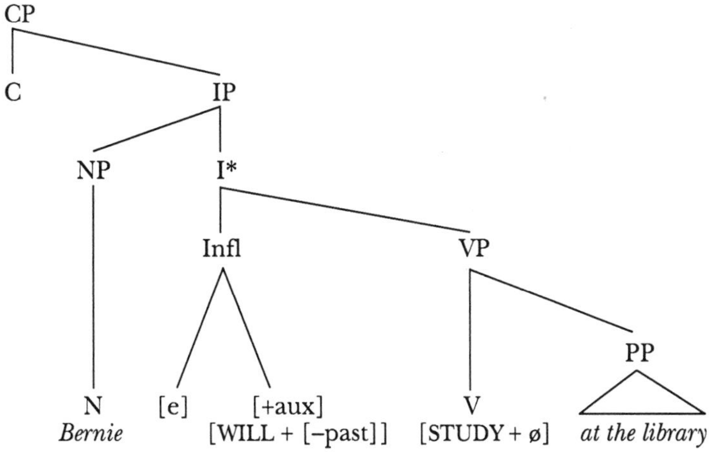


Note that [e] in (40c) represents the tense affix position under the assumption that no substitution (or adjunction) involves deleting the moved category. SAI then analyzes (40c) as shown in (41a) and maps it onto (41b).

(41) a.

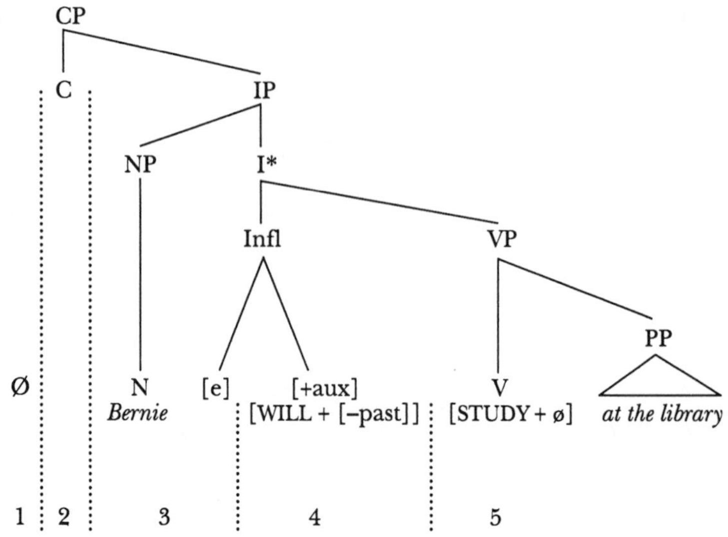


b.

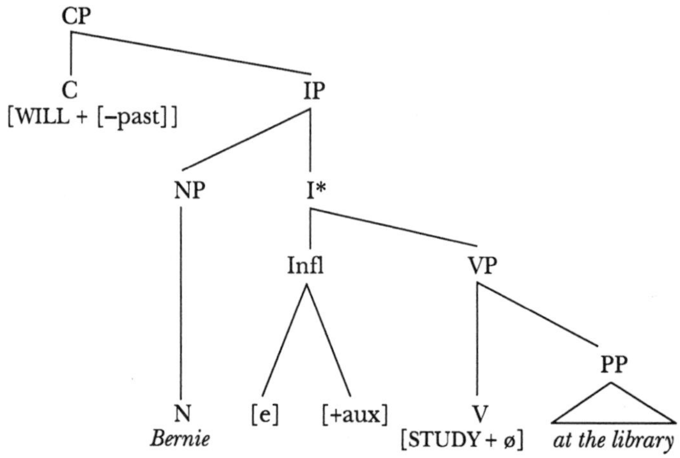


The actual morphological forms for the modal and the verb will then be determined by further rules of the morphological component.

In the above derivation, the rules of Affix Hopping and SAI were strictly ordered with respect to one another in that all applications of Affix Hopping occurred prior to the application of SAI. This is the only ordering possible for deriving (38). The application of SAI prior to Affix Hopping would leave the tense affix unconnected to any verbal stem, in violation of the DAC. That is, Affix Hopping would be unable to move the ø affix into the appropriate verbal form if the subject NP were to intervene.

We do not need to stipulate a strict order of application for these rules. Given the formulation of Affix Hopping that requires adjacency between the affix to be moved and the verbal stem it will be attached to, and given the DAC, the actual ordering facts of a correct derivation follow as a consequence.

---

**Exercise 4.3**

Consider the following examples:

(i) a. may I borrow your notes this evening
 b. will you be needing them before tomorrow

The derivation of (i.a) involves the application of Affix Hopping (twice) and SAI (once); the derivation of (i.b) involves an additional instance of Affix Hopping.

1. Give the underlying structure for each example and one derivation showing that the application of SAI can precede an application of Affix Hopping without violating the DAC.
2. Show how it follows from the DAC that SAI cannot apply prior to two or more applications of Affix Hopping.
3. What other ordering of the two rules will yield a good result?

---

The derivation of yes/no questions involving a modal auxiliary is straightforward since the modal auxiliary is base generated as a constituent of the Infl node that is fronted around the subject NP. Let us now examine the derivation of a yes/no question where the auxiliary form to be fronted is base generated in VP rather than Infl—in other words, it is one of the aspectual auxiliaries. In order for SAI to front an aspectual auxiliary, the auxiliary must first be moved into Infl. This requires the formulation of another rule, Auxiliary Raising (henceforth Aux Raising).

(42) **Auxiliary Raising**

$$X - [\text{+aux}] - \begin{bmatrix}\text{+aux}\\ \text{+aspect}\end{bmatrix} - Y$$

| | | | | |
|---|---|---|---|---|
| SD: | 1 | 2 | 3 | 4 |
| SC: | 1 | 3/2 | | 4 |

Because the substitution cannot occur unless term 2 is empty, there is no need to stipulate any condition on term 2. Aux Raising therefore moves an aspectual auxiliary that is adjacent to the empty auxiliary position in Infl into that empty position. This rule cannot then reapply to another aspectual auxiliary (i.e., the progressive auxiliary) and move it into the vacated perfective auxiliary position because there will be a mismatch of features between the two positions. (It is assumed here that these features that distinguish the perfective and progressive auxiliaries are part of their category designation.)

The derivation of (43) exemplifies the operation of Aux Raising and its interaction with Affix Hopping and SAI.

(43) have you seen Adam lately

(43) has the underlying structure (44), to which the transformations discussed above apply as indicated.

(44)
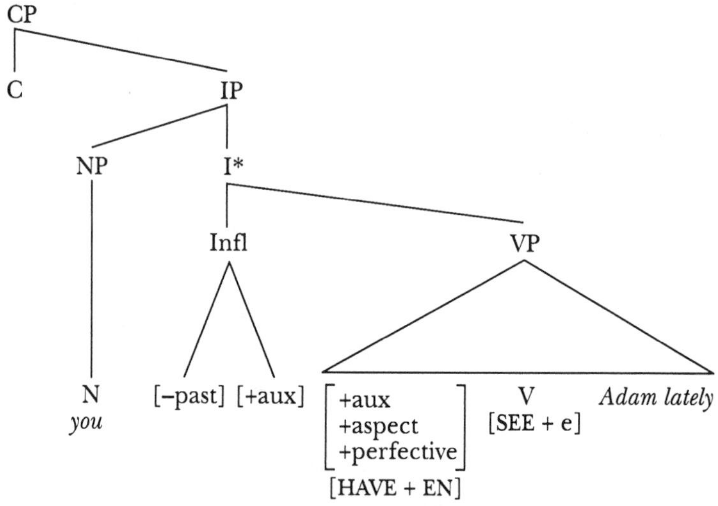


The derivation of (43) from (44) proceeds as follows.

(45) a.

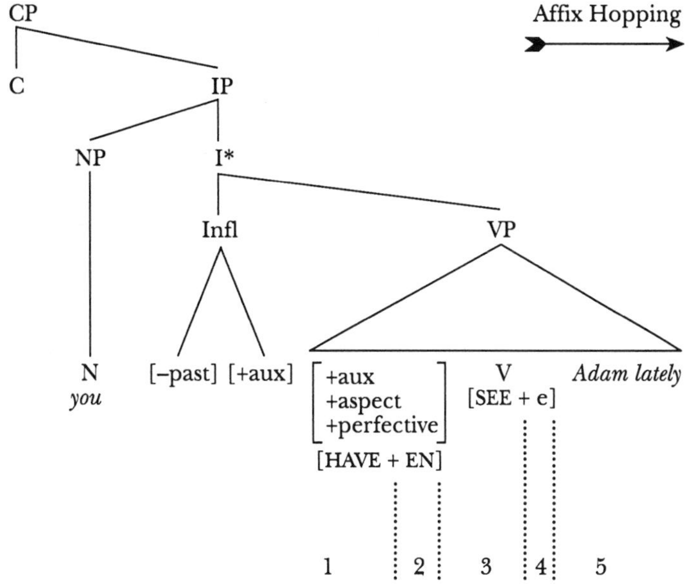
CP
Affix Hopping
C
IP
NP
I*
Infl
VP
N
you
[−past] [+aux]
+aux
+aspect
+perfective
[HAVE + EN]
V
[SEE + e]
Adam lately
1
2
3
4
5

b.

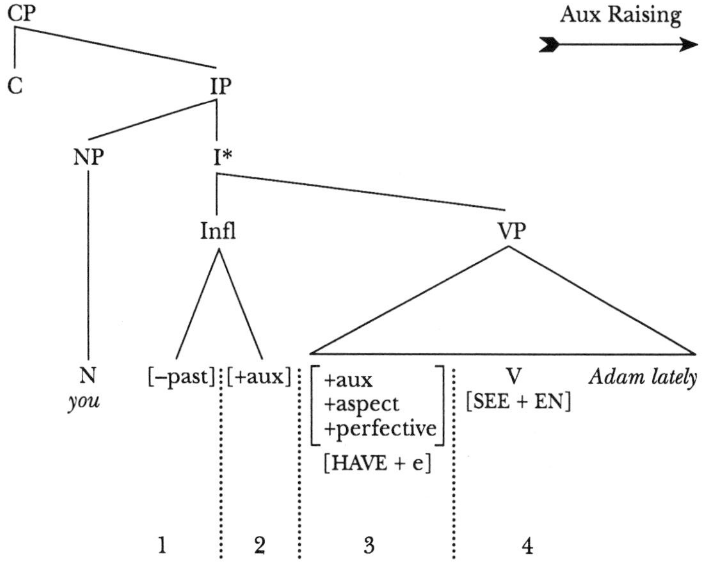
CP
Aux Raising
C
IP
NP
I*
Infl
VP
N
you
[−past]
[+aux]
+aux
+aspect
+perfective
[HAVE + e]
V
[SEE + EN]
Adam lately
1
2
3
4

(45) c.

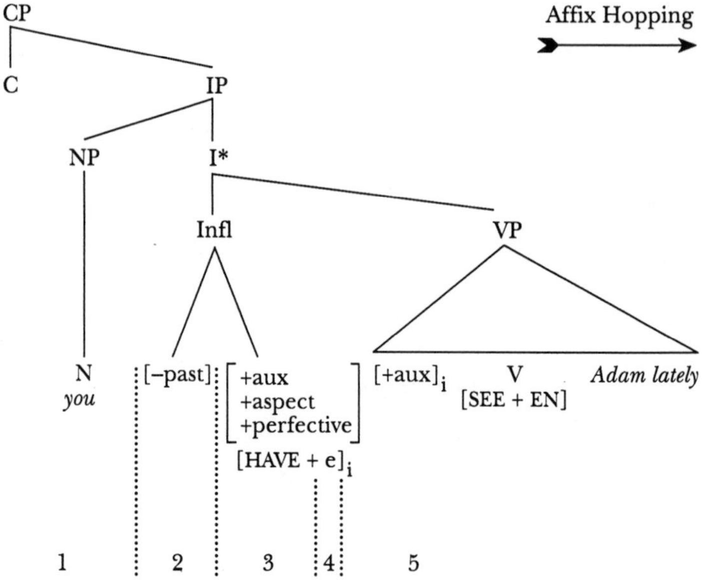
CP
Affix Hopping
C
IP
NP
I*
Infl
VP
N
you
[–past]
+aux
+aspect
+perfective
[HAVE + e]i
[+aux]i
V
[SEE + EN]
Adam lately
1
2
3
4
5

d.

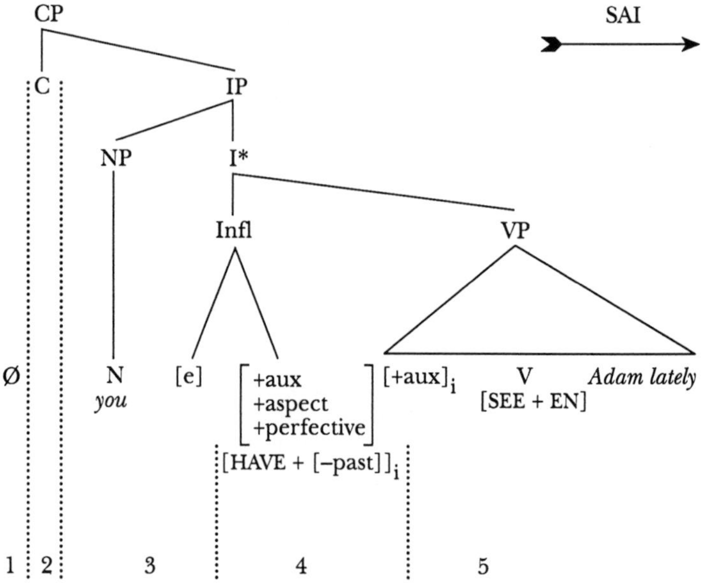
CP
SAI
C
IP
NP
I*
Infl
VP
Ø
N
you
[e]
+aux
+aspect
+perfective
[HAVE + [–past]]i
[+aux]i
V
[SEE + EN]
Adam lately
1
2
3
4
5

(45) e.

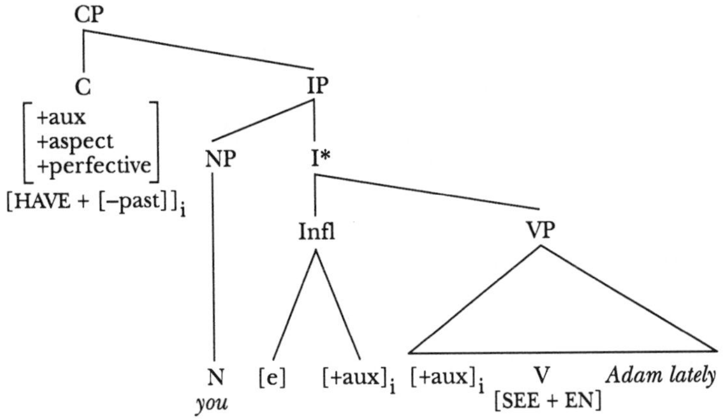


Again it is assumed that the actual forms *have* and *seen* will be determined by morphological rules.

In this regard it should be noted that the actual morphological form of the fronted auxiliary also depends on the person and number features of the surface subject. That is, we must account for the alternation between *has* and *have*, whereby first and second person pronouns (*I*, *we*, and *you*) take *have* regardless of plurality and third person pronouns take *has* in the singular (*he*, *she*, *it*) and *have* in the plural (*they*). Thus, the full derivation of the correct morphological forms would require a further rule of Subject-Verb Agreement (where "Verb" stands for the verbal form containing the tense affix at surface structure) that copies the relevant features of the subject NP head (number, person, and—in some languages—gender) onto the "Verb"—or alternatively, some device that checks the agreement of these features between subject and "Verb." Having noted the necessity for an agreement rule of some sort, I will stop short of giving an explicit formulation since this has no direct bearing on the distribution of auxiliaries and their affixes.

The derivation given in (45) has one interesting consequence with respect to rule ordering. Affix Hopping must apply both before and after Aux Raising. Thus, Affix Hopping must move the EN affix of HAVE onto the main verb prior to the raising of the perfective auxiliary ((45a) to (45b))—otherwise, this movement will be blocked since the raised auxiliary will no longer be adjacent to the verb. Furthermore, Affix Hopping can apply to the tense affix only after Aux Raising has applied ((45d) to (45e)) because prior to the movement of the auxiliary, the tense affix is not adjacent to the perfective auxiliary (i.e., the empty auxiliary position intervenes). Again, given the particular formulation of the rules and given their use in conjunction with the DAC, the ordering of the rules that produces the correct derivation need not be stipulated since it is the only ordering that does not lead to a DAC violation.

We have considered two possible cases with respect to yes/no question formation: the case where Infl contains a base generated modal, and the case where an aspectual auxiliary is raised from VP into Infl. The third and last case involves an underlying structure that contains no auxiliaries at all. Since the analysis of this construction introduces additional complexities into the formulation of the rules, we will delay discussing it until we have examined the interaction of the negative *not* with auxiliaries, which manifests properties similar to those we have encountered in yes/no questions.

### 4.4.2 Negative Sentences

One salient property of yes/no question constructions is that they involve the separation of the leftmost auxiliary from the rest of the verbal string by an intervening constituent—namely, the subject NP. In negative sentences, *not* separates the leftmost auxiliary from the rest of the verbal string in a similar fashion, as (46) illustrates.

(46) a. he *may* not *change* the proposal
b. he *is* not *changing* the proposal
c. he *has* not *changed* the proposal
d. he *may* not *be changing* the proposal
e. he *may* not *have changed* the proposal
f. he *has* not *been changing* the proposal
g. he *may* not *have been changing* the proposal

If *not* were base-generated by the phrase structure rules, then the rules of the auxiliary system—especially Affix Hopping—would have to be complicated considerably. Alternatively, *not* could be inserted by a transformational rule in such a way that the formulations of the other auxiliary system rules would remain unaffected. We will pursue the latter analysis.

Before considering how to formulate the rule that inserts *not* and investigating its interaction with the other rules for the auxiliary system, we might consider the status of a rule that inserts a negative element in a sentence and thereby affects the interpretation of that sentence. (Notice that SAI is another rule that affects the interpretation of a sentence—a statement and a corresponding yes/no question do not have the same meaning.) The question is, Which level or levels of syntactic representation are relevant for semantic interpretation?

Recall that within the model of grammar we have been exploring, which was diagrammed in figure 2.1, there are two basic levels of syntactic representation: the base-generated underlying structure (or D-structure), and the output of the transformational component (S-structure).[10] D-structure is relevant to semantic interpretation to the extent that the grammatical functions of constituents (e.g., subject and object) are determined at this level. Note that under trace theory the grammatical function of a constituent that has been displaced from its D-structure position by a movement transformation can be recovered at S-structure via trace binding. In (47), the constituent *which book by Feynman*, though occupying SPEC-CP at S-structure, will be properly interpreted as the object of *read* via trace binding.

(47) $[_{CP}$ $[_{NP:i}$ which book by Feynman] did $[_{IP}$ you read $e_i$ ]]]

The recoverability of such D-structure grammatical functions from S-structure indicates that semantic interpretation could be determined at S-structure.[11]

Empirical support for the hypothesis that S-structure is relevant for semantic interpretation comes from facts concerning the interaction of quantifiers and negatives. The specific case concerns the interpretation of *many* in (48).

(48) a. many arrows hit the target
b. not many arrows hit the target
c. many arrows did not hit the target
d. the arrows hit many targets
e. the arrows did not hit many targets
f. many targets were not hit by the arrows

The quantifier *many* in (48a) translates as 'numerous', whereas its negation *not many* in (48b) means 'few'. This difference is further highlighted in (49).

(49) a. many arrows hit the target, though many arrows didn't
b. %not many arrows hit the target, though many arrows did

(49b) is semantically anomalous (indicated by "%"). It is a contradiction—in contrast to (49a), which is not. The same difference in interpretation applies to (48d) versus (48e). Thus, the extension of (48d) as (50a) yields a semantically well-formed sentence; whereas the extension of (48e) as (50b) yields a semantically anomalous sentence (a contradiction, in this instance).

(50) a. the arrows hit many targets and missed many targets
b. %the arrows did not hit many targets and did not miss many targets

That is, given (48d) it is possible that the number of targets hit by an arrow and the number of targets not hit by an arrow are both comparatively large. Given (48e), however, few targets were hit by an arrow—which entails that most arrows missed the targets. To extend (48e) with a statement that few targets were missed by an arrow results in a contradiction of the entailment.

When *many* is negated by *not*, the interpretation of the negation *not . . . many* is 'few'. (48c) shows that the presence of *many* and *not* in the same sentence is not a sufficient condition for the negation of *many*. For example, (51) is not a contradiction.

(51) many arrows didn't hit the target, but many did

We will assume here that *not . . . many* is interpreted as 'few' when *many* is c-commanded by *not*.[12] If *not* is an immediate constituent of VP, then it will c-command the object NP but will not c-command the subject NP. This will account for the difference in interpretation of many with respect to (48c) versus (48e).

(48c) and (48f) show that the c-command relation between *not* and *many* that determines interpretation must be computed with respect to S-structure. The S-structure subject of (48f), *many targets*, functions semantically as the object of the verb *hit*, just as in (48e). If this identity of semantic function were the salient factor in the interpretation of *many*, then we would expect that the interpretations of (48e) and (48f) to be identical. Since they are not, we must distinguish the sentences in terms of their S-structures—which are distinct.

Since S-structure is apparently the level of representation relevant to the interpretation of negatives, it is not necessary that negatives be represented in D-structure. This allows for a model of grammar in which the negative *not* is transformationally introduced into a derivation; in other words, it is introduced between D-structure and S-structure. Likewise, it may not be necessary to distinguish between indicatives and interrogatives in D-structure. In this regard, notice that the interpretation of *many* is also affected by SAI, even when the sentence contains no negative. (52) does not allow the 'relatively many' reading found in (49a).

(52) did many arrows hit the target

Thus, it cannot be appropriately answered with either sentence in (53).

(53) a. yes, many arrows hit the target, though many didn't
b. no, many arrows didn't hit the target, though many did

When m*any* is in the scope of a logical operator (e.g., negation or an interrogative operator associated with yes/no questions), it has only the absolute interpretation (as opposed to the relative interpretation available in (49a)). Such facts again support a model of S-structure interpretation.

Let us now consider how to formulate the negative insertion rule, (keeping in mind that the following account does not constitute a complete analysis of negation in English, but is instead narrowly concerned with the distribution of *not* with respect to auxiliaries and main verbs). As noted earlier, base-generating a negative position would considerably complicate the statement of both Affix Hopping and also Aux Raising.

---

**Exercise 4.4**
Demonstrate this by discussing in detail the derivation of *Tom has not been studying.*

---

To avoid such complications, *not* can be introduced into the verbal string via an adjunction operation. Under the theory of elementary operations sketched in chapter 3, *not* must be adjoined to a maximal projection—in this instance VP. Furthermore, the adjunction will be optional, like all other transformations. The rule of Negative Insertion may be formulated as follows.

(54) **Negative Insertion**

| | | | |
|---|---|---|---|
| | X | - VP - | Y |
| SD: | 1 | 2 | 3 |
| SC: | 1 | *not* + 2 | 3 |

We are assuming here that *not* acts as a grammatical formative (like the aspectual auxiliaries and *'s* (see section 2.4)) rather than a lexical item. We are also assuming that under this model of grammar, lexical insertion occurs only in the base component and therefore never during the mapping from D-structure to S-structure.

The derivation of (55) illustrates the interaction of Negative Insertion with the other auxiliary rules.

(55) I have not read that article

Details aside, (55) has the underlying structure (56).

(56)

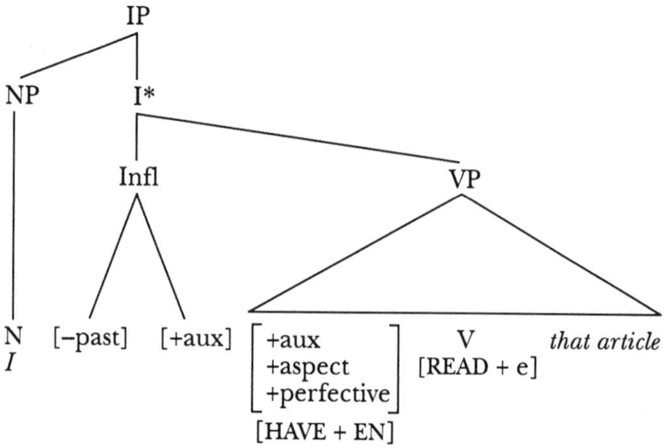


The derivation of (55) from (56) involves the application of Affix Hopping, Aux Raising, and Negative Insertion. Given that the application of both Affix Hopping and Aux Raising requires certain constant terms to be adjacent, Negative Insertion cannot apply until after the EN affix has been moved into the main verb and the perfective auxiliary has been raised into Infl. This stage in the derivation is illustrated in (57).

(57) a.

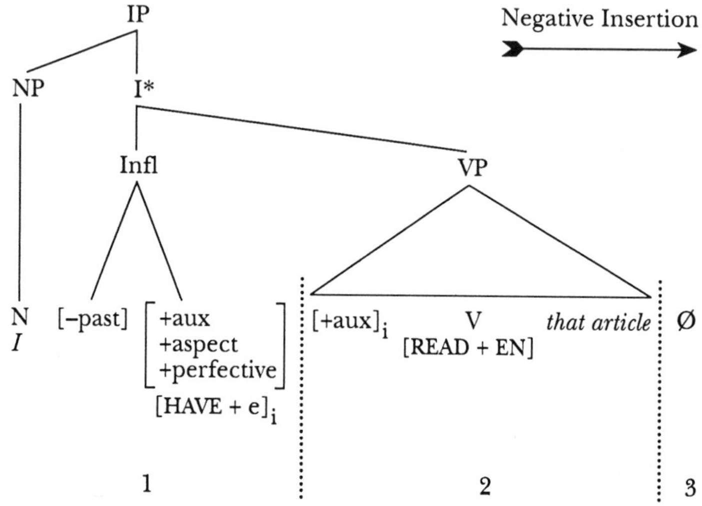

(57) b.

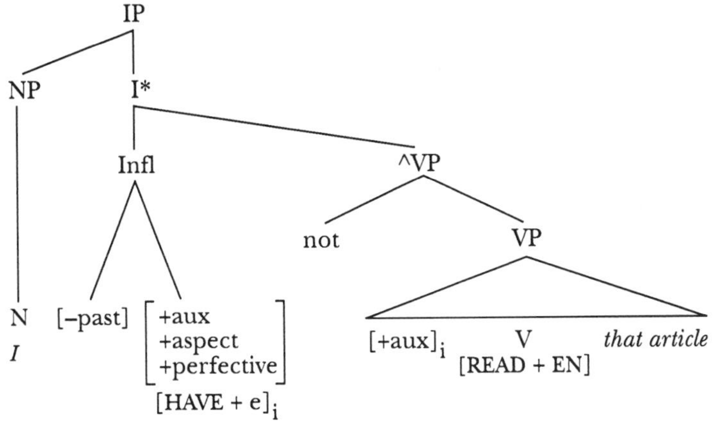


It should be clear that the DAC determines the order of rule application. In order that the negative formative *not* occur to the right of the aspectual auxiliary in S-structure, the auxiliary must be raised into Infl during the course of the derivation. Furthermore, this must occur before the insertion of *not*; otherwise, the SD of Aux Raising will not be met. (Note that if Aux Raising is allowed to move an auxiliary into a nonadjacent position (say, across a negative), it would be difficult to explain why a nonadjacent progressive auxiliary could not otherwise raise into Infl.) Given that Aux Raising must occur before Negative Insertion, it must also be the case that Affix hopping applies to the aspectual affix before raising. As with the derivation of questions involving Aux Raising, the operation that moves the aspectual auxiliary into Infl destroys the adjacency between the aspectual affix position and the following verbal element and therefore destroys the environment for the application of Affix Hopping. Were Aux Raising to apply first, the aspectual affix could not hop and therefore the tense affix would remain stranded—violating the DAC. Similarly, were Negative Insertion to apply before Aux Raising, the tense affix would again be stranded.

After Affix hopping and Aux Raising have applied, the order of application for Negative Insertion and the remaining application of Affix hopping (to the tense affix) is not crucial. Either order will suffice.

Recall that our base structures allow for the possibility that Infl contains only the tense affix (and no auxiliary position). A sentence like *Bernie has begun his Africa report* will then have two possible derived structures: one where the perfective auxiliary *has* occurs in Infl, and another where *has* remains in VP. The second possibility creates a problem for our formulation of Negative Insertion since the rules would generate the ungrammatical (58).

(58) *Bernie not has begun his Africa report

---

**Exercise 4.5**
Using the rules and base structures discussed so far, provide the derivation of (58).

---

To avoid this, it is necessary to reformulate Negative Insertion so that *not* can only be inserted when the tense affix is in Infl. This can be achieved by reformulating the SD of Negative Insertion in one of two ways: either VP must be adjacent to the tense affix, or VP must be adjacent to [+aux]—which would have the effect of blocking Affix Hopping of the tense affix into VP. Following the second option, the rule of Negative Insertion can be revised as (59).

(59) **Negative Insertion** (revised)

| | X | - | [+aux] | - | VP | - | Y |
|---|---|---|---|---|---|---|---|
| SD: | 1 | | 2 | | 3 | | 4 |
| SC: | 1 | | 2 | | *not* +3 | | 4 |

This formulation specifies a context in which *not* adjunction takes place that goes beyond just identifying the adjunction site (compare (54)). A rule like (59) requires a theory of transformations whose expressive power allows an SD to mention a constant that is unaffected by the operation of the rule. Whether such expressive power is needed generally for the formulation of transformations remains an open question. With respect to negation in English, the answer appears to be affirmative.

In addition to occurring as a grammatical formative *not*, the negative may also occur as an affix on the auxiliary form to its left, as in (60).

(60) Bernie hasn't begun his Africa report

The contraction of *not* to *n't* can be considered as the result of adjoining the formative *not* to the auxiliary or as a phonological result of this process. It is clear that *Not*-Contraction involves an actual movement operation since in negative interrogatives the negative is moved by SAI only when it is in the contracted form.

(61) a. has Bernie not begun his report yet
b. hasn't Bernie begun his report yet

c. *has not Bernie begun his report yet

In (61a) the negative remains in place while the auxiliary is shifted to the left of the subject; in (61b) the negative moves as part of the shifted auxiliary. It cannot remain an independent constituent and also move, as (61c) shows.

The rule of *Not*-Contraction is given in (62).

(62) ***Not*-Contraction**

| | | | | |
|---|---|---|---|---|
| | X – | [+aux] – | not – | Y |
| SD: | 1 | 2 | 3 | 4 |
| SC: | 1 | 2+3 | | 4 |

As formulated, *Not*-Contraction is a simple adjunction operation that adjoins *not* to an adjacent auxiliary to its left.[13] It is assumed that this results in the obligatory contraction of the form *not* to *n't*.

---

**Exercise 4.6**

Apply *Not*-Contraction to (57b). Then discuss how this accounts for the properties of the paradigm given in (61).

---

Assuming that the scope of the negative is determined at S-structure, the trace of the contracted *not* adjoined to VP plays a role in semantic interpretation similar to that of the trace of a *wh*-phrase in a grammatical function position.

This completes our analysis of interrogatives and negatives involving at least one base-generated auxiliary element. In the following section we will examine sentences containing no base-generated auxiliary element.

## 4.5 The Auxiliary *Do*

In yes/no interrogative or negative declarative sentences which contain no base-generated auxiliary, we find an auxiliary *do* that appears to have the sole function of bearing the tense marking of the sentence.

(63) a. does Barbie read science fiction
b. Barbie does not read science fiction

The distribution of this auxiliary element can be accounted for via a substitution transformation that inserts the auxiliary *do* (not to be confused with the verb *do*) into the empty auxiliary position in Infl. This rule is usually called *Do*-Support and can be formulated as in (64).

(64) ***Do*-Support**

$$
\begin{array}{lcccc}
 & X & - \ [+aux] \ - & \begin{bmatrix} +v \\ -n \\ -aux \end{bmatrix} & - \ Y \\
SD: & 1 & 2 & 3 & 4 \\
SC: & 1 & do/2 & 3 & 4
\end{array}
$$

Given that all rules are optional and unordered, it seems necessary to formulate *Do*-Support with a constant term 3 (corresponding to the main verb) that provides a specific context for the application of the rule. This analysis ensures that *do* will only occur in sentences that contain no other auxiliaries, and it therefore prevents the generation of ill-formed sentences such as **Mary did have left at noon.* The insertion of *do* can only occur when [+aux] is empty (under the Nondistinctness Condition on substitutions).

Let us assume that *do*, like the modal auxiliaries, has a zero affix. Therefore, *Do*-Support inserts the morphological form (65).

(65) [DO + [ø]]

In terms of feature specification, (65) is [+v, –n, +aux] like all the other auxiliaries. It is distinct from the modals in that it is [–modal], and also distinct from the aspectual auxiliaries by virtue of the feature [–aspect].[14]

As an illustration of how *Do*-Support applies, consider the derivation of (63b), with the D-structure (66).

(66)

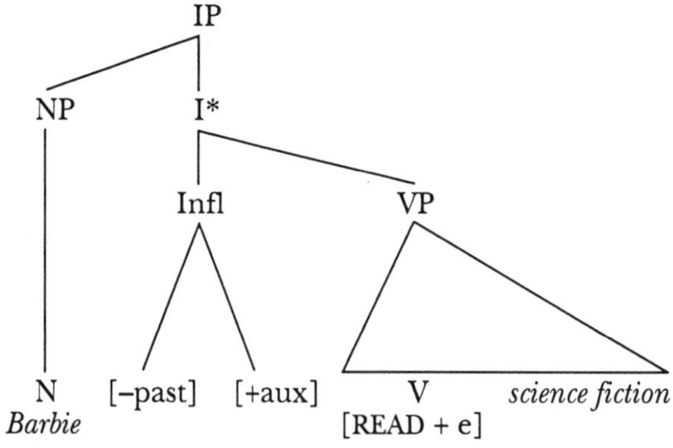


As formulated in (64), *Do*-Support would analyze (66) as (67a) and map it onto (67b).

(67) a.

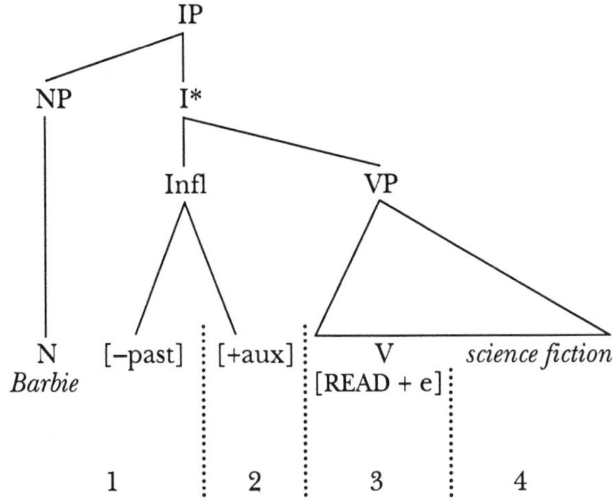


b.

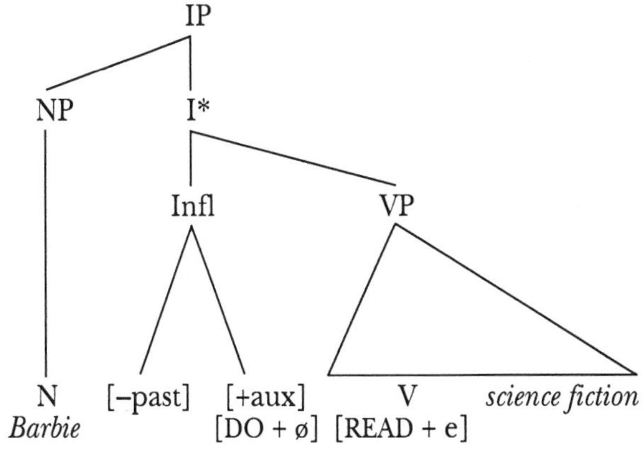


After *do* is inserted, Affix Hopping (of the ø affix) must apply before Negative Insertion applies; otherwise, the DAC will be violated. However, the movement of the tense affix can take place either before or after Negative Insertion.

---

**Exercise 4.7**

Explain why this is so. Show how this would not be the case if [+tense] instead of [+aux] were mentioned in the SD of Negative Insertion.

---

**Exercise 4.8**
Note that in the case of interrogatives involving *Do*-Support the proper order of application is not strictly determined by the formulation of the rules alone; that is, we must rely on the DAC as well. Discuss this with respect to the derivation of the question *Did John arrive on time?*

To recapitulate, in the analysis we have been examining, the [+aux] position in Infl can be filled in three distinct ways: (i) via lexical insertion of a modal auxiliary at D-structure, (ii) via a movement rule that moves a base-generated aspectual auxiliary into that position, or (iii) via a substitution operation that inserts the grammatical formative *do*. Options (ii) and (iii) are mutually exclusive; *Do*-Support will only occur when Aux Raising is not possible. This is captured in our formulation of *Do*-Support, which cannot apply when there is an aspectual auxiliary in VP.

So far the analysis of the auxiliary system has been relatively straightforward. There are, however, some residual problems that require comment. We have been assuming throughout that there is a clear distinction between auxiliary verbs [+v, –n, +aux] and main verbs [+v, –n, –aux]. Unfortunately this distinction appears to break down with respect to the copula *be*, as in (68).

(68) John is sarcastic

If we analyze the phrase *is sarcastic* as a VP consisting of a V *is* and an AP *sarcastic*, then there is no explanation in terms of the rules developed above for the behavior of *is* with respect to both Negative Insertion and SAI as indicated in (69a) and (69b), respectively, or with respect to *Do*-Support as indicated in (69c–e).

(69) a. John is not sarcastic
b. is John sarcastic
c. *John does be sarcastic
d. *John does not be sarcastic
e. *does John be sarcastic

Under the analysis developed above, *is* must be a constituent of Infl in order to have *not* occur to its right in (69a). Likewise, it must be a constituent of Infl in order to move to the left of the subject NP *John* in (69b). Therefore, the copula *is* must somehow be subject to Aux Raising. This could be achieved by analyzing the copular *be* as [+v, –n, +aux]. (We would then assume that a main verb (copular and noncopular) is distinct from a modal (i.e., that it is [–modal], so that a modal auxiliary could not be inserted in a main verb position.) Given the formulation of *Do*-Support in (64), (69c–e) could not be generated because the copula *be* is not [–aux] as term 3 requires.

With the formulation of *Do*-Support in (64) the auxiliary *do* should occur only with noncopular main verbs. The paradigm for imperative constructions as illustrated in (70) shows that this is incorrect—auxiliary *do* can occur with the copular *be*. (Examples (70b–c) are from Lasnik 1981a.)

(70) a. do be careful / be careful
b. do not be sarcastic
c. *be not sarcastic

(70a) shows that *Do*-Support is an option for affirmative imperatives, and (70c) shows that it is obligatory for negative imperatives. For imperatives (in contrast to indicatives) Aux Raising must be prohibited so that *Do*-Support can apply.

The facts that must be accounted for in our analyses are the following:

(71) a. Aux Raising must be allowed to apply to the copula in indicatives.
b. Aux Raising must be prevented from applying to the copula in imperatives.
c. *Do*-Support must apply in negative imperatives.

The term "indicatives" is used here to cover both propositions and questions.

---

**Exercise 4.9**

Note that Aux Raising need not apply to indicatives containing only the copula. Given our analysis (i) can have two distinct representations: one involving the copula as a constituent of Infl and another where the copula remains in VP.

(i) the President was nonplussed

Give the two representations for (i) and discuss why this occurs.

---

(71a–b) can be accommodated easily by revising Aux Raising so that it distinguishes between imperatives and indicatives. The distinction is based on the [±tense] feature of the initial affix in the verbal string. Indicatives are [+tense], whereas imperatives are [–tense]. To prevent imperatives from undergoing Aux Raising, we must reformulate the rule as (72).

(72) **Aux Raising** (revised)

| | | | | | | | | | |
|---|---|---|---|---|---|---|---|---|---|
| | X | – | [+tense] | – | [+aux] | – | [+aux] | – | Y |
| SD: | 1 | | 2 | | 3 | | 4 | | 5 |
| SC: | 1 | | 2 | | 4/3 | | | | 5 |

Main verbs other than the copula will not be affected by this rule since they are marked [–aux] and therefore are distinct from term 3. By mentioning [+tense] as part of the context in which Aux Raising applies, we ensure that it will not apply to imperatives.

(71c) requires reformulating *Do*-Support so that (70b) can be generated. Because we are forced to analyze copular *be* as [+aux] to account for its auxiliary-like behavior in yes/no questions and negative indicatives, it would appear that *Do*-Support cannot be restricted to contexts where [+aux] in Infl is adjacent to a [–aux] element (i.e., the main verb, as the rule is formulated in (64)). We therefore reformulate *Do*-Support as (73).

(73) ***Do*-Support** (revised)

| | | | | | |
|---|---|---|---|---|---|
| | X | – | [+aux] | – | Y |
| SD: | 1 | | 2 | | 3 |
| SC: | 1 | | *do*/2 | | 3 |

This formulation allows for the occurrence of auxiliary *do* in copular imperatives.

---

**Exercise 4.10**

To account for negative imperatives, we must revise the Negative Insertion rule. The formulation in (62) does not account for imperatives. Given (68), how could the rule of Negative Insertion be reformulated so that it accounts for imperatives and also distinguishes between the grammatical and ungrammatical pairs in (i) and (ii)? (Hint: See the discussion of (61) above.)

(i) a. do not run
  b. *not run

(ii) a. do not be ridiculous
  b. *not be ridiculous

Show how your reformulation generates (i.a) and (ii.a). Discuss what blocks the generation of (i.b) and (ii.b).

---

As formulated as (64), *Do*-Support accounted for the fact that the auxiliary *do* cannot occur in nonimperative sentences when either the perfective or progressive auxiliary occurs. In terms of our analysis, *Do*-Support cannot apply when Aux Raising is possible. Given the reformulation of *Do*-Support in (73) as required by imperatives containing the copula, this no longer follows. Any context in which Aux Raising can apply will also meet the structural description of *Do*-Support in (73). Under this analysis, we require a different way of accounting for the fact that auxiliary *do* may not coocur with an aspectual auxiliary in a nonimperative sentence.

If we are to maintain relatively simple formulations of the rules involved and avoid stipulations about when a given rule must apply, then the problem involving *Do*-Support and Aux Raising in indicatives must be solved in more general terms. As such a solution, Lasnik 1981a proposes the following general principle on rule application:

(74) If transformations T and T' are both applicable to a phrase marker P, and if the set of structures meeting the structural description of T is a proper subset of the set of structures meeting the structural description of T', then T' may not apply. (p. 169)[15]

Both *Do*-Support and Aux Raising affect the [+aux] position in Infl. The set of structures meeting the SD of Aux Raising is a proper subset of the set of structures meeting the SD of *Do*-Support since any structure meeting the SD of Aux Raising will also meet the SD of *Do*-Support but not conversely. Thus, (74) ensures that when a structure meets the SD of both rules, the application *Do*-Support will be blocked.

Though the rule system explored in this chapter accounts for the auxiliary verb phenomena we have looked at, it is far from clear that it is the optimal rule system. To determine whether it is the optimal rule system, we need to act on Feynman's methodological advice about the importance of investigating alternatives (see pages 88–89). In addition, one would like to know how much of this analysis generalizes to the auxiliary systems of other languages.

---

**Exercise 4.11**

For example, it has been suggested that in French V may raise to Infl, whereas in English it may not. Thus, we find the following contrasts between the two languages. (The examples are from Pollock 1989.)

(i) Placement of negatives
   a. *John likes not Mary
   b. Jean (n') aime pas Marie. [assume that *pas* is the negative]

(ii) Subject/verb inversion
   a. *likes he Mary
   b. aime-t-il Marie
(iii) Placement of adverbs
   a. *John kisses often Mary / John often kisses Mary
   b. Jean embrasse souvent Marie / *Jean souvent embrasse Marie
(iv) Placement of quantifiers
   a. *my friends love all Mary / my friends all love Mary
   b. mes amis aiment tous Marie / *mes amis tous aiment Marie

What would be the phrase structure analysis of the French data? How does this analysis lead to the conclusion that V raises to Infl in French (but not in English)?

---

**Exercise 4.12**
Given the analysis developed in this chapter, how is V to Infl raising prevented in English? How would the analysis of Infl have to be modified in order to allow V to Infl raising in French?

---

## Bibliographical Comments

Chomsky's analysis of the auxiliary system in English was one of the earliest transformational analyses (see Chomsky 1975b (written in 1955–56), 1957). Since then several transformational analyses of auxiliaries have been published, including Steele et al. 1981, Akmajian, Steele, and Wasow 1979, Lasnik 1981a, and Heny and Richards 1983. For work on the comparative syntax of auxiliaries, see Emonds 1978, Pollock 1989, and also Chomsky 1991.

# 5
# Infinitivals, Case, and Government

Having covered a fair amount of the syntax of finite clauses, we are now ready to turn to infinitival clauses (henceforth infinitivals), which are similar in basic structure but vary more widely in their surface realizations. Like embedded finite clauses, infinitivals can occur with a complementizer (*for*) and a lexical subject, as illustrated in (1a) (compare (1b)).

(1) a. it is unusual [for John to arrive on time]
    b. it is unusual [that John arrived on time]

Thus, they appear to have the same sentential structure that was assigned to finite clauses in chapter 4. Under this assumption, the sentential structure of the bracketed infinitival in (1a) would be given as (2).

(2)
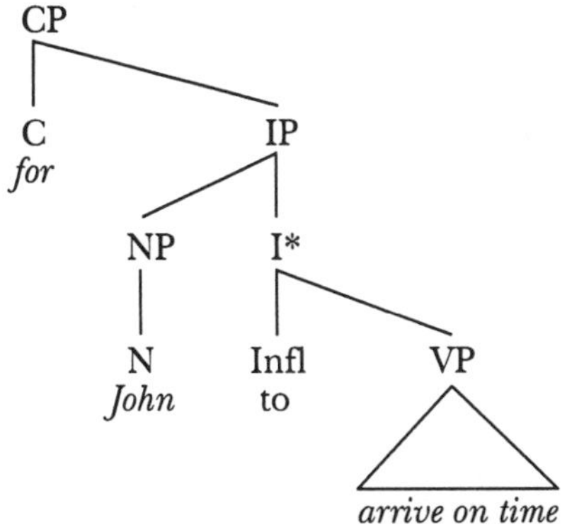


As noted in section 4.3 *for* is the complementizer for infinitivals that corresponds to the complementizer *that* in an embedded finite clause. The element *to* is analyzed here as a grammatical formative corresponding to the tense element in a finite clause.

Infinitivals differ from finite clauses in certain important respects. first, unlike finite clauses, which only occur with a lexical subject, infinitivals may occur either with a lexical subject (3a) or without a lexical subject (3b).

(3) a. With lexical subject
 i. Bernie expects [Adam to succeed]
 ii. Bernie wants very much [for Adam to help him]
 iii. it is possible [for Adam to lose at Othello]

 b. Without lexical subject
 i. Bernie expects [to succeed]
 ii. Bernie wants very much [to help Adam]
 iii. it is possible [to lose at Othello]

Second, under certain circumstances, infinitivals mu*st* occur without lexical subjects.

(4) a. I tried [to finish the review]
 b. *I tried [(for) Bill to finish the review]

(4) illustrates that an infinitival complement of *try* can only occur without a lexical subject. (4b) shows that this holds regardless of whether the infinitival contains the complementizer *for* or not.

A third difference involves the distribution of the complementizers *for* and *that.* As an illustration, consider the following paradigm for the predicate adjective *odd,* which can take either a finite or an infinitival clause complement.

(5) a. finite clause complement
 i. it is odd [that Mary is arriving on time]
 ii. it is odd [Mary is arriving on time]

 b. Infinitival complement
 i. it is odd [for Mary to be arriving on time]
 ii. *it is odd [Mary to be arriving on time]

Although the complementizer *that* is optional for the finite clause complement of *odd,* the complementizer *for* must occur in the infinitival complement. If we extend the paradigm to infinitivals without lexical subjects, then the converse requirement holds for the complementizer *for*—it may not occur without a lexical subject, as illustrated in (6).

(6) a. *it is odd [for to be arriving on time]
 b. it is odd [to be arriving on time]

A fourth difference between infinitivals and finite clauses concerns the Case marking of the subject NP. As illustrated in (7), a pronominal subject of a finite clause occurs in the nominative Case whereas the corresponding pronominal subject in an infinitival occurs in the objective Case.

(7) a. it is odd [that he is arriving on time]
b. it is odd [for him to be arriving on time]

In this way, the analysis of infinitivals connects with Case theory as sketched in section 2.4. In what follows we will explore an account of the properties of infinitivals based to a large extent on principles of Case theory.

## 5.1 Case Assignment

Before considering how Case is assigned to a lexical subject of an infinitival, let us briefly examine the conditions under which Case is assigned to other NP positions. To see this as clearly as possible, we will consider the distribution of English personal pronouns, which, unlike nonpronominal NPs in English, are overtly marked for Case. If, as we have been assuming, pronouns are inherently marked for Case in the lexicon, then "Case assignment" for pronouns is just Case licensing.[1] In what follows, "Case assignment" will be used as a cover term for either Case marking, a process that marks an NP for Case, or Case licensing, a process that checks whether an NP that is marked for Case bears the appropriate Case marking.[2]

Personal pronouns in English occur in several morphologically different forms that are distinguished in terms of Case. The third person masculine singular pronoun, for example, has the three distinct lexical realizations indicated in (8).

| | | | |
|---|---|---|---|
| (8) | *he* | *him* | *his* |
| | +n | +n | +n |
| | –v | –v | –v |
| | +pronoun | +pronoun | +pronoun |
| | 3rd person | 3rd person | 3rd person |
| | +masculine | +masculine | +masculine |
| | –plural | –plural | –plural |
| | NOMINATIVE | OBJECTIVE | GENITIVE |

Since these three forms occur in complementary distribution, the Case designations NOMINATIVE, OBJECTIVE, and GENITIVE are predictable on the basis of syntactic context.

Under our analysis of pronouns, Case assignment is determined on the basis of syntactic context. As discussed in chapter 2, this context is not simply one of string adjacency between an NP and some Case-assigning category. Consider the distribution of objective Case illustrated in (9) and (10).

(9) a. nobody recognized him
b. everyone has been talking about him

(10) a. nobody recognized [$_{NP}$ {his/*him} signature]
b. everyone has been talking about [$_{NP}$ {his/*him} book]

(9) shows that the pronominal object of a verb (9a) or a preposition (9b) occurs in the objective Case. Using the feature analysis of categories developed in section 2.3, we can state this as the following generalization:

(11) [–n] heads (i.e., V and P) assign objective Case to their NP objects.

(10) shows that objective Case assignment must be blocked from applying to an NP constituent of the object of a [–n] head. This follows if the [–n] head must govern NP in order to assign it objective Case. The definition of government is repeated in (12).

(12) A lexical head $\alpha$ *governs* a category $\beta$ iff $\alpha$ m-commands $\beta$ and $\beta$ m-commands $\alpha$.

Given (12), the verb in (10a) does not govern the pronoun *him* because it is not a constituent of NP. Therefore, the assignment of objective Case to the pronoun violates the government condition on objective Case assignment. Similarly, the preposition *about* in (10b) does not govern the pronoun *him.*

Pronouns in the objective Case also occur in NPs as illustrated in (13).

(13) we found [$_{NP}$ several pictures of him]

The grammatical formative *of* in (13) is inserted by a transformation (as discussed in section 2.4 ), so that the derived structure of the NP in (13) is (14), where $N^{max}$ stands for NP.

(14)

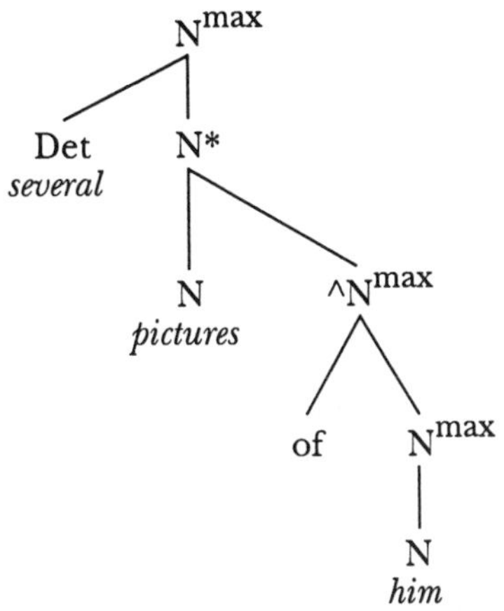


The assignment of objective Case to *him* is due to the presence of *of*, which can be analyzed as a [–n] segment though not a lexical head.

If *of* is the objective Case assigner in (14), then a Case assigner need not be a lexical head. With V and P, the objective Case assigner [–n] happens to be a lexical head; whereas with *of*, it is not. Nonetheless, Case assignment under government holds even for *of*, as illustrated in (15).

(15) several pictures of $[_{NP}$ {his/*him} guinea pig]

In this example *of* does not govern the NP headed by the pronoun because of the NP headed by *pig*. Since *of* is not a [–n] lexical head, we must restate (11) as (16).

(16) A [–n] nonphrasal segment assigns objective Case to an NP it governs.

As we will see, the government restriction generalizes to virtually all instances of Case assignment.

Before considering genitive Case assignment in English, we should note that in many languages, NP constituents of an NP occur in the genitive—the "adnominal genitive."

(17) German

a. der Bruder des Mädchens
the-NOM brother-NOM the-GEN girl-GEN
'the brother of the girl'

b. die Eltern jener Kinder
the-NOM parents-NOM those-GEN children-GEN
'the parents of those children'

(18) Russian

a. bol'šinstvo studentov
majority-NOM students-GEN
'most of the students'

b. sbornik statej
collection-ACC articles-GEN
'a collection of articles'

In these languages, an N functions as a genitive Case assigner in the appropriate syntactic configuration. Since this is not possible in modern English for some reason, *Of*-Insertion is required to introduce a Case assigner in N–NP noun phrases.

Genitive Case assignment in English has somewhat different properties than objective Case assignment. Genitive assignment does not depend on the presence of a Case-assigning element (e.g., [–n] for objective Case). Instead, genitive Case assignment depends on a syntactic configuration that contains no Case-assigning element. This configuration for genitive Case is given in the structural description for *'s*-Insertion—namely, $N^{max}$ followed by N* (as analyzed in (75) of chapter 2). The SC stipulates that the direction of Case assignment is to the left. Nonetheless, genitive and objective Case assignment are similar in that the relevant configurations involve a single government domain. Thus, the N* and the $N^{max}$ that is assigned genitive Case must occur in the same government domain, just as an $N^{max}$ and a Case-assigning [–n] must. Furthermore, they will be adjacent if the genitive $N^{max}$ is the only other immediate constituent of the $N^{max}$ that dominates it.

---

**Exercise 5.1**

Use the following examples to show how objective Case assignment occurs under conditions of adjacency and government with respect to the Case-assigning element.

(i) a. Jill met us in the park on Sundays
b. *Jill met in the park us on Sundays

(ii) a. we borrowed [$_{NP}$ his notes] for the weekend
b. *we borrowed [$_{NP}$ him notes] for the weekend

Which principles of Case theory do the ill-formed (b)-examples violate?

---

The assignment of nominative Case is also subject to government as illustrated in (19).

(19) a. [$_{NP:i}$ pictures of [$_{NP:j}$ {him/*he}]] annoy Susan
b. he annoys Susan

Under the IP analysis of clauses, Infl is the (nonlexical in this instance) head governing the subject NP ($NP_i$ in (19a) and *he* in (19b)). We assume therefore that whatever is responsible for nominative Case assignment must be a constituent of the Infl government domain. Thus, the pronominal $NP_j$ in (19a), which is in the government domain of the noun *pictures* and therefore cannot be governed by Infl, cannot occur in the nominative.

Although this account covers the facts of English, it is insufficiently general with regard to other languages. In Portuguese, for example, the pronominal subject of an infinitival (hence syntactically tenseless) IP will occur in the nominative if the infinitival verb is marked for agreement in number and person with the infinitival subject. (The examples are from Quicoli 1987.)

(20) a. e necessario [$_{IP}$ nɔs terminarmos a tarefa]
it is necessary we-NOM to finish-1st PL the task
'it is necessary for us to finish the task'
b. *e necessario [$_{IP}$ nos terminar a tarefa]

(20b), in contrast to (20a), shows that a nominative subject may not occur with a bare infinitive. In English, agreement occurs only with finite verbal forms. Thus, the evidence from Portuguese suggests that the presence of an agreement element, rather than tense, conditions the occurrence of nominative Case. Suppose therefore that an agreement marker AGR exists as a constituent of Infl, as in (21).

(21)

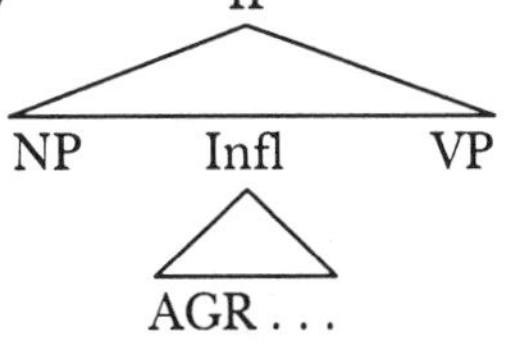


Given (21), nominative Case assignment also meets the adjacency and government conditions on Case assignment.

In section 2.4, *'s*-Insertion was interpreted as a rule of Case assignment with the following properties:

(22) a. Case is assigned to $N^{max}$. (as in chapter 2)
b. Case is assigned to all $N^{max}$.
c. Case is assigned under government and adjacency.
d. Case assignment is obligatory.

We will assume that these properties hold generally for all instances of Case assignment.[3] The fact that nominative and objective Case marking has overt morphological effects only for pronominal NPs in English simply reflects an idiosyncrasy of English. In languages with a rich morphological Case system all nouns are marked for Case (see section 5.3 for further discussion).

Recall that the obligatoriness of *'s*-Insertion follows from the general requirement that every NP is assigned Case (chapter 2, (80)). The examples discussed in chapter 2 all involved lexical NPs—NPs with phonetic content, as opposed to empty categories like trace. Given this observation, we will reformulate the Case filter as follows:

(23) **Case filter** (revised)
*NP, where NP is lexical and is not assigned Case.

(23) states that a lexical NP is ill formed if it does not bear Case. In addition to accounting for the obligatory application of *'s*-Insertion, (23) accounts for the nonoccurrence of lexical NPs in positions where NPs cannot be assigned Case. One such position is the subject of infinitivals in certain constructions.

(24) a. it is necessary [$_{CP}$ for politicians to tell the truth]
b. it is necessary [$_{CP}$ to tell the truth]
c. *it is necessary [$_{CP}$ politicians to tell the truth]

The Case filter (23) accounts for the ill-formedness of (24c) under the assumption that the lexical subject of the infinitival (*politicians*) is not assigned Case—in contrast to (24a) where it is. In the next section we will investigate in detail this Case theoretic analysis of infinitivals.

---

**Exercise 5.2**

Note again that the analysis for pronominal NPs will be somewhat different than for nonpronominal NPs. Under the assumption that pronouns are inherently marked for Case in the lexicon, discuss how the Case filter must be interpreted to rule out (i).

(i) *it is necessary [$_{CP}$ us to tell the truth]

Hint: Recall that the term "Case assignment" is being interpreted as either Case marking or Case licensing. How would (i) be excluded under the assumption that pronouns are not marked for Case in the lexicon and do not have a phonetic realization unless they are Case-marked? This would mean that the subject of the infinitival in (i) would be represented as a set of features [+n, –v, +plural, 1st person]. What problems arise for the interpretation of the notion "lexical NP" in the Case filter?

---

## 5.2 Case Assignment and the Subject of Infinitival Constructions

In this section we will explore in detail the conditions under which the lexical subject of an infinitival construction can be assigned Case. When these conditions are not met, lexical subjects of infinitivals will be prohibited by the Case filter. In situ, infinitival subjects will be marked with objective Case in the presence of a *for*-complementizer or a verb of a certain class whose lexical properties allow it to function as a Case assigner across a CP boundary. Alternatively, the lexical subject may be moved to a position that will be marked for Case.

### 5.2.1 The Complementizer *For*

In an infinitival CP, the complementizer *for* assigns objective Case to the subject, as in (25).

(25) a. it is $[_{AP}$ impossible $[_{CP}$ for $[_{IP}$ him to win]]]
b. $[_{NP}$ our desire $[_{CP}$ for $[_{IP}$ Bernie to succeed]]]

Like the grammatical formative *of* in NP, the complementizer *for* functions as a [–n] Case assigner. If this instance of Case assignment involves government between C and NP, then something more must be said about the government relation, because—since IP is taken to be the maximal phrasal projection of Infl—the subject NP does not m-command C. We can avoid this problem if only maximal phrasal projections of lexical heads count for determining m-command relations. Assuming that the infinitival *to* is a grammatical formative rather than a lexical head, infinitival IP does not count as a maximal phrasal projection for this purpose. Hence, in (25) C and NP would m-command each other and thus be in the appropriate government relation that allows Case assignment.[4]

The infinitival complements of adjectives and nouns as in (25) may also occur without the *for*-complementizer, but only when the infinitival subject is nonlexical. Thus, we have the following paradigm when *for* does not occur:

(26) a. it is $[_{AP}$ impossible $[_{CP}$ $[_{IP}$ PRO to win]]]
b. $[_{NP}$ our desire $[_{CP}$ PRO to succeed]]]

(27) a. *it is $[_{AP}$ impossible $[_{CP}$ $[_{IP}$ him to win]]]
b. *$[_{NP}$ our desire $[_{CP}$ $[_{IP}$ Bernie to succeed]]]

In (26) the subject of the infinitival is a base-generated nonlexical NP that is designated as PRO (chapter 6 provides further discussion of the structure and distribution of PRO). Because nonlexical NP is not subject to the Case filter, the structures in (26) are well formed with respect to Case. Similarly the lexical subjects of infinitival IP in (27) will not be marked for Case, thereby violating the Case filter.

As a lexical category C, the *for*-complementizer in infinitival constructions will be generated via optional lexical insertion. Because the lexicalization of the infinitival subject is independent of the introduction of the *for*-complementizer, the ill-formed structures in (28) will be generated by our rules.

(28) a. *it is $[_{AP}$ impossible $[_{CP}$ for $[_{IP}$ PRO to win]]]
b. *$[_{NP}$ our desire $[_{CP}$ for $[_{IP}$ PRO to succeed]]]

Following a proposal of Chomsky and Lasnik 1977, we can account for the ill-formedness of (28) in terms of the filter in (29).

(29) ***For-To* filter**
*[for - to]

This filter does not analyze the intervening empty subjects in (28)—that is, it analyzes only the phonetic string, which suggests that it functions as a condition on phonetic representations. It also covers structures in which the empty subject results from a movement operation, as in (30).

(30) *$[_{CP}$ $who_i$ $[_{IP}$ is it $[_{AP}$ impossible $[_{CP}$ $e_i$ for $[_{IP}$ $e_i$ to win]]]]]
(cf. it is impossible $[_{CP}$ for John to win])

(The trace in the embedded CP is required by the Subjacency filter of chapter 3.) Thus, the *For-To* filter does not analyze any empty subject, no matter how it is generated, so that the *for*-complementizer and the grammatical formative *to* are adjacent as required.

Could (30) also be a Case filter violation? This would require that movement apply prior to Case marking and further that a Case marking on a trace cannot be shared with the lexical antecedent of the trace. Evidence that this analysis is not tenable is given in (31).

(31) a. finite clause
i. $[_{CP}$ $who_i$ $[_{IP}$ is it likely $[_{CP}$ $e_i$ that $[_{IP}$John will recommend $e_i$]]]]
(cf. it is likely that John will recommend us)
ii. $[_{CP}$ $who_i$ $[_{IP}$ is it likely $[_{CP}$ $e_i$ $[_{IP}$ $e_i$ will recommend John]]]]
(cf. it is likely we will recommend John)

b. Infinitival

i. $[_{CP}$ who$_i$ $[_{IP}$ would it be odd $[_{CP}$ e$_i$ for $[_{IP}$ John to recommend e$_i$]]]]

(cf. it would be odd $[_{CP}$ for John to recommend us])

If (30) violated the Case filter (under the requisite assumptions), then so would the examples in (31). Given the grammaticality of these examples, we must assume either that Case marking applies before movement occurs or that the Case marking of a trace may be "inherited" by its lexical antecedent (often referred to in the literature as **case inheritance**). In section 5.2.2 we will examine evidence suggesting that Case marking may occur after movement—and therefore, Case inheritance is required to account for (31).

It is worth noting here that the infinitival example corresponding to (31b.i) constitutes a genuine Case filter violation.

(32) *$[_{CP}$ who$_i$ $[_{IP}$ would it be odd $[_{CP}$ e$_i$ $[_{IP}$ e$_i$ to recommend John]]]]
(cf. *it would be odd $[_{CP}$ us to recommend John])

Since neither the lexical NP *who* in the matrix CP nor its trace in the embedded IP is in a position to which Case is assigned, *who* has no way of being assigned Case, in violation of the Case filter.[5]

The analysis of the *for*-complementizer that we are considering is based on the assumption that complementizers are (optionally) lexically inserted. Once they are introduced into a derivation, they remain throughout the derivation (cf. note 5). Therefore, the *For-To* filter could apply immediately after the application of movement transformations (i.e., at S-structure).

We have seem that the *for*-complementizer must appear in certain constructions because of Case requirements imposed by the Case filter. Conversely, there are instances where the *for*-complementizer cannot occur with infinitival IP, as illustrated in (33).

(33) a. it is unclear $[_{CP}$ who$_i$ $[_{IP}$ PRO to believe e$_i$]]
b. it is unclear $[_{CP}$ whether $[_{IP}$ PRO to believe John]]
c. *it is unclear $[_{CP}$ for $[_{IP}$ us to believe the politicians]]

(33a–b) show that the predicate adjective *unclear* selects a [+Q] complementizer (recall the discussion of *wonder* in section 3.1). Therefore, (33c) violates the Principle of Lexical Satisfaction. This also accounts for the ill-formedness of examples containing both an overt *wh*-phrase and a *for*-complementizer in the same CP, as in (34).

(34) *it is unclear $[_{CP}$ who$_i$ for $[_{IP}$ Bill to believe e$_i$]]

However, it will not account for the ill-formedness of similar examples where the *for*-complementizer can otherwise occur.

(35) a. *it is impossible [$_{CP}$ who$_i$ for [$_{IP}$ Bill to annoy e$_i$]]
b. [$_{CP}$ who$_i$ is$_j$ [$_{IP}$ it e$_j$ impossible [$_{CP}$ e$_i$ for [$_{IP}$ Bill to annoy e$_i$]]]]

Since (35b) is well-formed, (35a) cannot be ruled out as a violation of the Principle of Lexical Satisfaction. Instead, it can be ruled out as a violation of SPEC-head agreement. The *for*-complementizer is marked [–Q] as required to explain (33c), whereas the *wh*-phrase *who* must be marked [+Q] as required for (33a). Thus, the SPEC of C and the head of C disagree with respect to the feature [±Q]. If (35a) constitutes a failure of SPEC-head agreement, then so does (34)—whatever else it violates. Note that this analysis generalizes to finite clauses as well and therefore rules out sentences containing CPs with both a *that*-complementizer and a wh-phrase, as in (36a).

(36) a. *Mary complained [$_{CP}$ who$_i$ that [$_{IP}$ she couldn't help e$_i$]]
b. [$_{CP}$ who$_i$ did$_j$ [$_{IP}$ Mary e$_j$ complain [$_{CP}$ e$_i$ that [$_{IP}$ she couldn't help e$_i$]]]]

As both (35b) and (36b) illustrate, the trace of a *wh*-phrase does not induce a failure of SPEC-head agreement and therefore presumably does not contain the lexical features that would produce the failure.[6]

---

**Exercise 5.3**
Give a complete phrase structure analysis for the infinitival complements in the following paradigms.

(i) a. they were uncertain who to visit
b. *they were uncertain for Bill to visit Mary
c. *they were uncertain who Bill to visit
d. *who were they uncertain for Bill to visit
e. *who were they uncertain to visit
f. ?who were they uncertain whether to visit
g. they were uncertain whether Bill to visit Mary

(ii) a. it was necessary for John to visit Mary
b. it was necessary to visit Mary
c. *it was necessary who to visit
d. *it was necessary whether to visit Mary
e. who was it necessary to visit

f. who was it necessary for Bill to visit
g. *it was necessary who Bill to visit

For each ill-formed example, state what principle of grammar is violated.

---

The examples considered above all involve sentential complements. Thus, the complementizer of the complement is selected by the verb or adjective that governs it. In relative clauses, the sentential forms are not complements of N-heads, and consequently the complementizer of the relative clause is not selected. Nonetheless, much of the previous analysis of sentential complements generalizes to relative clauses as well.

Since relative clauses do not subcategorize the nouns they modify and are not involved in selectional restrictions for nominals, a relative clause CP can be either finite or nonfinite, as (37) illustrates.

(37) a. $[_{NP}$ a clock $[_{CP}$ which$_i$ $[_{IP}$ Bernie can take apart $e_i]]]$
b. $[_{NP}$ a clock $[_{CP}$ that $[_{IP}$ Bernie can take apart $e_i]]]$
c. $[_{NP}$ a clock $[_{CP}$ for $[_{IP}$ Bernie to take apart $e_i]]]$
d. $[_{NP}$ a clock $[_{CP}$ $[_{IP}$ PRO to take apart $e_i]]]$

The SPEC-CP position of finite relative clauses contains either the relative pronoun (e.g., *which*) or the complementizer *that*, but never both.

(38) *$[_{NP}$ a clock $[_{CP}$ which$_i$ that $[_{IP}$ Bernie can take apart $e_i]]]$

The SPEC-head agreement analysis of (38) assumes there is a feature for which the complementizer and the relative pronoun have opposite values. In the infinitival relative, the *for*-complementizer must occur when the infinitival takes a lexical subject (to avoid a Case filter violation); alternatively, when the infinitival takes a PRO subject, neither the complementizer nor the *wh*-phrase may occur in CP. The absence of the complementizer is predictable from the *For-To* filter. Why the *wh*-phrase cannot occur in these constructions is so far unexplained. These properties will be discussed below.

The optionality of an overt relative pronoun can be accounted for in two different ways. The relative pronoun could be present at D-structure in all relative clauses and then deleted under the appropriate conditions. Alternatively, the missing relative pronoun could be interpreted as an empty NP that has moved into CP and binds a trace in IP. Given that we already have a base-generated null NP, namely PRO, it is not obvious that the second alternative can be prohibited in a principled way. And since we have not had to rely on any deletion operations thus far, let us put aside the first alternative for the time being.[7]

An infinitival relative with a lexical subject will have either an overt relative pronoun or a null NP in a grammatical function position at D-structure. Then, depending on whether or not the complementizer is lexicalized, four distinct S-structure representations could be derived, as illustrated in (39)–(40)—where the NPi in CP stands for a null NP and C stands for nonlexical C.

(39) a. *[$_{NP}$ a list [$_{CP}$ which$_i$ for [$_{IP}$ Bill to check e$_i$]]]
b. *[$_{NP}$ a list [$_{CP}$ which$_i$ C [$_{IP}$ Bill to check e$_i$]]]

(40) a. [$_{NP}$ a list [$_{CP}$ NP$_i$ for [$_{IP}$ Bill to check e$_i$]]]
b. *[$_{NP}$ a list [$_{CP}$ NP$_i$ C [$_{IP}$ Bill to check e$_i$]]]

To reconstruct the D-structures of these examples, we need only replace the trace in the embedded IP with the element that binds it. Both (b)-examples violate the Case filter because *Bill* is not Case-marked. (39a) constitutes a failure of SPEC-head agreement, as discussed earlier. (40a) is well formed—the only well-formed structure out of four possibilities.

The paradigm for infinitival relatives with a nonlexical (PRO) subject has somewhat different properties. Again there are four possible outcomes depending on whether the D-structure contains an overt relative pronoun (41) or a null NP (42).

(41) a. *[$_{NP}$ a list [$_{CP}$ which$_i$ for [$_{IP}$ PRO to check e$_i$]]]
b. *[$_{NP}$ a list [$_{CP}$ which$_i$ C [$_{IP}$ PRO to check e$_i$]]]

(42) a. *[$_{NP}$ a list [$_{CP}$ NP$_i$ for [$_{IP}$ PRO to check e$_i$]]]
b. [$_{NP}$ a list [$_{CP}$ NP$_i$ C [$_{IP}$ PRO to check e$_i$]]]

Because the subject in these constructions is nonlexical, the Case filter plays no role in this paradigm. Like (39a), (41a) constitutes a failure of SPEC-head agreement. (41b) remains unexplained. (42a) is excluded by the *For-To* filter. (42b) is well formed. This paradigm for infinitival relatives with null subjects shows that the only permissible pattern is for the infinitival VP to be phonetically adjacent to the N it modifies (that is, with no phonetic material intervening); recall that this is impossible for finite relative clauses. However, as the well-formed (43a) illustrates, this does not hold when the *wh*-phrase in CP is a PP. Only when CP contains a *wh*-NP, as in (43b), does the prohibition against phonetic material between infinitival IP and the N it modifies seem to hold.

(43) a. [$_{NP}$ a topic [$_{CP}$ [$_{PP:i}$ on which] [$_{IP}$ PRO to write a term paper e$_i$]]]
b. *[$_{NP}$ a topic [$_{CP}$ which$_i$ C [$_{IP}$ PRO to write a term paper on e$_i$]]]
c. [$_{NP}$ a topic [$_{CP}$ NP$_i$ C [$_{IP}$ PRO to write a term paper on e$_i$]]]

Whereas in the other paradigms for infinitival relatives there was only one well-formed outcome among four possible structures, the paradigm for movement out of a PP yields two well-formed outcomes. (43c) is equivalent to (42b); however, (43a) is unique to this paradigm. The relevant factor appears to be the NP status of the *wh*-phrase in CP and not the pied piping of non-*wh* material, as illustrated by the ungrammaticality of (44), where *book* has been pied-piped into CP.

(44) *[$_{NP}$ an author [$_{CP}$ [$_{NP:i}$ whose book] C [$_{IP}$ PRO to read $e_i$]]]

Further evidence suggests that perhaps it is (43a) that is odd since not all complex *wh*-PPs are well formed in these constructions, as (45) illustrates.

(45) *[$_{NP}$ an author [$_{CP}$ [$_{PP:i}$ about whose book] [$_{IP}$ PRO to write $e_i$]]]

Thus, as Chomsky (1981:chap. 2, n. 31) proposes, it may be that infinitival relatives with PRO subjects generally do not allow *wh*-phrases in CP. How this follows from a theory of grammar has yet to be explained.

One last infinitival relative paradigm remains to be examined: the one involving relativization of the subject position. The examples in (46) contain an overt relative pronoun and the ones in (47) do not.

(46) a. *[$_{NP}$ a man [$_{CP}$ who$_i$ for [$_{IP}$ $e_i$ to fix the sink]]]
b. *[$_{NP}$ a man [$_{CP}$ who$_i$ C [$_{IP}$ $e_i$ to fix the sink]]]

(47) a. *[$_{NP}$ a man [$_{CP}$ NP$_i$ for [$_{IP}$ $e_i$ to fix the sink]]]
b. [$_{NP}$ a man [$_{CP}$ NP$_i$ C [$_{IP}$ $e_i$ to fix the sink]]]
(cf. John found [$_{NP}$ a man to fix the sink])

(46a) violates the SPEC-head agreement requirement; (46b) violates the Case filter since *who* is not Case marked, and (47a) violates the *For-To* filter. (47b) is well formed. Once again, out of four possible structures only one is permissible.

Examples like those in (48) and (49) call into question the trace-binding analysis of (47b).

(48) a. *a man [$_{CP}$ who$_i$ [$_{IP}$ it was reported [$_{CP}$ $e_i$ C [$_{IP}$ $e_i$ to accept our offer]]]]
b. *a man [$_{CP}$ NP$_i$ [$_{IP}$ it was reported [$_{CP}$ $e_i$ C [$_{IP}$ $e_i$ to accept our offer]]]]

(49) a. a man [$_{CP}$ who$_i$ [$_{IP}$ it was reported [$_{CP}$ $e_i$ C [$_{IP}$ $e_i$ accepted our offer]]]]
b. a man [$_{CP}$ NP$_i$ [$_{IP}$ it was reported [$_{CP}$ $e_i$ C [$_{IP}$ $e_i$ accepted our offer]]]]

Although there is a sharp contrast in acceptability between (46b) and (47b), there is no contrast between similar structures given in (48)—both are equally unacceptable. In contrast to (48), both corresponding finite constructions in (49) seem perfectly acceptable.[8] (48a) is a clear Case filter violation—the lexical NP *who* is not marked for Case. Since (48b) does not involve a Caseless lexical NP, it ought to be well formed. One way to account for (48b) would be to extend the Case filter to the trace bound by an element in CP. Then the subject trace in (48b) would be Caseless, in contrast to the subject traces in (49), which would be marked nominative. However, since this analysis now excludes the apparently well-formed (47b), it is probably not the correct analysis for infinitival relatives.

An alternative to the trace-binding analysis of (47b) would be to take the infinitival subject to be PRO. (42b) and (43a,c) have already established that an infinitival relative can take a PRO subject. Suppose then that (47b) is reanalyzed as (50), and (48b) as (51).

(50) $[_{NP}$ a man $[_{CP}$ C $[_{IP}$ PRO to fix the sink]]]

(51) *$[_{NP}$ a man $[_{CP}$ $[_{IP}$ it was reported $[_{CP}$ C $[_{IP}$ PRO to accept our offer]]]]]

In (50) the PRO subject is anaphorically linked to the noun *man*. The relationship is local in that the head N *man* governs the clause containing the PRO subject. In contrast the head N in (51) does not govern the clause containing the PRO subject because several maximal phrasal projections intervene (at least IP and VP, if not the higher CP). If this is on the right track, then (51) is ruled out by a locality condition on PRO binding rather than by the Case filter.

So far the Case filter in conjunction with the *For-To* filter and SPEC-head agreement have provided a fairly straightforward account of the distribution of lexical NP subjects in infinitival constructions. The problematic cases concern infinitivals with nonlexical subjects. At this point we will leave our discussion of the latter constructions where it stands and return to the former.

### 5.2.2 Exceptional Case Marking

Lexical subjects of infinitivals can occur when the *for*-complementizer is absent as well as when it is present, as the paradigm for *want* illustrates.

(52) a. we very much want [for him to be there]
b. we very much want [him to be there]
c. we want very much [for him to be there]
d. *we want very much [him to be there]

(52a–b) show that *want* can take an infinitival complement with a lexical subject with or without the *for*-complementizer. However, when an adverb separates the verb from its complement, as in (52c–d), the complementizer must occur.

We can give a Case-theoretic analysis of the lexical infinitival subjects in (52) as follows. In (52a) *him* is assigned Case via the *for*-complementizer; in (52b) *him* must be assigned Case in some other way. Recall that under our revised definition of m-command (with respect to government) infinitival IP does not constitute a maximal phrasal projection because it is not projected from a lexical head. Therefore, infinitival IP will not be a **barrier** to government like VP, NP, AP, PP, CP, and finite IP. From this it follows that a verb that takes an infinitival complement may govern the infinitival subject provided there are no other barriers (e.g., CP, which is usually a barrier to government). If *want* governs *him* in (52b), then the infinitival subject can be assigned Case. When an adverb intervenes between the verb and the infinitival subject as in (52c–d), the subject NP and the Case-assigning V are not adjacent, and Case assignment is blocked. (52d) then violates the Case filter because there is no way to assign Case to the infinitival subject, whereas in (52c) *him* is assigned Case by the *for*-complementizer.

The kind of Case assignment illustrated in (52b) is referred to in the literature as **exceptional Case marking** (henceforth ECM), under the assumption that Case marking across a clause boundary is exceptional, and verbs allowing such infinitival complements are referred to as "ECM verbs." Given our analysis of government, however, there is nothing exceptional about a verb governing the subject of its infinitival complement. Furthermore, this government relation appears to hold across certain CP boundaries as well, as we see in (53).

(53) a. who does Adam want us to visit
b. $[_{CP}$ who$_i$ does$_j$ $[_{IP}$ Adam e$_j$ want $[_{CP}$ e$_i$ C $[_{IP}$ us to visit e$_i$]]]

(53) shows that ECM constructions cannot be accounted for under the hypothesis that the ECM verbs subcategorize for an IP (as opposed to a CP) complement. Given the Subjacency analysis of the boundedness of movement formulated in chapter 3, *who* in (53) must move through a CP of the complement of *want*—thus, (53a) must have the representation (53b) at S-structure, where the Subjacency filter applies.

If we assume that CP is always a barrier to government,[9] then to account for Case assignment of the infinitival subject by the matrix verb, (53a) will have another representation, shown in (54).

(54) $[_{CP}$ who$_i$ does$_j$ $[_{IP}$ Adam e$_j$ want $[_{IP}$ us to visit e$_i$]]]

(54) is derived from (53b) by a process of **CP-deletion**, which results in the elimination of both the trace in CP and the nonlexical C so that the

adjacency requirement on Case assignment is satisfied. Thus, the Case filter will apply at a different level of representation than the Subjacency filter. Since the latter applies at S-structure, the Case filter must apply at a later level of representation: S'-structure.

Although CP-deletion is optional for some verbs (e.g., *want* and *expect*), it is obligatory for others (e.g., *believe* and *consider*). Compare the paradigm for *believe* in (55) with the one for *want* in (52).

(55) a. *we sincerely believe [for him to be telling the truth]
b. we sincerely believe [him to be telling the truth]
c. *we believe sincerely [him to be telling the truth]
d. *we believe sincerely [for him to be telling the truth]

(52b) and (55b) respectively show that CP-deletion is optional for *want* (and other verbs of its type) but not optional for *believe* (and other verbs of its type). The fact that the *for*-complementizer never occurs with the infinitival complement of *believe* can be explained as the result of a lexical property—namely, obligatory CP-deletion. When the CP deletes, the complementizer (and any trace in SPEC-CP) must also delete. The differences between the two paradigms are thus predictable on the basis of a single difference in lexical properties.

---

**Exercise 5.4**
Recast the paradigms in (52) and (55) with interrogative pronouns rather than personal pronouns (e.g., *who* instead of *him*). Discuss the analysis of these paradigms as done above for (52) and (55).

---

The requirement that the infinitival complement of certain verbs must undergo CP-deletion instantiates an (idiosyncratic) lexical property of those verbs. The ability of other verbs to take infinitival complements that optionally undergo CP-deletion seems less like a lexical property of those verbs and more like the standard case in grammar—namely, that grammatical processes (in this case CP-deletion) apply optionally. If this is correct, then we need not stipulate anything further about verbs that allow both CP and CP-deletion complements.[10]

---

**Exercise 5.5**
Lasnik and Uriagareka 1988 propose that the underlying presence of *for* blocks CP-deletion. They assume that the *for*-complementizer is option-

ally inserted in D-structure and that the infinitival complements of *believe*-type verbs never occur with an underlying *for*-complementizer. Show how the paradigms (52) and (55) are analyzed under this set of assumptions. Can you think of any reason why the presence of a lexical complementizer would block CP-deletion?

---

### 5.2.3 Case Assignment via Movement

In the previous two sections we have seen that the lexical subject of an infinitival IP can be assigned Case in situ by an adjacent Case assigner (*for*-complementizer or V) under government. Another way lexical subjects of infinitival constructions may receive Case is by moving to a position that is governed by a Case assigner. Consider the paradigm for predicate adjectives that allow this option—where a is either IP or CP.

(56) a. he$_i$ is likely [$_\alpha$ e$_i$ to be telling the truth]
b. it is likely [$_{CP}$ (that) he is telling the truth]
c. *it is likely [$_{CP}$ for him to be telling the truth]
d. *it is likely [$_\alpha$ him to be telling the truth]
e. *he$_i$ is likely [$_\alpha$ e$_i$ is telling the truth]

Predicate adjectives like *likely* can take either infinitival or finite clause complements (as in (56a) and (56b) respectively). In (56a) the lexical subject *he* has moved from its D-structure position as subject of the complement IP to the main clause subject position. (Such a movement operation, often referred to as "subject raising" since it results in the raising of the subject to a higher position in the phrase–marker, is a form of **NP-movement**, which occurs when an NP moves from one grammatical function position to another.) In this position it is assigned nominative Case under the usual conditions. When *likely* takes an infinitival complement, the infinitival subject cannot remain in the complement clause, as illustrated by (56c) and (56d). (56d) would violate the Case filter under either interpretation of α. Even if the adjective *likely* governs the pronoun *him* in (56d), it does not assign objective Case to the pronoun since it is [+n] rather than [–n]. (56c), in contrast, would satisfy the Case filter since the lexical subject of the complement is in a Case marked position and is assigned objective Case by the *for*-complementizer. To explain the ungrammaticality of (56c), we would say that *likely* shares with *believe*-type verbs the lexical property of requiring obligatory CP-deletion. Then (56c) violates the Principle of Lexical Satisfaction.

Since (56c) demonstrates that the infinitival complement of *likely* undergoes CP-deletion obligatorily, then α in (56a) can only be IP. This is required independently by the Empty Category Principle (ECP) of chapter 3 (restated as (57)).

(57) **Empty Category Principle**
A trace must be lexically governed.

Given that a in (56a) is IP, the predicate adjective lexically governs the trace of the NP *he*. In this way the CP-deletion analysis of infinitivals is motivated by the ECP, as well as by the Case filter with respect to Case assignment.

---

**Exercise 5.6**
The ill-formedness of (56e) remains to be explained. Is there any way to force the analysis of α as CP or IP? What problems arise? Could (56e) under either interpretation of a be accounted for as a violation of the Case Uniqueness Principle?

---

In contrast to predicate adjectives that require obligatory CP-deletion, there is another class of predicate adjectives that prohibit CP-deletion. For this class, subject raising is not possible.[11]

(58) a. *he$_i$ is unusual [$_\alpha$ e$_i$ to be telling the truth]
b. it is unusual [$_{CP}$ (that) he is telling the truth]
c. it is unusual [$_{CP}$ for him to be telling the truth]
d. *it is unusual [$_\alpha$ him to be telling the truth]
e. *he$_i$ is unusual [$_\alpha$ e$_i$ is telling the truth]

(58a) is ruled out by the ECP if a is CP and CP is a barrier to government, but not if α is IP. To exclude the IP interpretation, we must postulate the nonapplication of CP-deletion as a lexical property of *unusual*-type predicate adjectives. Aside from this, the ill-formed examples in (58) will be accounted for in the same way as the corresponding examples in (56).

---

**Exercise 5.7**
Compare the analysis of the paradigms (56) and (58). Which properties of the two follow from general principles of grammar? Which properties do not, and therefore must be stipulated as idiosyncratic lexical properties?

---

Subject raising out of infinitival complements also occurs with passive participle counterparts of active verbs that allow CP-deletion. Consider the paradigm for *report,* another *believe*-type verb.

(59) a. active
    i. John reported [$_{IP}$ Rex to have finished his thesis]
    ii. *John reported [$_{CP}$ for [$_{IP}$ Rex to have finished his thesis]]
  b. passive
    i. Rex$_i$ was reported [$_{IP}$ e$_i$ to have finished his thesis]
    ii. *it was reported [$_{IP}$ Rex to have finished his thesis]
    iii. *it was reported [$_{CP}$ for Rex to have finished his thesis]
    iv. it was reported [$_{CP}$ that Rex had finished his thesis]

(59a) establishes that *report* requires obligatory CP-deletion. Assuming that this lexical property holds for the passive participle of *report* as well, we can see that (59b.iii) is ill formed because it violates the Principle of Lexical Satisfaction. (59b.ii) shows that the passive participle *reported* does not assign Case to the NP *Rex* even under adjacency and government—in contrast to the active form of the verb in (59a.i). Thus, the passive participle behaves like an adjective rather than a verb with respect to Case assignment.[12] The fact is that passive morphology generally blocks Case assignment.[13] Hypothesizing that passive morphology induces a category change from verb to adjective is one way of accounting for this, since adjectives are not Case assigners.

In both (56a) and (59b.i) the movement from the infinitival subject position to the matrix subject position is motivated solely on the basis of structural considerations—that is, Case assignment. Movement is from a Caseless position to a Case-marked position. This operation is simply an instance of "Substitute α for β," where α and β are NPs that bear grammatical functions with respect to their IPs—that is, both NP positions bear the grammatical function "subject." This is not a necessary condition for NP-movement since in simple passive constructions movement is from grammatical function object position to grammatical function subject position.[14]

(60) a. they$_i$ were arrested e$_i$ by the police
  b. *it was arrested them by the police

Assume that *it* in (60b) stands for the nonreferential pleonastic element that occurs in (56c), (58c–d), and (59b.iv). Then the reason why (60b) is ill formed is that the object NP *them* is not assigned Case, and the reason why the underlying object NP in a passive construction must move is so that it can be assigned Case.

**Exercise 5.8**

Movement between Caseless positions is also possible, but only as an intermediate step in a derivation. Show how this works by discussing the derivation of (i).

(i) they were expected to be reported to have been arrested
(cf. it was expected that it would be reported that they had been arrested)

Note too that an infinitival subject is not necessarily raised to the subject position of a finite clause. Give an analysis of the examples in (ii) and discuss how they demonstrate this.

(ii) a. it is impossible for Rex to have been reported to have finished his thesis.
b. we believe Rex to have been reported to have finished his thesis.

Be sure to include the relevant traces.

---

So far we have seen that a verb and its passive participle share the same lexical property with respect to CP-deletion. Thus, if a verb requires CP-deletion, so does its passive participle. What about the passive participles of verbs that allow optional CP-deletion? We might expect that an infinitival complement of the corresponding passive predicate would optionally allow CP-deletion. This appears to be false, since full *for*-NP-*to*-VP complements do not occur naturally with the passive participles of optional CP-deletion verbs like *expect* and *want*.[15]

(61) a. *expect*
i. Rex$_i$ is expected [$_{IP}$ e$_i$ to finish his thesis by September]
ii. *it is expected [$_{CP}$ for Rex to finish his thesis by September]
(cf. we expect Rex to finish his thesis by September)

b. *want*
i. *Rex$_i$ is wanted [$_{IP}$ e$_i$ to finish his thesis by September]
ii. *it is wanted [$_{CP}$ for Rex to finish his thesis by September]
(cf. we want Rex to finish his thesis by September)

One difference between the active and passive forms of *expect* and *want* is that the former, but not the latter, can act as a Case assigner. Suppose that the *for*-complementizer can assign Case to the subject of an infinitival complement only when its CP is governed by a Case-assigning element. Then the failure of optional CP-deletion verbs to take full *for*-NP-*to*-VP complements in the passive form would follow from a violation of the Case filter. This analysis relates the Case-assigning property of the *for*-complementizer to the more canonical Case-assigning elements. The contrast in acceptability between (61a.ii) and (62) appears to support this analysis.

(62) [$_{CP}$ for Rex to finish his thesis by September] is expected

It is assumed that the infinitival CP is in the government domain of AGR and that this licenses the assignment of Case to *Rex* by the *for*-complementizer.[16]

---

**Exercise 5.9**

As illustrated in (53), a CP-deletion construction that is the complement of an active verb allows for *wh*-movement from the infinitival to the matrix clause. This is also possible with the passive form of a verb that allows CP-deletion.

(i) what is Rex expected to finish

Discuss the analysis of (i) and give the appropriate representations for it at S-structure and S'-structure. Given that the Subjacency filter on S-structure requires that the *wh*-phrase move through the infinitival SPEC-CP and given that *wh*-movement is optional, what accounts for the ill-formedness of (ii)?

(ii) *Rex is expected what to finish

(ii) does not violate the Case filter. There will be two different accounts to discuss, depending on whether or not you assume that (ii) involves CP-deletion.

---

This completes our discussion of CP-deletion phenomena with respect to the analysis of Case and government.

## 5.3 Lexical Case Phenomena

In the preceding sections we have dealt exclusively with what can be called **configurational Case**—Case that is assigned on the basis of syntactic configuration. In languages with a richer morphological Case system than English, Case assignments often depend on the particular lexical item that assigns Case. Where the actual lexical item involved determines the Case which is assigned, rather than the syntactic configuration, we have an instance of **lexical Case**.

### 5.3.1 Russian

Russian is one language that exhibits an interesting range of lexical Case phenomena. In general, the object of a verb is Case-marked in the accusative on the basis of configuration. Yet there are some verbs that require their object to be marked in some other Case (e.g., dative, instrumental, or genitive). (63) provides one specific set of examples.[17]

(63) a. Configurational Case

| | | | | | |
|---|---|---|---|---|---|
| i. | Ivan | poceloval [$_{NP}$ | ètu | krasivuju | devušku] |
| | Ivan-NOM | kissed | that-ACC | pretty-ACC | girl-ACC |
| | 'Ivan kissed that pretty girl' | | | | |

b. Lexical Case

| | | | | | |
|---|---|---|---|---|---|
| i. | Ivan | pomog [$_{NP}$ | ètoj | krasivoj | devuške] |
| | Ivan-NOM | helped | that-DAT | pretty-DAT | girl-DAT |
| | 'Ivan helped that pretty girl' | | | | |
| ii. | *Ivan | pomog [$_{NP}$ | ètu | krasivuju | devušku] |
| | Ivan-NOM | helped | that-ACC | pretty-ACC | girl-ACC |
| iii. | *Ivan | pomog [$_{NP}$ | ètu | krasivuju | devuške] |
| | Ivan-NOM | helped | that-ACC | pretty-ACC | girl-DAT |

The predicate *pomog* requires that its object be marked for dative Case, rather than accusative, as illustrated in (63b.i) and (63b.ii). Note that this lexical requirement is not satisfied if the head of the object NP is marked dative but other constituents of the object are marked in the accusative, as shown in (63b.iii).

Let us assume that all Case, lexical as well as configurational, is assigned to Nmax and spreads (or "percolates") to the constituents of $N^{max}$. (To ensure that Case percolates from $N^{max}$ to its relevant constituents (i.e., the [+n] segments), we must reformulate the Case filter to prohibit any Caseless lexical [+n] segment with phonetic content.) Further, let us assume that the lexical Case requirement holds for the head of the NP as a selectional restriction. The lexical requirement that the object of *pomogs* must be marked with dative Case will be stated as a lexical feature (64).

(64) [+___ [DAT]]

The assignment of Case to $N^{max}$ in conjunction with the lexical requirement in (64) forces the percolation of lexical Case from $N^{max}$ to its head. We can assume that satisfaction of such lexical features follows from the more general Principle of Lexical Satisfaction, which guarantees that such properties will be met. As stated, this principle predicts that when there is a potential conflict between structural properties of a sentence and lexical properties of the words it contains, lexical properties take precedence.

Although Case splitting as in (63b.iii) is usually impossible, there is a construction in Russian involving NPs containing a numeral where Case splitting occurs when the NP is configurationally Case-marked, but not when it is lexically Case-marked.

(65) a. Configurational Case

| | | | | | |
|---|---|---|---|---|---|
| i. | Ivan | vidit | [$_{\text{NP}}$ pjat' | čërnyx | knig] |
| | Ivan-NOM | sees | five-ACC | black-GEN | books-GEN |
| ii. | *Ivan | vidit | [$_{\text{NP}}$ pjat' | čërnye | knigi] |
| | Ivan-NOM | sees | five-ACC | black-ACC | books-ACC |

b. Lexical Case[18]

| | | | | | |
|---|---|---|---|---|---|
| i. | Ivan | dovolen | [$_{\text{NP}}$ pjat'ju | čërnymi | knigami] |
| | Ivan-NOM (is) | satisfied-with | five-INST | black-INST | books-INST |
| ii. | *Ivan | dovolen | [$_{\text{NP}}$ pjat'ju | čërnyx | knig] |
| | Ivan-NOM (is) | satisfied-with | five-INST | black-GEN | books-GEN |
| iii. | *Ivan | dovolen | [$_{\text{NP}}$ pjat'ju | čërnye | knigami] |
| | Ivan-NOM (is) | satisfied-with | five-INST | black-GEN | books-INST |

For configurationally Case-marked NPs, the numeral occurs in the relevant configurational Case and the remaining constituents to the right occur in the genitive. Genitive marking for these constructions is obligatory, as the contrast between (65a.i) and (65a.ii) indicates. When an NP is lexically Case-marked, the words following the numeral cannot be marked genitive. Like NPs that do not contain numerals, such lexically Case-marked NPs must have all constituents in the government domain of the head marked in the required lexical Case. Thus, it is not possible for the numeral to occur in the required lexical Case and the remainder of the NP to be marked in the genitive, as in (65b.ii).

With the Case filter and the Principle of Lexical Satisfaction, we can predict that lexical Case will be assigned uniformly to all constituents within the government domain of the head of the lexically Case-marked NP. The fact that the numeral shows up in the expected configurational Case strongly supports the idea that $N^{max}$ receives the initial Case marking.

What remains unexplained is how genitive Case is assigned within a configurationally Case-marked NP containing a numeral (henceforth a "quantified NP," as they are designated in the literature)—in other words, how in a structure like (66) where the numeral Q is marked for a configurational Case (e.g., NOM or ACC), the lexical elements of N* are marked genitive.[19]

(66) [$_{\text{NP}}$ . . . Q N*]

If Q were actually the head of NP in (66), then the genitive marking on N* could be interpreted as the configurational adnominal genitive. The distribution of lexical Case within an NP shows, however, that the numeral is not the head of a maximal phrasal projection. If it were, then (65b.ii) should be well formed instead of (65b.i). Therefore, N* cannot be analyzed as an $N^{max}$ and cannot be assigned Case directly by the rule "Assign Case" (to $N^{max}$).

In Old Russian, though, numerals did function as lexical heads and so even the complements of lexically Case-marked numerals occurred in the genitive—in this instance a configurational Case since an NP that is a complement of an N is marked in the "adnominal genitive."

(67) a. Old Russian

| | | | | |
|---|---|---|---|---|
| i. | toi | pjati | krasivyx | devušek |
| | that-DAT/SG | five-DAT | pretty-GEN | girls-GEN |
| ii. | ta | pjat' | krasivyx | devušek |
| | that-NOM/SG | five-NOM | pretty-GEN | girls-GEN |

b. Modern Russian

| | | | | |
|---|---|---|---|---|
| i. | tem | pjati | krasivym | devuškam |
| | those-DAT/PL | five-DAT | pretty-DAT | girls-DAT |
| ii. | te | pjat' | krasivyx | devušek |
| | those-NOM/PL | five-NOM | pretty-GEN | girls-GEN |

As illustrated in (67a.ii) and (67b.ii), Old Russian and Modern Russian exhibit the same Case-marking pattern for NPs containing numerals where the numeral is marked with configurational Case. The striking difference between the two concerns the distribution of lexical Case. In Old Russian, as illustrated in (67a.i), lexical Case marking on the numeral satisfies the lexical property of a verb that assigns dative Case to its object. Presumably *krasiv- devuš-* cannot occur in the dative in Old Russian in the construction shown in this example. This would follow if the phrase constituted an NP in itself—in which case percolation of dative would be blocked. The fact that the percolation of lexical Case is not blocked in this way for NPs containing numerals in Modern Russian suggests that the phrase *krasiv- devuš-* is not analyzed as an NP. It seems then that some sort of reanalysis occurred between Old and Modern Russian.

As noted above, the precise mechanism for genitive Case marking in quantified NPs remains to be determined. Putting aside this question, let us turn to some consequences of the Principle of Lexical Satisfaction for Case assignment in Russian. As noted above, it follows from this principle that lexical properties take precedence over structural properties where the two might appear to conflict. Another consequence of the principle as applied to Case distribution is that whereas configurational Case may alternate with some other (nonlexical) Case—apparently in free variation—this alternation is prohibited for lexical Case.

Partitive genitives in Russian provide one striking example of this phenomenon.

(68) a. Configurational Case
   i. ja xoču vodu
      I want water-ACC
      'I want the water'
   ii. ja xoču vody
      I want water-GEN
      'I want some water'
   b. Lexical Case
   i. Ivan prišel [$_{PP}$ s vodoj]
      Ivan arrived with water-INST
      'Ivan arrived with water'
   ii. *Ivan prišel [$_{PP}$ s vody]
      Ivan arrived with water-GEN
      'Ivan arrived with some water'

In (68a) accusative Case alternates with genitive, and this alternation correlates with a difference in interpretation: 'the water' versus partitive 'some water'. In (68b), an instance of lexical Case assignment, the same Case is interpreted (68b.i) as either 'the water' or partitive 'some water'; however, as (68b.ii) shows, the genitive cannot be used in this lexical Case context to express the partitive meaning. Therefore, the the inability of an NP to occur in the partitive genitive Case in a lexical Case context cannot be attributed to semantic reasons.

The genitive of negation is another phenomenon in Russian involving alternations between configurational Case and genitive as well as changes in interpretation.[20] This phenomenon can involve either a subject or an object. The alternation for a subject is given in (69).

(69) a. pticy bol'še ne pojavljalis'
      birds-NOM any-more NEG appeared
      'the birds didn't come again'
   b. ptic bol'še ne pojavljalos'
      birds-GEN any-more NEG appeared
      'no birds came again'

The genitive Case marking on the subject in (69b) indicates that it is the subject that is being negated. When the genitive of negation does not occur, the scope of the negative is determined by its position in the sentence. Although this alternation is found with configurationally Case-marked objects as well (70a), it is prohibited for lexically Case-marked objects (70b).

(70) a. Configurational Case

i. oni ne odobrjajut inostrannye metody
they-NOM NEG approve-of foreign-ACC methods-ACC
'they do not approve of (the) foreign methods'

ii. oni ne odobrjajut inostrannyx metodov
they-NOM NEG approve-of foreign-GEN methods-GEN
'they approve of no foreign methods'

b. Lexical Case

i. oni ne podražajut inostrannym metodam
they-NOM NEG imitate foreign-DAT methods-DAT
'they do not imitate foreign methods'

ii. *oni ne podražajut inostrannyx metodov
they-NOM NEG imitate foreign-GEN methods-GEN

iii. oni ne upravljajut inostrannymi mašinami
they-NOM NEG drive foreign-INST cars-INST
'they do not drive foreign cars'

iv. *oni ne upravljajut inostrannyx mašin
they-NOM NEG drive foreign-GEN cars-GEN

The impossibility of using the genitive of negation in lexical Case contexts is quite general. Neither the object of *podražajut* 'imitate', which must be marked dative (as in (70b.i)) nor the object of *upravljajut* 'drive', which must be marked instrumental (as in (70b.iii)), may be marked with the genitive of negation. Again there appears to be no reason why this should be prohibited on semantic grounds. Instead, these facts follow from the Principle of Lexical Satisfaction.

The same situation holds in passive constructions. As in English, passivization in a simple sentence in Russian involves the assignment of nominative Case to the NP that corresponds to the accusative object in its active counterpart.

(71) a. Configurational Case

i. Ivan čitaet knigu
Ivan-NOM reads book-ACC
'Ivan is reading the book'

ii. kniga čitaetsja (Ivanom)
book-NOM is-being-read Ivan-INST
'the book is being read (by Ivan)'

iii. *knigu čitaetsja (Ivanom)
book-ACC is-being-read Ivan-INST

b. Lexical Case

i. rabotnik podražaet inostrannym metodam
worker-NOM copies foreign-DAT methods-DAT
'the worker is copying foreign methods'

ii. *inostrannye metody podražajutsja rabotnikom
foreign-NOM methods-NOM are-copied worker-INST
'foreign methods are being copied by the worker'

iii. *inostrannym metodam podražajutsja rabotnikom
foreign-DAT methods-DAT are-copied worker-INST

iv. *rabotnik podražajutsja inostrannym metodam
worker-NOM are-copied foreign-DAT methods-DAT

As illustrated in (71a.ii–iii), when a verb has passive morphology, its object must be marked nominative. That is, the object cannot appear in the accusative no matter where it occurs in the sentence. This shows that passive morphology in Russian, as in English, blocks Case assignment. This blocking also appears to affect lexical Case assignment. Thus, a verb like *podražaet* that assigns dative to its object has no corresponding grammatical passive—whether or not the NP corresponding to the object in the active occurs in the nominative (71b.ii) or the appropriate lexical Case (71b.iii–iv). If we assume that passive morphology blocks Case assignment generally, then (71b.ii) follows from the Principle of Lexical Satisfaction and (71b.iii–iv) follow from the blocking effect of passive morphology. This analysis accounts for the Russian facts, but will require some modification when we examine lexical Case in Icelandic.

### 5.3.2 Icelandic

Lexical Case in Icelandic differs from lexical Case in Russian in one crucial respect. In Icelandic, but not in Russian, subjects may be lexically Case-marked. (72) gives some indication of the range of possibilities for lexical Case marking in Icelandic.[21]

(72) a. Objects

i. Egill hjálpaði barninu
Egill-NOM helped the-child-DAT
'Egill helped the child'

ii. stúlkan beið mín
the girl-NOM awaited me-GEN
'the girl awaited me'

b. Subjects

i. verkjanna gætir ekki
the-pains-GEN is-noticeable not
'the pains are not noticeable'

ii. mér batnaði veikin
me-DAT recovered-from the-disease-NOM
'I recovered from the disease'

iii. mig vantar peninga
me-ACC lacks money-ACC
'I lack money'

These examples indicate that the following selectional restrictions are active in Icelandic.

(73) a. [+___[DAT]]
b. [+___[GEN]]
c. [+[GEN] ___ ]
d. [+[DAT] ___ ]
e. [+[ACC] ___ ]

Note in particular that ACC, which in object position is a configurational Case, may occur as a lexical Case in subject position. The occurrence of nominative Case in object position in (72b.ii) is not an instance of lexical Case marking, but rather some other process that takes place when the subject occurs in the dative. (See Andrews 1982 for further discussion.)

Not only does Icelandic allow lexically Case-marked subjects, but those subjects may undergo movement as in the following raising constructions:

(74) a. mig$_i$ virðist [$_{IP}$ e$_i$ vanta peninga]
me-ACC seems to-lack money-ACC

b. barninu$_i$ virðist [$_{IP}$ e$_i$ hafa batnað veikin]
the-child-DAT seems to-have recovered-from the-disease-NOM

c. verkjanna$_i$ virðist [$_{IP}$ e$_i$ ekki gæta]
the-pains-GEN seems not to-be-noticeable

In these raising constructions, where the complement subject is lexically Case-marked by the complement predicate, the raised subject must occur in the requisite lexical Case rather than the nominative. This shows that the Case marking, which occurs in the complement subject position, is distinct from Case licensing, which occurs in the subject position of the finite main clause. As in English, the verb for "seem" does not license Case for the subject position in its infinitival complement. Therefore, a lexical subject must move to a position that is Case-licensed. In contrast, the matrix subject of a finite clause is licensed for Case and thus the matrix subjects in (74) satisfy the licensing requirement as well as the lexical requirement of the complement predicates.

Exceptional Case marking in Icelandic exhibits a similar pattern.

(75) a. hann telur [$_{IP}$ mig vanta peninga]
he-NOM believes me-ACC to-lack money-ACC

b. hann telur [$_{IP}$ barninu hafa batnað veikin]
he-NOM believes the-child-DAT to-have recovered-from the-disease-NOM

c. hann telur [$_{IP}$ verkjanna ekki gæta]
he-NOM believes the-pains-GEN not to-be-noticeable

The subjects of the infinitival complements in (75) receive their specific lexical Case marking by virtue of being subjects of the different complement predicates; however, they are licensed to receive overt lexical Case by virtue of being governed by the matrix verb. In contrast to the raising constructions with *virðist*, where the lexical complement subjects must raise to the matrix subject position, these examples allow the lexical complement subjects to remain in situ. Therefore, we must assume that this position is Case licensed, in contrast to the infinitival complement subject position of a *seem*-type verb. As in the raising cases, the lexically Case-marked subjects are assigned Case by one element and licensed for bearing Case (or having a phonetic matrix) by another.

This phenomenon is also found in passive constructions where a lexically Case marked object shows up in subject position *bearing the requisite lexical Case.*[22] ["PPP" = passive past participle]

(76) a. barninu$_i$ var hjálpað e$_i$
the-child-DAT was helped-PPP

b. *barnið var hjálpað
the-child-NOM was helped-PPP

In (76a) *barninu* receives dative Case by virtue of being the underlying object of the passive predicate *hjálpað.* (76b) violates the Principle of Lexical Satisfaction.

Passive morphology also blocks Case licensing with respect to exceptional Case marking. Thus, compare (75) with (77), where the lexically Case-marked subject is forced to raise to the matrix subject position when the verb *telur* has passive morphology.

(77) a. mig$_i$ er talið [$_{IP}$ e$_i$ vanta peninga]
me-ACC is believed to-lack money-ACC

b. barninu$_i$ er talið [$_{IP}$ e$_i$ hafa batnað veikin]
the-child-DAT is believed to-have recovered-from the disease-NOM

c. verkjanna$_i$ er talið [$_{IP}$ e$_i$ ekki gæta]
the-pains-GEN is believed not to-be-noticeable

For Icelandic it is clear that a distinction between Case assignment and Case licensing is required to account for lexical Case phenomena where the lexically Case-marked NP occurs in a position that is not directly assigned lexical Case.

If, as Icelandic shows, lexical Case assignment is not blocked by passive morphology, then the reason why a lexically Case-marked NP cannot occur in object position in Russian (e.g., (71b.iv)) is not that passive morphology blocks the assignment of lexical Case, but that Case is not licensed in that position. The fact that a lexically Case-marked object cannot occur as the subject of a Russian passive construction would have to follow from the fact that in Russian subject position is not independently a position of lexical Case. This, then, would be our explanation for the ill-formedness of (71b.iii). In Icelandic on the other hand, lexical Case may occur indefinitely far away from the predicate that determines it because in that language subject position is also a position of lexical Case. If a lexically Case-marked NP can move at all, then subject to structural conditions it may move indefinitely far away, like any configurationally Case-marked NP.

In conclusion, it should be noted that lexical Case phenomena in Icelandic do not contradict the Case filter; rather, as illustrated in (78), they show that the Case filter does not account for the distribution of lexical NPs marked for lexical Case.

(78) a. Jóni batnaði veikin
John-DAT recovered-from the-disease-NOM

b. ég tel [$_{IP}$ Jóni hafa batnað veikin]
I believe John-DAT to-have recovered-from the-disease-NOM

c. [$_{CP}$ að [$_{IP}$ PRO batna veikin]] er venjulegt
PRO-DAT to-recover-from the-disease-NOM is usual

d. *[$_{CP}$ að [$_{IP}$ Jóni batna veikin]] er mikilvægt
John-DAT to-recover-from the-disease-NOM is important

As illustrated in (78a), the verb *batna* requires a dative subject. From (78c), it appears that PRO (suitably Case-marked dative) can satisfy this requirement even though it is not lexical. In fact, the lexically Case-marked NP in this position cannot be lexical, as (78d) shows. The subject of the infinitive in (78d) is not appropriately governed by a Case-assigning element, in contrast to (78b) where the dative NP is governed by the matrix verb *tel* (assuming the infinitival has undergone CP-deletion).

---

**Exercise 5.10**

The same situation holds under movement from object position, as illustrated in (i).

(i) a. ég tel [$_{IP}$Jóni$_i$ hafa verið hjálpað e$_i$]
I believe John-DAT to-have been helped

b. [$_{CP}$ að [$_{IP}$ PRO$_i$ vera hjálpað e$_i$] er erfitt
PRO-DAT to-be helped is difficult

c. *[$_{CP}$ (að) [$_{IP}$Jóni$_i$ vera hjálpað e$_i$] er erfitt
John-DAT to-be helped is difficult

Discuss the analysis of each example in detail and state how the paradigm demonstrates that PRO may satisfy a lexical Case requirement in a position where a lexical item would violate the Case filter.

---

**Exercise 5.11**

Given the representations in (74) and (77), it looks like the ECP also motivates CP-deletion in Icelandic. Discuss this in detail. Show how the paradigms in (75), (78), and exercise 5.10 support the CP-deletion analysis. The following example shows that when the infinitive does not lexically determine the Case of its subject, the subject occurs in the standard configurational Case.

(i) Jón telur mig hafa étið hárkarlinn
John-NOM believes me-ACC to have eaten the-shark-ACC

The same holds for the NP-movement cases, as in (ii).

(ii) a. þeir telja hanna (vera) sagða (vera) vinsæla
they-NOM believe her-ACC (to-be) said-ACC (to-be) popular-ACC

b. hún er talin (vera) sögð (vera) vinsæl
she-NOM is believed-NOM (to-be) said-NOM (to-be) popular-NOM

Discuss (ii) in light of the earlier analysis of English. Note that the passive participles are Case-marked. How does this support the analysis of passive participles as adjectives? Be sure to consider the feature analysis of categories (as presented in chapter 2).

---

We have seen in this chapter how notions of Case and government play an important role in determining the distribution of lexical NPs and some nonlexical NPs (trace and PRO) in a variety of constructions cross-linguistically. We have also seen that these basic notions interact with idiosyncratic lexical properties of verbs and adjectives to produce the paradigms found in various languages. The analysis of Case-related phenomena is one area in grammar that clearly demonstrates the interaction of lexical and structural properties of languages.

## Bibliographical Comments

The analysis of infinitivals presented in this chapter is based largely on Chomsky and Lasnik 1977, which provides an extensive and systematic treatment of the syntax of infinitivals—both sentential complements and infinitival relatives. It is a landmark paper dealing with the distribution of complementizers and the structure of clauses, as well as the psychological ramifications of the proposed analysis. The *For-To* filter was introduced there, along with several others (see note 6). Although much of its analysis has been superseded (see Chomsky 1980b for a critique of part of the analysis), in particular by Case theory, many of the problems and issues raised in the paper remain with us.

The analysis of the distribution of lexical subjects in infinitivals in terms of Case and government is due to Jean-Roger Vergnaud (letter to Chomsky and Lasnik dated April 17, 1977; see also Rouveret and Vergnaud 1980 and Vergnaud 1985). Vergnaud's Case theory is adapted and extended in Chomsky 1980b. For some criticism and extension of the "On Binding" theory, see Lasnik and Freidin 1981 and Kayne 1980. The analysis of lexical Case in terms of the Principle of Lexical Satisfaction was first proposed in Freidin and Babby 1984, based on Babby 1980a,b (which provide the first extensive application of Case theory to a language with a rich morphological Case system). This principle is extended to Icelandic in Freidin and Sprouse 1991, based on studies of Icelandic Case presented in Thráinsson 1979, Andrews 1976, 1982, and Zaenen, Maling, and Thráinsson 1985.

# 6
# The Analysis of Empty Categories

The theory of grammar we have been exploring involves two kinds of empty category: trace and PRO. A trace is an empty category that is produced when a constituent is moved to another position in a phrase marker. So far we have seen four varieties of trace:

(1) a. $[_{CP}$ $[_{NP:i}$ which report] will$_j$ $[_{IP}$ John $e_j$ read $e_i$ carefully]]
  b. $[_{IP}$ $[_{NP}$ a man $e_i$] $[_{VP}$ $[_{VP}$ is coming to dinner] $[_{CP:i}$ who$_j$ I want to meet $e_j$]]]
  c. Adam$_i$ is certain $[_{IP}$ $e_i$ to love your squid salad]

In (1a) $e_i$ is the trace of a *wh*-phrase (*which report*) and $e_j$ is the trace of the modal auxiliary (*will*); in (1b) $e_i$ is the trace of an extraposed CP (*who I want to meet*); and in (1c) $e_i$ is the trace of an NP (*Adam*). The other kind of empty category, PRO, is a base-generated empty NP that remains empty at S-structure.

(2) a. it is important [PRO to complete all the exercises]
  b. [PRO to complete all the exercises] is important
  c. John tried [PRO to leave on time]

In (2a–b) the reference of PRO cannot be linked to that of any other NP in IP, whereas in (2c) the reference of PRO is linked to the matrix subject and consequently is coreferential with the subject. The relationship between the matrix subject and PRO in (2c) is called **control**, and the NP that is interpreted as the antecedent of PRO is called the **controller**. For some verbs (e.g., *try*), a PRO subject in the infinitival complement is obligatory; for others (e.g., *want*), a PRO subject is optional. The latter case is illustrated in (3), where the infinitival may also occur with a lexical subject.

(3) a. Bernie wants $[_{IP}$ me to understand *Inside Macintosh*]
  b. Bernie wants $[_{\alpha}$ PRO to understand *Inside Macintosh*]

(We will return to the question of whether α in (5a) is a CP or an IP (or possibly either).) Where there is no overt controller, as in (2a–b), PRO is referred to as noncontrol PRO.

As preparation for attempting a formal analysis of the distribution of PRO, let us consider some basic facts about the distribution of PRO in various constructions.[1]

(4) a. *PRO will receive a message from Bill
b. *Mary will receive PRO from Bill
c. *Mary will receive a message from PRO

As these examples show, in finite clauses PRO cannot occur in any grammatical function position. As is easily verified, this is true for embedded finite clauses as well. In infinitival complements PRO can only occur in subject position, as illustrated in (5).

(5) a. we expect [$_{\alpha}$ PRO to receive a message from Bill]
b. *we expect [$_{IP}$ Mary to receive PRO from Bill]
c. *we expect [$_{IP}$ Mary to receive a book from PRO]

(4a) shows that PRO cannot be the subject of a finite IP; (4b) and (5b), that it cannot be the object of a verb; and (4c) and (5c), that it cannot be the object of a preposition. Since these are all Case-licensed positions, we can account for the ill-formedness of (4a–c) and (5b–c) simply by saying that PRO cannot occur in a Case-licensed position.[2] If this is the correct analysis, then α in (5a) could not be IP because then PRO would occur in a Case-licensed position, as illustrated in (6).

(6) we expect [$_{IP}$ her to receive a message from Bill]

The infinitival subject *her* is lexical and therefore must be Case-licensed to satisfy the Case Filter. In (6) Case licensing proceeds under government by the matrix verb *expect*, and therefore infinitival IP cannot be a barrier to government (as discussed in chapter 5).

If PRO cannot occur in a Case-licensed position, then CP must be a barrier to government even when it has no overt lexical head. This analysis correlates with the fact that the infinitival complement of a predicate that does not allow CP-deletion should take a PRO subject.

(7) a. [$_{IP}$ it is possible [$_{CP}$ for [$_{IP}$ John to write a book in a month]]]
b. *[$_{IP}$ John$_i$ is possible [$_{CP}$ C [$_{IP}$ e$_i$ to write a book in a month]]]
c. [$_{IP}$ it is possible [$_{CP}$ C [$_{IP}$ PRO to write a book in a month]]]

(7a) establishes that the predicate adjective *possible* takes a full infinitival CP complement. (7b) shows that CP-deletion is not possible. If it were, then the subject trace would be governed by the predicate adjective (since infinitival IP is not a barrier to government) and (7b) could not be analyzed as an ECP violation. This suggests that CP must be a barrier to government even when it contains no overt lexical head. Suppose that selection by a lexical head (e.g., V or A) identifies even a nonovert (i.e., not phonetically realized) C as lexical. Then a complement CP will be a barrier to government unless it undergoes CP-deletion.

Our analysis of the distribution of PRO in terms of Case licensing also correctly predicts that verbs that require obligatory CP-deletion cannot take infinitivals with PRO subjects or the *for*-complementizer.

(8) a. we believe [$_{IP}$ him to be telling the truth]
b. *we believe [$_{IP}$ PRO to be telling the truth]
c. *we believe (sincerely) [$_{CP}$ for [$_{IP}$ him to be telling the truth]]

PRO in (8b) would be in a Case-licensed position just as *him* is in (8a). Note, however, that calling *believe* an obligatory CP-deletion verb is inaccurate for finite clause complements since (9), with an overt complementizer, is perfectly grammatical.

(9) we believe [$_{CP}$ that he is telling the truth]

Limiting CP-deletion to infinitivals only would be highly stipulative and ad hoc for a rule of grammar. Alternatively, the absence of the *for*-complementizer (see (8c)) would follow if *believe* selected infinitival *to* rather than infinitival C. Then there could be no CP-deletion in the infinitival complement of *believe* since it could never be realized as a CP.[3]

---

**Exercise 6.1**

Consider the possibility that a PRO in D-structure may be moved to another NP position, leaving behind a trace. Decide whether the following examples demonstrate this:

(i) a. John wants Mary to appear to be happy
b. John expects Mary to appear to be happy

(ii) a. John wants to appear to be happy
b. John expects to be promoted

In the derivation of (i.a–b), the movement of the lexical NP *Mary* is required by Case theory. What, if anything, would force the similar movement of PRO?

---

The analysis of the the paradigms discussed above reveals a fundamental complementarity between trace and PRO: (i) a trace must be governed by an overt lexical head, but (ii) a PRO cannot be governed by an overt lexical head. The qualification "by an overt lexical head" in (i) and (ii) is necessary to account for (7b) and (7c). If nonovert C in (7b) counted as a lexical governor for the infinitival complement subject trace, the deviance of the example would not follow from the ECP. Nonetheless, a nonovert C must count as a lexical head so that CP will be a barrier to government in (7c). Therefore, C will govern PRO, but will not Case-license it. (i) follows from the ECP with the appropriate revision concerning overt lexical heads. (ii), however, is just a stipulation at this point. (For a discussion of how (ii) might be derived from principles of grammar, see section 8.3.3.)

---

**Exercise 6.2**

It is always good to test the strength of an analysis by trying to work out alternative analyses. In this spirit, consider an alternative approach to the distribution of PRO. Suppose that PRO can be lexically governed, but not minimally governed by a lexical head. Interpret this to mean that the closest governor cannot be a lexical head. In a structure like (i), PRO would be governed by both V and Infl, but minimally governed by Infl.

(i). . . V $[_{IP}$ PRO $[_{Infl}$ to] VP] . . .

It follows from this proposal that PRO can only occur as the subject of an infinitival construction. What problems arise now, given the examples discussed so far? Can you propose any solutions to these problems? Must we continue to analyze CP as a barrier to government when it contains no overt complementizer?

---

Returning to the distribution of traces, we note that a trace in object position is always governed by a lexical head and therefore always satisfies the ECP. The distribution of subject trace in finite clauses is somewhat more complicated. There are two distinct cases to consider: NP-trace and *wh*-trace. NP-trace is generally excluded, whereas *wh*-trace is allowed unless it is adjacent to an overt complementizer (compare (10) with (11)).

(10) a. *Mary$_i$ is expected $[_{CP}$ that $[_{IP}$ e$_i$ will win]]
 b. *Mary$_i$ is expected $[_{CP}$ C $[_{IP}$ e$_i$ will win]

(11) a. *$[_{CP}$ who$_i$ do$_j$ $[_{IP}$ you e$_j$ think $[_{CP}$ e$_i$ that $[_{IP}$ e$_i$ likes Mary]]]]
 b. $[_{CP}$ who$_i$ do$_j$ $[_{IP}$ you e$_j$ think $[_{CP}$ e$_i$ C $[_{IP}$ e$_i$ likes Mary]]]]

In many analyses (see Chomsky 1981, 1986a) the ill-formed examples in (10)–(11) are considered to be ECP violations. This assumes that the subject trace of a finite clause is not lexically governed. The analysis depends, of course, on how lexical government is characterized. Given our analysis of the auxiliary system in chapter 4, a finite Infl containing an auxiliary verb should count as a lexical head. Thus, the subject traces in (10) are lexically governed under our analysis. If we assumed that Infl can be realized as a lexical head via Affix-Hopping onto the main verb, then the subject traces in (11) would be lexically governed as well. If we included "directionality" in the analysis of government, as has sometimes been proposed—in other words, if we claimed that head government in English is always rightward—then all the traces in (10)–(11) would violate the ECP. Although this interpretation of the ECP correctly predicts that a subject trace in the presence of an adjacent complementizer (e.g., (10a) and (11a)) yields an ill-formed sentence, it incorrectly rules out (11b)—showing that the ECP must be modified to account for the distribution of subject traces in finite clauses.

In the remainder of this chapter we will address these and other problems regarding the distribution of trace and PRO. In section 6.1 we will pursue the ECP analysis for subject traces in finite clauses. We will be dealing with two sets of constructions that have somewhat different properties: main clauses and sentential complements on the one hand versus relative clauses and cleft constructions on the other. In section 6.2 we will examine the distribution of traces from some considerations about predicate-argument relations in sentences. In section 6.3 we will look at an alternative account of NP-trace based on conditions on trace binding and how these conditions overlap with other conditions we have been considering. In section 6.4 we will return to the PRO/trace distinction.

## 6.1 Subject Traces in Finite Clauses

The ECP analysis is based on the assumption that the subject of a finite clause is not a lexically governed position. Thus, the ECP alone accounts for the impossibility of extracting plain NPs out of subject position as illustrated in (10). However, the movement of *wh*-phrases poses a problem for the formulation of the ECP which states simply that a trace must be lexically governed. (12) exemplifies the simplest case where this problem arises.

(12) $[_{CP}$ who$_i$ $[_{IP}$ e$_i$ left]]

(12) would be improperly ruled out by the ECP since the trace in IP is not lexically governed. This can be prevented by extending the ECP as a disjunctive condition (13).

(13) **Empty Category Principle** (revised)
A trace must be
a. lexically governed *or*
b. locally bound from CP.

A trace meeting either of these conditions is said to be **properly governed** in the terminology of Chomsky 1981. Recall that a trace is bound when it is coindexed with a c-commanding element. It is locally bound when the structural distance between the trace and its closest binder crosses no more than one IP. Thus, the subject trace in (12) is locally bound since the binding crosses only one IP. Under this definition, CP-to-CP movement will result in local binding if the movement obeys Subjacency. Part (b) of this revised formulation is usually referred to as "antecedent government"—though an element in CP does not "govern" an adjacent subject in the strict sense of the term, which is limited to relations between a head of a phrasal projection and the constituents of the projection (see (86) in chapter 2).[4] The subject trace in (12) is locally bound and therefore does not violate the ECP.[5]

Local binding effects also show up in more complicated cases—for example, (11b), where the subject trace is bound by an adjacent trace in CP (instead of a *wh*-phase as in (12)).

(11) b. $[_{CP}$ who$_i$ do$_j$ $[_{IP}$ you e$_j$ think $[_{CP}$ e$_i$ C $[_{IP}$ e$_i$ likes Mary]]]]

Note that the trace in CP also satisfies the ECP in (13) since it is locally bound to the *wh*-phrase in the external CP.[6] When the complementizer is adjacent to the subject trace, as in (11a), an ill-formed structure results.

(11) a. *$[_{CP}$ who$_i$ do$_j$ $[_{IP}$ you e$_j$ think $[_{CP}$ e$_i$ that $[_{IP}$ e$_i$ likes Mary]]]]

Whatever is wrong with such structures, it cannot be simply that the embedded CP contains both a *wh*-trace and an overt complementizer since the corresponding object movement construction (14) is well formed and has exactly the same CP structure.

(14) $[_{CP}$ who$_i$ do$_j$ $[_{IP}$ you e$_j$ think $[_{CP}$ e$_i$ that $[_{IP}$ Mary likes e$_i$]]]]

The problem with (11a) results from the cooccurrence of the lexical complementizer with a *subject* trace.[7] Following standard practice, we can refer to the problem with (11a) as a ***that*-trace effect**.

**Exercise 6.3**

The so-called *that*-trace effects may be extended to complementizers in general under the heading of complementizer trace effects. In English this will include the complementizer *for*, thereby relating the *For-To* Filter discussed in chapter 5 to the ECP. Discuss the following examples in terms of the ECP.

(i) a. *[$_{IP}$ John$_i$ is expected [$_{CP}$ for [$_{IP}$ e$_i$ to win]]]
 b. *[$_{CP}$ who$_i$ do$_j$ [$_{IP}$ you e$_j$ want very much [$_{CP}$ e$_i$ for [$_{IP}$ e$_i$ to win]]]]

Although *For-To* Filter violations involving movement can be subsumed under the ECP, violations of the filter involving PRO subjects cannot. Thus, if we are to eliminate the *For-To* Filter entirely, some further explanation is needed to account for examples like (ii).

ii) *Bernie wants [$_{CP}$ for [$_{IP}$ PRO to take apart the computer]]

Would a prohibition against Case-marked PRO provide a solution to this problem?

If the ECP alone accounts for the *that*-trace effect, then subject trace in constructions like (11a) should be neither lexically governed nor locally bound. However, the trace in SPEC-CP c-commands the subject trace in IP and the binding is local—in fact, just as local as the binding between the subject trace and the embedded CP trace in (11b). On the other hand, the presence of the lexical complementizer appears to block antecedent government. Therefore, the subject trace would be in violation of the ECP, in which case the ECP analysis would cover the *that*-trace effect.[8]

With respect to empty subject phenomena, the properties of relative clauses and cleft constructions differ somewhat from those of sentential complements. For example, both constructions allow a *that*-complementizer followed by a subject trace in single clauses and therefore do not show *that*-trace effects. The relative clause paradigm is given in (15).

(15) Relative clause
 a. the student [$_{CP}$ who$_i$ C [$_{IP}$ e$_i$ knows John]]
 b. the student [$_{CP}$ NP$_i$ that [$_{IP}$ e$_i$ knows John]]
 c. *the student [$_{CP}$ NP$_i$ C [$_{IP}$ e$_i$ knows John]]
 d. *the student [$_{CP}$ who$_i$ that [$_{IP}$ e$_i$ knows John]]

In single-clause finite relatives with subject relativization there are two viable options for CP: either the relative pronoun is lexicalized (15a) or the complementizer is lexicalized (15b). Having both a lexical relative pronoun and a lexical complementizer in CP (15d) violates SPEC-head agreement, as in sentential complements. Having neither a relative pronoun nor a lexical complementizer in CP (15c) is also prohibited. This holds for subject relativization only; the corresponding structure for object relativization, (16), is well formed.

(16) the student $[_{CP}$ $NP_i$ C $[_{IP}$ John knows $e_i]]$

The contrast between the ill-formed (15c) and the well-formed (16) constitutes a subject-object asymmetry for traces. The asymmetry is captured to some extent by the ECP since object traces are always lexically governed, whereas subject traces in finite clauses never are. From this perspective, (15c) could be characterized as yet another ECP effect, as will be discussed below.

What needs to be explained are (i) why *that*-trace effects do not occur in single-clause relatives (that is, why (15b) is well formed), and (ii) what prohibits a single-clause relative from having both a null NP and a null complementizer in CP (in contrast to sentential complements such as (11b), where this is allowed). A complete account of the *that*-trace effect should explain why these structures are ill formed in sentential complements, but allowed in single-clause relatives.[9]

Consider an ECP analysis of the paradigm in (15). In (15a) the relative pronoun *who* locally binds the subject trace so that this trace satisfies the ECP. Given that constructions like (15b) do not violate the ECP, then the subject trace in these constructions also meets the condition for antecedent government—that is, it is locally bound. Moreover, if the null NP in CP of (15b) is the binder for antecedent government, then we should expect a *that*-trace effect as in (11a). Since there is none, a different analysis is required. The alternative is to designate the complementizer *that* as the antecedent governor, which is plausible to the extent that the complementizer in relative clauses (as opposed to sentential complements) seems to have some pronominal flavor.[10] This means that the null NP cannot act as the antecedent governor of the subject trace. As a result, (15c) violates the ECP.

When relativization occurs out of a sentential complement, *that*-trace effects show up. There are six possible structures to consider—ignoring the two where both the relative pronoun and the complementizer are lexicalized in the outermost CP in violation of SPEC-head agreement.

(17) a. the student $[_{CP}$ $who_i$ C $[_{IP}$ you think $[_{CP}$ $e_i$ C $[_{IP}$ $e_i$ knows John]]]]
b. the student $[_{CP}$ $NP_i$ that $[_{IP}$ you think $[_{CP}$ $e_i$ C $[_{IP}$ $e_i$ knows John]]]]
c. the student $[_{CP}$ $NP_i$ C $[_{IP}$ you think $[_{CP}$ $e_i$ C $[_{IP}$ $e_i$ knows John]]]]

d. *the student [$_{CP}$ who$_i$ C [$_{IP}$ you think [$_{CP}$ e$_i$ that [$_{IP}$ e$_i$ knows John]]]]
e. *the student [$_{CP}$ NP$_i$ that [$_{IP}$ you think [$_{CP}$ e$_i$ that [$_{IP}$ e$_i$ knows John]]]]
f. *the student [$_{CP}$ NP$_i$ C [$_{IP}$ you think [$_{CP}$ e$_i$ that [$_{IP}$ e$_i$ knows John]]]]

The complement CP can contain either a trace plus the null complementizer (17a–c) or a trace plus the complementizer *that* (17d–f). The latter option produces a *that*-trace effect, so (17d–f) violate the ECP. In the outermost CP three structures are possible: (i) a relative pronoun plus a null complementizer (17a,d), (ii) a null NP plus the complementizer *that* (17b,e), or (iii) a null NP plus a null complementizer (17c,f). These three structures are all permissible when the internal CP does not contain a *that*-trace violation. Thus, (17c) patterns like (16) and not (15c) even though it is an example of subject relativization like (15c) and not object relativization like (16).

(17) shows that when relativization occurs out of a sentential complement, subject ECP violations occur. The *that*-trace effects in (17d–f) violate the ECP for the reason discussed above. The problem that remains is to explain why the subject trace in (17a–c) does not violate the ECP on a par with (15c). A comparison of the examples shows that, unlike the null NP, a trace in SPEC-CP can antecedent-govern a subject trace. Note, however, that if intermediate traces in CP must satisfy the ECP, then the null NP in (17b–c) must be able to antecedent-govern the trace in CP. Why the null NP cannot antecedent-govern a trace in a grammatical function position (e.g., subject) remains to be determined.

The same properties also show up in cleft constructions, which are complex sentences whose matrix subject is a nonreferential *it* and whose matrix verb is some form of the copula, *be*. The VP of this construction consists of the copula followed by an NP and a CP that contains a gap in a grammatical function position.[11] The relation between the NP and CP can be characterized as topic-comment. The relevant paradigm is given in (18).

(18) Cleft constructions
a. it was Mary [$_{CP}$ who$_i$ C [$_{IP}$ e$_i$ recommended *Perelandra*]]
b. it was Mary [$_{CP}$ NP$_i$ that [$_{IP}$ e$_i$ recommended *Perelandra*]]
c. *it was Mary [$_{CP}$ NP$_i$ C [$_{IP}$ e$_i$ recommended *Perelandra*]]
d. *it was Mary [$_{CP}$ who$_i$ that [$_{IP}$ e$_i$ recommended *Perelandra*]]

As we can see by comparing (15) and (18), the properties of embedded CPs in a single clause construction have identical properties to single clause relatives. In the case of complex embedded clauses, we again find perfect parallelism with complex clause relatives.

(19) a. it was Mary [$_{CP}$ who$_i$ C [$_{IP}$ he thought [$_{CP}$ e$_i$ C [$_{IP}$ e$_i$ recommended *Perelandra*]]]]
b. it was Mary [$_{CP}$ NP$_i$ that [$_{IP}$ he thought [$_{CP}$ e$_i$ C [$_{IP}$ e$_i$ recommended *Perelandra*]]]]
c. it was Mary [$_{CP}$ NP$_i$ C [$_{IP}$ he thought [$_{CP}$ e$_i$ C [$_{IP}$ e$_i$ recommended *Perelandra*]]]]
d. *it was Mary [$_{CP}$ who$_i$ C [$_{IP}$ he thought [$_{CP}$ e$_i$ that [$_{IP}$ e$_i$ recommended *Perelandra*]]]]
e. *it was Mary [$_{CP}$ NP$_i$ that [$_{IP}$ he thought [$_{CP}$ e$_i$ that [$_{IP}$ e$_i$ recommended *Perelandra*]]]]
f. *it was Mary [$_{CP}$ NP$_i$ C [$_{IP}$ he thought [$_{CP}$ e$_i$ that [$_{IP}$ e$_i$ recommended *Perelandra*]]]]

(19a–c) are well-formed (cf. (17a–c)), whereas (19d–f) manifest *that*-trace effects and are deviant (cf. (17d–f)).

---

**Exercise 6.4**
Show how the analysis of cleft constructions in (18) relates to the analysis of relative clauses in (15).

---

Although (19c) is well formed, there is an alternative analysis of the sentence *It was Mary he thought recommended Perelandra* that is not. If the string h*e thought* is taken to be a parenthetical phrase as indicated in (20), then the resulting structure should have the same properties as (18c), which does violate the ECP.

(20) *it was Mary, he thought, recommended *Perelandra*

Given this, speaker judgments regarding the string *It was Mary he thought recommended Perelandra* could vary depending on which structure a given speaker assigns to the string.

---

**Exercise 6.5**
The same problem arises with respect to (18d). Show how this works by giving the alternative analysis and discussing it.

---

Thus far our investigation of relative clauses and cleft constructions shows that a complementizer followed by a subject trace can occur when the embedded CP is not a sentential complement. For English we have proposed that the complementizer binds the adjacent empty subject in relative clauses and cleft constructions, an arrangement that satisfies the ECP. It appears that this analysis can be extended to relative clauses in other languages.

In Norwegian, for example, where complementizer-trace configurations are prohibited in sentential complements, as in (21a), a complementizer-trace sequence can occur in a relative clause, as in (21b). ((21a) is from Nordgård 1986; it is cited there as being grammatical for some dialects, though impossible for the standard language. (21b–d) are from Taraldsen 1986.)

(21) a. *[$_{CP}$hvem$_i$ [$_{IP}$ du tror [$_{CP}$ som [$_{IP}$ e$_i$ har vært her]]]]
who you believe that has been here
b. vi kjenner [$_{NP}$ den mannen [$_{CP:i}$ Ø som] [$_{IP}$e$_i$ snakker med Marit]]
we know the man that is-talking with Mary
c. *vi kjenner [$_{NP}$den mannen [$_{CP}$ Ø [$_{IP}$ e$_i$ snakker med Marit ]]
we know the man is-talking with Mary
d. vi kjenner den mannen [$_{CP}$ Ø (som) [$_{IP}$ Marit snakker med e$_i$]]
we know the man (that) Mary is-talking with

(21c) shows that Norwegian, like English, does not allow relative clauses with empty subjects and no complementizer. (21d) demonstrates that relative clause complementizer is optional when trace is in a nonsubject position, as in English.[12] Thus, English and Norwegian relative clauses appear to have similar properties with respect to empty subjects—properties that can be accounted for by the same grammatical mechanisms.

Like Norwegian, French exhibits a complementizer alternation with respect to relative clauses.

(22) a. l' homme que Marie aime
the man that Mary loves
b. *l' homme que aime Marie
the man that loves Mary
c. l'homme qui aime Marie

In French, *que* is the usual complementizer for finite clauses—both sentential complements and relative clauses (see (22a) and (23)). Unlike English, however, French exhibits complementizer-trace phenomena quite generally with respect to both sentential complements and relative clauses. Data for sentential complements are provided in (23).

(23) a. i. qui est-il évident que Marie aime bien
ii. qui$_i$ est-il évident [$_{CP}$ e$_i$ que [$_{IP}$ Marie aime e$_i$ bien]]
who is it evident that Marie likes well

b. i. *qui crois-tu que est parti
   ii. $qui_i$ crois-tu [$_{CP}$ $e_i$ que [$_{IP}$ $e_i$ est parti]]
   who do you believe that left

c. i. qui crois-tu qui est parti
   ii. $qui_i$ crois-tu [$_{CP}$ $e_i$ qui [$_{IP}$ $e_i$ est parti]]
   who do you believe that left

As (22a) and (23a) illustrate, the complementizer *que* occurs when a nonsubject is extracted. However, as (22b) and (23b) show, when a subject is extracted and the complementizer *que* occurs, a complementizer trace violation results. What is distinct about the French data is that when *qui* is substituted for the complementizer *que* (as in (22c) and (23c)), no complementizer trace violation results. In French, the ability of a complementizer to antecedent-govern an adjacent subject trace somehow depends on the form of the complementizer—that is, the complementizer *que* cannot bind an adjacent subject trace, whereas the complementizer *qui* can.

As is true for many syntactic constructions, no definitive account exists for these relative clause phenomena. The purpose of this discussion is simply to suggest that cross-linguistically, relative clause constructions have somewhat special properties with respect to finite clause subjects. Exactly how these properties are to be accommodated in terms of language particular mechanisms—and indeed with respect to general principles of grammar—is still an open question.

Before we leave this topic, it is also worth noting that complementizer-trace phenomena vary cross-linguistically as well. In Spanish, for example, complementizer-trace sequences are possible even in sentential complements; compare (24) with its English counterpart (25). (The following example is adapted from Chomsky and Lasnik 1977.)

(24) a. quién tú creiste que vio a Juan
   b. [$_{CP}$ $quién_i$ [$_{IP}$ tú creiste [$_{CP}$ ($e_i$) que [$_{IP}$ $e_i$ vio a Juan]]]]
   who you thought that saw John

(25) *who did you think that saw John

One possible explanation for this difference involves the fact that Spanish, unlike English, permits subject pronouns to occur optionally, as illustrated in (26).

(26) a. yo creo que él partió
   I think that he left
   b. creo que partió

The missing subject pronouns are recoverable from the verbal morphology which indicates that the subject of the matrix clause is first person singular and that the subject of the complement is third person singular. Languages with such properties are referred to as **pro-drop languages**. If the missing subject pronouns result from actual deletions, and not merely from optional lexical insertion, then we can explain why examples like (24a) are not ECP violations in Spanish. After deletion, the representation of (24a) will be (27) rather than (24b).

(27) [$_{CP}$ quién$_i$ [$_{IP}$ tú creiste [$_{CP}$ Ø que [$_{IP}$ Ø vio a Juan]]]]

If the ECP applies after the deletion of the subject pronoun (or trace subject in (24b)), then representation (27) of (24a) will no longer contain the relevant trace and therefore will not violate the ECP.[13] The prediction, made by Perlmutter (1971) for a different theoretical framework, is that no pro-drop language should display *that*-trace effects.

## 6.2 Empty Categories and Thematic Structure

In this section we will investigate further principles of trace binding that are needed in addition to the ECP and Subjacency. Although the ECP accounts for most problems involving the binding of subject traces, it does not cover improper trace binding relations involving objects. Consider (28), derived via NP-movement from the underlying structure (29), where NP is a base-generated empty category.[14]

(28) *it is odd [$_{CP}$ C [$_{IP}$ John$_i$ to find e$_i$ in a friendly mood]]

(29) it is odd [$_{CP}$ C [$_{IP}$ NP to find John in a friendly mood]]

Given that all phrase structure rules are optional, there is no particular difficulty in base generating an empty underlying subject as in (29). In fact, we require this option for the derivations of both the simple passive construction (e.g., (30a)) and the raising construction (e.g., (30b)).

(30) a. Seymour$_i$ was [$_{VP}$ arrested e$_i$ in Shanghai]
b. Roger$_i$ seems [$_{IP}$ e$_i$ to be enjoying his new job]

Thus, the rules of grammar as formulated so far will have to be allowed to base-generate structures like (29) and produce derived structures like (28).

As it stands, (28) does not violate any conditions we have examined up to this point. Since the trace in object position is properly governed by V (*like*), the ECP does not explain the ill-formedness of (28). Since the trace binding is "local" (in the sense of "subjacent"), Subjacency does not explain it either. And finally, the Case Filter is inoperative here since the surface subject *John* is marked for Case once and once only by virtue of its trace in object position. Notice that in English, the viable examples of Case inheritance via the binding of a trace in a Case-marked position are generally restricted to *wh*-movements. Nonetheless, seems to be no principled reason to exclude Case inheritance between a lexical NP and its trace when both occupy grammatical function positions (as in (28)). Therefore, under the set of assumptions we have adopted, the ill-formedness of constructions like (28) must fall outside the domain of bounding theory, Case theory, and the theory of government (as embodied in the ECP).

To understand what is wrong with (28), it is useful to compare it with well-formed examples of NP-movement like (30a) and (30b). There are two differences to consider. First, in the well-formed constructions the trace occupies a Caseless position and its lexical antecedent occupies a Case-marked position, whereas the converse is true of (28). We cannot, however, exclude (28) solely on the basis that it contains a Case-marked trace, because such traces are required for *wh*-NPs that are moved into CP. Rather, we would have to stipulate a distinction between NP-trace and *wh*-NP trace and then say that no NP-trace can occur in a Case-marked position.

An alternative approach to (28) can be formulated on the basis of the second difference between (28) and (30). This difference involves a distinction between grammatical function positions that are also **thematic** positions and those that are **nonthematic**. A position is thematic if it is assigned an **argument function** with respect to some predicate. Consider the following examples.

(31) a. John left.
b. Bill mentioned the book to Mary
c. Bernie gave Adam a rocket
d. the Goldberg Variations are intricate
e. the mayor criticized the city council
f. the mayor's criticism of the city council was premature

The verb leave in (31a) is a one-place predicate (in the sense of standard predicate calculus) with a single argument *John* in subject position. The verb *mention* in (31b) is a three-place predicate with three arguments, *Bill* (subject), *the book* (object), and *Mary* (in the PP complement). The verb *give* in (31c) is also a three-place predicate involving the grammatical functions of subject (*Bernie*), indirect object (*Adam*), and direct object (*a rocket*). In (31d) the adjective *intricate* functions as a one-place predicate for the single argument *the Goldberg Variations.* In (31e) the verb *criticize* is a two-place predicate with the arguments *the mayor* (subject) and *the city council* (object). In (31f) the nominal *criticism* functions as a predicate with respect to the same two arguments and assigns the same argument functions to them. Note also that in (31f) the NP headed by the nominal *criticism* is itself assigned an argument function as the subject of the adjective *premature.*[15]

At this point it will be useful to make the notion "argument function" more concrete by discussing some specific examples. Let us assume that argument functions are determined with respect to semantic classes of predicates. For example, predicates of motion (e.g., *go, give,* and *receive*) will assign certain argument functions, and predicates of propositional attitude (e.g., *believe* and *know*) will assign others. Predicates of motion involve the following argument functions:

(32) a. Theme: 'object which moves'
b. Source: 'place from which the object moves'
c. Goal: 'place to which the object moves'

These functions, also called **thematic relations** or **theta-roles** (henceforth θ-roles), are assigned on the basis of lexical properties of the particular predicates of motion.

(33) a. John went to the concert
b. Jim gave a cookbook to Bob
c. Bob received a cookbook from Jim

Thus, the subjects in (33a–c) are assigned the θ-roles Theme, Source, and Goal, respectively. In both (33b) and (33c) *a cookbook* functions as a Theme. There appears to be no specific correlation between grammatical function and thematic relation with respect to predicate class. For example, although *the concert* in (33a), *Bob* in (33b), and *Jim* in (33c) all function as object of a preposition, they are not all assigned the same θ-role: *the concert* and *Bob* are assigned the θ-role Goal, and *Jim* is assigned Source. Presumably it is not necessary that each predicate of motion assign the full set of thematic relations associated with that class to an overt lexical argument. So, for example, the θ-roles Goal and Source are not expressed in (34a) and (34b) respectively.

(34) a. John left the meeting in a hurry
b. Mary arrived at the meeting on time

In all of these examples, however, the θ-role Theme is lexically realized. This seems to be required for all predicates of motion.

---

**Exercise 6.6**

Assume that the verb *tell* is a predicate of motion like the verb *give.* Identify the θ-roles of the NPs in the following examples:

(i) a. John told Bill a story
b. John told a story to Bill
c. Bill was told a story by John
d. a story was told to Bill by John

How do these examples illustrate that the θ-role of an NP does not correlate directly with a syntactic grammatical function position?

---

Not only is there no specific correlation between grammatical function and thematic relation; it is also the case that lexical NPs bearing a single thematic relation may occur in different grammatical function positions for the same predicate. Consider the following active-passive pairs.

(35) a. Barbie sent Bernie a letter
b. Bernie was sent a letter by Barbie

(36) a. Barbie sent a letter to Bernie
b. a letter was sent to Bernie by Barbie

In all these example sentences, Barb*ie* functions as a Source, *a letter* functions as a Theme, and *Bernie* functions as a Goal. In terms of grammatical functions, however, the Source *Barbie* is a grammatical subject in (35a) and (36a), but a prepositional object in (35b) and (36b). Similarly, the Theme *a letter* is a direct object in (35a–b) and (36a), but a grammatical subject in (36b). The NP that functions as the Goal in these examples (i.e., *Bernie*) is configurationally an indirect object in (35a), a subject in (35b), and an object of a preposition in (36a–b).

Although there may be no correlation between θ-roles and grammatical function positions, the assignment of θ-roles for each individual predicate will be determined in part in terms of underlying grammatical functions. For example, in (35a) the fact that the indirect object functions as a Goal will have to be stipulated in the lexical structure of *give*—unless of course this fact follows from a general principle of (perhaps) lexical structure. Thus, we might expect that the verb *give* is associated with a thematic template like (37), which assigns the appropriate θ-roles to positions on the basis of grammatical configuration.

(37) GIVE: [Source ___ Goal Theme]

Alternatively, θ-roles can be determined on the basis of which preposition governs an argument. For motional predicates, the preposition *to* always governs a Goal, whereas the preposition *from* always governs a Source.

The passive preposition *by* always assigns the θ-role associated with the subject of the corresponding active predicate. This holds across predicate classes. If θ-roles are assigned at D-structure and the NP object of a passive *by*-phrase is base-generated in subject position and subsequently moved into the prepositional phrase, the θ-role of the NP will be assigned to the D-structure subject position. Alternatively, the passive *by*-phrase is base-generated with a lexical object and the θ-role associated with the active subject must be assigned to the object of the *by*-phrase. The first alternative encounters difficulties with respect to nominal counterparts (e.g., (38b–c) of passive sentences (e.g., (38a)).

(38) a. Harry was acquitted by the jury
b. Harry's acquittal by the jury
c. the acquittal of Harry by the jury

Consider how the nominal (38c) would have to be derived under this proposal. The assumption that the lexical object of a *by*-phrase is derived via NP-movement of an underlying lexical subject into the prepositional phrase requires that (39) be an intermediate representation in the derivation of (38c).

(39) $[_{NP}$ $[_{NP}$ $e_i]$ acquittal of Harry by $[_{NP:i}$ the jury]]

The problem under this analysis is how to account for the presence of the determiner *the*. An operation that substitutes a lexical determiner for an NP-trace would violate the Nondistinctness Condition on substitutions. The alternative is to base-generate the passive *by*-phrase for nominals—in which case there is little reason to assume that this is not also the case for sentential forms.

Given that the passive *by*-phrase is base-generated, the object of this phrase must be a thematic position in its own right. If the object of the *by*-phrase is assigned the θ-role associated with the subject position in active sentences, then we need an explanation for the deviance of (40).

(40) *the police arrested John by the FBI

The interpretation of (40) should be that both the police and the FBI arrested John. Although the interpretation is perfectly coherent, the sentence is deviant. This suggests that the θ-role of *arrest* associated with the subject position in the active and with the *by*-phrase in the passive cannot be assigned to two different syntactic positions in the same sentence. So if the object of the *by*-phrase in the passive construction is the syntactic position to which this θ-role of *arrest* is assigned, then the subject position in passive constructions will be nonthematic—that is, no θ-role will be assigned to that position—under the assumption that a predicate can assign each of its θ-role once only.[16] The prohibition against multiple assignments of the same θ-role is captured by the following principle:

(41) **Unique Assignment**
Each θ-role of a predicate may be assigned only once.[17]

If the subject θ-role is assigned to either *the police* or *the FBI* in (40), then one of these NPs will not be assigned a θ-role. To account for (40) we will postulate a principle of Functional Relatedness that prohibits lexical arguments that bear no θ-role.

(42) **Functional Relatedness**
Each lexical argument must bear a θ-role.

A **lexical argument** is an NP (or CP, in the case of propositional arguments) that is semantically nonnull.[18] Functional Relatedness also accounts for the fact that lexical arguments cannot be base-generated in positions where semantically null lexical NPs occur.

(43) a. *John was expected that Mary would win
b. it was expected that Mary would win

(44) a. *John seems that Mary will win
b. it seems that Mary will win

The ill-formedness of (43a) and (44a) seems to be attributable solely to the fact that the lexical argument *John* occurs in a nonthematic position and bears no θ-role. These examples provide independent motivation for the principle of Functional Relatedness—that is, independent of the earlier facts concerning the passive *by*-phrase.

**Exercise 6.7**

There are ill-formed constructions that can be interpreted as violations of both the Case Filter and Functional Relatedness. Discuss the following example in this light.

(i) *Lestrade was astounded Watson by Holmes's uncanny deduction

Could the empirical effects of one be subsumed under the other? Consider (43)–(44) in this regard. Then examine the following paradigm.

(ii) a. *it is not possible [$_{CP}$ [$_{IP}$ it to be established that John lied]]
b. ?it is not possible for it to be established that John lied
c. it is not possible that it will be established that John lied

What does (ii) show regarding the possibility of subsuming the effect of the Case Filter under Functional Relatedness?

How is a θ-role assigned to the S-structure subject of a passive construction? Consider the following S-structure representations of the passive sentences (35b) and (36b):

(45) a. [$_{NP:i}$ Bernie] was sent $e_i$ a letter by Barbie
b. [$_{NP:i}$ a letter] was sent $e_i$ to Bernie by Barbie

As mentioned earlier (see note 18), the analysis we are exploring assumed that although the nonovert object position in a passive construction remains a thematic position (i.e., one to which a θ-role is assigned), the subject position in a passive construction is not assigned any thematic relation of its own. Thus, it follows that if the subject of a passive construction contains a lexical NP that is assigned a θ-role, the assignment must be indirect—via trace binding to a position that is assigned a θ-role. Given that the indirect object position in (45a) is assigned the θ-role of Goal, the NP *Bernie* is designated as a Goal via trace binding. Similarly, the NP *a letter* in (45b) would be designated as a Theme.

What we have observed so far is that instances of NP-movement resulting in well-formed structures generally involve movement from a thematic to a nonthematic position.

**Exercise 6.8**

Show how this holds for the grammatical examples of NP-movement discussed in section 5.2.3.

If the principle of Functional Relatedness applies at D-structure, lexical arguments will not be base-generated in nonthematic positions.[19]

**Exercise 6.9**

Note, however, that trace binding between two nonthematic positions is possible. Demonstrate this by discussing the analysis of (i).

(i) it was believed to be likely that John was lying

Be sure to give the relevant examples that show that the two positions involved in the trace binding are nonthematic.

As we saw in chapter 5, Case theory determines when a lexical argument must appear in a nonthematic position at S-structure: namely, when the lexical argument is base-generated in a position to which Case cannot be assigned, it must move to a position where it can receive Case.

Although it is possible to move an NP from a thematic position to a nonthematic position, it is not possible to move NPs between thematic positions. This is illustrated by examples like (28) (repeated here).

(28) *it is odd [$_{CP}$ C [$_{IP}$ John$_i$ to find e$_i$ in a friendly mood]]

So far (28) violates no principle of grammar that we have discussed. The NP *John* would be assigned Case via its trace in object position. The trace of *John* is lexically governed by the verb *like*, which satisfies the ECP, and the trace binding does not violate Subjacency. The lexical argument *John* occupies a thematic position in S-structure (the subject of *like*) and is linked to another thematic position (the object of *like*) via trace binding. Thus, the problem appears to be that the argument *John* is assigned two θ-roles. To exclude the possibility of movement between thematic positions, as in (28), we can postulate another principle of predicate-argument structure that prohibits a lexical argument from having more than one θ-role.

(46) **Functional Uniqueness**
A lexical argument may bear only one θ-role.

With respect to trace binding, this principle will hold at S-structure or LF where antecedent-trace relations are expressed.

In (28) Functional Uniqueness is violated by a lexical argument that receives two θ-roles from a single predicate. It applies as well where a lexical argument receives two θ-roles from different predicates.

(47) *John reported to like Mary

(47) would have the S-structure representation (48).

(48) $[_{IP}$John$_i$ reported $[_{IP}$ e$_i$ to like Mary]]

Here *John* would be assigned the θ-role of the subject of *report* in the matrix clause and would also be assigned the θ-role of the subject of *like* in the embedded clause.

Notice that (48) would also violate the Case Uniqueness Principle if *John* were doubly Case-marked—once as the subject of the finite matrix clause and again by the matrix verb, which governs the trace of *John*. If the trace of *John* were not governed, then (48) would violate the ECP. However, there are examples that do not violate Case Uniqueness.

(49) *it is odd $[_{CP}$ C $[_{IP}$John$_i$ to report $[_{IP}$ e$_i$ to like Mary]]]

The NP *John* in (49) would be Case-marked via its trace, which is governed by the active verb *report* (to satisfy the ECP), so that this example violates only Functional Uniqueness.

Thus, far we have the following conditions on predicate-argument structure: each lexical argument must be assigned one θ-role (Functional Relatedness) and only one θ-role (Functional Uniqueness), and each θ-role of a predicate may be assigned only once (Unique Assignment).

Chomsky (1981:36) combines these three conditions on predicate-argument structure, together with one additional condition as the **θ-Criterion**.

(50) **θ-Criterion**
Each argument bears one and only one θ-role, and each θ-role is assigned to one and only one argument.

The first half of (50) incorporates Functional Relatedness and Functional Uniqueness, and the second half combines Unique Assignment with a principle requiring each θ-role of a predicate to be assigned to some argument. It is not clear exactly how this last requirement is to be interpreted. For example, truncated passives—those lacking an overt *by*-phrase—presumably involve predicates for which a θ-role (the one that would be assigned to the subject of the corresponding active) cannot be assigned to an overt argument.

---

**Exercise 6.10**

Identify which part of the θ-Criterion is violated in each of the following examples and explain exactly what is wrong:

(i) a. *Bill was told a story to Mary by John
b. *John seems Mary to be winning
c. *John told Bill a story by Mary
d. *Bill was told Mary a story by John

---

The exact implementation of these conditions on predicate-argument structure will depend on the level of representation at which θ-roles are assigned. For example, if θ-roles are assigned at D-structure, then Functional Uniqueness is violated by the movement of a θ-marked NP into a θ-marked position, assuming a θ-role can be assigned to an empty position (e.g., subject position). Under this implementation trace binding need not be mentioned. If, however, θ-marking occurs at either S-structure or LF, then the proper implementation of Functional Uniqueness will depend on the inheritance of θ-roles via trace binding—specifically, that the argument binder of a trace receives the θ-role assigned to the position occupied by the trace.

Several distinct proposals about where and how θ-roles are assigned are possible. Strong empirical and/or methodological arguments for any one of them remain to be constructed. As discussed above, different proposals will force different implementations for Functional Uniqueness. This may hold for Functional Relatedness as well. If we assume that these conditions should be grouped together and therefore apply at the same level of representation, we can eliminate analyses in which they apply solely at D-structure: Functional Uniqueness cannot be violated at D-structure because each θ-role will be assigned to a different syntactic position.

Having noted the open-endedness of these proposals, we turn to yet another way of dealing with the problems of unconstrained NP-movement.

### 6.3 Alternative Conditions on NP-Movement

In the preceding sections we have been investigating constraints on NP-movement based on (i) Case considerations with respect to lexical NPs, (ii) government considerations with respect to the empty category that is left behind at a movement site, and (iii) thematic considerations with respect to NPs that move from one thematic position to another. In addition to Case, government, and thematic structure, binding is another natural grammatical notion that can be applied to constrain NP-movements. Since a lexical NP that is moved from a position is said to bind a trace in that position via coindexing, we may explore the limitations on NP-movements in terms of constraints on binding. These binding constraints on NP-trace overlap to a large extent with previously discussed principles of grammar, as we will see in section 6.3.1.2. Nonetheless, a binding theory of NP-movement seems to be motivated by consideration of raising constructions in Portuguese involving inflected infinitives.

### 6.3.1 Conditions on Trace Binding

In all the well-formed examples of trace binding between two NP positions that we have considered so far, the lexical antecedent c-commands its trace. Examples are provided in (51).

(51) a. $[_{IP}$ Mary$_i$ $[_{VP}$ was amused $e_i$ by Bill's antics]
b. $[_{IP}$ Max$_i$ seems $[_{IP}$ $e_i$ to be prevaricating]]

(51a) is an instance of passivization; (51b) is an instance of raising. In both cases the matrix subject c-commands its trace. Suppose now that the positions of the trace and lexical antecedent are reversed in each example, yielding (52).

(52) a. *$[_{IP}$ $e_i$ $[_{VP}$ was amused Mary$_i$ by Bill's antics]
b. *$[_{IP}$ $e_i$ seems $[_{IP}$ Max$_i$ to be prevaricating]]

Neither example violates either the Case Filter or Functional Uniqueness. The traces in (52) are in nonthematic positions, so that their lexical antecedents are assigned only one θ-role—the one assigned to their S-structure position. Although these lexical antecedents are not in Case-marked positions, they are linked to Case-marked positions via trace binding; therefore, they will be Case-marked nominative via Case inheritance. Both traces in (52) do, however, violate the ECP—though this is not inevitable, as illustrated in (53).

(53) a. *it was likely $[_{IP}$ $e_i$ to $[_{VP}$ be amused Mary$_i$ by Bill's antics]
b. *it was likely $[_{IP}$ $e_i$ to seem $[_{IP}$ Mary$_i$ to be prevaricating]]

By changing the matrix verbs in (52) to infinitivals and embedding the resulting structures as complements of a CP-deletion predicate adjective like *likely*, we neutralize the effects of the ECP since the subject trace is now lexically governed. Of course, (53) now violates the Case Filter.

Since in (52)–(53) the lexical antecedents are c-commanded by their traces, whereas in the well-formed (51) the reverse is true, we may also attribute their ill-formedness to a condition on trace binding such that a trace may not c-command its lexical antecedent.

---

**Exercise 6.11**

An alternative formulation, "A trace must be c-commanded by its antecedent," may be problematic for extraposition. Consider the derived structures of (i) and (ii) in this regard (cf. the discussion of extraposition in section 3.2.1).

(i) a. a man who I want to meet is coming to dinner
b. a man is coming to dinner who I want to meet

(ii) a. how many reports which John had written did Mary like
b. how many reports did Mary like which John had written

How do the S-structures of these examples provide an argument against the alternative formulation of the trace binding constraint given above?

---

Generally in well-formed constructions the trace of an NP is **bound**—that is, c-commanded by the NP it is coindexed with. In (52)–(53) the subject traces are not bound according to this definition. Note that we are assuming that an NP-trace (i.e., a trace in a grammatical function NP position) is an element that *must* be bound. Let us say that an NP-trace must be bound to an antecedent—although the immediate (i.e., local) binder may itself be a trace, as shown in (54).

(54) [$_{IP}$ Smith$_i$ is believed [$_{IP}$ e$_i$ to have been reported [$_{IP}$ e$_i$ to be traveling under an alias]]]

The subject trace of the infinitival complement of *report* is bound by the subject trace of the infinitival complement of *believe* (which in turn is bound by the NP *Smith*).

**6.3.1.1 Binding Domains** Bound NP-traces are subject to further restrictions, as illustrated in the following paradigm.

(55) a. Finite clause complements
i. *John$_i$ was reported [$_{CP}$ [$_{IP}$ e$_i$ had recommended Mary]]
ii. *Mary$_i$ was reported [$_{CP}$ [$_{IP}$ John had recommended e$_i$]]

b. Infinitival complements
i. John$_i$ was reported [$_{IP}$ e$_i$ to have recommended Mary]
ii. *Mary$_i$ was reported [$_{IP}$ John to have recommended e$_i$]

Each trace in (55) is coindexed with a c-commanding NP and therefore is bound according to the definition provided in the preceding paragraph. To distinguish the well-formed (55b.i) from the ill-formed (55a.i-ii) and

(55b.ii), we will make a further distinction between traces that are bound (all four traces in (55)) and those that are **properly bound** (only the trace in (55b.i)). A trace is properly bound when it is bound in a particular domain, known as a **binding domain**. Thus, the constraint that an NP-trace must be properly bound can be stated as a prohibition against an NP-trace that is **free** (i.e., not bound) in its binding domain.

To formalize a constraint on proper binding, we must characterize what constitutes a binding domain. From the paradigm in (55) we can identify two such domains. (55a) illustrates that finite clauses constitute binding domains. Thus, the traces in (55a) are free in the domain of finite Infl—that is, where Infl c-commands the trace.[20] By defining the binding domain for NP-trace as the c-command domain of finite Infl, we are able to distinguish between the ill-formed (55a.i–ii) and the well-formed (55b.i). This leaves the ill-formedness of (55b.ii) to be accounted for.

Before turning to an account of (55b.ii), we might consider an alternative characterization of the binding domain for finite clauses—namely, the domain of AGR. Since for English, finite Infl always entails the presence of AGR and conversely, there is no way to distinguish these proposals empirically in this language. However, in languages such as Turkish that have agreement phenomena in infinitivals and movement phenomena involving infinitival subjects, the two proposals do have distinct empirical consequences. If finite Infl is the relevant factor for defining binding domains, then movement of infinitival subjects in the domain of AGR should be permissible. Since such movements are prohibited, as shown in (56), then the more general account will formulate binding domains in terms of AGR. (The examples in (56) are adapted from George and Kornfilt 1981.)

(56) a. i. dinleyici-ler [$_{IP}$ e$_i$ viski-yi iç-ti]
auditor-PL whisky-ACC drink-PAST-(no AGR)

san-ɨyor-lar biz-i$_i$
believe-PRES-3RD/PL we-ACC
'the auditors believe us to have drunk the whisky'

ii. (biz$_i$) [$_{IP}$ e$_i$ viski-yi iç-ti]
we whisky-ACC drink-PAST-(no AGR)

san-ɨl-ɨyor-uz
believe-PASSIVE-PRES-1st/PL
'we are believed to have drunk the whisky'

b. i. *dinleyici-ler $[_{IP}\ e_i$ viski-yi iç-ti-k]
auditor-PL whisky-ACC drink-PAST-1st/PL

san-ɨyor-lar $biz_i$
believe-PRES-3rd/PL we-NOM

ii. *(biz) $[_{IP}\ e_i$ viski-yi iç-ti-k]
we whisky-ACC drink-PAST-1st/PL

san-ɨl-ɨyor-uz
believe-PASSIVE-PRES-1st/PL

In (56b) the subject trace is free in the domain of the AGR element in the sentential complement, whereas in (56a) there is no AGR element in the sentential complement. In (56a) the subject trace is in the domain of the AGR element of the matrix clause, but it is bound by the matrix subject and therefore meets the requirement for proper binding. The formulation of binding domains in terms of AGR cuts across the more traditional distinction between finite clauses and infinitivals.

Because there is no agreement in English between an infinitival subject and its corresponding verb (or auxiliary), the proper binding violation in (55b.ii) must be accounted for in terms of a different characterization of binding domain. With the exception of (55b.i), it appears that clausal domains constitute binding domains. The c-command domain of AGR is one way to characterize a clausal domain; the c-command domain of subject (i.e., syntactic subject) is another.[21] With respect to trace binding, any syntactic subject creates a binding domain. The subject may be lexical, or it may be nonlexical (e.g., trace or PRO).

(57) a. Lexical subjects[22]
i. *$John_i$ is expected $[_{CP}$ for $[_{IP}$ Mary to like $e_i]]$
ii. *$[_{NP}$ a unicorn$]_i$ is expected $[_{CP}$ for $[_{IP}$ there to be $e_i$ in the garden$]]$
(cf. there is expected to be a unicorn in the garden)

b. Non-lexical subjects[23]
i. *$[_{CP}\ who_i\ was_k\ [_{IP} John_j\ e_k$ expected $[_{CP}\ e_i\ [_{IP}\ e_i$ to like $e_j]]]]$
(cf. $[_{CP}\ who_i\ was_k\ [_{IP} John_j\ e_k$ expected $[_{CP}\ e_i\ [_{IP}\ e_j$ to like $e_i]]]]$)
ii. *$[_{IP} John_i$ was persuaded $Mary_j\ [_{CP}[_{IP}\ PRO_j$ to nominate $e_i]]]$

In (57a.i) the complement object trace is free in the domain of the lexical subject *Mary*, which is an argument. In (57a.ii), the trace of the NP *a unicorn* is free in the domain of the pleonastic (and hence nonargument) subject *there.* In (57b.i) the trace of *John* in complement object position is free in the domain of the trace of *who* in the complement subject. In (57b.ii) the trace of *John* in complement object position is free in the domain of PRO, the complement subject.

Since we must allow for a trace subject of an infinitival to be properly bound across a clause boundary (see (55b.i)), it is not possible to give the simplest formulation of binding domain: namely, IP. Instead, we posit two distinct but overlapping domains: the domain of AGR and the domain of subject. The domains overlap with respect to object position in finite clauses, which are in the domain of both AGR and subject. Thus, in (55a.ii) the trace in object position is in the domain of both the complement subject (*John*) and AGR.

At this point we may formulate the condition on trace binding as (58).

(58) **Proper Binding Condition**
*[$_{NP}$ e], where [$_{NP}$ e] is a trace that is free in its binding domain.

The binding domain of a trace resulting from NP-movement is the c-command domain of either a c-commanding AGR or a c-commanding syntactic subject. If an NP-trace is bound in the minimal (or smallest) binding domain, then it will be bound in all binding domains. It is the minimal domain that determines whether an NP-trace is properly bound.

---

**Exercise 6.12**

Note that the Proper Binding Condition overlaps with the θ-Criterion. Consider the following cases:

(i) a. *John expects [$_{IP}$ e$_j$ will like Mary]
(cf. John expects he will like Mary)
b. *John expects [$_{IP}$ Mary will like e$_j$]
(cf. John expects Mary will like him)

Explain how each example violates the Proper Binding Condition and identify exactly which part of the θ-Criterion each one violates.

---

As it stands, the Proper Binding Condition incorrectly predicts that the following cases of *wh*-movement will be ill formed.

(59) a. [$_{CP}$ who$_i$ [$_{IP}$ e$_i$ AGR was reported [$_{IP}$ e$_i$ to be winning]]]
b. [$_{CP}$ [$_{NP:i}$ which book] did$_j$ [$_{IP}$ you AGR$_j$ borrow e$_i$]]
c. [$_{IP}$ it is not obvious [$_{CP}$ who$_i$ [$_{IP}$ PRO to blame e$_i$]]]

The matrix subject trace in (59a) is free in the domain of AGR, as is the object trace in (59b). The complement object trace in (59c) is free in the domain of the syntactic subject PRO. Since the examples in (59) are grammatical, it is necessary to distinguish between traces created by NP-movement and traces created by *wh*-movement. What we have been calling NP-movement always involves movement between grammatical function positions, whereas *wh*-movement involves movement to SPEC-CP, which is not a grammatical function position. Let us say that all grammatical function positions are **A-positions** (positions where arguments are assigned θ-roles—basically, grammatical function positions), whereas all other positions are **Ā-positions** (read "A-bar positions").[24] With this terminology we can now distinguish between NP-movement and *wh*-movement in terms of trace binding. A trace is **A-bound** when its most local antecedent is in an A-position; it is **Ā-bound** when its most local antecedent is in an Ā-position. NP-movement creates A-binding; *wh*-movement creates Ā-binding. For example, the complement subject trace in (59a) is A-bound by the trace in matrix subject position; the matrix subject trace in (59a) and the object trace in (59b) are both Ā-bound by a *wh*-phrase in CP. If the Proper Binding Condition is restricted to A-binding, then (59) poses no problem for our analysis.

This distinction between A- and Ā-binding will be explored further in chapter 7, when we formulate a binding condition on lexical anaphors, and in chapter 8 when we compare conditions on the binding of lexical items (e.g., reciprocals and pronouns) with binding conditions on empty categories. Since the framework developed here accomplishes both NP- and *wh*-movement with a single rule (Substitute α for β), the different properties of the resulting constructions must be established in terms of binding configuration. As we will see in chapter 8, A-bound traces have different properties from Ā-bound traces, so that this distinction is empirically justifiable.

**6.3.1.2 Overlapping Conditions** As noted earlier, the binding conditions for NP-trace overlap with other independently motivated conditions. Consider, for example, the overlap between the ECP and the Proper Binding Condition as they apply to trace subjects of finite clauses. A relevant example is (55a.i) (repeated here).

(55) a. i. *John$_i$ was reported [$_{CP}$ [$_{IP}$ e$_i$ had recommended Mary]]

Here the complement subject trace is neither properly bound nor properly governed and therefore violates both the Proper Binding Condition and the ECP.[25] If constructions like (55a.i) are the only cases covered by the Proper Binding Condition as formulated in terms of the domain of AGR, then we might justifiably eliminate this part of the Proper Binding Condition from our theory since the empirical results of this part are derivable from the more general ECP (which applies to *wh*-trace as well as traces in adjunction structures, see section 3.3. Recall that (55) violates the ECP only because we have stipulated that a trace will be locally bound only if it is locally Ā-bound. If we eliminate the qualification "from CP" regarding local binding in our formulation of the ECP (13), then the trace in (55), being locally bound (i.e., locally Ā-bound), will indeed satisfy the ECP. To rule out (55) now, we will have to employ the Proper Binding Condition.

Next we must consider whether there is any independent motivation for the Proper Binding Condition with respect to the domain of AGR. This part of the condition will be independently motivated if there is at least one construction whose ungrammaticality results solely from a trace that is free in the domain of AGR. Since finite IP is always a barrier to government within the framework we have developed, an A-bound NP-trace in subject position will invariably violate the ECP—that is, unless local A-binding satisfies the ECP. To motivate the domain of AGR (as distinct from the domain of subject) as relevant to the proper binding of traces, we would have to examine infinitival constructions that involve AGR. An analysis of inflected infinitive constructions in Portuguese provides some relevant data.

Portuguese has raising constructions with properties similar to those of English. (The following Portuguese examples are from Quicoli 1987.)

(60) a. Uninflected infinitival complements
   i. eles parecem ter razão
      they seem to-have reason
      *they seem to be right*
   ii. [$_{IP}$ eles$_i$ AGR-parecem [$_{IP}$ e$_i$ ter razão]]

   b. Inflected infinitival complements
   i. *eles parecem terem razão
   ii. [$_{IP}$ eles$_i$ AGR-parecem [$_{IP}$ e$_i$ AGR-terem razão]]

c. Finite clause complements
   i. *eles parecem tem razão
   ii. [$_{IP}$ eles$_i$ AGR-parecem [$_{CP}$ que [$_{IP}$ e$_i$ AGR-tem razão]]]

(60a.i) shows that raising can occur with uninflected infinitival complements of *parecer.* Assuming that the ECP holds in Portuguese as well as English, the verb *parecer* must allow CP-deletion so that the trace in complement subject position of (60a.ii) is properly governed by the matrix verb. When the infinitival complement of *parecer* contains an inflected infinitive (e.g., *terem*, versus the uninflected *ter*), raising is prohibited, as illustrated in (60b.i). If we suppose that *parecer* allows CP-deletion, then (60b.i) does not violate the ECP since the subject trace is lexically governed, as shown in (60b.ii). (60c.i) demonstrates that raising out of a finite complement of *parecer* is also prohibited. (60b.i) is ill formed because the trace (which is A-bound by the matrix subject) is free in the domain of AGR and hence violates the Proper Binding Condition.[26]

A similar situation arises with clitic pronoun constructions in Portuguese where the clitic pronoun subject of an infinitival complement is raised into the matrix VP.[27] Consider the paradigm in (61) and (62) where the (a)-examples have regular common nouns as complement subjects and the (b)-examples have clitic pronouns in that position.

(61) Uninflected infinitival complements
   a. i. José viu os meninos sair
         José saw the boys to-leave (–AGR)
      ii. [$_{IP}$ José viu [$_{IP}$ os meninos sair]]
   b. i. José nos viu sair
         José us saw to-leave (–AGR)
      ii. [$_{IP}$ José nos$_i$ viu [$_{IP}$ e$_i$ sair]]

(62) Inflected infinitival complements
   a. i. José viu os meninos sairem
         José saw the boys to-leave (+AGR)
      ii. [$_{IP}$ José viu [$_{IP}$ os meninos sairem]]
   b. i. *José nos viu sairmos.
         José us saw to-leave (+AGR)
      ii. [$_{IP}$ José nos$_i$ viu [$_{IP}$ e$_i$ sairmos]]

Given Case theory, the uninflected infinitival complement in (61a.i) must be subject to CP-deletion so that the lexical NP subject *os meninos* is assigned Case via government by the matrix verb *viu*. Let us assume that the inflected infinitival complement in (62a.i) also undergoes CP-deletion.

---

**Exercise 6.13**

We can block double Case assignment (via the matrix verb and the complement AGR) in this case by invoking the Minimality Condition on government (see note 8) with respect to Case assignment. (61) has properties similar to Case structures in Icelandic (like those in section 5.3) where Case is assigned by one element and licensed by another. Suppose that AGR assigns nominative Case as the minimal governing Case assigner, but that AGR is not sufficient to license Case—thus, CP-deletion is necessary so that the matrix V can license Case on the infinitival subject. In this regard it is interesting to consider the additional following structures for infinitival complements of *parecer.* (The example sentences are from Quicoli 1987.)

(i) Inflected infinitive
   a. parece terem eles razão
      it-seems to-have (+AGR) they reason
      'it seems they are right'
   b. *parece eles terem razão

(ii) Uninflected infinitive
   a. *parece ter eles razão
      it-seems to-have (–AGR) they reason
   b. *parece eles ter razão

How does the suggested analysis apply to (i) and (ii)?

---

In both clitic constructions the clitic has moved from the infinitival subject position to the matrix VP. In the uninflected infinitival construction we must assume that the clitic is assigned Case by the matrix verb *viu* just like the nonclitic subject in (61a.i). The clitic moves to a position that is not Case-marked. In the inflected infinitival construction the clitic is assigned Case via AGR. Since the position it moves to is not Case marked, the ill-formedness of (62b.i) cannot be attributed to Case Uniqueness as was possible with (60b.i). Therefore, (62b.i) looks like a Proper Binding Condition violation, since it does not violate Case theory, the ECP, the θ-Criterion, or Subjacency.

**Exercise 6.14**

The following paradigm (from from Quicoli 1987) provides further evidence for the analysis we have been building.

(i) Uninflected infinitive

a. *nos parece ter razão

b. [$_{IP}$ NP [$_{VP}$ nos$_i$ parece [$_{IP}$ e$_i$ ter razão]]]
us seems to-have reason
'we seem to be right'

(ii) Inflected infinitive

a. *nos parece terem razão

b. [$_{IP}$ NP [$_{VP}$ nos$_i$ parece [$_{IP}$ e$_i$ AGR-terem razão]]]

NP represents a null subject corresponding to English nonreferential *it.* (ii.a) cannot involve Case Uniqueness. Explain why not and show the relevance of this example to a binding theory approach to movement. Finally, compare (i.a) with (61b.i) and show how Case theory accounts for the ill-formedness of the former.

---

Let us now try to discover independent motivation for the Pro-per Binding Condition with respect to subject domain effects. The ill-formedness of example (55b.ii), in which a trace is free in the domain of a subject can also be explained in terms of Case theory.

(55) b. ii. *Mary$_i$ was reported [$_{IP}$ John to have recommended e$_i$]

Here the infinitival subject *John* will not be assigned Case, in violation of the Case Filter. If we change the matrix predicate from passive to active, then *John* will undergo exceptional Case marking by the matrix verb via CP-deletion; however, *Mary* will then be assigned two distinct θ-roles in violation of Functional Uniqueness, since the active verb *report* has a subject θ-role to assign.[28]

To establish the Proper Binding Condition with respect to the domain of subject, we must find a subject domain effect that does not also involve either Case theory violations or predicate-argument structure violations. As long as we are dealing with trace in object position, the ECP will not be violated. (63a) has the relevant properties.

(63) a. *Mary$_i$ is unusual [$_{CP}$ for [$_{IP}$ John to help e$_i$]]
b. it is unusual [$_{CP}$ for [$_{IP}$ John to help Mary]]
c. [$_{CP}$ for [$_{IP}$ John to help Mary]] is unusual

(63b–c) establish that the predicate adjective *unusual* occurs with a full *for*–NP–*to*–VP infinitival complement.[29] The matrix subject position is nonthematic, as illustrated by the presence of pleonastic *it* in (63b), so (63a) cannot be a violation of Functional Uniqueness with respect to *Mary*. Since the trace in (63a) is free in the domain of a subject, it could be counted as a violation of binding theory—in particular, a subject domain effect. But here too Case Uniqueness could be raised as an alternative explanation. *Mary* is marked nominative as the subject of the matrix IP and inherits objective Case via its trace, which is the object of *help*. However, if we replace the verb *help* with the predicate *be proud*, the Case Uniqueness explanation is no longer possible.

(64) a. *$\text{Mary}_i$ is unusual $[_{CP}$ for $[_{IP}$ John to be proud $e_i]]$
b. it is unusual $[_{CP}$ for $[_{IP}$ John to be proud of Mary$]]$

This analysis is based on the assumption that *of* in (64b) results from the application of *Of-I*nsertion, as discussed in section 2.4. Because that transformation has to be optional, it is possible for it not to apply in the derivation of (64a). Then the trace will not be in a Case-marked position and *Mary* will not violate Case Uniqueness. (64a) will be unequivocally only a binding theory violation—specifically, it will manifest a subject domain effect.

The evidence for conditions on trace binding in addition to Case theory (i.e., the Case Filter, the Case Uniqueness Principle, and the Principle of Case Licensing), the ECP, and Functional Uniqueness is not overwhelming. The fact that there is at least some indicates that we should keep thinking about traces in terms of a binding theory—just in case. (See chapter 8, appendix B for further discussion and Koster 1987 for an attempt to reduce bounding (Subjacency) to binding.)

---

**Exercise 6.15**

In note 17 of chapter 3 it was suggested that all violations of the Strict Cycle Condition (72) would fall under independently motivated conditions on representations. The discussion in that chapter was limited to *wh*-movement cases. (i) is a case involving NP-movement, assuming that *John* is the D-structure subject of *give*.

(i) a. *John was reported a book to have been given
b. $[_{IP}$ $\text{John}_i$ was reported $[_{IP}$ a $\text{book}_j$ to have given Bill $e_j]]$

Construct the derivation of (i) that violates the Strict Cycle Condition. Show that there is another derivation of (i) that does not violate this condition. Discuss how (i.b) satisfies or violates principles of Case theory, the ECP, Functional Uniqueness, Functional Relatedness, and the Proper Binding Condition.

---

## 6.4 The PRO/Trace Distinction

Having developed a relatively detailed analysis of the distribution of traces, we now return to the distribution of PRO.

Although trace and PRO have different derivational histories, they share two properties. First, both enter into binding relations with an antecedent.[30] That PRO must enter into binding relations, like trace, is demonstrated in the following corresponding paradigms, which involve agreement between a reflexive pronoun (or predicate nominal) and its trace/PRO antecedent.

(65) a. i. $he_i$ seems $[_{IP}\ e_i$ to have consoled $himself_i$ with another beer]
ii. *$he_i$ seems $[_{IP}\ e_i$ to have consoled $herself_i$ with another beer]
b. i. $he_i$ tried $[_{CP}\ [_{IP}\ PRO_i$ to console $himself_i$ with another beer]]
ii. *$he_i$ tried $[_{CP}\ [_{IP}\ PRO_i$ to console $herself_i$ with another beer]]

(66) a. i. $they_i$ appear $[_{IP}\ e_i$ to have become $[_{NP:i}$ brain surgeons]]
ii. *$he_i$ appears $[_{IP}\ e_i$ to have become $[_{NP:i}$ brain surgeons]]
b. i. $they_i$ expect $[_{IP}\ PRO_i$ to become $[_{NP:i}$ brain surgeons]]
ii. *$he_i$ expects $[_{IP}\ PRO_i$ to become $[_{NP:i}$ brain surgeons]]

(67) a. i. $he_i$ seems $[_{IP}\ e_i$ to have consoled $himself_i$ with another beer]
ii. *$I_i$ seem $[_{IP}\ e_i$ to have consoled $himself_i$ with another beer]
b. i. $I_i$ failed $[_{CP}\ [_{IP}\ PRO_i$ to console $myself_i$ with another beer]]
ii. *$I_i$ failed $[_{CP}\ [_{IP}\ PRO_i$ to console $himself_i$ with another beer]]

The paradigm in (65) concerns gender agreement. Both the antecedent of the trace and the controller of PRO must have the same gender feature as the reflexive pronoun, which is bound by trace in the (a)-examples and by PRO in the (b)-examples. Thus, the (ii)-examples in (65) are ill formed because the antecedent of trace and the controller of PRO (*he*) does not agree in gender with the reflexive *herself.* The paradigms in (66)–(67) involve similar analyses, where (66) concerns number agreement with a predicate nominal and (67) concerns person agreement. These paradigms thus demonstrate a second common property of trace and PRO—namely, that they bear (or transmit) the agreement features of their antecedents.

---

**Exercise 6.16**

It is worth noting at this point that the paradigms for PRO and NP-trace binding in sentential complements are identical: proper binding is possible only with respect to infinitival subject position. Give the paradigm for PRO corresponding to (55) for trace. Discuss how the facts are accounted for without reference to binding conditions. Remember that trace, but never PRO, can occur as an object in a simple sentence.

---

Binding aside, the distribution of PRO differs from that of trace in three ways:

1. PRO is not subject to the ECP.
2. PRO binding is always between thematic positions.
3. PRO binding is not subject to Subjacency.

In contrast, a trace must satisfy the ECP, as demonstrated in this chapter and in chapters 3 and 5. Given that trace binding involves the transmission of a θ-role to the antecedent of the trace, Functional Uniqueness prohibits trace binding between thematic positions. Finally, as demonstrated in chapter 3, trace binding is constrained by the Subjacency Condition.

The fact that PRO cannot occur in certain lexically governed positions is one piece of evidence suggesting that PRO cannot be subject to the ECP.

(68) a. *John saw PRO
b. *John gave a book to PRO
c. *John believes [$_{IP}$ PRO to be lying]

Thus, PRO cannot be lexically governed by V (in (68a,c)) or P (in (68b)).[31] (68c) has been interpreted as showing that PRO cannot occur as the infinitival subject of an obligatory CP-deletion verb where it will be governed by the matrix verb. In contrast, PRO does occur in positions that are not lexically governed.

(69) a. [$_{CP}$ [$_{IP}$ PRO to arrive on time]] is very important
b. it is very important [$_{CP}$ [$_{IP}$ PRO to arrive on time]]

If the infinitival IP in (69a) is not lexically governed, there is no way for PRO to be lexically governed. The impossibility of CP-deletion in (69b) is illustrated by the ill-formedness of the raising option in (70).

(70) *John$_i$ is very important [$_{CP}$ [$_{IP}$ e$_i$ to arrive on time]]

The trace violates the ECP if CP is a barrier to government. Given this, the distribution of PRO follows under the hypothesis that all infinitivals with PRO subjects are CP structures as well as IPs.

The fact that PRO binding is always between thematic positions is shown in the following examples of control PRO.

(71) a. John$_i$ tried [$_{CP}$ [$_{IP}$ PRO$_i$ to leave on time]]
b. Mary$_i$ wants [$_{CP}$ [$_{IP}$ PRO$_i$ to leave on time]]
c. Mary persuaded John$_i$ [$_{CP}$ [$_{IP}$ PRO$_i$ to leave on time]]
d. John$_i$ was persuaded e$_i$ [$_{CP}$ [$_{IP}$ PRO$_i$ to leave on time]]
e. John$_i$ promised Mary [$_{CP}$ [$_{IP}$ PRO$_i$ to leave on time]]

The fact that PRO is in a thematic position can be demonstrated with verbs that allow either PRO or lexical NP as the subject of their infinitival complement; compare (71b) and (72).

(72) Mary wants John to leave on time

By Functional Relatedness, the subject *John* must be assigned a θ-role. Thus, the subject of the infinitival is a thematic position just like the subject of the matrix clause. In the cases of *persuade* and *promise*, the structures with finite complements (corresponding to infinitivals with PRO subjects) contain a lexical subject that is distinct from the matrix subject.

(73) a. Mary persuaded John that Bill should leave on time
b. John was persuaded that Bill should leave on time
c. John promised Mary that Bill would leave on time

Again the conclusion that PRO in (71c–e) is in a thematic position holds.

The third difference between PRO and trace concerns the locality conditions relating to their binding. Although trace binding is subject to Subjacency, PRO binding seems not to be. The examples in (74) provide a contrast.[32]

(74) a. after the accident John$_i$ found [$_{CP}$ that [$_{IP}$ it was difficult [$_{CP}$ [$_{IP}$ PRO$_i$ to shave himself$_i$]]]]
b. *after the accident John$_i$ seemed [$_{CP}$ that [$_{IP}$ it was likely [$_{IP}$ e$_i$ to shave himself$_i$]]]

In (74a) *John* is bound to PRO across two bounding nodes (the two embedded IPs). Because the example is grammatical, we must conclude that PRO binding is not subject to Subjacency. In contrast, the matrix subject *John* in the ill-formed (74b) binds its trace across the same two bounding nodes, violating Subjacency. Thus, it appears that Subjacency must distinguish between trace and PRO if the grammar is to account for the grammaticality differences between (74a) and (74b).[33]

A structural difference between PRO and trace might account for why PRO binding is immune to the principle of Functional Uniqueness. By "immune to Functional Uniqueness" we do not mean that the binder of PRO may carry more than one θ-role. Rather, we mean that although trace binding necessarily involves the transfer of a θ-role from a position occupied by a trace to its lexical antecedent, PRO binding appears to involve no such transfer. Why should this be so?

We can clarify this issue by a more detailed examination of how θ-roles are assigned. Let us assume for concreteness that θ-roles are assigned at LF to grammatical positions. In (75), for example, the θ-role Goal will be assigned to the position occupied by the trace and then transferred to the surface subject.

(75) $\text{Peter}_i$ was given $e_i$ a head of lettuce by one of the students

If a θ-role must be associated with a head, then we might have an explanation for why trace binding necessarily entails θ-role transfer. A trace is a maximal phrasal projection without a head. Therefore, a trace must have a θ-role assigned to its antecedent, which does have a head. To prevent the transfer of θ-roles in PRO binding, we need only analyze PRO as a headed empty NP—thereby creating a structural distinction between PRO and trace, as given in (76).

(76) Trace: $[_{NP}\ e]$
PRO: $[_{NP}\ [_{N}\ e]]$

The hypothesis is that a headed NP, whether or not it contains lexical material, retains the θ-role assigned to the position it occupies.

The structural PRO/trace distinction suggested in (76) might be used in a related way to explain why trace but not PRO must be subject to the ECP. As a bearer of a θ-role, PRO is an identified empty category. Trace under our analysis never bears a θ-role, and so cannot be identified in that way. Perhaps the ECP provides another way for empty categories to be identified. Since PRO is identified in one way, it need not be identified in another.

**Bibliographical Comments**

The ECP originated in Chomsky 1981, as did the ECP analysis for trace subjects of finite clauses. The ECP analysis is clarified and extended in Lasnik and Saito 1984; see also Lasnik and Saito, 1992. Chomsky 1986a provides a somewhat different approach to the ECP. See also Aoun 1985 for an analysis that attempts to derive ECP effects from a generalization of binding theory, and Kayne 1983a and Pesetsky 1982a for attempts to derive these effects from conditions on the geometry of phrase structure. The notion of proper government plays a role in another principle of grammar, the **Constraint on Extraction Domains** (standardly referred to as the CED), which accounts for certain asymmetries concerning extractions from complements versus extractions from subjects of finite clauses and from adjuncts.[34]

The concept of thematic relation (or θ-role) distinct from that of grammatical relation originated in Gruber 1965. For a theory of semantic interpretation that makes extensive use of thematic relations, see Jackendoff 1972—and see also Freidin 1975a and Hust and Brame 1976 for some critical discussion. The principle of Unique Assignment is due to Freidin 1975b. The principles of Functional Uniqueness and Functional Relatedness come from Freidin 1978b, where they are formulated in terms of arguments rather than θ-roles. The θ-Criterion of Chomsky 1981 incorporates these three conditions (translating the latter two in terms of thematic relations) and adds a fourth condition requiring that each thematic relation of a predicate be discharged.

The binding-theoretic approach to movement rules is due to Fiengo 1974 (summarized in Fiengo 1977) and developed in Chomsky 1976. The Tensed-S and Specified Subject Conditions originate in Chomsky 1973; see also Chomsky 1977a and 1980b for discussion and alternative formulations. See Kayne 1975 and Quicoli 1976a,b for demonstrations of how the TSC and SSC apply to Romance clitic and quantifier movement constructions.

For further discussion of the PRO/trace distinction, see chapter 8 and the references cited there.

# 7
# Binding Theory

In chapter 6 we were concerned with constructing a theory of grammar that accounts for the distribution of empty categories in sentential representations. As we have seen, this theory makes crucial use of Case, government, and the locality principle known as Subjacency. It is also possible to constrain the distribution of NP-trace and control PRO—empty categories that require a coindexed lexical antecedent—in terms of proper binding violations, where the trace or bound PRO is free in a bind-ing domain. Unlike the ECP or the Case Filter, the Proper Binding Condition generalizes across two apparently distinct domains of grammar, movement (trace binding) and interpretation (PRO binding). Thus, in spite of the redundancy between the Proper Binding Condition and other independently motivated principles of grammar, it is useful to consider whether there is some general principle that determines possible binding configurations. The question is whether there is some justification for postulating a general principle that limits all coindexing under c-command.

In this chapter we will pursue this question by investigating the binding of lexical NPs, which involves further instances of coindexing under c-command. Such binding occurs with respect to reflexive pronouns (as illustrated in (1)) and nonreflexive pronouns (as illustrated in (2)).

(1) a. John$_i$ believes [$_{IP}$ himself$_i$ to be clever]
    b. the men$_i$ considered [$_{IP}$ each other$_i$ to be responsible for the accident]

(2) a. John$_i$ believes [$_{CP}$ (that) [$_{IP}$ he$_i$ is clever]]
    b. I$_i$ consider [$_{CP}$ (that) [$_{IP}$ I$_i$ am responsible for the accident]

For the purposes of discussion, we will distinguish between reflexive pronouns and nonreflexive pronouns by referring to the former as **anaphors** and the latter as **pronouns**. An anaphor differs from a pronoun in that it must have an antecedent in the sentence in which it occurs, whereas a pronoun may or may not have an antecedent in the same sentence.[1] The requirement that an anaphor have an antecedent in a sentence is presumably a syntactic one because in certain contexts, some lexical anaphors—for example, first and second person reflexive pronouns—may be interpreted as designating unique individuals.

(3) a. I bought myself a present
b. *John bought myself a present

(4) a. you should buy yourself a present
b. *I will buy yourself a present

Within the context of a conversation between two people, the reflexive pronoun *myself* uniquely designates the speaker and the reflexive pronoun *yourself* uniquely designates the addressee. Therefore, it does not seem that the requirement for an antecedent is motivated by considerations of interpretability. Rather, (3b) and (4b) are syntactically ill formed because they do not satisfy the requirement that an anaphor have an antecedent in the sentence in which it occurs.

In contrast, a pronoun does not require an antecedent within the sentence in which it occurs. The sentence (5) may be represented as either (2a) or (6), where the different indices on *John* and *he* indicate that the pronoun is not anaphoric on the name.

(5) John believes (that) he is clever

(6) $\text{John}_i$ believes $[_{CP}$ (that) $[_{IP}$ $\text{he}_j$ is clever$]]$

The interpretation of a pronoun can be established independently of the sentence in which it occurs.[2] Let us say that a pronoun is "bound" when it is c-commanded by its antecedent and not otherwise.[3]

The distribution of anaphors and bound pronouns is limited to certain configurations, as we can see by substituting pronouns for anaphors in (1)—giving (7)—and conversely in (2)—giving (8).

(7) a. *$\text{John}_i$ believes $[_{IP}$ $\text{him}_i$ to be clever$]$
b. *the $\text{men}_i$ considered $[_{IP}$ $\text{them}_i$ to be responsible for the accident$]$

(8) a. *$\text{John}_i$ believes $[_{CP}$ (that) $[_{IP}$ $\text{himself}_i$ is clever$]]$
b. *$\text{I}_i$ consider $[_{CP}$ (that) $[_{IP}$ $\text{myself}_i$ am responsible for the accident$]]$

Although each anaphor in (8) has a c-commanding antecedent, the sentences in (8) are ill formed presumably because the syntactic relation between the anaphor and its antecedent is not licit, as we will see in section 7.1.1. The anaphors in (8) are bound, but not properly bound—and similarly with the pronouns in (7).

The paradigm consisting of (1)–(2) and (7)–(8) suggests a complementarity in the distribution: bound pronouns may not occur in configurations where anaphors may, and conversely. This complementarity also holds for the simple sentence paradigm, as illustrated in (9), where the anaphor, but not the bound pronoun, may occur as the object of a verb.

(9) a. *$\text{John}_i$ promoted $\text{him}_i$
b. $\text{John}_i$ promoted $\text{himself}_i$

There is, however, another paradigm that appears to contradict the complementarity of anaphors and bound pronouns. In the subject position of NP (i.e., [NP,NP]), either an anaphor (10a) (in this instance, a reciprocal) or a bound pronoun (10b) may occur.

(10) a. $\text{they}_i$ have read [$_{NP}$ each $\text{other's}_i$ books]
b. $\text{they}_i$ have read [$_{NP}$ $\text{their}_i$ books]

In this chapter we will investigate these and other facts concerning the distribution of anaphors and bound pronouns and develop an account of proper binding for anaphors and pronouns from which all the facts discussed above follow—one that reconciles (10) with the apparent complementarity of anaphors and bound pronouns. In section 7.1 we will begin with an analysis of the distribution of lexical anaphors and then consider how the analysis applies cross-linguistically. In section 7.2 we will deal with bound pronouns, looking first at the distribution of bound pronouns and then at indexing for plural pronouns, which is essential to a full account of pronoun binding.

## 7.1 Lexical Anaphors

In this discussion we will assume that indexing applies freely to NP so that an anaphor can be coindexed with another NP. With respect to anaphor binding, coindexing expresses the relation of antecedence between an anaphor and another expression (see note 1). If two NPs are appropriately coindexed, then they must share the same grammatical features—for example, number, gender, and person—where relevant. This requirement excludes the following ill-formed sentences, which will be generated by the rules of grammar under the assumption that indexing of NPs (including coindexing) is free.

(11) a. $*I_i$ shaved $himself_i$
b. $*she_i$ amused $himself_i$
c. $*he_i$ annoyed $themselves_i$

Coindexing in (11) is prohibited because of a failure of agreement in person features (11a), gender features (11b), and number features (11c).

Although coindexing under feature agreement is necessary for anaphor binding, it is not sufficient. We also need to rule out cases like (12a), where there is coindexing under feature agreement and the sentence is ill formed.

(12) a. $*himself_i$ promoted $John_i$
b. $John_i$ promoted $himself_i$ (= (9b))

In (12a) the anaphor c-commands the NP it is coindexed with, whereas in the grammatical (12b) the coindexed NP c-commands the anaphor. For anaphor binding, the antecedent must c-command the anaphor.

---

**Exercise 7.1**

In (12a) the anaphor c-commands its antecedent. Perhaps the requirement for anaphor binding should be stated as "An anaphor may not c-command its antecedent" rather than as "The antecedent must c-command the anaphor." Discuss the following examples in light of the two proposals:

(i) $*[_{NP}$ $John's_i$ wife] likes $himself_i$

(ii) a. $*[_{NP}$ $our_i$ mothers] like $[_{NP}$ each $other's_i$ recipes]
b. $[_{NP:i}$ our mothers] like $[_{NP}$ each $other's_i$ recipes]

Another way to account for (12a) is to say that an anaphor may not occur to the left of its antecedent. How do the examples in (i)–(ii) show that this is not the correct account?

---

The above examples show that anaphor binding requires at least permissible coindexing with a c-commanding antecedent. In the remainder of the discussion we will say that an anaphor that meets this requirement is bound. As we saw in (8), certain configurations for anaphor binding are not licit. In the following section we will investigate the conditions that distinguish licit from illicit anaphor binding.

### 7.1.1 Proper Binding

The sentences in (8) contain anaphors that are bound (have c-commanding antecedents) but are nonetheless ill formed. Though the anaphor is bound, it is not properly bound. The examples cited involve complex sentences where the anaphor occurs in the embedded IP and its antecedent in the matrix IP. The paradigm for proper binding violations involving complex sentences is given in (13).[4]

(13) a. Finite clause complement
i. *we$_i$ expect [$_{CP}$ (that) [$_{IP}$ each other$_i$ will win]]
ii. *we$_i$ expect [$_{CP}$ (that) [$_{IP}$ Mary will admire each other$_i$]]

b. Infinitival complement
i. *we$_i$ expect [$_{IP}$ Mary to admire each other$_i$]

(13a.i–ii) show that an anaphor in a finite clause complement cannot be properly bound by an external antecedent (i.e., one that is not contained in that clause), and (13b.i) shows that an object in an infinitival complement cannot be bound by an external antecedent. This suggests that an anaphor in IP must have its antecedent in the same IP. However, this formulation is not quite adequate. In contrast to (13b.i), proper binding can occur between an infinitival subject anaphor and an external antecedent, as illustrated in (14) and also in (1a).

(14) we$_i$ expect [$_{IP}$ each other$_i$ to win]

Therefore, an account of proper binding for anaphors must capture the difference in structure between (13) and (14).

The proper binding violations show that when anaphor binding occurs, it must occur within a specific subdomain of a sentence. When an anaphor is bound in a sentence, but is not bound within the appropriate subdomain of the sentence, proper binding is violated. That is, the anaphor cannot be free (i.e., not coindexed with a c-commanding expression) in this subdomain. An account of proper binding then requires a principle of the form (15).

(15) An anaphor must be bound in domain D.

To account for the limitations on proper binding, we will have to characterize domain D in terms of the relevant subdomain(s) in which an anaphor must be bound (or equivalently, cannot be free—but see exercise 7.6).

The examples in (13a) show that an anaphor cannot be free in a finite clause—in these cases the embedded finite clause containing the anaphor. (13b) shows that the characterization of domain D in (15) must also include infinitivals where the anaphor is not the subject. In this case the anaphor is c-commanded by the infinitival subject, so domain D for (13b.i) is the domain in which the anaphor is c-commanded by a subject (or "the c-command domain of subject" for short). This characterization also covers (13a.ii) since the anaphor in the finite clause is similarly c-commanded by a subject (*Mary*) that is not its antecedent. Let "c-command domain of subject" be defined as the set of categories that are c-commanded by the subject. This includes all categories dominated by IP, minus the subject itself, given that the c-command relation holds only between categories in a linear precedence relation.[5]

Although the set-of-categories definition of domain seems less problematic than the single-category definition, it is still possible to use the latter by making the notion of subject (relevant to binding) more precise. The domain of the complement subject in (13a.ii) and (13b.i) is a binding domain, whereas the domain of the complement subject in (14) is not. The difference between the examples is that in the former the subject and the anaphor are distinct, whereas in the latter the anaphor is the subject. Although the complement subjects in (13a.ii) and (13b.i) can act as antecedents for the anaphor in the complement object, the infinitival subject in (14) cannot act as its own antecedent. Let us say, then, that the complement subjects in (13a.ii) and (13b.i) are **accessible antecedents** (i.e., possible though not actual antecedents). In contrast, the anaphor subject in (14) is not an accessible antecedent to itself. Therefore, if we sharpen our characterization of the binding domain D in (15) as "c-command domain of an accessible subject," then (13a.ii) and (13b.i) violate (15) as before, and (14) does not. The infinitival IP does not contain a subject accessible to the anaphor, so it is not the binding domain for the anaphor. The matrix IP does, and in that domain the anaphor is bound to the matrix subject, so no binding violation occurs.

---

**Exercise 7.2**

Consider the analysis of the following grammatical example:

(i) they told me lies about each other

Assume that *tell* is a double object verb and that both the NP object *lies* and the PP *about each other* occur in the subcategorization domain. How does the analysis of this example distinguish between the two possibilities for the formulation of binding domain: accessible antecedent versus accessible subject?

---

To account for the proper binding violation in (13a.i), we will have to revise our formulation of binding domain further. As it stands, our formulation allows a subject anaphor in a finite complement to be properly bound by an antecedent outside the complement—contrary to fact. This happens with finite subject complements under our formulation for exactly the same reason that infinitival complement subject anaphors can be bound by an antecedent in the matrix—namely, there is no "accessible antecedent" for the anaphor in the complement. This shows that some other concept (in addition to or perhaps instead of the notion "antecedent") is at work in binding phenomena.

For excluding bound anaphor subjects of finite clauses under the proper binding condition (15), there are two elements that could play a role: finite Infl and Infl containing the AGR element, as we discussed in section 6.3.1.1 with respect to proper binding for NP-trace. The data from English do not distinguish between the two proposals. However, data from languages that manifest subject-verb agreement phenomena in nonfinite sentential constructions suggest that the AGR element rather than finite Infl is the relevant factor in determining binding domains. Turkish is one such language that illustrates this effect. (The following examples are from George and Kornfilt 1981.)

(16) *yazar-lar$_i$ [$_\alpha$ birbir-lerin-in$_i$ viski-yi
author-PL each-other=their-GEN whisky-ACC

iç-tik-lerin]-i san-ɨyor-lar
drink-GER-3PL-ACC believe-PRES-3PL

'the authors believe that each other drank whisky'

The phrase a is a gerundive sentential complement containing a verb form *iç* to which the gerund-forming morpheme *-tik* has been affixed. The third person suffix *-lerin* on the verb *iç* indicates agreement with the sentential subject of the gerund, *bibir-lerin* 'each other'. In this instance the binding of the anaphor by an antecedent outside the domain of the agreement element is not well formed. When the agreement element is not present, the anaphoric subject of a sentential complement may be bound by an external antecedent, as illustrated in (17) for nonfinite complements.

(17) a. (biz$_i$) [$_{IP}$ bibir-imiz-i$_i$ viski-yi
we each-other=our-ACC whisky-ACC

iç-ti] san-ɨyor-uz
drink-PAST-(no AGR) believe-PRES-1PL

'we believe each other to have drunk the whisky'

b.* (biz$_i$) [$_{IP}$ bibir-imiz-i$_i$ viski-yi
we each other-1PL-ACC whisky-ACC

iç-ti-**k**] san-ɨyor-uz
drink-PAST-1PL believe-PRES-1PL

In (17a), where the sentential complement lacks the agreement element, the matrix subject may properly bind the anaphor in complement subject position. This binding relationship is not permissible when the sentential complement contains AGR, as illustrated in (17b). In other words, the anaphor *bibir-* is free (i.e., not bound) in the domain of AGR. Thus, the Turkish facts indicate that it is the domain of AGR that is relevant to binding.

In light of this discussion, domain D in the condition of proper binding (15) may now be specified as the domain of an accessible subject or AGR. Since the occurrence of AGR is always linked to the syntactic subject of a clause (via subject-verb agreement), we might consider AGR to be a "subject" in some sense. Given the intrinsic connection, we can designate syntactic subject and AGR as instances of **SUBJECT** (read "capital subject") (following Chomsky 1981).[6] Under this characterization, domain D of the proper binding condition is now the domain of an accessible SUBJECT.

Because the binding domain for anaphors now includes AGR in Infl, it cannot be formulated in terms of c-command under the usual definition (see note 3). Given the structure of IP where IP immediately dominates the NP subject and I*, and I* immediately dominates Infl and VP, Infl does not c-command the subject position since I* is the first branching category that dominates Infl. Although AGR in Infl does not c-command the subject in IP, it does m-command that position. Suppose that the proper binding condition (15) is now reformulated in terms of the m-command domain of an accessible SUBJECT. IP is the first maximal phrasal projection that dominates a subject NP and also AGR in Infl. Therefore, the m-command domain of AGR is IP, as is the m-command domain of a syntactic subject.

Consider now how (15) with domain D characterized as "the m-command domain of an accessible SUBJECT" accounts for proper binding violations involving an anaphor subject of a finite clause complement. The link between AGR and the syntactic subject, which shows up as morphological agreement between the subject and the finite form of the verb or auxiliary, can be represented by coindexation of the subject with Infl. Under this analysis, (13a.i) would be represented as (18).

(18) *$\text{we}_i$ expect [$_{CP}$ (that) [$_{IP}$ each $\text{other}_i$ $\text{Infl}_i$ will win]]

Because the anaphor in (18) is both coindexed with and m-commanded by Infl, it is technically speaking bound in the domain of an accessible SUBJECT. However, Infl is not an appropriate binder for an anaphor since an anaphor is an NP and therefore only stands in for another NP. The relation of anaphora involves expressions of the same category. To rule out (18), we need to say something more about the relation "bound" that distinguishes binding by Infl from binding by NP. Since NPs that can bind anaphors are always arguments (of a predicate), whereas Infl is never an argument, the requisite distinction for binding can be given in terms of A-binding versus $\bar{A}$-binding. Binding by Infl is an instance of $\bar{A}$-binding. Therefore, (18) can be excluded if the condition on proper binding is limited to A-binding. The anaphor is not A-bound in the domain of an accessible SUBJECT and therefore violates the condition on proper binding.

We have been assuming that the condition on proper binding applies only to anaphors that are bound in a sentence but not properly bound. However, as formulated in (19), this condition accounts for all the violations of anaphor binding discussed so far—including some cases where an anaphor is not bound in the sentence in which it occurs.

(19) **Proper Binding Condition** (revised)
An anaphor must be A-bound in the domain of an accessible SUBJECT.[7]

Consider the case where an anaphor occurs as the subject in a simple sentence with an intransitive verb.

(20) a. *each other left
b. $[_{IP}$ each $\text{other}_i$ $\text{Infl}_i$ left]

The anaphor fails to satisfy (19) because it is not A-bound in the domain of Infl. (19), apparently correctly, makes no distinction between (18) and (20). What is relevant to anaphor binding is whether an anaphor is A-bound within the relevant domain. If it is not, the sentence containing the anaphor will be ill formed whether or not the anaphor has an antecedent elsewhere in the sentence. That is, the domain D of (15)—or more precisely, the domain of an accessible SUBJECT (in (19))—constitutes a **binding domain** (the domain in which an anaphor must be bound).

---

**Exercise 7.3**

Discuss how the revised Proper Binding Condition (19) accounts for the following cases:

(i) a. *each $\text{other}_i$ admires $\text{us}_i$
b. *John admires each $\text{other}_i$

Now consider example (ii) from exercise 7.1 (repeated here).

(ii) *[$_{NP}$ John's$_i$ wife] likes himself$_i$

How does (19) apply in this case?

---

In what follows we will see that (19) is the only principle of anaphor binding we need to cover all the cases.

The examples considered thus far have involved anaphors in grammatical function positions in sentences. Henceforth the full paradigm for these cases will be referred to as the **IP-paradigm**. We now turn to another class of cases involving anaphors that occur as constituents of NP, which we may designate the **NP-paradigm**.

The binding principle as formulated in (19) applies correctly to the simple sentence cases of the NP-paradigm, as illustrated in (21).

(21) a. Anaphor in subject of NP position[8]
  i. they$_i$ never read [$_{NP}$ each other's$_i$ books]

 b. Anaphor in object position
  i. they$_i$ have read [$_{NP}$ books about each other$_i$]
  ii. *they$_i$ have read [$_{NP}$ John's/his books about each other$_i$]
  iii. John has read [$_{NP}$ their$_i$ books about each other$_i$]

(21b.ii) violates proper binding because the anaphor is A-free in the m-command domain of an accessible SUBJECT—namely, *John/his* in NP. Thus, an NP with a syntactic subject is a binding domain for an anaphor. When the NP contains no subject and thus no accessible SUBJECT, as in (21a.i) and (21b.i), the NP does not constitute a binding domain and an anaphor in the NP may be properly bound by an antecedent outside of the NP.

In the NP-paradigm cases involving complex sentences, the domain of a syntactic subject continues to act as a binding domain for anaphors, as (22) illustrates.

(22) Anaphor in subject of NP position
 a. *they$_i$ expected [$_{CP}$ that [$_{IP}$ John would favorably review [$_{NP}$ each other's$_i$ books]]]
 b. *they$_i$ expected [$_{CP}$ that [$_{IP}$ John would read [$_{NP}$ books about each other$_i$]]]
 c. *they$_i$ expected [$_{IP}$ John to favorably review [$_{NP}$ each other's$_i$ books]]
 d. *they$_i$ expected [$_{IP}$ John to read [$_{NP}$ books about each other$_i$]]

In (22a,c) the anaphor is in the subject position of NP, and in (22b,d) it is in the adjunct position of NP. The NPs containing the anaphor are objects of finite clause complements in (22a–b), but objects of infinitival complements in (22c–d). In all cases the anaphor is A-free in the domain of the (accessible) syntactic subject *John* and each example is ungrammatical for that reason.

---

**Exercise 7.4**

The following examples show that for anaphor binding the domain of syntactic subject includes the subject of NP.

(i) *$\text{they}_i$ liked [$_{NP}$ John's books about each $\text{other}_i$]

(ii) *$\text{they}_i$ expected [$_{IP}$ [$_{NP}$ John's books about each $\text{other}_i$] to receive rave reviews]]

(iii) *$\text{they}_i$ expected [$_{CP}$ that [$_{IP}$ [$_{NP}$ John's books about each $\text{other}_i$] would receive rave reviews]]]

Notice that (i) is just like (21b.ii). Discuss how each example violates the Proper Binding Condition.

---

In contrast to the domain of syntactic subject cases cited in (22), the domain of AGR does not appear to function as a binding domain for the NP-paradigm. Some relevant examples are given in (23).

(23) a. $\text{they}_i$ expected [$_{CP}$ that [$_{IP}$ [$_{NP}$ each other's$_i$ books] would receive rave reviews]]
b. $\text{they}_i$ expected [$_{CP}$ that [$_{IP}$ [$_{NP}$ books about each $\text{other}_i$] would receive rave reviews]]

(23a–b) show that the position of the anaphor within NP does not affect grammaticality. In both examples the anaphor will be A-free in the domain of the complement AGR (instantiated in the modal auxiliary *would*). (23a–b) seem as grammatical as (24a–b), which satisfy (19).

(24) a. $\text{they}_i$ expected [$_{IP}$ [$_{NP}$ each other's$_i$ books] to receive rave reviews]
b. $\text{they}_i$ expected [$_{IP}$ [$_{NP}$ books about each $\text{other}_i$] to receive rave reviews]

In (24) there is no possibility of a binding principle violation since the anaphor is A-bound in the domain of an accessible SUBJECT—the domain of matrix IP. The lack of contrast in grammaticality between (23) and (24) poses a problem for the account of binding developed thus far: namely, to explain why (23) is not a binding violation.

To solve this problem, we must come to terms with why (18) violates proper binding and (23a–b) do not. In terms of binding, the contrast between (18) and (23) shows that the domain of AGR constitutes a binding domain for an anaphor in subject position when AGR and the subject are directly linked, but not when they are not. When an anaphor is properly contained in the subject NP, as in (23a–b), it is not directly linked to AGR.

An explanation will have to address the difference in well-formedness between the following two configurations, where α is an anaphor:

(25) a. *. . . $NP_i$ . . . $[_{CP}\ [_{IP}\ \alpha_i$ AGR . . . ]] (≈ (18))
b. . . . $NP_i$ . . . $[_{CP}\ [_{IP}\ [_{NP}$ . . . $\alpha_i$ . . . ] AGR . . . ]] (≈ (23))

One difference between the two configurations is that in (25a) the AGR element is construed as a link between the subject $\alpha_i$ and the finite verb of IP. The link is determined on the basis of a set of shared features: [α number, β gender, γ person], so-called **ϕ-features**. In this way the AGR element looks like a partially specified index, since like other indices it consists of a feature matrix containing at least these three features. Let us assume therefore that the AGR element is actually an index on Infl, as suggested above. The representations of (25) now translate into those of (26).

(26) a. *. . . $NP_i$ . . . $[_{CP}\ [_{IP}\ \alpha_i\ Infl_i$ . . . ]]
b. . . . $NP_i$ . . . $[_{CP}\ [_{IP}\ [_{NP:k}$ . . . $\alpha_i$ . . . ] $Infl_k$ . . . ]]

In (26a) α will be coindexed with Infl via agreement, and so NP, α, and Infl will all bear the same index. In contrast, α and Infl in (26b) will not be coindexed via agreement. Rather, Infl and the NP containing α will be coindexed.

If the index *k* in (26b) must be distinct from the index *i*, then the difference between the IP-paradigm and the NP-paradigm with respect to the domain of AGR is explained. In both (26a) and (26b) there is a direct connection via agreement between Infl and the NP it is coindexed with. In (26b), however, there is no direct connection between α and Infl. Moreover, there *cannot* be any direct connection between these two elements. In some way the grammar must exclude the possibility that agreement will occur between α and Infl in (26b) whether or not α is an anaphor bound by an antecedent in a higher clause. That is, the grammar must generally prohibit examples of the following sort where agreement occurs between Infl and an NP properly contained in the adjacent subject rather than with the subject itself:

(27) a. *$[_{NP}$ reactions to $[_{NP:i}$ the proposal]] $Infl_i$ $[_V$ BE + e] mixed
b. *reactions to the proposal was mixed

The ungrammatical (27b) would result from (27a). Like nominative Case assignment, indexing of Infl requires that the Infl containing AGR and the NP it gets its index from occur in the same government domain. Under this characterization, a is not available for the indexing of Infl in (26b), in contrast to (26a).

Using this contrast between (26a) and (26b), we can now show how the contrast between (18) and (23) follows from our proper binding condition simply by sharpening the concept of accessibility. Let us say that a SUBJECT is *accessible* to an anaphor when a direct coindexing connection is possible. Direct coindexing connections are possible for any pair of NPs; therefore, any syntactic subject will be accessible to an anaphor in the same sentence. Since AGR can only be directly coindexed with the subject NP of its clause, AGR will be an accessible SUBJECT for only the syntactic subject of its clause. The contrast between (18) and (23) now follows from our formulation of the Proper Binding Condition given in (19).[9] In (18) AGR constitutes an accessible SUBJECT for the anaphor in subject position. Since the anaphor is not A-bound in the domain of AGR, the sentence violates (19). In (23) AGR is not accessible to either anaphor; therefore, AGR does not constitute an accessible SUBJECT with respect to them. The syntactic subject of the matrix is, however, an accessible subject with respect to these anaphors properly contained in the complement subject position. Yet in the domain of this accessible SUBJECT (= matrix syntactic subject), the anaphors are A-bound and therefore satisfy (19).

---

**Exercise 7.5**

Under this analysis of "accessible SUBJECT," the domain of AGR will not constitute a binding domain for nonsubject anaphors or for subject anaphors in a different clause. To see how this works, consider how the revised Proper Binding Condition (19) applies to the following examples with respect to (19):

(i) a. *they$_i$ Infl$_i$ said John$_j$ Infl$_j$ believes each other$_i$ to be lying
    b. *they$_i$ Infl$_i$ said John$_j$ Infl$_j$ believes [$_{NP}$ pictures of each other$_i$] to have appeared in the newspaper
    c. *they$_i$ Infl$_i$ said John$_j$ Infl$_j$ believes that [$_{NP:k}$ pictures of each other$_i$] Infl$_k$ would eventually appear in the newspaper

Distinguish the SUBJECTs in each example from the accessible SUBJECTs. State how each example violates (19).

---

We have been assuming that the definition of SUBJECT covers all syntactic subjects. This is correct for "referential" lexical subjects, their empty category counterparts (i.e., trace), and PRO.

(28) a. NP-trace
*Adam$_i$ seems to us$_j$ [$_{IP}$ e$_i$ to like each other$_j$]
b. *wh* trace
*which man$_i$ do they$_j$ expect [$_{IP}$ e$_i$ to like each other$_j$]
c. PRO
*we$_i$ persuaded Mary$_j$ [$_{CP}$ [$_{IP}$ PRO$_j$ to like each other$_i$]]

In (28a–b) the anaphor *each other* is A-free in the m-command domain of a trace subject, and in (28c) it is A-free in the domain of a PRO subject. In contrast, pleonastic *it* (also called "nonreferential" *it*) does not appear to behave like an accessible SUBJECT with respect to anaphor binding (see Freidin and Harbert 1983 for a detailed discussion). For example, (29a.ii) seems relatively well formed compared with the ungrammatical (29a.i), and similarly for the corresponding examples in (29b).[10]

(29) a. Infinitival complements
i. *they$_i$ expect [$_{IP}$ John$_j$ to seem to each other$_i$ [$_{IP}$ e$_j$ to be crazy]]
ii. they$_i$ expect [$_{IP}$ it to seem to each other$_i$ [$_{CP}$ that John is crazy]]

b. Finite clause complements
i. *they$_i$ expected [$_{CP}$ that John$_j$ AGR$_j$ would seem to each other$_i$ [$_{IP}$ e$_j$ to be crazy]]
ii. they$_i$ expected [$_{CP}$ that it AGR$_j$ would seem to each other$_i$ [$_{CP}$ that John is crazy]]

As indicated in (29), the well-formedness of these constructions is not significantly affected by the addition of AGR to the complement of *expect*.

The contrast in grammaticality of the examples in (29) suggests that the definition of "accessible SUBJECT" for anaphor binding should take account of the distinction between pleonastic NPs, which have no semantic content, and NPs that do have semantic content. This distinction can be formulated in terms of θ-roles as follows. A subject that bears a θ-role constitutes a θ-subject, in contrast to non-θ-subjects like pleonastic *it*. Apparently, only θ-SUBJECTS (including Infl that is bound to a θ-subject) qualify as accessible SUBJECTs for the proper binding condition given in (19). This formulation has some intuitive appeal in that an anaphor also bears a θ-role and therefore could not be anaphoric on (i.e., stand in for) an NP that could not bear a θ-role.

**Exercise 7.6**

The precise formulation of the proper binding condition in (19) is crucial to a correct account of the binding facts. To see this, consider how an alternative formulation of the condition given in (i) fails to account for (ii).

(i) An anaphor cannot be A-free in the domain of an accessible SUBJECT.

(ii) *[$_{NP:j}$ each other's$_i$ books] Infl$_j$ have been selling well

Discuss in detail why (ii) is problematic for (i) and how it is accounted for under (19).

Following standard practice in the literature, let us designate the proper binding condition for anaphors (19) as **Principle A** of the binding theory. Having established a working version of Principle A for a wide range of facts concerning anaphor binding in English, we turn now to anaphor binding in other languages. As will become clear in the following sections, Principle A is subject to some parametric variation cross-linguistically.

### 7.1.2 Cross-linguistic variation

The analysis of anaphor binding given in the previous section was based almost exclusively on data from English. In other languages the patterns for proper binding of anaphors often seem quite different. Yet they are by and large variations on a theme. Thus, the basic component of the binding theory with respect to anaphors is some condition requiring that they be A-bound within a binding domain. The variation across languages concerns how binding domains are determined and which lexical items fall under Principle A. In English it appears that the binding domain for anaphors is computed in terms of an accessible SUBJECT and that both reflexive pronouns and reciprocals are subject to Principle A. There are other possibilities, some of which are sketched briefly in the following three subsections.

**7.1.2.1 Russian** Like English, Russian has two types of lexical anaphor, reciprocals and reflexives. The reciprocal in Russian is *drug druga.* It does not morphologically distinguish number, person, or gender—though it does show Case, being able to occur in any case except the nominative. The citation form *drug druga* is in the accusative. The reflexive has two distinct morphological forms, the personal pronoun *sebja* and the possessive *svoj.* Neither form undergoes morphological changes with respect to the number, gender, or person of its antecedent.

Unlike the corresponding English anaphors, the two Russian anaphors manifest distinctly different binding patterns. Within a single clause where both the subject and the object c-command the anaphor,[11] either subject or object may be interpreted as the antecedent of the reciprocal, whereas only the subject may bind the reflexive. This contrast is shown in (30) versus (31). (The examples in this section are from Rappaport 1986.)

(30) milicionery rassprašivali ix drug o drug-e
policemen-NOM questioned them-ACC each about other-LOC
'the policemen$_i$ questioned them$_j$ about each other$_{\{i,j\}}$'

(31) a. milicioner rassprašival arestovannogo o sebe
policeman-NOM questioned suspect-ACC about self-LOC
'the policeman$_i$ questioned the suspect$_j$ about himself$_{\{i,*j\}}$'

b. my dovezli rebenka do svoego doma
we-NOM took child-ACC to self's home-GEN
'we$_i$ took the child$_j$ to our$_i$/*his$_j$ home'

In contrast to reciprocal binding in (30), reflexive binding in (31) appears to be limited to subjects—that is, reflexive binding is subject-oriented, as is the case for the Japanese reflexive *zibun* (see Koster 1982 for discussion and references).[12]

Another difference between reflexives and reciprocals in Russian concerns binding across syntactic subjects. Although neither anaphor may be bound across the subject of a finite clause, reflexives—but not reciprocals—may be bound across a PRO subject (i.e., the subject of a nonfinite clause). (32) gives the paradigm for finite clauses and (33) the paradigm for nonfinite clauses.

(32) a. Reflexive binding
Vanja znaet, [$_{CP}$ čto Volodja ljubit sebja]
Vanja-NOM knows that Volodja-NOM loves self-ACC
'Vanja$_i$ knows that Volodja$_j$ loves himself$_{\{*i,j\}}$'

b. Reciprocal binding
roditeli dumali, [$_{CP}$ čto deti ljubjat drug drug-a]
parents-NOM thought that children-NOM love each other-ACC
'the parents$_i$ thought that the children$_j$ loved each other$_{\{*i,j\}}$'

(33) a. Reflexive binding

on ne razrešaet mne
he-NOM not permit me-DAT

[$_{CP}$ PRO proizvodit' opyty nad soboj]
to-perform experiments on self-INST

'he$_i$ does not allow me$_j$ [$_{CP}$ PRO$_j$ to perform experiments on himself$_i$/myself$_j$]'

b. Reciprocal binding

my proprosili ix
we-NOM asked them-ACC

[$_{CP}$ PRO nalit' drug drug-u čajku]
to-pour each other-DAT tea-ACC

'we$_i$ asked them$_j$ [$_{CP}$ PRO$_j$ to pour each other$_{\{*i,j\}}$ tea]'

Reciprocal binding for the IP-paradigm in Russian appears to have the same properties as in English—namely, a reciprocal must be bound in the domain of a SUBJECT. (We will refer to this as **SUBJECT effects**, and to the analogous situation with subjects as **subject effects**.) Reflexive binding for the IP-paradigm in Russian is less restrictive than in English since the domain of a PRO subject in infinitival complements does not count as a binding domain. In (33a) the reflexive pronoun in the infinitival complement is free in the domain of a subject PRO but can be bound by either the subject or the object of the matrix IP. The corresponding English construction is ill formed (see (28c)).

There is also a lack of subject effects in the NP-paradigm in Russian with respect to lexical NP subjects.

(34) ja čital [$_{NP}$ ego stat'ju o sebe]
I-NOM read his article-NOM about self-LOC
'I$_i$ read [$_{NP}$ his$_j$ article about myself$_i$/himself$_j$]'

In (34) the reflexive in the NP can be properly bound by a sentential subject even when the NP contains its own subject NP.

One way to account for the reflexive paradigm would be to modify the domain statement for Principle A. The modification must be based on a distinction between the syntactic subjects of finite and nonfinite clauses. Under the analysis of AGR given above, this distinction is manifested in terms of coindexing (i.e., binding) with Infl. The subject of a finite clause will be bound by Infl (and conversely), whereas the subject of an infinitival complement will not be bound within its clause and the subject of an NP will not be bound within the minimal NP that contains it. Given this, the modification of Principle A in (35) will account for the examples of reflexive binding in Russian cited above.

(35) **Principle A** (for Russian reflexives)
A reflexive pronoun must be bound in the domain of a bound SUBJECT.

In (33a) the domain where PRO is bound is the matrix IP; hence, the reflexive in the complement can take either the matrix subject or the matrix object as an antecedent.[13] It is necessary to include AGR in the formulation of the domain statement (hence "SUBJECT" and not "subject") to account for the absence of nominative reflexive pronouns in Russian.

In contrast to reflexive binding, reciprocal binding in Russian does show subject effects for the NP-paradigm.

(36) a. oni čitali $[_{NP}$žaloby drug na drug-a]
they-NOM read complaints-ACC each against other-ACC
'they$_i$ were reading $[_{NP}$ complaints against each other$_i$]'

b. *oni čitali $[_{NP}$moi žaloby drug na drug-a]
they-NOM read my complaints-ACC each against other-ACC
'they$_i$ were reading $[_{NP}$ my$_j$ complaints against each other$_i$]'

In (36b) the subject *moi* of the object NP blocks proper binding between the anaphor and the sentential subject *oni.*

One final difference between English and Russian concerns the notion of accessibility as it applies to binding for the NP-paradigm. Accessibility as defined for AGR in English does not play a role in determining the binding domains for either reciprocals or reflexives in Russian. In both cases Russian shows that the domain of AGR is a binding domain for anaphors properly contained in the subject that is linked to AGR.

(37) a. *dissidenty dumali, $[_{CP}$ čto$[_{IP}[_{NP}$ stat'i
dissidents-NOM thought that articles-NOM

drug o drug-e] pojavilis' v zapadnoj presse]]
each about other-LOC appeared in Western press-LOC

'dissidents$_i$ thought $[_{CP}$ that $[_{IP}[_{NP}$ articles about each other$_i$] appeared in the Western press'

b. *Vanja znaet, $[_{CP}$ čto $[_{IP}[_{NP}$ stat'ja o
Vanja-NOM knows that article-NOM about

sebe / svoej žene] pojavilas' v gazete]]
self-LOC/ self's wife-LOC appeared in newspaper-LOC

'Vanja$_i$ knows [$_{CP}$ that [$_{IP}$ [$_{NP}$ an article about himself$_i$/his own$_i$ wife] appeared in the paper]]'

As (37) demonstrates, AGR functions as a SUBJECT for reciprocal binding and as a bound SUBJECT for reflexive binding.

To summarize, Russian anaphor binding differs from English anaphor binding in the following ways:

1. Reflexives and reciprocals have different opaque domains in Russian: for reciprocals, any SUBJECT defines a binding domain; for reflexives, only bound SUBJECTs define binding domains.
2. Anaphor binding in Russian does not involve a notion of "accessible SUBJECT" as defined for English.

In this way, the two languages differ in the possibilities for proper binding of anaphors, yet they utilize essentially the same concepts and mechanisms to establish the pattern.

**7.1.2.2 Icelandic** Icelandic reflexives show the same binding pattern in indicative clauses as Russian reflexives. A Subject coindexed with Infl creates a binding domain for reflexives, and and Infl itself creates a binding domain for a coindexed subject anaphor. As with reflexive binding in Russian, the Icelandic data can be accounted for under the assumption that the domain of a "bound SUBJECT" constitutes the binding domain for reflexives. The domain of a subject not coindexed with Infl (e.g., the subject of an infinitival) is not a binding domain. This is illustrated in (38). (Examples (38a) and (40) are from Thráinsson 1990, (38b), (39), (42a,c), (43) and (44) are from Thráinsson 1979, (41) and (42b) are from Anderson 1986.)

(38) a. *Jón$_i$ upplysti [$_{CP}$ hver hafði barið sig$_i$]
John revealed who had-IND hit self
'John$_i$ revealed [$_{CP}$ who had hit himself$_i$]'

b. Jon$_i$ telur [$_{IP}$ mig$_j$ hafa svikið sig$_i$]
John believes me to have betrayed self
'John$_i$ believes [$_{IP}$ me$_j$ to have betrayed himself$_i$]'

In (38b) the reflexive *sig* is properly bound across a sentential subject *mig*, whereas in (38a) the reflexive cannot be properly bound from outside the indicative clause. Assuming that the subject of the indicative is coindexed with Infl, it is then a "bound subject." The absence of the nominative reflexive in Icelandic can be explained as a binding theory effect if AGR that is coindexed with a subject is considered a bound "subject" as well.

The definition of bound SUBJECT in Icelandic may extend to bound PRO as well. This would account for the ungrammaticality of the reflexive in the following example:

(39) *ég$_i$ lofaði Haraldi$_j$ [$_{CP}$ að PRO$_i$ raka sig$_j$]
I promised Harold to shave self
'I$_i$ promised Harold$_j$ [$_{CP}$ PRO$_i$ to shave himself$_j$]'

Since PRO in (39) is a bound subject, it induces a binding domain with respect to the reflexive even though CP in this instance is nonfinite. In contrast to the Russian example (33a), in (39) the domain of bound PRO constitutes a binding domain, not the domain in which the PRO is bound.[14]

Icelandic and Russian reflexive binding also differ in that subjunctive clauses do not seem to be binding domains in Icelandic. Thus, compare (38a) and (40) which constitute a syntactic minimal pair—the only difference being that (38a) contains the indicative form of the verb 'have' and (40) contains the subjunctive.

(40) Jón$_i$ upplysti [$_{CP}$ hver hefði barið sig$_i$]
John revealed who had-SUBJ hit self
'John$_i$ revealed [$_{CP}$ who had hit himself$_i$]'

Long-distance binding of this sort can occur indefinitely far away just as long as the intervening clauses have subjunctive verbs. (41) provides a striking example.

(41) Jón$_i$ segir [$_{CP}$ að María telji
John$_i$ says-IND that Maria believes-SUBJ
[$_{CP}$ að Haraldur vilji [$_{CP}$ að Billi heimsaeki sig$_i$]]]
that Harold wants-SUBJ that Billy visit-SUBJ himself$_i$

Note that whatever the mechanism is that accounts for such long-distance binding, it cannot be that sentential complements containing subjunctive verbs lack AGR, since the subjunctive participates in subject-verb agreement and involves a rich morphological system. (See Maling 1986 for a more detailed discussion of these constructions.)

Reciprocal binding in Icelandic differs from reflexive binding. The kind of long-distance binding that is available for reflexives in subjunctive clauses is not possible with reciprocals. The reciprocal *hvor annan* must be bound within a finite clause. Thus, (42a) is well formed, but (42b-c) are not.

(42) a. mennirnir$_i$ hata hvor annan$_i$
the-men hate each other

b. *þeir$_i$ vita [$_{CP}$ að ég$_j$ hef sent hvor öðrum$_i$ bréf]
they know that I have-IND sent each other letters

c. *mennirnir$_i$ sögðu [$_{CP}$ að ég$_j$ hefði rakað hvor annan$_i$]
the-men said that I had-SUBJ shaved each other

The more restrictive nature of reciprocal binding is also highlighted in the contrast between the following near minimal syntactic pair.

(43) a. Jón$_i$ skipaði mér$_j$ [$_{CP}$ að PRO$_j$ raka sig$_i$]
John ordered me to-shave himself

b. *þeir$_i$ skipuðu mér$_j$ [$_{CP}$ að PRO$_j$ raka hvor annan$_i$]
they ordered me to-shave each other

In contrast to the reflexive in (43a), the reciprocal in (43b) cannot be properly bound across a bound PRO subject even though the PRO is itself bound by a nonsubject. (44) shows that even an unbound subject creates a binding domain for Icelandic reciprocals.

(44) *mennirnir$_i$ töldu [$_{IP}$ mig$_j$ hata hvor annan$_i$]
the-men believed me to-hate each other
'the meni believed [$_{IP}$ me$_j$ to hate each other$_i$]'

Thus, the binding domain for reciprocals is apparently the domain of SUBJECT.

**7.1.2.3 Korean** Like Icelandic and Russian, Korean also distinguishes between reflexive binding and reciprocal binding, manifesting stronger restrictions on the latter than on the former. Furthermore, the restrictions on reflexive binding are different from those in Icelandic and Russian. The brief sketch that follows is based on Hong 1985, from which the examples are also taken.

Korean is apparently a language in which reflexive binding is free provided the binder is a c-commanding NP. That is, in Korean, Principle A will not specify a domain in which the reflexive (*caki*) must be bound. Nonetheless, we will want to analyze *caki* as an anaphor because it must be antecedent-bound, as indicated by the ill-formedness of (45).

(45) *[$_{NP}$ casin-etahan kisa-ka] naoetta
self-about an article-NOM came out
'[$_{NP}$ an article about self$_i$] came out'

Reflexive binding does not exhibit subject effects.

(46) a. John-i [$_{NP}$ Mary-ɨy casin-etahan kisa-ka] ilketta
John-NOM Mary-GEN self-about article-ACC read
'John$_i$ read [$_{NP}$ Mary's$_j$ article about self$_{\{i,j\}}$]'

b. John-i [$_{CP}$ [$_{NP}$ Mary-ɨy casin-etahan kisa-ka] kecitira-ko] malhetta
John-NOM Mary-GEN self-about article-NOM false-COMP said
'John$_i$ said [$_{CP}$ that [$_{NP}$ Mary's$_j$ article about self$_{\{i,j\}}$] is false]'

As illustrated in (46), the subject of an NP does not induce a binding domain for reflexives whether or not the NP containing the reflexive is in the same clause as the antecedent. In (46a) the NP containing the reflexive is in the same clause as the antecedent; and in (46b) they are in different clauses. (Note that both examples are ill formed in English.) Furthermore, AGR does not appear to induce a binding domain for reflexives since long-distance binding is possible.

(47) Fred-nin John-i Mary-ka caki-ka
Fred-TOP John-NOM Mary-NOM self-NOM

toktokhata-ko malhanket-il siinheta-ko sengakheta
smart-comp said-COMP-ACC admitted-COMP thought

'Fred$_i$ thought that John$_j$ admitted that Mary$_k$ said that self$_{\{i,j,k\}}$ is smart'

Thus, it appears that there is no domain restriction on proper binding of reflexives in Korean.

However, the Korean reflexive must be bound by a c-commanding NP.

(48) a. [$_{NP}$ John-ɨy emma-ka] casin-il pipanheta
John-GEN mother-NOM self-ACC criticized
'[$_{NP}$John's$_i$ mother]$_j$ criticized self$_{\{*i,j\}}$'

b. John-i Bill-eke [$_{CP}$ caki-ka toktokhata-ko malhetta]
John-NOM Bill-to self-NOM be-smart-COMP said
'John$_i$ told Bill$_j$ [$_{CP}$ that himself$_{\{i,*j\}}$ (was) smart]'

In (48a) the possessive NP *John-ɨy* does not c-command the reflexive and therefore cannot properly bind it. In (48b) the object *Bill* will fail to c-command the complement subject *caki* if we interpret the phrase *Bill-eke* as a PP. However, an object may bind a reflexive where c-command holds between the two, as illustrated in (49).

(49) a. John-i Fred-lil casin-ɨy pang-e kaduetta
John-NOM Fred-ACC self-GEN room-at locked-in
'John$_i$ locked Fred$_j$ in self's$_{\{i,j\}}$ room'

b. John-i Fred-lil casin-ɨy cip-ero tolreponeta
John-NOM Fred-ACC self-GEN house-to returned
'John$_i$ returned Fred$_j$ to self's$_{\{i, j\}}$ house'

Given that the accusative object can properly bind the reflexive, it would appear that examples like (48b) cannot be ruled out on the grounds that reflexive binding in Korean is subject-oriented—that is, that only subjects may serve as antecedents to reflexives.[15]

In contrast to reflexive binding, reciprocal binding in Korean manifests binding domain effects. Like the reflexive *caki*, the reciprocal *sero* must be A-bound. Thus, (50) is ill-formed because the reciprocal lacks an antecedent.

(50) *sero-ka tenaetta
each other-NOM left

Unlike the reflexive, the reciprocal shows subject effects in both the NP-paradigm and the IP-paradigm. For example, the matrix subject in (51) cannot properly bind the reciprocal across the subject of NP.

(51) *wuri-ka [$_{NP}$ Mary-ɨy sero-etehan kisa]-lil ilketa
we-NOM Mary-GEN each other-about article-ACC read
'we$_i$ read [$_{NP}$ Mary's$_j$ article about each other$_i$]'

The IP-paradigm in Korean shows no AGR effects, as illustrated by the fact that (52) is well formed.

(52) haksentil-i sero-ka toktokhata-ko malhetta
students-NOM each other-NOM be-smart-COMP said
'students$_i$ said that each other$_i$ (are) smart'

(Given that (52) is well formed, the ungrammaticality of (50) cannot be attributed to the notion that the subject of a finite clause must be A-bound in that clause.) In light of (52), the ungrammaticality of (53) should be attributed to a subject effect, where proper binding between the matrix subject and complement object is blocked because the domain of the complement subject is a binding domain.

(53) wuri-nin kitil-i sero-lil pinanheta-ko malhetta
we-TOP they-NOM each other-ACC criticized-COMP said
'we$_i$ said that they$_j$ criticized each other$_{\{*i, j\}}$'

(51)–(53) together establish that the domain of syntactic subject is a binding domain for reciprocals. (54) shows that reciprocal binding in Korean is more constrained than in English, Russian, or Icelandic.

(54) kitil-i [$_{NP}$ John-kwa Mary]-lil sero-eke sogehetta
they-NOM John-and Mary-ACC each other-to introduced
'they$_i$ introduced [$_{NP}$ John and Mary]$_j$ to each other$_{\{*i, j\}}$'

Unlike what happens in English, for example, where both interpretations of (54) are possible (cf. also *We told John lies about each other*), in Korean the domain of any c-commanding NP constitutes an opaque domain for reciprocal binding. Thus, it appears that in Korean, the subject versus nonsubject distinction is not relevant for defining binding domains.

**7.1.2.4 Summary** Among the languages investigated above, the characterizations of binding domains for anaphors appear to cluster around the various ways we can designate c-commanding binders. Thus, we have the following characterizations:

(55) a. c-commanding NP (Korean reciprocals)
b. c-commanding SUBJECT (Russian and Icelandic reciprocals)
c. c-commanding bound SUBJECT (Russian and Icelandic reflexives)
d. c-commanding accessible SUBJECT (English reciprocals)

These alternatives merely indicate the possible variation. Whether other patterns exist remains to be determined. For example, is there a language for which "bound subject" constitutes a binding domain—that is, a language in which anaphor binding exhibits no AGR effect and also does not exhibit a subject effect for nonfinite clauses? These are questions of fact, as is the more interesting question of why human languages vary in the way they do and not otherwise. That is, is there some theory of grammar that might give a principled explanation for the range of cross-linguistic variation in anaphor binding? At present we have no clear answers to such questions.

## 7.2 Pronouns

In this section we will deal with two separate but related issues concerning pronoun binding. One involves the conditions under which a pronoun may be bound to a c-commanding antecedent. The other involves the indexing of NPs with respect to pronoun binding and the interpretation of indices.

### 7.2.1 Proper Binding

As we established at the beginning of this chapter, the distribution of bound pronouns, like the distribution of bound anaphors, is limited to certain configurations. Moreover, the examples from the IP-paradigm cited in (1)–(9) suggested that there is a complementarity in the distribution of bound anaphors and bound pronouns. These examples showed that if an anaphor is properly bound with respect to an antecedent, a bound pronoun cannot be substituted—and conversely. The paradigm is summarized in (56)–(57).

(56) Simple sentences:
 a. *Mary$_i$ admires her$_i$
 a'. Mary$_i$ admires herself$_i$

(57) Complex sentences
 a. Pronoun in subject position
  i. Mary$_i$ expects [$_{CP}$ (that) [$_{IP}$ she$_i$ will win]]
  i'.*Mary$_i$ expects [$_{CP}$ (that) [$_{IP}$ herself$_i$ will win]]
  ii.*Mary$_i$ expects [$_{IP}$ her$_i$ to win]
  ii'. Mary$_i$ expects [$_{IP}$ herself$_i$ to win]
 b. Pronoun in object position
  i. Mary$_i$ expects [$_{CP}$ (that) [$_{IP}$ John will admire her$_i$]]
  i'.*Mary$_i$ expects [$_{CP}$ (that) [$_{IP}$ John will admire herself$_i$]]
  ii. Mary$_i$ expects [$_{IP}$ John to admire her$_i$]
  ii'.*Mary$_i$ expects [$_{IP}$ John to admire herself$_i$]

To account for proper binding of anaphors, it was necessary to specify the domain in which an anaphor *must* be bound. This approach will not work for proper binding of pronouns because pronoun binding, unlike anaphor binding, is optional. With pronouns, the question is, Under what conditions is binding prohibited? In other words, if pronoun binding is optional, then why is it ruled out in (56a) and (57a.ii)? The answer is, presumably, that within certain syntactic domains a pronoun cannot be bound to an antecedent and therefore must be antecedent-free in that domain. This would be a proper binding condition for pronouns, on a par with the one we have explored for anaphors.

A principle that accounts for proper binding for pronouns can be stated schematically in (58).

(58) **Principle B**
 A pronoun must be A-free in domain D.

(58) appears to be a mirror image of Principle A for anaphor binding (cf. (15) with the appropriate modification regarding A-binding).

Let us turn now to the formulation of the domain statement for Principle B with respect to the IP-paradigm.[16] To account for the simplest case in the IP-paradigm (simple sentences, as in (56a)), the domain statement of Principle B can be specified as "the domain of subject." If a pronoun must be A-free in the domain of subject, then (56a) will be excluded because the pronoun *her* is A-bound in the domain of the clause subject *Mary*. This domain statement suffices to account for the complex sentence cases as well, with the exception of (57a.i).

---

**Exercise 7.7**

Show how Principle B so formulated accounts for the complex sentence cases of this paradigm, with the single exception of (57a.i). Discuss how each ungrammatical sentence violates this formulation of Principle B, in contrast to each grammatical sentence. State why this formulation fails for (57a.i).

---

To account for (57a.i), it is necessary to incorporate the domain of AGR in the domain statement of Principle B so that pronoun subjects of finite clause complements can be properly bound by an antecedent in a matrix clause. As with anaphor binding, AGR can be incorporated into the domain statement in terms of the notion SUBJECT.

If the domain statements for Principles A and B are identical, then the domain statement for Principle B must be "the domain of an accessible SUBJECT." If this is correct, then pronoun binding should be sensitive to accessibility as defined for anaphor binding, and also to the θ versus pleonastic subject distinction discussed in section 7.1.1. It turns out that pronoun binding is sensitive to neither.[17]

Pleonastic subjects induce binding domains for pronouns, as illustrated in (59).

(59) Holmes$_i$ expects it to be reported to him$_i$ that Moriarty has fled to Paris

If the θ versus pleonastic subject distinction were relevant for pronoun binding, as it appears to be for anaphor binding, then pronoun binding in (59) should be prohibited (just as anaphor binding is allowed in similar constructions—for example, (29a.ii)). The grammaticality of (59) suggests that the θ versus pleonastic subject distinction is not relevant for pronoun binding. Thus, Principle B is satisfied if a pronoun is A-free in the domain of any subject or AGR.[18]

A further lack of complementarity between anaphor binding and pronoun binding occurs in the NP-paradigm. Consider first the simple sentence cases of pronoun binding where complementarity fails.

(60) a. $John_i$ read $[_{NP}$ $his_i$ books]

(61) a. $John_i$ does not read $[_{NP}$ books about $him_i]$
b. $John_i$ does not read $[_{NP}$ books about $himself_i]$

(60) shows that in a simple sentence, a pronoun in the subject position of the object NP may be bound. When the pronoun occurs in an adjunct of NP position, the pronoun may be bound by the matrix subject—as illustrated by (61a).[19] This is problematic for a theory in which Principles A and B have the same domain statements since anaphors can be properly bound in both positions, as illustrated in (61b) for the adjunct position. Although the noncomplementarity cannot be shown for subject of NP position with reflexive pronouns—because the form *himself's* does not exist in English—the case can be made with the reciprocal and a corresponding plural pronoun, as in (62).[20]

(62) a. $they_i$ read $[_{NP}$ each $other's_i$ books]
b. $they_i$ read $[_{NP}$ $their_i$ books]

Thus, (60)–(61) indicate that NP constitutes a binding domain for pronouns regardless of the presence of a syntactic subject.[21]

The NP-paradigm involving complex sentences also provides evidence against the total complementarity of anaphors and bound pronouns. The relevant examples concern the subjects of infinitival complements, as illustrated in (63).

(63) a. $Mary_i$ expected $[_{IP}$ $[_{NP}$ $her_i$ book] to receive rave reviews]
b. $Mary_i$ expected $[_{IP}$ $[_{NP}$ books about $her_i]$ to be popular]

In both cases a pronoun (*her*) that is properly contained in the subject of the infinitival may be bound by an antecedent (*Mary*) in the matrix clause.[22] As illustrated in (24) (repeated here), anaphor binding is also permissible in the same configurations.

(24) a. $they_i$ expected $[_{IP}$ $[_{NP}$ each $other's_i$ books] to receive rave reviews]
b. $they_i$ expected $[_{IP}$ $[_{NP}$ books about each $other_i]$ to receive rave reviews]

From the IP-paradigm, we know that IP is not a binding domain for pronouns in the infinitival subject position (e.g., (57a.ii)). This leaves NP as the possible binding domain in which the pronoun is A-free, thereby satisfying Principle B. If NP is a binding domain for pronouns, most of the NP-paradigm is accounted for without reference to the domain of subject of NP.

Although the domain of SUBJECT may be irrelevant to pronoun binding involving the NP-paradigm, it does account for pronoun binding within the IP-paradigm as discussed above. If we are to have a unified account for pronoun binding within both paradigms, it will be necessary to provide an alternative account of the IP-paradigm.

Within the IP-paradigm, IP acts as a binding domain except for the subject of infinitivals. To construct a solution to the problem of unifying the IP- and NP-paradigms, let us begin with an analysis of what is common to IP and NP. Aside from the fact that IP and NP both take syntactic subjects, both are domains in which θ-roles are assigned by verbs, predicate nominals and adjectives, and certain (nonpredicate) nominals. This is illustrated by the sentence-nominal pair in (64).

(64) a. the mayor criticized the city council
b. the mayor's criticism of the city council

Presumably *criticize* and *criticism* assign the same θ-roles to the subject *the mayor* and to the object *the city council*. Let us say that IP and NP constitute **θ-domains**—that is, the domain in which the θ-roles of a predicate are assigned to arguments.

(65) A *θ-domain* is the minimal domain in which a predicate $\pi$ ($\pi$ = V, A, or N) assigns its θ-roles to arguments.[23]

Since V and A may assign a θ-role to an NP outside of their maximal projections (VP and AP)—that is, to a subject of IP, VP and AP do not count as θ-domains.

By characterizing the binding domain for pronouns as the minimal θ-domain containing the pronoun, we can provide a unified account of the IP- and NP-paradigms, with the exception of infinitival subjects. We must assume that IP constitutes a θ-domain even when its sentential subject is a nonthematic position. Consider (66).

(66) *$\text{Mary}_i$ seems to $\text{her}_i$ $[_{IP}\ e_i$ to be happy]

To account for (66) as a violation of Principle B under the proposed analysis, we must consider the matrix IP as the minimal θ-domain containing the pronoun, and not just the VP. The fact that the subject of *seems* is not a position to which a θ-role is assigned appears to be irrelevant to determining the binding domain in this instance. All phrases of the type IP are θ-domains.

**Exercise 7.8**

It should be clear that VP and AP do not constitute θ-domains and therefore are not binding domains for pronouns. Use the following examples to demonstrate this:

(i) a. *John$_i$ is [$_{AP}$ proud of him$_i$]
b. *John$_i$ [$_{VP}$ likes him$_i$]

The status of PP is less obvious. If the distribution of bound pronouns can be used as a diagnostic for when a category constitutes a θ-domain, then some PPs are θ-domains and some are not. Discuss this in light of the following examples:

(ii) a. *John$_i$ sent a book [$_{PP}$ to him$_i$]
b. John$_i$ brought a book [$_{PP}$ with him$_i$]
c. John$_i$ discovered the money [$_{PP}$ near him$_i$]

Try additional examples with other prepositions.

Although the notion "θ-domain" picks out NP and IP, it does not account for the fact that the binding domain for a pronoun subject of an infinitival is the matrix IP containing the infinitival. By definition, the minimal θ-domain containing an infinitival subject is the infinitival IP itself. One difference between a finite and an infinitival complement is that the lexical subject of the former is assigned Case within the complement IP, whereas the lexical subject of the latter when it remains in subject position can only receive Case via exceptional Case marking from the matrix verb. As we saw in chapter 5, Case marking requires government; thus, the pronominal subject of an infinitival must be governed by the matrix verb.

An account of the binding domain of pronoun subjects in infinitival complements can be achieved by incorporating the notions of θ-domain and government in the formulation of Principle B.

(67) **Principle B** (revised)
A pronoun must be A-free in the minimal θ-domain containing its governor.

When the governor of a pronoun subject of an infinitival is the matrix V, the minimal θ-domain of that V will always be the matrix IP. Therefore, the binding domain for a pronoun subject of an infinitival will always be the matrix IP.[24]

**Exercise 7.9**
Explain how (67) accounts for the NP-paradigm—in other words, that NP is a binding domain for pronouns. Now explain how (67) applies to the IP-paradigm in (56)–(57). Is there any advantage or disadvantage to substituting "Case assigner" for "governor" in this formulation of Principle B?

**Exercise 7.10**
Is the following construction ruled out by the formulation of Principle B in (67)?

(i) *John$_i$ wants very much [$_{CP}$ for [$_{IP}$ him$_i$ to win]]

Explain.

In section 7.1 we investigated a wide variety of facts showing cross-linguistic variation in binding domains for anaphors. We will not attempt to do this for pronouns, partly because the subject has yet to be studied in as much detail as anaphor binding. However, some evidence has been discussed in the literature. In Icelandic, for example, bound pronouns appear to be in complementary distribution with bound anaphors with respect to the IP-paradigm. Thus, although the object of an infinitival complement may be bound across a syntactic subject, as in (43a), a pronoun cannot be bound in the same configuration, as illustrated in (68).

(68) *Jón$_i$ skipaði mér$_j$ [$_{CP}$ að PRO$_j$ raka hann$_i$]
John ordered me to shave him

Cross-linguistic studies of such variation are extremely important for a deeper understanding of binding theory.

### 7.2.1 Pronoun Binding and Interpretation

Unlike anaphor binding, pronoun binding allows for the possibility that a plural pronoun can have more than one antecedent in a sentence. This is illustrated in (69), where on one reading the plural pronoun *they* can be interpreted as having both the subject and the object of *tell* as its antecedents.

(69) Adam$_i$ told Bernie$_j$ that they$_k$ would be leaving in an hour

Under this interpretation, the NPs *Adam* and *Bernie* constitute a **split antecedent**. They occur in different syntactic positions (grammatical function positions) and have different θ-roles.[25] In contrast, anaphor binding does not permit split antecedents.

(70) a. *Adam$_i$ told Bernie$_j$ about themselves$_k$
b. Adam$_i$ told Bernie$_j$ about himself$_j$
c. Adam$_i$ told Bernie$_j$ about himself$_i$

(70b–c) indicate that either *Adam* or *Bernie* may be an antecedent for the anaphor in the *about*-phrase, and (70a) shows that both cannot be antecedents of an anaphor in that position.[26]

Pronoun-binding also differs from anaphor binding in another way. Consider the relation between the pronoun and the name in (71).

(71) Adam$_i$ said that they$_k$ would be leaving in an hour

Under one interpretation of (71), the NP *Adam* can be construed as an antecedent of the plural pronoun *they*. Let us call such an NP a **partial antecedent** of a pronoun. Each part of the split antecedent in (69) is a partial antecedent.

We can represent the relation between a pronoun and a partial antecedent in terms of indexing by representing the index of a plural term as a set (of letters). For the sake of uniformity we can assume that the index of a singular term is also given as a set—namely, a set consisting of one member. Under this analysis, the indexing representation for the split antecedent case (69) would be (72).

(72) Adam$_{\{i\}}$ told Bernie$_{\{j\}}$ that they$_{\{i,\,j\}}$ would be leaving in an hour

In (72) the index of the pronoun *they* contains the indices of both *Adam* and *Bernie*. Where a sentence contains only a partial antecedent of a pronoun (e.g., (71)), the indexing representation could be given as (73).

(73) Adam$_{\{i\}}$ said that they$_{\{...i...\}}$ would be leaving in an hour

The index of *they* contains the index of the NP *Adam* as a proper subset (since it is plural and the NP *Adam* is singular).[27]

Partial antecedence for plural pronouns is prohibited in the same domain as binding for singular pronouns. Just as a pronoun cannot be interpreted as coreferential with an antecedent within a binding domain (e.g., (74a)), so a pronoun cannot be interpreted as intersecting in reference with a partial antecedent within a binding domain (e.g., (74b) and (75b)).

(74) a. *Holmes$_{\{j\}}$ was spying on him$_{\{i\}}$
b. *Holmes$_{\{j\}}$ was spying on them$_{\{...i...\}}$

(75) a. *Holmes$_{\{j\}}$ believes [$_{IP}$ him$_{\{i\}}$ to be involved in a crime]
b. *Holmes$_{\{j\}}$ believes [$_{IP}$ them$_{\{...i...\}}$ to be involved in a crime]

To account for (74b) and (75b) under Principle B, the cases of partial antecedence must be treated as instances of pronoun binding. The (a)-examples in (74)–(75) show that within its binding domain a pronoun may not be interpreted as anaphoric on a c-commanding antecedent. *Holmes* and *him* must be interpreted as "noncoreferential."[28] This requirement is satisfied in the (b)-examples in (74)–(75), since *Holmes* and *them* do not corefer. The ungrammaticality of these examples demonstrates that the constraint on pronoun binding is stronger than a requirement of noncoreference. A pronoun must in fact be **disjoint in reference** from all NPs within its binding domain. This will also account for the (a)-examples in (74)–(75) since noncoreference between two singular terms is synonymous with the two terms being disjoint in reference.[29]

**Bibliographical Comments**

The binding conditions for anaphors and pronouns presented in this chapter are essentially those developed in Freidin 1986, which is based (with some modifications) on the binding theory of Chomsky 1981. (See also Chomsky 1986b for a similar analysis.) For a historical overview of the development of Chomsky's binding theory, see chapter 1 of Lasnik 1989b. The account given here for the fact that pleonastic subjects do not induce strong binding domains for anaphors is based on Freidin and Harbert 1983. The idea that the interpretation of pronouns involves the more restrictive notion "disjoint in reference" (as opposed to "noncoreferential") is due to Lasnik 1976. The notion of "nonintersecting in reference" is utilized in Chomsky 1973 for his rule of interpretation RI (a precursor of Principle B). For some alternative views about a binding theory for anaphors and pronouns, see Pica 1987, Burzio forthcoming, and Reinhart and Reuland 1991.

# 8
# Extensions of Binding Theory

## 8.1 The Assignment of Indices

In chapter 7 we established that a certain subclass of nouns (or NPs) called anaphors may occur in sentences only when they are bound by antecedents under certain structural conditions (which we designated as Principle A of the binding theory). Another subclass of nouns called pronouns may be bound to antecedents in sentences subject to different conditions (as stated in Principle B of the binding theory). Given that the binding of an anaphor or a pronoun by an antecedent is accomplished through the mechanism of coindexing, let us assume that coindexing results from the optimally general rule "Index NP." Thus, indices are assigned freely to NPs and any assignment that results in an unacceptable sentence should be ruled out by a principle of grammar that constrains representations with coindexed NPs, like Principles A and B of the binding theory. The question now arises, What happens when NPs that are name-like, and hence neither pronouns, nor anaphors, nor pleonastic elements, receive identical indices? The answer involves yet another principle of binding theory.

We will begin with a discussion of this third principle of binding theory, how it applies in English, and how its formulation varies in other languages. We will then consider how the three principles of binding theory are organized in the grammar. Given that principles of binding function as well-formedness conditions on syntactic representations, it is necessary to determine which level (or levels) of syntactic representation are subject to the binding principles. We will investigate this issue in section 8.2 . In section 8.3 we will look at the evidence for extending the domain of binding theory to empty categories. Binding theory extended in this way shows that empty categories with different derivational histories have distinct syntactic properties.

### 8.1.1 R-expressions and Binding

With free indexing of NPs, coindexing between NPs that are name-like (called **R-expressions** in contemporary literature) is automatically available. As illustrated in (1), there are sentences of English whose interpretation seems to require this possibility.

(1) a. [$_{NP}$ John's$_i$ best friend] just told me that [$_{IP}$ John$_i$ is unreliable]
b. [$_{NP}$ Mary's$_i$ mother-in-law] [$_{VP}$ adores Mary$_i$]
c. that story [$_{PP}$ about John$_i$] [$_{VP}$ made John$_i$ angry]
d. Bill returned [$_{NP}$ Sam's$_i$ bicycle] to [$_{NP}$ Sam's$_i$ house]

The coindexing of the R-expressions distinguishes the interpretation where the sentence is about one person (e.g., *John* in (1a)) from the interpretation where the sentence is about two different people with the same name. In (1), where the c-command domain of the indexed R-expression is indicated with labeled brackets, neither of the coindexed R-expressions is in the c-command domain of the other. Therefore, neither of the R-expressions is bound by the other.

In fact, an R-expression may not be bound (coindexed with a c-commanding NP), as (2)–(3) demonstrate.

(2) Simple sentences
*Mary$_i$ admires Mary$_i$

(3) Complex sentences
a. R-expression in subject position
i. *Mary$_i$ expects [$_{CP}$ (that) [$_{IP}$ Mary$_i$ will win]]
ii. *Mary$_i$ expects [$_{IP}$ Mary$_i$ to win]
b. R-expression in object position
i. *Mary$_i$ expects [$_{CP}$ (that) [$_{IP}$ John will admire Mary$_i$]]
ii. *Mary$_i$ expects [$_{IP}$ John to admire Mary$_i$]

((2)–(3) gives the IP-paradigm corresponding to the one for pronouns and anaphors given in (56)–(57) of chapter 7.) The paradigm indicates that an R-expression cannot be coindexed with a c-commanding NP. This restriction holds for the NP-paradigm also, as illustrated in (4)–(5).

(4) Simple sentences
a. R-expression in subject position
i. *John$_i$ read [$_{NP}$ John's$_i$ books]
b. R-expression in object position
i. *John$_i$ doesn't read [$_{NP}$ books about John$_i$]

ii. *John$_i$ doesn't read [$_{NP}$ Mary's books about John$_i$]
iii. *Mary doesn't read [$_{NP}$John's$_i$ books about John$_i$]

(5) Complex sentences
a. R-expression in subject position
i. *Mary$_i$ expected [$_{CP}$ that [$_{IP}$ [$_{NP}$ Mary's$_i$ books] would be favorably reviewed]]
ii. *Mary$_i$ expected [$_{IP}$ [$_{NP}$ Mary's$_i$ books] to be favorably reviewed]
iii. *Mary$_i$ expected [$_{CP}$ that [$_{IP}$John would favorably review [$_{NP}$ Mary's$_i$ books]]]
iv. *Mary$_i$ expected [$_{IP}$John to favorably review [$_{NP}$ Mary's$_i$ books]]
b. R-expression in object position
i. *Mary$_i$ expected [$_{CP}$ that [$_{IP}$ [$_{NP}$ books about Mary$_i$] would be popular]]
ii. *Mary$_i$ expected [$_{IP}$ [$_{NP}$ books about Mary$_i$] to be popular]
iii. *Mary$_i$ expected [$_{CP}$ that [$_{IP}$ [$_{NP}$ John's books about Mary$_i$] would be popular]]
iv. *Mary$_i$ expected [$_{IP}$ [$_{NP}$ John's books about Mary$_i$] to be popular]]
v. *Mary$_i$ expected [$_{CP}$ that [$_{IP}$John would write [$_{NP}$ books about Mary$_i$]]]
vi. *Mary$_i$ expected [$_{IP}$ John to write [$_{NP}$ books about Mary$_i$]]

In comparison with the IP- and NP-paradigms for pronoun-binding, (2)–(5) show that the prohibition against a bound R-expression is without qualification—that is, unmodified by a domain statement that allows for some configurations in which an R-expression can be bound.

This evidence supports the postulation of a third binding principle that we will refer to, following standard practice, as Principle C of the binding theory.

(6) **Principle C**
An R-expression must be free.

As noted above, R-expressions must be free in all domains—in contrast to pronouns and anaphors, which can be bound in some domains and not others. The term "free" here means 'not coindexed with a c-commanding category'. Principle C is like Principles A and B in that all three are formulated in terms of the same structural relations, c-command and coindexing.

**Exercise 8.1**
If the following sentences violate Principle C, what must be true of the phrase structure analysis of these examples?

(i) a. *Mary's$_i$ remark about Mary$_i$ surprised us
b. *Mary's$_i$ claim that Mary$_i$ was telling the truth surprised us.

What does Principle C tell us about the phrase structure analysis of the following examples under the assumption that the two instances of *John* are coindexed?

(ii) a. when John$_i$ arrived, John$_i$ was eating a sandwich
b. ?John$_i$ was eating a sandwich when John$_i$ arrived

Although (ii.b) is somewhat odd, it is clearly better than the corresponding ungrammatical sentence where the matrix subject is a pronoun, as in (iii.a)—in contrast to the grammatical (iii.b).

(iii) a. *he$_i$ was eating a sandwich [$_{CP}$ when John$_i$ arrived]
b. John$_i$ was eating a sandwich [$_{CP}$ when he$_i$ arrived]

Can (iii.a) be accounted for as a Principle C violation, if (ii.b) is fully grammatical? Give the reasoning for your answer.

Since Principle C, unlike Principles A and B, contains no domain statement, we might wonder whether it really is a constraint on the syntax or whether its empirical effects can be derived from some other principle of interpretation (to which we will return). Consider the case where the c-commanding NPs in the paradigms above are replaced with corresponding pronouns (e.g., (7) corresponding to (5a.i)).

(7) *she$_i$ expected [$_{CP}$ that [$_{IP}$ [$_{NP}$ Mary's$_i$ books] would be favorably reviewed]]

It follows from Principle C that the pronoun cannot be interpreted as anaphoric on the R-expression it binds. Embedding (7) in a discourse where *she* can easily be interpreted as anaphoric on the R-expression *Mary* in a preceding sentence does not change the unacceptability of (7).

(8) *Mary was happy. She expected that Mary's books would be favorably reviewed.

In the discourse, the pronoun is anaphoric on the instance of *Mary* in the preceding sentence. Therefore, in (8) the pronoun need not be construed as anaphoric on the instance of *Mary* that it c-commands. Although repeating a name in two contiguous sentences in a discourse may be infelicitous, it is certainly not impossible, so the repetition of the name in (8) does not explain why (8) is ill formed. (8) is ill formed because it violates a principle of syntactic binding, Principle C. So it appears that the ill-formedness of (7) is also due to a syntactic fact—namely, that an R-expression cannot be bound. The ill-formedness of (7)–(8) is syntactic and not a problem of sentence interpretation.

We could speculate further that the reason an R-expression cannot be bound (c-commanded by a coindexed NP) is that it receives its interpretation from its lexical content—as opposed to bound anaphors and bound pronouns, which receive their interpretations via the lexical content of another NP (see Higginbotham 1983). This cannot be the full explanation, however, because an **anaphoric epithet** (e.g., *the idiot* and *the genius*), yet another kind of NP, obeys the same binding conditions as R-expressions and also receives a significant part of its interpretation from an NP that is construed as its antecedent. If we take the examples in (1), where two R-expressions may bear the same index, and substitute an anaphoric epithet for the second one, the resulting sentences are well formed.

(9) a. $[_{NP}$John's$_i$ best friend$]$ $[_{VP}$just told me that the idiot$_i$ is unreliable$]$
b. $[_{NP}$ Mary's$_i$ mother-in-law$]$ $[_{VP}$ adores the angel$_i$$]$
c. $[_{NP}$ that story about John$_i$$]$ $[_{VP}$ made the idiot$_i$ angry$]$
d. Bill returned $[_{NP}$ Sam's$_i$ bicycle$]$ $[_{PP}$ to $[_{NP}$ the jerk's$_i$ house$]]$

In each sentence in (9) the epithet is interpreted as anaphoric on the name it is coindexed with. And when we substitute an anaphoric epithet for the bound R-expression in the IP-paradigm given in (2)–(3), the resulting sentences are all ill formed too—thereby indicating that an anaphoric epithet cannot be bound.

(10) Simple sentences
*Mary$_i$ admires the angel$_i$

(11) Complex sentences
a. Epithet in subject position
i. *Mary$_i$ expects $[_{CP}$ (that) $[_{IP}$ the angel$_i$ will win$]]$
ii. *Mary$_i$ expects $[_{IP}$ the angel$_i$ to win$]$
b. Epithet in object position
i. *Mary$_i$ expects $[_{CP}$ (that) $[_{IP}$John will admire the angel$_i$$]]$
ii. *Mary$_i$ expects $[_{IP}$John to admire the angel$_i$$]$

**Exercise 8.2**
Construct the NP-paradigm for anaphoric epithets to show how it patterns exactly like the corresponding paradigm for R-expressions. There is a potential difference between (i) coindexing between R-expressions and (ii) coindexing between an R-expression and an anaphoric epithet. What happens when the linear order of R-expression and anaphoric epithet is reversed in (7)? Construct the examples and discuss. Note that judgments of acceptability may vary from speaker to speaker.

---

Like a pronoun (and unlike an R-expression), an anaphoric epithet can be anaphoric on another NP; but like an R-expression, it cannot be bound. Given that Principle C applies to both R-expressions and anaphoric epithets, the two NP-types share the common property that they may not be bound—presumably a syntactic property since their interpretive properties are distinct.[1]

In addition to the c-command constraint on the coindexing of anaphoric epithets, as illustrated in the IP-paradigm given in (10)–(11), there also seems to be a strong linear order effect with respect to coindexing between epithets and R-expressions. Consider the following pair of sentences:

(12) a. $[_{IP}$ $[_{I^*}$ John$_i$ was slicing onions] $[_{CP}$ when the idiot$_i$ cut his finger]]
b. *$[_{IP}$ $[_{I^*}$ the idiot$_i$ was slicing onions] $[_{CP}$ when John$_i$ cut his finger]]

Given that an anaphoric epithet cannot be bound by an R-expression, (12a) must not be an instance of binding (i.e., the subject of the matrix clause, *John*, does not c-command the epithet).[2] Thus, the bracketed CPs in (12) are sisters to the projection of Infl containing the subject NP. Under this analysis, the epithet in (12b) does not c-command the R-expression. Therefore, (12b) cannot be ruled out by Principle C. These facts correspond exactly to those concerning coindexing between an R-expression and a pronoun.

(13) a. $[_{IP}$ $[_{I^*}$ John$_i$ was slicing onions] $[_{CP}$ when he$_i$ cut his finger]]
b. *$[_{IP}$ $[_{I^*}$ he$_i$ was slicing onions] $[_{CP}$ when John$_i$ cut his finger]]

Again, assuming that c-command does not hold in either direction for the two coindexed positions (as established in (12a)), (13b) cannot be ruled out as a violation of Principle C. This suggests that the distribution of coindexed but unbound pronouns is similar to that of unbound anaphoric epithets. However, the extension of this paradigm shows that the distribution of coindexed anaphoric epithets is more restricted than that of coindexed pronouns.

(14) a. [$_{CP}$ when John$_i$ cut his finger], he$_i$ was slicing onions
b. [$_{CP}$ when he$_i$ cut his finger], John$_i$ was slicing onions

(15) a. [$_{CP}$ when John$_i$ cut his finger], the idiot$_i$ was slicing onions
b. *[$_{CP}$ when the idiot$_i$ cut his finger], John$_i$ was slicing onions

If the fronted CP in these examples were c-commanded by the matrix subject, then (14a) should violate Principle C. Since (14a) is well-formed, we must assume that the matrix subject pronoun in (14a) does not c-command the R-expression in the fronted subordinate clause.[3] (15b) then cannot be explained as a Principle C violation since neither of the coindexed NPs in this construction c-commands the other.

The paradigms discussed above illustrate that some failures of antecedence involving pronouns and anaphoric epithets cannot be ascribed to binding—that is, coindexation with c-command.

---

**Exercise 8.3**

As analyzed, (13b) and (15b) suggest that the analysis of anaphoric relations involves more than just c-command. Discuss. Try to formulate a condition of linear precedence that accounts for (13b).[4] Can this condition be generalized to account for (15b), and if not, why not? Does this condition overlap with Principle C, and if so, how?

---

### 8.1.2 Parametric Variation of Principle C

The following discussion concerns Thai and Vietnamese and is based on the work of Howard Lasnik (1989a). In these languages, unlike in English, R-expressions may be bound under certain conditions. In Vietnamese anaphoric epithets and R-expressions may be bound under the same conditions, whereas in Thai the conditions on binding of anaphoric epithets are more restrictive than for R-expressions.

In Vietnamese, R-expressions may be bound across a clause boundary, as illustrated in (16a), but not within a single clause (16b).

(16) a. John$_i$ tin John$_i$ sẽ thắng
John believes John will win

b. *John$_i$ thương John$_i$
John likes John

This paradigm extends to anaphoric epithets as well.

(17) a. John$_i$ tin cái thằng chó đẻ$_i$ sẽ thắng
John believes CLASS the son of a bitch will win

b. *John$_i$ thương cái thằng chó đẻ$_i$
John likes CLASS the son of a bitch

It would appear that anaphoric epithets and R-expressions fall together under Principle C, appropriately modified to allow binding across clauses. Following Lasnik, we can account for this variation with the following modification of Principle C (indicated by italics):

(18) **Principle C** (Vietnamese)

An R-expression must be free in the *θ-domain of its governor.*

This formulation of Principle C is very similar to the formulation of Principle B for English given in (67) in chapter 7, which also prohibits binding within a clause, but not across a finite clause boundary.[5]

As formulated in (18), Principle C for Vietnamese does not block the binding of R-expressions by pronouns. Such binding, however, is virtually universally impossible. The paradigm for Vietnamese is given in (19).

(19) a. R-expressions

i. *nó$_i$ tin John$_i$ sẽ thắng
he thinks John will win

ii. *nó$_i$ thương John$_i$
he likes John

b. Anaphoric epithets

i. *nó$_i$ tin cái thằng chó đẻ$_i$ sẽ thắng
he thinks CLASS the son of a bitch will win

ii. *nó$_i$ thương cái thằng chó đẻ$_i$
he likes CLASS the son of a bitch

(19) demonstrates that both R-expressions and anaphoric epithets cannot be bound by pronouns. As Lasnik notes, this indicates that what we have been calling Principle C actually has two parts, one of which is (20).

(20) **Principle C'**

An R-expression must be pronoun-free.

(19b) in conjunction with Principle C' provides a reasonably strong argument that anaphoric epithets must be analyzed as having the same property as R-expressions.

If anaphoric epithets are also pronominal, then they cannot bind R-expressions given Principle C'. The evidence from Vietnamese supports this conclusion.

(21) a. *cái thằng chó đẻ$_i$ thương John$_i$
CLASS the son of a bitch likes John
b. *cái thằng chó đẻ$_i$ tin John$_i$ sẽ thắng
CLASS the son of a bitch thinks John will win

Binding of an R-expression by an anaphoric epithet is not possible either within a single clause (21a) or across a clause boundary (21b). This behavior indicates that anaphoric epithets in Vietnamese are pronominal. However, an anaphoric epithet may bind another anaphoric epithet across a clause boundary.

(22) cái thằng chó đẻ$_i$ tin cái thằng chó đẻ$_i$ sẽ thắng
CLASS the son of a bitch thinks CLASS the son of a bitch will win

(22) violates Principle C' under the interpretation of anaphoric epithets as pronominal R-expressions. The problem is that if Principle C' excludes both binding of an anaphoric epithet by a pronoun and also binding of an R-expression by an anaphoric epithet, then it should also exclude (22). If we try to modify Principle C' (e.g., replace "R-expression" with "non-pronominal R-expression"), then we lose the fact that pronouns cannot bind anaphoric epithets. Lasnik's solution is to generalize Principle C' in terms of a hierarchy of referential expressions—specifically, an inherently less referential NP type in the hierarchy may not bind a more referential NP-type. The hierarchy for Vietnamese would be as follows:

(23) a. Names (R-expressions)
b. Anaphoric epithets (pronominal R-expressions)
c. Pronouns/anaphors

Given the hierarchy in (23) and the generalized Principle C', it should follow that anaphors and pronouns cannot bind anaphoric epithets or names, and that anaphoric epithets cannot bind names.[6] This leaves open the possibility that anaphoric epithets can bind anaphoric epithets as in (22). That such binding cannot occur within a single clause will follow from Principle C for Vietnamese (or alternatively Principle B—since anaphoric epithets are also pronominal).

Unlike Vietnamese, Thai appears to have no Principle C type restrictions. Not only can an R-expression be bound across a clause boundary (e.g., (24b)), but such binding can also occur within a single clause (e.g., (24a)). (ɔ stands for a lax mid back vowel—that is, open *o*.)

(24) a. Cɔɔn$_i$ chɔ̂ɔp Cɔɔn$_i$
John likes John

b. Cɔɔn$_i$ khít wâa Cɔɔn$_i$ chàlāat
John thinks that John is smart

Anaphoric epithets in Thai do not, however, pattern exactly like R-expressions. An anaphoric epithet in Thai may be bound across a clause boundary (e.g., (25b); yet it cannot be bound within a single clause (e.g., (25a)).

(25) a. *Cɔɔn$_i$ chɔ̂ɔp ˀâybâa$_i$
John likes the nut

b. Cɔɔn$_i$ khít wâa ˀâybâa$_i$ chàlāat
John thinks that the nut is smart

In this way anaphoric epithets in Thai pattern like those in Vietnamese. Nonetheless, (25a) cannot be a Principle C violation since Principle C does not hold in Thai, as (24) shows. Therefore, (25a) provides evidence that anaphoric epithets in Thai are pronominal—in which case (25a) can be analyzed as a Principle B violation. Even so, it is clear that anaphoric epithets in Thai must be higher on the referential hierarchy than pronouns since they cannot be bound by pronouns, and lower than R-expressions since they cannot bind R-expressions . The relevant paradigms are given in (26).

(26) a. R-expressions

i. *ˀâybâa$_i$ chɔ̂ɔp Cɔɔn$_i$
the nut likes John

ii. *ˀâybâa$_i$ khít wâa Cɔɔn$_i$ chàlāat
the nut thinks that John is smart

iii. *khǎw$_i$ chɔ̂ɔp Cɔɔn$_i$
he likes John

iv. *khǎw$_i$ khít wâa Cɔɔn$_i$ chàlāat
he thinks that John is smart

b. Anaphoric epithets

i. *khǎw$_i$ chɔ̂ɔp ˀâybâa$_i$
he likes the nut

ii. *khǎw$_i$ khít wâa ˀâybâa$_i$ chàlāat
he thinks that the nut is smart

As in Vietnamese, the presence of a clause boundary between the bound NP and its binder has no effect. Here too, pronouns cannot bind anaphoric epithets (26b) or R-expressions (26a.iii–iv), so that anaphoric epithets and R-expressions pattern together in this regard. And also as in Vietnamese, anaphoric epithets in Thai cannot bind R-expressions (26a.i–ii), thereby exhibiting a characteristic of pronouns.

At this point we have reviewed a variety of evidence from English, Vietnamese, and Thai that indicates that anaphoric epithets share properties of both R-expressions and pronouns. For Vietnamese and Thai the referential hierarchy appears to distinguish among the three with respect to principles of the binding theory. English, in contrast, appears to group R-expressions and anaphoric epithets together under Principle C.

A comparative analysis of these three languages also reveals that what we have been calling Principle C for English apparently involves two distinct conditions. One, designated above as Principle C', prohibits binding of a more referential expression by a less referential expression. This principle applies without exception in all three languages. The other part of Principle C concerns the prohibition on binding between two R-expressions or two anaphoric epithets. The application of this part of Principle C varies across languages. In Vietnamese it holds within a restricted domain (cf. (18)), in English it holds in all domains, and in Thai it does not apply at all. Thus, one part of Principle C is parameterized, whereas the other appears to be an absolute prohibition that holds across languages.

## 8.2 Binding Theory and Levels of Representation

As formulated, the principles of the binding theory constitute a set of filters that determine the well-formedness of syntactic representations at some level (or levels) of representation. Which levels are relevant is an empirical issue. In most discussions it has been assumed that Principles A, B, and C apply as a single unit.[7] This assumption may be correct, as we will see. Let us consider the levels of D-structure, S-structure, and LF.[8]

The evidence from NP-movement shows that D-structure alone cannot be the relevant level of representation at which well-formedness of binding is determined. In the case of pronouns and R-expressions, the S-structure representations and not the D-structure representations of ungrammatical sentences violate Principles B and C of the binding theory.

(27) Principle B

a. $[_{IP}$ $[_{NP}$ e] seems to $\text{her}_i$ $[_{CP}$ $[_{IP}$ $\text{Jill}_i$ to be happy]]]

b. *$[_{IP}$ $\text{Jill}_i$ seems to $\text{her}_i$ $[_{CP}$ $[_{IP}$ $e_i$ to be happy]]]

(28) Principle C

a. $[_{IP}$ $[_{NP}$ e] seems to $\text{John}_i$ $[_{CP}$ $[_{IP}$ $\text{he}_i$ to be happy]]]

b. *$[_{IP}$ $\text{he}_i$ seems to $\text{John}_i$ $[_{CP}$ $[_{IP}$ $e_i$ to be happy]]]

In (27a) there is no c-command relation between *her* and *Jill* and therefore neither Principle B nor Principle C is violated. In (27b) however, the NP *Jill* c-commands and therefore binds the pronoun *her* in the θ-domain of its governor (the preposition *to*)—hence in the matrix IP. This constitutes a violation of Principle B at S-structure.[9] Similarly, with (28a) the pronoun *he* does not c-command the R-expression at D-structure. However in the S-structure (28b), *he* binds the *John*, in violation of Principle C.

With respect to anaphor binding, the NP-movement case shows that there are grammatical sentences where the anaphor is bound only at S-structure, but not at D-structure.

(29) Principle A
   a. $[_{IP}$ $[_{NP}$ e] seem to each $other_i$ $[_{CP}$ $[_{IP}$ the $men_i$ to be happy]]]
   b. $[_{IP}$ the $men_i$ seem to each $other_i$ $[_{CP}$ $[_{IP}$ $e_i$ to be happy]]]

In the S-structure (29b) the anaphor *each other* is properly bound by the matrix subject *the men*, whereas in the D-structure (29a) the anaphor is not bound at all. The example suggests that Principle A holds at S-structure.

By contrast, in some *wh*-movement constructions the anaphor is bound at D-structure, but not at S-structure.

(30) a. $[_{CP}$ $[_{IP}$ $they_i$ were $[_{AP}$ how angry $[_{PP}$ at each $other_i$]]]]
   b. $[_{CP}$ $[_{AP:j}$ how angry $[_{PP}$ at each $other_i$]] $were_k$ $[_{IP}$ $they_i$ $e_k$ $e_j$]]

In (30a) prior to *wh*-movement the anaphor *each other* is properly bound by the subject *they*. After the *wh*-phrase has been moved into CP, the matrix subject no longer c-commands the anaphor and hence does not bind it. Contrary to (29), (30) indicates that S-structure alone cannot be the level at which Principle A is satisfied, since it is at D-structure and not S-structure that the anaphor is bound. Since (30b) is well formed, it should not violate Principle A.

This problem can be solved by identifying some other single level of representation where Principle A holds such that the anaphors in both (29) and (30) would be bound at that level. The obvious candidate would be LF. Under this hypothesis, the LF representation of the sentence in (29) would be similar to its S-structure with respect to anaphor binding, whereas the LF representation of the sentence in (30) would have to be similar to its D-structure representation. Thus, the LF representation for (30) would have to reconstruct something like the D-structure configuration (30a) from the S-structure (30b). To make this proposal concrete, suppose that the S-structure of (30a) maps onto the following representation at LF:

(31) (to what degree $x$) were $[_{IP}$ they$_i$ $[_{AP}$ $x$ angry at each other$_i$]]

This analysis is based on the assumption that in LF, quantifier-variable relations are expressed overtly in terms of a quantifier (given in parentheses) that binds a variable in IP (indicated by the letter $x$). In the phrase *how angry at each other* the interrogative *how* is interpreted as a quantifier of degree. If we take (31) to be the LF representation of (30b) and the S-structure (29b) to be essentially identical to its own LF representation, Principle A applied at LF accounts for (29)–(30).[10]

The LF reconstruction solution also accounts for constructions where Principle A would be violated at D-structure, but satisfied at S-structure. Such constructions are ill formed, as illustrated in (32).

(32) *$[_{IP}$ they$_i$ knew $[_{CP:j}$ $[_{AP}$ how angry at each other$_i$] $[_{IP}$John was e$_j$]]]

In the D-structure of (32) the anaphor will be bound across an accessible subject (*John*) in violation of Principle A. At S-structure, the level shown in (32), the anaphor is bound by the matrix subject (*they*) and not free in the domain of an accessible SUBJECT. Therefore, the S-structure (32) satisfies Principle A. Since the LF representation of (32) would have essentially the same binding properties as its D-structure, Principle A applied at LF would rule out (32).

---

**Exercise 8.4**

Consider a sentence with the opposite property from (32)—namely, where the anaphor is properly bound at D-structure but violates Principle A at S-structure. Discuss how this holds for (i).

(i) $[_{IP}$ the women$_i$ said $[_{IP}$John knew $[_{CP}$ $[_{AP:j}$ how angry at each other$_i$] $[_{IP}$ they$_i$ were e$_j$]]]

Now consider the following examples:

(ii) a. how angry at each other did Mary say they were
b. *how angry at each other did they say Mary was

(iii) a. Mary knows how angry at each other they were
b. *they know how angry at each other Mary was

Give the S-structure and LF analyses of each example and discuss how the LF reconstruction analysis for Principle A works for these cases.

---

A similar case can be made for Principle B as well. Consider (33)–(34), which correspond to (29)–(30) above.

(33) a. $[_{IP}$ $[_{NP}$ e] seem to them$_i$ $[_{CP}$ $[_{IP}$ the men$_i$ to be happy]]]
b. *$[_{IP}$ the men$_i$ seem to them$_i$ $[_{CP}$ $[_{IP}$ e$_i$ to be happy]]]

In the S-structure (33b) the pronoun *them* is bound by the matrix subject *the men* in violation of Principle B, whereas in the D-structure (29a) the pronoun is not bound at all. The example indicates that Principle B holds at S-structure. In contrast to the NP-movement case in (33), the *wh*-movement construction in (34) illustrates that Principle B applies at D-structure (or LF if that level has the relevant structure) since the pronoun violates Principle B at D-structure (34a) but not at S-structure (34b).

(34) a. $[_{CP}$ $[_{IP}$ the men$_i$ were $[_{AP}$ how angry $[_{PP}$ at them$_i$]]]]
b. *$[_{CP}$ $[_{AP:j}$ how angry $[_{PP}$ at them$_i$]] were$_k$ $[_{IP}$ the men$_i$ e$_k$ e$_j$]]

At S-structure the pronoun is not bound and therefore should satisfy Principle B. However, Principle B requires that a pronoun be A-free in the minimal θ-domain containing its governor (recall that a θ-domain is either IP or NP). By this definition, the pronoun in (34b) is not in any θ-domain and Principle B therefore cannot apply to this structure because its structural description is not met. The examples (33-34) show that Principle B must apply at both D-structure and S-structure.

The problem with this dual-level analysis for Principle B involves the paradigm (35)–(36), constructed from (ii)–(iii) of exercise 8.4, where the third person plural pronoun has been substituted for the anaphor and the NP *the men* has been substituted for the intended antecedent of the anaphor.

(35) a. *how angry at them$_i$ did Mary say the men$_i$ were
b. how angry at them$_i$ did the men$_i$ say Mary was

(36) a. *Mary knows how angry at them$_i$ the men$_i$ were
b. the men$_i$ know how angry at them$_i$ Mary was

The pronoun in (36b) is A-bound in the minimal θ-domain containing its governor—that is, the matrix IP. Thus, (36b) should violate Principle B. Since (36b) is well formed, the dual-level analysis does not work for the formulation of Principle B we have adopted.

**Exercise 8.5**
Give the analysis of the D-structures and S-structures of (35)–(36) and explain why only (36b) constitutes a problem for the dual-level analysis.

As with anaphors, an LF reconstruction analysis accounts for the pronoun-binding facts. This works if for the *wh*-movement cases (34)–(36) the moved phrase containing the pronoun is restored to its D-structure grammatical function position—in contrast to the NP-movement cases, where the moved NP remains in its derived position.

---

**Exercise 8.6**

Discuss the proposal that Principle B holds only at LF. In particular, show how Principle B applies to the LF representations of (34) and (36b).

---

In this way, Principles A and B apply at the same level of representation—a welcome result to the extent that we are interpreting both as conditions on bound elements (i.e. as principles of proper binding).

Principle C manifests the same behavior as Principles A and B with respect to the level of syntactic representation at which it applies. Thus, we can construct the same argument that binding applies at S-structure for Principle C that we have for Principles A and B. In (37) (which corresponds in structure to (29) and (33)), the indexed R-expression in (37a) is not bound by the pronoun, so that the D-structure of the ill-formed (37b) does not violate Principle C.[11]

(37) a. $[_{IP}\ [_{NP}$ e$]\ [_{VP}$ seemed $[_{PP}$ to John$_i]\ [_{CP}\ [_{IP}$ he$_i$ to be happy$]]]]$
 b. *$[_{IP}$ he$_i\ [_{VP}$ seemed $[_{PP}$ to John$_i]\ [_{CP}\ [_{IP}$ e$_i$ to be happy$]]]]$

In (37b) the matrix subject *he* binds the object of the preposition *to*, violating Principle C. Hence, (37) provides evidence that Principle C holds at S-structure.[12]

Again, as with the other binding principles, the *wh*-movement constructions in (38)–(39) indicate that Principle C applies at D-structure (or LF if that level of representation is reconstructed with the relevant D-structure properties).

(38) i. $[_{CP}\ [_{IP}$ he$_i$ was $[_{AP}$ how angry at John$_i]]]$
 ii. $[_{CP}\ [_{AP:j}$ how angry at John$_i]$ was$_k\ [_{IP}$ he$_i$ e$_k$ e$_j]]$
 iii. *how angry at John$_i$ was he$_i$

(39) i. $[_{CP}\ [_{IP}$ he$_i$ said $[_{CP}\ [_{IP}$ Mary was $[_{AP}$ how angry at John$_i]]]]]$
 ii. $[_{CP}\ [_{AP:j}$ how angry at John$_i]$ did$_k\ [_{IP}$ Mary e$_k$ say $[_{CP}$ e$_j\ [_{IP}$ he$_i$ was e$_j]]]]$
 iii. *how angry at John$_i$ did Mary say he$_i$ was

In the D-structures of both examples the R-expression in the *wh*-AP is bound, in violation of Principle C; whereas at S-structure that R-expression is no longer bound.

So far, what we have said about the application of Principle C is on a par with the analysis we gave for Principles A and B—namely, that it too seems to apply at both D-structure and S-structure. However, we cannot use structures like (32) or (36b) to argue against a dual-level analysis of Principle C. This is because because an R-expression cannot be bound in any domain, and in all these structures the R-expression is bound at D-structure.

---

**Exercise 8.7**
Construct the S-structure representations of the Principle C cases corresponding to (35)–(36)—that is, substitute *John* for the pronoun, and *he* for the coindexed NP *the men* in each example. Discuss why none of the resulting examples poses any problem for the dual-level hypothesis for Principle C.

---

There is, however, evidence that Principle C does not apply at D-structure. This involves *wh*-movement that carries along a relative clause, as in (40).

(40) a. $[_{CP}$ $[_{IP}$ he$_i$ submitted $[_{NP}$ which report$_j$ $[_{CP}$ that $[_{IP}$ John$_i$ revised e$_j$]]]]]]
b. $[_{CP}$ $[_{NP:k}$ which report$_j$ $[_{CP}$ that $[_{IP}$ John$_i$ revised e$_j$]]] did$_m$ $[_{IP}$ he$_i$ e$_m$ submit e$_k$]]
c. which report that John$_i$ revised did he$_i$ submit

In the D-structure (40a) of the grammatical sentence (40c) the R-expression *John* is bound by the pronoun *he*, whereas at S-structure it is coindexed but not bound. (The ungrammatical sentence **He$_i$ submitted several reports that John$_i$ revised e$_j$*, which corresponds to (40a), violates Principle C. Thus, Principle C cannot hold at D-structure since that would rule out the perfectly acceptable (40c).[13]

If Principle C cannot hold at D-structure as indicated by (40), and if holding at S-structure will not account for the *wh*-movement cases in (38)–(39), then it must apply at some other level of representation. Again, the obvious candidate is LF. Suppose that the S-structure of (38) (for example) maps onto the following representation at LF (cf. (31)):

(41) (to what degree *x*) was$_j$ $[_{IP}$ he$_i$ e$_j$ $[_{AP}$ *x* angry at John$_i$]]

Here the D-structure relation between the pronoun and the R-expression is "reconstructed" at LF. If this solution is viable, then evidence for the

D-structure application of Principle C can be subsumed under an LF analysis. In contrast to (41), the relative clause remains with the quantifier at LF and does not reconstruct back into its D-structure position.[14]

The conclusion that Principle C cannot apply at D-structure forces an LF interpretation in yet another way. Whereas a relative clause containing a bound R-expression at D-structure does not violate Principle C, a sentential complement containing a bound R-expression at D-structure does, as illustrated in (42).

(42) a. $[_{CP}$ $[_{IP}$ he$_i$ submitted $[_{NP}$ which report $[_{CP}$ that $[_{IP}$ John$_i$ was a genius]]]]]

b. $[_{CP}$ $[_{NP:k}$ which report $[_{CP}$ that $[_{IP}$ John$_i$ was a genius]]] did$_j$ $[_{IP}$ he$_i$ e$_j$ submit e$_k$]]

c. *which report that John$_i$ was a genius did he$_i$ submit

Given our analysis so far, the sentential complement of *report* in (42), in contrast to the relative clause in (40), must undergo reconstruction at LF if Principle C is to account for the deviance of (42c).[15]

The analysis presented in this section supports the conclusion that the three binding principles apply at LF and illustrates some problems with applying them at other levels of representation. Thus, the assumption that these principles apply as a single unit is compatible with some rather intricate facts about syntactic binding.

## 8.3 Binding Theory and Empty Categories

Having established a set of principles for bound lexical elements in chapter 7 and section 8.1, we turn to the possibility of extending binding theory to those empty categories that are also bound.[16] This extension provides a more fine-grained analysis that distinguishes empty category types in correspondence with lexical NP-types. In the pages that follow we will investigate the binding interactions of *wh*-trace and pronouns, which indicates that *wh*-trace, which is $\bar{A}$-bound, is subject to Principle C (appropriately extended to trace), and apparently not to Principle A. (In contrast, NP-trace, which is A-bound, is subject to Principle A, as discussed in Appendix B.)

The status of a *wh*-trace can be elucidated by investigating its binding interactions with a pronoun. To begin, let us consider a standard case of pronoun binding, as given in (43).

(43) Adam wants Barbie to take him to the pool

(43) can have two different readings, one in which the pronoun *him* is anaphoric on the matrix subject *Adam* (henceforth the bound reading) and another in which it is not. Thus, in the bound reading the sentence is about two people, and in the unbound reading it is about three people. If we replace the name with an interrogative pronoun, as in (44), we still have two possible readings, which can be represented in terms of the indexing of the pronoun (given in (45).

(44) who wants Barbie to take him to the pool

(45) a [$_{CP}$ who$_i$ [$_{IP}$ e$_i$ wants [$_{IP}$ Barbie$_j$ to take him$_i$ to the pool]]]
b. [$_{CP}$ who$_i$ [$_{IP}$ e$_i$ wants [$_{IP}$ Barbie$_j$ to take him$_k$ to the pool]]]

(45a) represents the bound reading, and (45b), where the pronoun and the trace of the *wh*-phrase have different indices, represents the unbound reading.

When we switch the positions of the pronoun and the name (in the matrix subject position), yielding (46), only one reading is possible—namely, the unbound reading.

(46) he wants Barbie to take Adam to the pool

Sentence (46) can only be about three people, not just two. The bound reading for this sentence is excluded because it would involve the binding of the name *Adam*, an R-expression, which violates Principle C.

Interestingly, we get the same effect when we switch the positions of the pronoun and the trace in (44). The sentence (47) has only one possible reading (the unbound reading) and hence only one representation, (48b).

(47) who does he want Barbie to take to the pool

(48) a. *[$_{CP}$ who$_i$ does$_m$ [$_{IP}$ he$_i$ e$_m$ want [$_{CP}$ e$_i$ [$_{IP}$ Barbie$_j$ to take e$_i$ to the pool]]]]
b. [$_{CP}$ who$_i$ does$_m$ [$_{IP}$ he$_k$ e$_m$ want [$_{CP}$ e$_i$ [$_{IP}$ Barbie$_j$ to take e$_i$ to the pool]]]]

That is, (47) cannot have the bound reading of (44) (i.e., (45a)). Examples like (47) are referred to in the literature as **crossover phenomena** on the grounds that *wh*-movement over the pronoun affects possibilities for the anaphoric interpretation of the pronoun. The question to be answered is, Why does (47) have only one reading while a similar sentence, (44), has two?

To answer this question, we might begin by observing that the declarative sentence (43), which corresponds to the interrogative (44), has essentially the same two possible readings. In contrast, the declarative sentence (46) has only one reading, which corresponds to the only possible reading for its interrogative counterpart, (47). As we have already discussed, the fact that (46) has only the unbound reading follows from Principle C of the binding theory. If we could extend this analysis to (47), then we would have not only an answer to our question, but also an explanation for the phenomenon in terms of binding theory.

If *wh*-trace has the status of an R-expression, then the bound interpretation of (47) would be excluded because the pronoun *he* binds the *wh*-trace in the complement object position in violation of Principle C. To establish the hypothesis that *wh*-trace has the status of an R-expression, we need to eliminate two other possibilities—namely, that a *wh*-trace has the status of an anaphor, or of a pronoun. Let us consider why these two possibilities are not viable.

Suppose that a *wh*-trace is an anaphor, and hence subject to Principle A of the binding theory. Notice that this hypothesis would account for (48a). The *wh*-trace in complement object position would be A-free in the domain of an accessible subject (*Barbie*) in violation of Principle A. However, this cannot be the correct explanation for (48b), since the same trace in (48b), a grammatical sentence, violates Principle A in exactly the same way. Hence, a *wh*-trace is not an anaphor subject to Principle A.

The hypothesis that a *wh*-trace is a pronoun, and hence subject to Principle B, would account for (48b). The wh-trace in complement object position is A-free in the $\vartheta$-domain of its governor (the embedded IP), and therefore the representation for the unbound reading of (47) would not constitute a problem for this hypothesis. However, this cannot be the full explanation for the phenomenon because it fails to rule out (48a).

Whereas each of the preceding hypotheses is able to account for only one of the representations in (48), the hypothesis that a *wh*-trace has the status of an R-expression can account for both. In (48a) the *wh*-trace is A-bound by the pronoun *he* in the matrix subject position in violation of Principle C. In (48b) the *wh*-trace is not A-bound and therefore satisfies Principle C. Of course, the *wh*-trace is $\bar{A}$-bound in both representations of (48), but since Principle C says nothing about $\bar{A}$-binding, this poses no problem. Thus, the reason why similar interrogative questions (e.g., (44) and (47)) do not have the same interpretations is that a *wh*-trace has the status of an R-expression and is therefore subject to Principle C of the binding theory. In this way, binding theory provides an explanation for this (crossover) phenomenon.

This analysis for the traces of interrogative pronouns (or interrogative *wh*-phrases more generally) also holds for *wh*-traces in relative clauses.

This is worth noting because a relative pronoun and an interrogative pronoun are not semantically equivalent in any sense. Recall that an interrogative pronoun is interpreted as a quasi-quantifier at LF and therefore the *wh*-trace is translated as a variable. If the *wh*-trace in a relative clause can also be analyzed as some form of variable, then we get the generalization that a variable at LF is the empty category analogue of an R-expression.

---

**Exercise 8.8**

Consider the following pair of sentences, which provides another crossover case.

(i) a. who said she won the contest
 b. who did she say won the contest

Give the S-structure representations for each sentence, showing how (i.a) allows two possible interpretations whereas (i.b) allows only one. Given these examples, what could we conclude from the hypothesis that the *wh*-trace is an anaphor or, alternatively, a pronoun?

---

**Exercise 8.9**

So far we have considered only crossover cases involving interrogative pronouns. Notice that virtually the same analysis holds for the analogous cases involving relative pronouns. Consider the following pairs of sentences:

(i) a. the woman who said she won the contest received an award
 b. the woman who she said won the contest received an award

(ii) a. the boy who wants Barbie to take him to the pool is very insistent
 b. the boy who he wants Barbie to take to the pool is very insistent

Discuss the analyses of these examples in detail, showing how the analysis that accounts for the interrogative pronoun cases also holds for the relative pronoun cases.

---

As noted by Lasnik and Uriagereka (1988:41), this analysis provides an argument that movement rules leave traces, the basic tenet of trace theory. If there were no traces in the representations of sentences like (44) and (47), then Principle C could not apply.

The hypothesis that a *wh*-trace is subject to Principle C also provides a binding-theoretic explanation for why *wh*-movement must be SPEC-CP to SPEC-CP (henceforth CP-to-CP) once a *wh*-phrase has moved into SPEC-

CP position. One example that violates this requirement is given in (49).

(49) a. *who decided Barbie likes
b. *[$_{CP}$ who$_i$ [$_{IP}$ e$_i$ decided [$_{CP}$ e$_i$ [$_{IP}$ Barbie$_j$ likes e$_i$]]]]

In (49) the *wh*-phrase begins as the grammatical object of the sentential complement. It is moved into the SPEC of the complement CP, then into the subject of matrix clause, and finally from subject position into the SPEC of the matrix CP. The movement from SPEC-CP to a grammatical function position in IP is prohibited by the CP-to-CP requirement. Given that a *wh*-trace cannot be A-bound and that the trace object of *like* in (49b) is a *wh*-trace—that is, created by movement from a grammatical function position to an $\bar{A}$-position—(49a) violates Principle C.[17] (49) also violates both the Functional Uniqueness requirement of the θ-Criterion and the Case Uniqueness Principle. Functional Uniqueness is violated because the interrogative pronoun binds traces in two thematically marked positions (object of the complement IP and subject of the matrix IP). Case Uniqueness is violated under the assumption that the *wh*-phrase in the matrix CP inherits two Case assignments—one from its trace in complement object position and the other from its trace in matrix subject position. Thus, (49) is ill formed for three distinct reasons under the theory we are developing.

In contrast to (49), (50) violates only the prohibition against movement from SPEC-CP to a grammatical function position in IP.

(50) a. *who is it possible to have been odd for John to choose
b. *[$_{CP}$ who$_i$ is$_k$ [$_{IP}$ it e$_k$ possible [$_{CP}$ e$_i$ [$_{IP}$ e$_i$ to have been odd [$_{CP}$ e$_i$ for [$_{IP}$ John$_j$ to choose e$_i$]]]]]]

Assuming that the predicate adjective *odd* does not assign a θ-role to the syntactic subject of its clause, (50a) does not violate Functional Uniqueness. Nor does it violate Case Uniqueness or the ECP. However, it does violate the constraint on CP-to-CP movement of *wh*-phrases in the same way that (46) does. Among the principles of grammar we have considered, only Principle C of the binding theory applied to the *wh*-trace object of *choose* accounts for the ill-formedness of the construction.

In this way, the analysis of *wh*-trace as the empty category analogue of an R-expression is motivated in two distinct domains: constraints on movement (the CP-to-CP constraint on *wh*-movement) and constraints on interpretation (the effect of crossover on the interpretation of pronouns).[18] This analysis provides further evidence that there is more than one type of empty category and that distinct types of empty category have distinct properties (recall section 6.4 on the PRO/trace distinction). A *wh*-trace cannot be A-bound, whereas an NP-trace is always A-bound (as is control PRO).[19]

The theory of grammar we have been exploring has led to the postulation of at least three distinct empty categories (NP-trace, *wh*-trace, and PRO). As these empty categories play a significant role in the mental computation of language, we might ask how such elements, which have no physical realization in speech, are acquired by the individual language learner. Since presumably they cannot be acquired from the environment, they must be part of the human language faculty, which is itself part of our human genetic endowment. Thus, the study of empty categories in the mental representation of language constitutes yet another topic in the study of knowledge acquisition that relates directly to the issue of poverty of the stimulus.

## 8.4 In Lieu of a Conclusion

In the course of this book we have explored in some detail the basic concepts of generative grammar and how these concepts have been incorporated into principles of grammar that apply across a wide range of phenomena. One of the most central concepts is government, which intimately relates the theory of phrase structure and the theory of transformations (or more specifically, movement operations). The notion of government is based on the concept of phrasal projection, which in turn lies at the heart of phrase structure theory. Given that traces, which are created by movement rules, are subject to the ECP, a well-formedness condition involving government, the concept of government now stands at the core of a theory of syntactic representations. In addition, the theory requires some concept of binding—which could also relate to government, depending on whether the command relation involved is stated in terms of branching categories (c-command) or maximal phrasal projections (m-command). The notions of Case marking and Case licensing also crucially involve government. In effect, the concept of government provides a locality restriction between elements in a syntactic representation. Whether all locality restrictions (including binding and bounding (i.e., Subjacency)) can be formulated in terms of government remains a topic of debate.[20]

In addition to government, which is a purely structural notion, there are also principles more closely related to the properties of specific lexical items in a syntactic representation. The interaction of lexical properties and syntactic structure is mediated in part by such principles as Lexical Satisfaction, the Projection Principle, and the θ-Criterion.

Although this text has aimed at a clear and precise explication of what continues to be a promising approach to the theory of grammar, it still has its loose ends and to-be-justified (and sometimes unstated) assumptions. As with any theoretical enterprise, it is virtually impossible to justify every assumption and explore every alternative so that the definitive theory can be constructed. Nonetheless, it is important to try to justify assumptions and explore alternatives, for only by trying will we increase our understanding of the strengths and weaknesses of the theory we are investigating.

The science of grammar as we know it today is relatively young—hardly more than three decades old. Even so, it displays some of the same characteristics as its more mature cousins in the natural sciences. Witness Bertrand Russell's comparison of classical and modern science in terms of the work of Newton and Einstein.

> Newton's *Principia* proceeds in the grand Greek manner: from the three laws of motion and the law of gravitation, by purely mathematical deduction, the whole solar system is explained. Newton's work is statuesque and Hellenic, unlike the best work of our own time. The nearest approach to the same classical perfection among moderns is the theory of relativity, but even that does not aim at the same finality, since the rate of progress is so great. (1931:36–37)

Russell relates how Newton conceived the law of gravitation in 1665 and then spent twenty-one years thinking about it before publishing it.

> No modern would dare to do such a thing, since twenty-one years is enough to change completely the scientific landscape. Even Einstein's work has always contained ragged edges, unresolved doubts, and unfinished speculations. I do not say this as a criticism; I say it only to illustrate the difference between our age and that of Newton. We aim no longer at perfection, because of the army of successors whom we can scarcely outstrip, and who are at every moment ready to obliterate our traces. (1931:37)

## Appendix A: Two Kinds of Crossover

The crossover phenomenon discussed in section 8.3 involves the movement of a *wh*-phrase over a pronoun that c-commands it, with the result that the pronoun binds the *wh*-trace. The fact that the *wh*-trace cannot be bound by such a pronoun was shown to follow straightforwardly from the extension of Principle C to *wh*-trace. Consider now a similar case.

(51) a. who loves his mother
b. who does his mother love

(51a) can have two different interpretations: as a question about three different people (where someone loves someone else's mother) or as a question about only two different people (where someone loves his own mother). In terms of indexing, the different interpretations would be represented as (52a–b) respectively.

(52) a. $\text{who}_i$ loves $[_{NP:k}$ $\text{his}_j$ mother]
b. $\text{who}_i$ loves $[_{NP:k}$ $\text{his}_i$ mother]

In (52b) the pronoun *his* is taken to be anaphoric on the interrogative pronoun *who.* In striking contrast, (51b) has only one interpretation—the question is about three different people. The anaphoric interpretation (who is it such that his own mother loves him) is not available.

(53) a. $[_{CP}$ $\text{who}_i$ $\text{does}_m$ $[_{IP}$ $[_{NP:k}$ $\text{his}_j$ mother] $e_m$ love $e_i$]]
b. *$[_{CP}$ $\text{who}_i$ $\text{does}_m$ $[_{IP}$ $[_{NP:k}$ $\text{his}_i$ mother] $e_m$ love $e_i$]]

(53b) can also be described as an instance of crossover since the movement of the *wh*-phrase over the pronoun correlates with a reduction in possible interpretations, just as we found with the constructions discussed in section 8.3.

Although (51b) involves the crossover property of (47), it is also distinct because the impossible interpretation does not involve binding of a *wh*-trace. In (53b) the pronoun *his* does not c-command (and hence bind) the *wh*-trace object of *love.* Therefore, we cannot account for (53b) as a Principle C violation. Because binding between the pronoun and the *wh*-trace is not involved in these constructions, there is no Principle C violation in the corresponding declarative sentence where the interrogative pronoun is replaced by a name, as in (54).

(54) a. his friend admires Holmes
b. ?$[_{IP}$ $[_{NP}$ $\text{his}_i$ friend] admires $\text{Holmes}_i$]

The anaphoric reading of (54a) as represented in (54b) is marginal at worst, and certainly not on a par with the ungrammatical examples where the pronoun binds the name, as in (46). Thus, we can distinguish the two cases of crossover as **strong crossover** (when the pronoun binds the *wh*-trace) and **weak crossover** (when the *wh*-trace is coindexed with but not bound by the pronoun).[21]

As noted above, although strong crossover falls under the binding theory, weak crossover does not because the *wh*-trace in these cases is not

A-bound. This means that weak crossover must be accounted for in terms of some other principle. One of the earliest proposals in the literature was the condition given in (55).

(55) **Leftness Condition**
A variable cannot be the antecedent of a pronoun to its left.[22]

Assuming that a *wh*-trace is interpreted as a variable at LF, then the Leftness Condition applies at LF. The Leftness Condition blocks the weak crossover case (53b), which would have the LF representation (56).

(56) (for which $x$: $x$ = a person) $[_{IP}$ [ $his_i$ mother$]_k$ loves $x_i]$

Given the coindexing of the pronoun and the variable in (56), the variable would be interpreted as the antecedent of the pronoun, violating the Leftness Condition.

The parallelism between *wh*-trace binding and variable binding is indicated in part by a correspondence of binding paradigms, where quantified NPs occupy the same positions as *wh*-traces at S-structure.[23]

(57) *Wh*-trace
a. $[_{CP}$ $who_i$ $[_{IP}$ $e_i$ loves $[_{NP}$ $his_i$ mother]]]
b. ?$[_{CP}$ $[_{NP:j}$ $whose_i$ mother] $[_{IP}$ $e_j$ loves $him_i$]]
c. *$[_{CP}$ $who_i$ $does_j$ $[_{IP}$ $[_{NP}$ $his_i$ mother] $e_j$ love $e_i$]]
d. *$[_{CP}$ $[_{NP:j}$ $whose_i$ mother] $does_k$ $[_{IP}$ $he_i$ $e_k$ love $e_j$]]

(58) Quantified NP
a. every $boy_i$ loves $[_{NP}$ $his_i$ mother]
b. ?$[_{NP}$ every boy's$_i$ mother] loves $him_i$
c. *$[_{NP}$ $his_i$ mother] loves every $boy_i$
d. *$he_i$ loves $[_{NP}$ every boy's$_i$ mother]

The (a)-examples contain bound pronouns, so the anaphoric interpretation of the pronoun is straightforward. In the (b)-examples the pronoun is not bound and the anaphoric interpretation is noticeably weaker than in the bound pronoun cases. The (c)-examples are the weak crossover cases (assuming that the quantifier at LF has moved across the pronoun by adjoining to IP).[24] In these constructions neither the pronoun nor the *wh*-trace/quantified NP binds the other. This contrasts with the (d)-examples, which are strong crossover constructions where the pronoun binds the *wh*-trace/quantified NP.

Now consider the corresponding paradigm for names.

(59) Names

a. $John_i$ loves $[_{NP}$ $his_i$ mother]

b. $[_{NP}$ $John's_i$ mother] loves $him_i$

c. ?$[_{NP}$ $his_i$ mother] loves $John_i$

d. *$he_i$ loves $[_{NP}$ $John's_i$ mother]

This paradigm differs from the other two in two ways. First, whereas a pronoun object may be anaphoric on a name properly contained in the matrix subject, as in (59b)), the anaphoric interpretation is distinctly less acceptable when an interrogative pronoun or quantified noun replaces the name, as in (57b) and (58b). Second, it is possible for a pronoun to the left of a name to be coindexed with the name when the pronoun does not c-command the name, as in (59c). This is not possible if the name is replaced with a *wh*-trace or a quantified NP—the weak crossover cases. Given that quantified NPs are subject to movement in LF via the rule of Quantifier Raising (QR), which adjoins a quantified NP to IP (see note 15), then (58c) is the LF equivalent of a weak crossover violation for QR. Similarly, (58d) is the LF equivalent of a strong crossover violation for QR. Presumably the LF representation for this example will be (60), where the matrix subject *he* binds the variable.

(60) $(\forall x\text{: } x = \text{a boy})$ $[_{IP}$ $he_i$ loves $[_{NP}$ $x\text{'s}_i$ mother]]

In the *wh*-trace example, reconstruction will have to apply if the variable is to be bound at LF. Thus, the LF representation of (57d) should be (61), under the assumption that the correspondence between the paradigms (57) and (58) is not accidental.

(61) (for which $x$: $x$ = a person) $[_{IP}$ $he_i$ loves $[_{NP}$ $x\text{'s}_i$ mother]]

If reconstruction applies in these cases, then (57b) and (58b) will also involve reconstruction at LF. The two examples would be represented as (62a–b) respectively.

(62) a. (for which $x$: $x$ = a person) $[_{IP}$ $[_{NP}$ $x\text{'s}_i$ mother] loves $him_i$]

b. $(\forall x\text{: } x = \text{a boy})$ $[_{IP}$ $[_{NP}$ $x\text{'s}_i$ mother] loves $him_i$]

The question is why these should be marginal and why they are clearly more acceptable than the weak crossover cases. They are like the weak crossover cases in that binding is not involved—there is no c-command between coindexed NPs. They differ with respect to the linear order of pronoun and variable. Whereas the weak crossover cases are prohibited by the Leftness Condition, the examples in (62) are not.[25]

The analysis of weak crossover cases given above should be treated as a preamble rather than a complete account (see Jacobson 1977 for an extensive discussion of the phenomena). It should be noted that the Leftness Condition covers the strong crossover cases as well—and therefore overlaps with the binding-theoretic approach to strong crossover.[26]

One further remark seems in order here. The binding-theoretic approach to strong crossover will cover constructions where "crossover" does not occur. For example, consider a construction where a pronoun binds a *wh*-trace, though the *wh*-phrase has not been moved over the pronoun, as in (63a).

(63) a. he wonders who Mary has recommended
b. who wonders whether Mary has recommended him

(63b) can be interpreted as a sentence about two or three different people. (63a) can only be interpreted as a sentence about three people. This follows from the fact that the pronoun in (63a) cannot bind the *wh*-trace object of the complement IP, given Principle C. These examples involve the same facts and the same analysis as the strong crossover paradigm, yet no crossover is involved. Thus, it appears that crossover is not the essential property of these constructions that requires an explanation.[27]

---

**Exercise 8.10**
A similar case can be made for weak crossover. The relevant examples are given in (i).

(i) a. his mother wonders who Mary has recommended
b. who wonders whether Mary has recommended his mother

Discuss the interpretations of these examples and provide the relevant indexing representations. Show how the Leftness Condition applies with respect to (i.a) to exclude the impossible interpretation.

---

## Appendix B: The Binding-Theoretic Approach to Empty Categories

In this appendix we will consider further the possibility of extending binding theory to other empty categories besides *wh*-trace. In the first section we will discuss a binding-theoretic account for the distribution of NP-trace, and in the second we will look at a similar account for the distribution of PRO.

**NP-Trace and Binding Theory**

Although a *wh*-trace cannot be A-bound, an NP-trace is typically A-bound, as illustrated in (64).

(64) John$_i$ seems [$_{IP}$ e$_i$ to be irritable this morning]

The standard cases of NP-movement discussed in chapters 5 and 6 show that an NP-trace is not the empty category analogue of an R-expression—if it were, then NP-movement would be prohibited by Principle C of the binding theory.

Recall that in section 6.3.1.1 we proposed a proper binding condition as one way to account for the distribution of NP-traces. This proper binding condition is very similar to Principle A of the binding theory as formulated in chapter 7. For the basic IP-paradigm, NP-trace binding mirrors lexical anaphor binding.

(65) Simple sentences
  a. John$_i$ was criticized e$_i$
  b. John$_i$ criticized himself$_i$

(66) Finite clause complements
  a. i. *John$_i$ was believed [$_{CP}$ (that) [$_{IP}$ e$_i$ is helping Mary]]
    ii. *John$_i$ believed [$_{CP}$ (that) [$_{IP}$ himself$_i$ is helping Mary]]
  b. i. *Mary$_i$ was believed [$_{CP}$ (that) [$_{IP}$ John is helping e$_i$]]
    ii. *Mary$_i$ believed [$_{CP}$ (that) [$_{IP}$ John is helping herself$_i$]]

(67) Infinitival complements
  a. i. John$_i$ was believed [$_{IP}$ e$_i$ to be helping Mary]
    ii. John$_i$ believed [$_{IP}$ himself$_i$ to be helping Mary]
  b. i. *Mary$_i$ was believed [$_{IP}$ John to be helping e$_i$]
    ii. *Mary$_i$ believed [$_{IP}$ John to be helping herself$_i$]

(65) illustrates that both a lexical anaphor and an NP-trace can be A-bound within a clause. Binding across a clause boundary is ruled out when the clause is finite, as in (66). It is also ruled out when the clause is an infinitival and the binding is across a syntactic subject, as in (67b). However, both an NP-trace and a lexical anaphor can be properly bound across a clause boundary as the subject of an infinitival clause, as shown in (67a). This correspondence suggests that NP-trace should be considered the empty category analogue of a lexical anaphor, and hence subject to Principle A of the binding theory.

There is, however, a difference between the behavior of lexical anaphors and the behavior of NP-traces within the IP-paradigm extended to binding across pleonastic subjects. As noted in section 7.1.1, reciprocal binding across a pleonastic subject seems significantly more acceptable than binding across a nonpleonastic subject. This contrast was illustrated in (29a) of chapter 7 (repeated here as (68 a–b)).

(68) a. *they$_i$ expect [$_{IP}$ John$_j$ to seem to each other$_i$ [$_{IP}$ e$_j$ to be crazy]]
b. they$_i$ expect [$_{IP}$ it to seem to each other$_i$ [$_{CP}$ that John is crazy]]

No such contrast exists with respect to NP-trace binding across the pleonastic subject of an infinitival complement, as (69) shows.

(69) a. *[$_{IP}$ Al$_i$ was likely [$_{CP}$ for [$_{IP}$ it [$_{VP}$ to be mentioned e$_i$]]]]
(cf. it was likely for Al to be mentioned; Al was likely to be mentioned)
b. *[$_{IP}$ Al$_i$ was likely [$_{CP}$ for [$_{IP}$ Bill [$_{VP}$ to mention e$_i$]]]]

(69a) is interesting as a construction that violates no principle of grammar discussed so far other than possibly Principle A (modulo the θ-subject proviso)—see also example (63a) of chapter 6. The ECP is not violated, because the trace in the complement VP is properly governed. The Case Filter is not violated, because the matrix subject *Al* moves from a Caseless to a Case-marked position, and the pleonastic complement subject is Case-marked by the *for*-complementizer. Subjacency is not involved provided that IP is the only sentential bounding node for English. θ-theory is also satisfied since *Al's* moves from a θ-position (the object of *mention*) to a nonthematic position (the subject of a predicate adjective that takes a pleonastic subject with a finite clause complement). (69a) is unquestionably a case of "illicit movement" (also called "improper movement"; see Chomsky 1986b) and therefore should be ruled out by some general principle of grammar.[28]

To account for (69a) as a Principle A violation, the definition of "accessible SUBJECT" for NP-trace, in contrast to lexical anaphor, must include pleonastic subjects. Alternatively, the binding domain for anaphors generally is the domain of SUBJECT. The issue of accessibility arises for lexical anaphors (for reasons to be specified), but not for empty anaphors. In the NP-paradigm cases where accessibility is relevant for lexical anaphor binding the Subjacency Condition is also violated.

(70) Finite clause complement
a. they$_i$ expected [$_{CP}$ that [$_{IP}$ [$_{NP}$ each other's$_i$ books] would receive rave reviews]]
b. *John$_i$ was expected [$_{CP}$ that [$_{IP}$ [$_{NP}$ e$_i$ books] would receive rave reviews]]

(71) Infinitival complement
a. they$_i$ expected [$_{IP}$ [$_{NP}$ each other's$_i$ books] to receive rave reviews]
b. *John$_i$ was expected [$_{IP}$ [$_{NP}$ e$_i$ books] to receive rave reviews]

In both (b)-examples the NP-trace in the subject-of-NP position is bound across two bounding categories (NP and IP), violating Subjacency. However, these trace binding violations seem worse than standard island violations and therefore may be deviant for additional reasons—for example, binding theory as applied to NP-trace.

With this in mind, let us consider a case of illicit movement that appears to circumvent the binding theory.

(72) *[$_{IP}$ Bill$_i$ was likely [$_{CP}$ that [$_{IP}$ he$_i$ would [$_{VP}$ be proud e$_i$]]]][29]

(72 is not a Subjacency violation because the trace is bound across only one bounding category (IP). Since the NP-trace is lexically governed by the predicate adjective *proud,* the trace satisfies the ECP. Since the trace is in a Caseless position, and its lexical antecedent is Case-marked as the subject of a finite IP, the sentence does not violate Case theory. Taking *Bill* to be the antecedent of the trace, the θ-Criterion is satisfied because the movement is from a thematic position to a nonthematic position. Principle A seems to be satisfied because the NP-trace, an empty category analogue of a lexical anaphor, is properly bound by the pronoun subject of the sentential complement. Furthermore, the binding relation between the pronoun and the matrix subject *Bill* satisfies Principle B. Still the example is ill formed.

One way to account for (72) would be to derive some bad consequence from taking the coindexed pronoun as the lexical antecedent of the trace. Given that trace binding involves the transfer of a θ-role from a trace to its binder (as discussed section 6.2), the pronoun complement subject would be assigned two θ-roles in violation of the Functional Uniqueness requirement of the θ-Criterion. In addition, the matrix subject *Bill* would be assigned no θ-role at all, in violation of Functional Relatedness. To ensure that the θ-role of the trace *is* assigned to the pronoun and not *Bill,* we must assume that NP binding involves θ-role transfer and that there is a condition on NP-trace binding that prohibits the main clause subject from properly binding the trace. This could be achieved with the following proper binding condition:

(73) An NP-trace must be A-bound in the minimal θ-domain containing its governor.

Recall from the discussion of pronoun binding in section 7.2.1 that the notion θ-domain equates IP and NP. Therefore an NP-trace must be A-bound within the smallest NP or IP that contains its governor. (73) not only achieves the correct result with respect to (72), but also accounts for the ill-formed examples of NP-trace binding in (65)–(67) and (69).

---

**Exercise 8.11**
Discuss how (73) applies with respect to the examples in (65)–(67) and (69). Be sure to discuss how the grammatical sentences satisfy (73) as well as how the deviant examples violate it.

---

Regarding the conclusions we can draw from this discussion, we must exercise some caution. It is clear from our formulation of (73) that the proper binding condition for NP-trace is not identical to Principle A for lexical anaphors. The domain statements are different; moreover, the domain statement of (73) is identical to that of Principle B in chapter 7. Clearly we cannot conclude from this that an NP-trace is therefore an empty category pronominal, since Principle B would prohibit grammatical sentences with NP-trace binding (e.g., (65a) and (67a.i)). Yet designating an NP-trace to be the empty category analogue of a lexical anaphor does little more than identify a common property—the requirement that both must be A-bound within their respective binding domains. It is still necessary to distinguish lexical anaphors from NP-traces in the application of proper binding conditions. Hence, calling an NP-trace an empty category anaphor does not lead to a generalization (as would be the case if Principle A for lexical anaphors applied without modification to NP-traces). This does not, however, refute the analysis of NP-trace as the empty category analogue of a lexical anaphor. Given the binding-theoretic analysis of *wh*-trace in section 8.3, it is necessary to distinguish between NP-trace and *wh*-trace, and designating NP-trace as an empty category anaphor is one way to make the distinction. Furthermore, constructions like (69a) provide some evidence that NP-trace, like lexical anaphors, is subject to a proper binding condition.

**PRO and Binding Theory**
Assuming that the control relationship between a PRO and its antecedent constitutes yet another binding relation like trace binding, we might ask whether the distribution of PRO can be accounted for in terms of the

binding theory. As noted at the outset of chapter 6, the distribution of PRO is distinct from the distribution of trace in that PRO can never be lexically governed. The question arises, Does this fact follow from some application of the binding theory to PRO? As a basis for discussion we will begin by comparing the distribution of bound PRO with that of lexical bound elements (anaphors and pronouns).

PRO binding exhibits the same IP-paradigm as lexical anaphors with respect to binding across clause boundaries (as can be demonstrated by substituting the reciprocal *each other* for PRO in the following examples).

(74) Finite clause complement
  a. *$we_i$ expect [$_{CP}$ (that) [$_{IP}$ $PRO_i$ will see Mary at the meeting]]
  b. *$we_i$ expect [$_{CP}$ (that) [$_{IP}$ Mary will see $PRO_i$ at the meeting]]

(75) Infinitival complement
  a. $we_i$ expect [$_{IP}$ $PRO_i$ to see Mary at the meeting]
  b. *$we_i$ expect [$_{IP}$ Mary to see $PRO_i$ at the meeting]

Bound PRO may occur as the subject of an infinitival complement (75a), but not as the object of an infinitival complement (75b) or as the subject or object of a finite sentential complement (74a–b). There is a further similarity that PRO may be bound across a pleonastic subject (i.e., that a pleonastic subject does not induce a binding domain for PRO (cf. (69a)).[30]

(76) $John_i$ knows [$_{CP}$ that [$_{IP}$ it isn't easy [$_{CP}$ C [$_{IP}$ $PRO_i$ to shave $himself_i$ in the dark]]]]

This constitutes the evidence for analyzing PRO as an empty category anaphor subject to Principle A of the binding theory.

The evidence against this analysis consists of three points. First, bound PRO cannot occur in the VP of a simple sentence—that is, unlike lexical anaphors, it cannot be bound within a single clause.

(77) a. *$John_i$ admires $PRO_i$
  b. *$Sarah_i$ is always talking to $PRO_i$
  c. *$Adam_i$ gave $PRO_i$ a new toy

Thus, the examples in (77) cannot have the interpretation that would result from substituting the appropriate reflexive pronoun for $PRO_i$. Second, bound PRO cannot occur in NP, and therefore PRO binding does not correspond to lexical anaphor binding for the NP-paradigm (cf. (21) in chapter 7).

(78) a. *we$_i$ read [$_{NP}$ PRO('s)$_i$ books]
b. *we$_i$ read [$_{NP}$ several books about PRO$_i$]

Thus, the examples in (78) cannot have the interpretation that would result from substituting the appropriate pronoun (or reflexive pronoun in the case of (78b)) for PRO$_i$. Finally, PRO need not be bound at all.

(79) it is difficult [$_{CP}$ C [$_{IP}$ PRO to form an opinion with so few facts]]

In other words, PRO cannot occur in (77)–(79) whether or not it is bound.

For the moment, let us consider only bound PRO. We have some evidence that PRO patterns like a lexical anaphor (74)–(76), and other evidence that it does not (77)–(79). The nonoccurrence of PRO-binding within a single clause would follow from the binding theory if PRO were analyzed as a pronominal subject to Principle B. Then the examples in (77) would all constitute Principle B violations. This analysis cannot be extended to the IP-paradigm involving sentential complements, as illustrated by comparing (74)–(75) with the corresponding paradigm for pronouns, given in (80)–(81).

(80) Finite clause complement
a. we$_i$ expect [$_{CP}$ (that) [$_{IP}$ we$_i$ will see Mary at the meeting]
b. we$_i$ expect [$_{CP}$ (that) [$_{IP}$ Mary will see us$_i$ at the meeting]]

(81) Infinitival complement
a. *we$_i$ expect [$_{IP}$ us$_i$ to see Mary at the meeting]
b. we$_i$ expect [$_{IP}$ Mary to see us$_i$ at the meeting]

A bound pronoun cannot occur in the subject of an infinitival complement where a bound PRO can (compare (81a) with (75a)). Furthermore, PRO binding cannot occur where pronominal binding is allowed; that is, it cannot occur in the subject of a finite sentential complement (compare (80a) with (74a)) or the VP of any sentential complement (compare (80b) and (81b) with (74b) and (75b)). Within a single IP, PRO binding behaves like pronoun-binding, whereas across an IP boundary, PRO binding behaves like lexical anaphor binding. However, PRO binding is not allowed across an NP boundary, unlike either pronoun binding or lexical anaphor binding—though exactly like NP-trace binding.

To account for this behavior, Chomsky (1981) analyzes PRO as a pronominal anaphor and therefore subject to Principles A and B of the binding theory. Thus, although PRO binding within a single IP, as in (77) satisfies Principle A, it violates Principle B. Similarly, although the binding in (74), for example, satisfies Principle B, it violates Principle A. In order to allow for PRO binding in (75a) something more must be said. Chomsky's analysis assumes that the binding domains for Principles A and B are virtually identical and that they are formulated in terms of government—thus, the binding domain is called the *governing category*, defined as the NP or IP in which the anaphor/pronoun is governed. It is further assumed that PRO is not governed and therefore does not have a governing category—in which case the binding principles do not apply, with the result that PRO binding can occur in the subject of an infinitival complement.[31] This binding-theoretic approach to the distribution of PRO, which derives the fact that PRO cannot occur in a governed position, is referred to as the *PRO Theorem*.[32]

## Bibliographical Comments

Principle C of the binding theory is essentially a reformulation of Lasnik's noncoreference rule (or more accurately, disjoint reference rule); see Lasnik 1976. For some alternative approaches, see Higginbotham 1983, and Reinhart 1983—and, for some critical discussion of these alternatives, Lasnik and Uriagereka 1988. The parametric analysis of Principle C comes from Lasnik 1989a. The discussion of binding theory and levels of representation in section 8.3.2 is adapted from Freidin 1986—see also Chomsky 1981, 1982, and Lasnik and Uriagereka 1988 for further commentary.

The discussion of crossover phenomena is introduced into generative grammar in Postal 1971, which considers a wider range of phenomena within an earlier framework for transformational grammar. The trace-theoretic analysis of strong crossover originates with Wasow 1979 [a revised version of his 1972 MIT dissertation, *Anaphoric relations in English*]. This analysis is also discussed in some detail in Chomsky 1976 and in Freidin and Lasnik 1981. The distinction between weak and strong crossover is also due to Wasow 1979. The Leftness Condition as a solution to weak crossover is proposed in Chomsky 1976. For criticism of and alternatives to the Leftness Condition see in particular Higginbotham 1980a,b, 1983, Koopman and Sportiche 1982, Safir 1984, and Lasnik and Stowell 1991.

The seminal text on the possible relation between government and binding is Chomsky 1981: chap. 3.

The extension of binding theory to all empty categories has been a topic of discussion and debate from the beginnings of trace theory (circa 1973). For discussion of the binding-theoretic approach to the distribution of

PRO, see Manzini 1983 and Huang 1989. The binding-theoretic account of the distribution of empty categories involves two related issues: the feature analysis of empty categories and the determination of empty categories. The feature analysis is motivated both by the necessity of distinguishing *wh*-trace from NP-trace and also by the necessity of distinguishing PRO from trace. For further discussion, see Chomsky 1981, 1982. Empty categories may be determined (i.e., interpreted with respect to type) via their derivation or the way they are locally bound (also called "functional determination"). For discussion of functional determination of empty categories, see Chomsky 1982 and Bouchard 1984. For some critical discussion, see Freidin 1986, and Lasnik and Uriagereka 1988, and in particular Brody 1984, which proposes that the theory of grammar should be able to rule out all inappropriate interpretations of empty categories, thereby rendering both derivational determination and functional determination beside the point.

# Notes

## Chapter 1

1. Note that in the case of *orange juice* the two possible syntactic analyses will have different phonological representations. In the case of *orange* the noun, *orange* receives a heavier stress than *juice*, whereas in the case of *orange* the adjective, *juice* receives the heavier stress. In this way, the phonological assignment of stress for this example depends on syntactic structure, as does the assignment of meaning.

2. Note that there are several ways a child's language faculty could "come up with" the correct grammar. It could "select" the grammar from a range of possible grammars compatible with its own properties and the primary data the child is exposed to. Alternatively, it might simply construct the correct grammar on the basis of the primary linguistic data.

3. Two other senses of "universal grammar" are in use as well. In one sense, "universal" refers to aspects of grammar that apply to every human language (see Greenberg 1963 and Comrie 1981). For example, one might talk about the "universality" of construction types like "relative clause." Supposing that every human language has such a construction, we might then proceed to study what properties are shared by relative clauses in the languages of the world. Whether such "universals" have any status under the psychological interpretation of grammar remains to determined. Unless they are instantiated as part of the theory of grammar, they are merely historical artifacts of the languages under investigation. Yet another sense of "universal grammar" is discussed in Richmond Thomason's introduction to Montague 1974, where the focus is mathematical properties of language and hence the universality of grammar derives from the universality of mathematics.

4. Note that movement rules of this sort (i.e., rules that reposition elements in the phrase structure of a sentence) are distinct from phrase structure rules. Such rules constitute a special class of rules called "transformations," which are discussed in later chapters.

**Chapter 2**

1. Note, however, that tree diagrams and labeled bracketings may contain more information than phrase markers. In the case where a category A rewrites as a single nonterminal category B, the phrase marker does not show that B is a constituent of A. In fact, such a phrase marker could be interpreted with A as a constituent of B. Thus, the phrase marker will be ambiguous in this case, while the tree diagram and labeled bracketing cannot be.

See also Kupin 1978 for a proposal concerning a "reduced" phrase marker consisting of the terminal string of a derivation and only those strings containing exactly one nonterminal category. See Lasnik and Kupin 1977 for additional discussion.

2. Richard Kayne (1983) has proposed that binary branching constitutes an upper limit and that the maximal number of immediate constituents a category can take is therefore two. See Kayne 1983 for discussion of the ramifications of this proposal.

3. The triangle in the tree diagram (6) indicates that the NP has further internal structure that is not specified.

4. The formulation of nondistinctness given in the text differs slightly from that given in Chomsky 1965. There two matrices are distinct just in case the values of features that both matrices contain have the same value. Thus, two matrices that had different features would be nondistinct under this definition, but not under the definition adopted here.

5. An exact characterization of the nature of such linking is complicated. For further discussion of predicate-argument structure, see Grimshaw 1990, Jackendoff 1990, and Ravin 1990.

6. How to determine the correct set of word classes for languages has been debated since antiquity. In Plato's *Cratylus* only two classes are mentioned, *ónoma* (ὄνομα) and *rhêma* (ρημα)—roughly, words that are noun-like and verb-like. Aristotle added a third class *syndesmoi* (συνδεσμοι), covering conjunctions, the article, pronouns, and possibly prepositions. (See Robins 1966, 1979 for interesting discussions of the history of grammatical analysis concerning word classes.)

7. In the classical literature of generative grammar, the distinction between lexical and phrasal categories is made in terms of the bar notation, where a phrasal category bears one or more bars on top (see Chomsky 1970 for the original proposal). In some papers, bars are replaced with primes (N', N", and so on). The star notation used here is equivalent to the bar and prime notations; however, we will not be differentiating levels of phrasal projection in terms of different numbers of stars for reasons that will be presented in this section.

8. In the original X-bar theory, levels of projection were distinguished in terms of number of bars. Thus, the first level of projection had a single bar; the next, a double bar; and so on. Under this analysis, the maximal phrasal projection is rigidly fixed in terms of a particular number of bars. This means that each phrasal projection is in some sense categorially distinct from the others. In contrast, the proposal being discussed in the text assumes that only one phrasal

category is projected by a lexical head and that any distinctions among instances of this phrasal category follow from the configuration in which the instance of the category occurs.

9. The motivation for assuming that the specifier *the* is a constituent of a higher level of phrasal projection than the adjunct PP is rather minimal. So far we have no compelling evidence *for* the analysis given in (37) or *against* an alternative in which Det and PP are immediate constituents of the same projection. What will be established in the following discussion is that evidence exists for a level of structure that is intermediate between the lexical head and its maximal phrasal projection.

10. For the moment we will define a "bound anaphor" as an NP that, having no reference of its own, must get its reference from some other NP in a sentence—referred to as its **antecedent**. Thus, a bound anaphor cannot occur as the sole NP in a sentence: **Each other are/is happy.*

11. A historical note: (45) is a simplification of the original definition of c-command proposed by Reinhart 1976, which declares that α c-commands β if *the first branching node* that dominates α also dominates β, and neither dominates the other. This definition assumes that nonbranching categories do not create c-command domains (hence the stipulation about "first branching category"). This distinction does not affect the current discussion.

12. For discussion of the grammatical relation "subject," see Stowell 1983.

13. If we include N as a category that may take an NP object as defined in the text, then the question of A(djective)s arises. The adjective *proud* as in *proud of Bernie* has been suggested as a candidate for an English adjective that takes an NP object (see Chomsky 1981:49). The evidence that A takes an NP object in English is weak. In languages such as German and Russian, however, the evidence is stronger. See Freidin and Babby 1984 for some discussion of Russian.

14. Here "*of*-insertion" refers to the phenomenon of inserting the grammatical formative *of* in a phrase marker, in contrast to the rule of grammar "*Of*-Insertion," which carries out the insertion. This usage occurs throughout the text.

15. Note that the strings in (69) would be well formed if *Mary's* is interpreted as an elliptical NP standing for *Mary's X*, where X is the head of the NP. This is not the interpretation given to (69). Rather, it is assumed that *Mary's* is the lexical head of the subject NP in (69a) and of the object NPs in (69b-c); hence, the elliptical interpretation is not available.

16. Given that such forms are possible, relative clauses that do not end with a noun (as in (i)) should also be able to occur with *'s*.

(i) the mathematician who is happy's hat

Although (i) is certainly more awkward than (73a), the simplest grammatical rule for inserting *'s* will generate both NPs. Thus, they will both be designated as grammatical in this regard. The unacceptability of (i) may be explained in terms of the *'s* forming a "word" with an adjective. If this is prohibited by some rule or principle of word formation (morphology), then (i) could be designated as ungrammatical by virtue of morphology, independent of syntax. Note that this account could not be extended to (73a), however.

17. S-structure is similar, though not always identical, to what was called "surface structure" in earlier work on transformational grammar. The differences need not concern us here.

18. Following standard practice, the word "case" will be capitalized when it refers to the grammatical notion, in order to distinguish it from other lexical items with the same spelling.

19. The Case Filter is also a condition on syntactic representations. As such, it acts as a filter that excludes representations containing any lexical NP that is not marked for Case in some way.

20. How the grammatical formative *of* is involved in Case assignment will be discussed in section 5.1. Note however that it is different from *'s* in that it can cooccur with personal pronouns (e.g., *a portrait of her* versus **a portrait her*).

21. One alternative to the Case-theoretic account is to stipulate the restrictions on *Of*-Insertion in terms of the SD of the rule. This would involve replacing the SD of (62) with (i).

(i) $X\ [_{N*}\ N\ N^{max}]\ Y$

(i) extends the descriptive power of transformational rules by allowing dominance relations among terms to be expressed in their SDs (in contrast to the SD of (62) which only expresses linear precedence relations between constant terms). (i) is to be interpreted as a conjunction of two string conditions that the phrase marker must meet.

(ii) $X_i\ N^*\ Y_j$ AND $X_i\ N\ N^{max}\ Y_j$

The variables X and Y are indexed with subscripts in (ii) to indicate that they stand for the same strings in each case. *AND* is a Boolean connective used to state a condition on analyzability of a phrase marker by a transformation. *OR, NOT, ONLY IF,* and *IF AND ONLY IF* are other Boolean connectives that might be employed in the statement of SDs for transformations. If negation (*NOT*) and either conjunction (*AND*) or disjunction (*OR*) are allowed, then we have the full power of the propositional calculus for stating SDs of transformations, since from either pair we can derive the others. For arguments against incorporating these connectives into a theory of transformations, see Lasnik 1981a.

Such extensions of descriptive power are generally to be avoided. If our descriptive system allows for possibilities that are not realized in the grammars of natural languages, then it will not explain why languages exhibit certain grammatical properties and not others. Therefore, the more restrictive our system of grammatical rules and principles, the better our chances of achieving some level of explanation for why languages are the way they are.

22. Note that this departs from the previous usage of categorial features where a feature [+X] represents a category X.

23. This feature analysis embodies an empirical claim that {A, P} and {N, V} do not constitute natural classes. So far, linguists have not discovered any evidence that {A, P} or {N, V} are analyzed as natural classes with respect to grammatical rules.

## Chapter 3

1. For some speakers it is also possible to ask a nonecho question with the form of (9), where the *wh*-form is uttered with a quick falling intonation (similar to the mid-falling tone in Mandarin Chinese).

2. See Baltin 1978a, 1982 for further discussion of this notion.

3. In earlier work in the 1970s and thru the mid to late 1980s it was assumed that sentential constructions consisited of an "S-bar" that immediately dominated the nodes COMP and S. COMP was analyzed as a constituent that contained positions for the complementizer and a *wh*-phrase. This analysis is less well motivated than the one presented here.

4. The auxiliary verb system of English is investigated in detail in chapter 4.

5. In current work in generative grammar, this result is guaranteed by the following principle of grammar:

(i) **The Projection Principle**
Lexical structure must be represented categorially at every syntactic level. (Chomsky 1986b:84)

One effect of the Projection Principle is that subcategorization properties of lexical heads (e.g., verbs, nouns, adjectives, and prepositions) must be represented at D-structure and S-structure. Hence there must be traces in complement positions that subcategorize heads when the complement has been moved by a transformation. For further discussion of this principle, its formulation, and its consequences, see Chomsky 1986b and the works cited there.

6. An even stronger constraint on the formulation of grammatical transformations would be to exclude all compounding of elementary operations. This would mean that each transformational rule in a grammar consists of only one elementary operation, and it would exclude rules that involve multiple applications of a single elementary operation or combinations of elementary operations. Whether the stronger constraint is viable remains an empirical issue. The analyses presented in this book are consistent with this constraint, and so we will consider it as a working hypothesis. That each grammatical transformation consists of a single elementary operation was first proposed in Hasegawa 1968:sec. 5 and is mentioned again with respect to trace theory in Chomsky 1980b.

7. "*Wh*-phrase" is an informal designation. The rule as formulated in (28) makes no distinction between *wh*-NPs and non-*wh*-NPs. If only *wh*-NPs are moved into CP (and similarly for *wh*-PPs and *wh*-APs versus their non-*wh* counterparts), then this must follow from some principle of grammar since it is not stipulated in the rule. (We will discuss this further in section 3.3.) Basically, (28) formalizes a generic substitution operation—of which what we have been calling *Wh*-Movement is just one instance.

8. This notion of cyclic domain is due to Edwin Williams 1974.

9. The basis for this designation is the correspondence between such an NP in a nominal (e.g., *the professor's interpretation of Beckett*) and in the corresponding

sentence (e.g., *The professor interpreted Beckett*). Thus, just as the NP *the professor* functions as the subject of the sentence, so it functions analogously as the subject of the nominal. Following standard practice, we will extend the designation to all NPs in this position even when there is no corresponding sentence (as in *the boy's cap*, for example).

10. We cannot take both IP and CP to be bounding categories. If we did, then Subjacency would rule out long-distance *wh*-movement which crosses both CP and IP when moving from CP to CP.

11. There is another asymmetry between leftward and rightward movements, however. Leftward but not rightward movements can apply successive cyclically, thereby giving the appearance of being unbounded. We return to this issue below in section 3.3.

12. Compare:

(i) a. John asked us whether the boy who gave the dog to Mary had talked to Susan.

b. John asked us [$_{CP}$ who$_i$ the boy who gave the dog to Mary had talked to e$_i$]

13. Compare:

(i) John asked us whether the report that the committee had recommended Princeton had been circulated

14. The analysis is based on the assumption that relative clauses, like *wh*-questions, undergo *Wh*-Movement. See Chomsky 1977a for discussion. Nonetheless, given that relative pronouns are different from interrogative pronouns, (61) might be accounted for independently of Subjacency. Suppose that whereas (60) is well formed when *who* is a relative pronoun, it is ill formed when *who* is an interrogative pronoun. Then (61) would be subject to two different interpretations: (i) *who* is an interrogative pronoun, and (ii) *who* is a relative pronoun. (i) would be excluded by whatever excludes (60) under the same interpretation of *who*. (ii) requires yet another prohibition against a relative pronoun that occurs outside of the NP it is associated with. Of course, this prohibition follows from Subjacency.

15. Grammaticality judgments for these examples may differ between speakers. The basis for this variation remains to be determined.

One mechanism for handling (62) that has been suggested in the literature is "**reanalysis.**" The intuitive idea is that the syntactic structure of (62) is reanalyzed so that *who* is interpreted as a direct object of the verb. Although a more formal account of the reanalysis mechanism will not be attempted here, it should be noted that reanalysis would be a lexically determined process; that is, it could apply only with certain verbs.

16. In fact, this may be the case for all movements. See Freidin 1978b for discussion; section 6.3.1.2 for cases involving (non-*wh*) NP-movement; and Browning 1991 for another, independent argument for construing Subjacency as a condition on representations.

17. Since Italian appears not to allow sentences containing multiple interrogative pronouns, the corresponding cases involving extraction of an interrogative pronoun out of an indirect question do not occur. See Adams 1984 for further discussion of multiple interrogatives in Italian. The examples that follow are from Rizzi 1980.

18. It should be noted, however, that there are constructions in Italian where a *wh*-phrase may not be extracted out of an NP that properly contains it. The following examples are from Cinque 1980:

(i) NP in object position

a. *il paese $[_{PP:i}$ a cui] ricordiamo $[_{NP}$ un/l'attacco $e_i$ ] (è la Polonia)
a country on which (we) remember an/the attack is Poland

b. *non è posto $[_{PP:i}$ da cui] possano minacciarci
it is not a position from which (they) can threaten us
$[_{NP}$ il licenziamento $e_i$ ]
the dismissal

(ii) NP in subject position

a. *una persona $[_{PP:i}$ a cui] $[[_{NP}$ l'attaccamento $e_i$ ] potrebbe rovinarci . . .
a person to whom the attachment could ruin us

b. *quel posto $[_{PP:i}$ da cui] $[[_{NP}$ un/il licenziamento $e_i$ ]
that position from which a/the dismissal

ci è stato minacciato
has been threatened

It appears that the *wh*-PPs *a cui* and *da cui* may not be extracted out of NP in either subject or object position. In contrast, it is possible to extract the *wh*-PP *di cui* from an NP, as the following examples illustrate.

(iii) NP in object position

una persona $[_{PP:i}$ di cui] apprezziamo $[_{NP}$ la grande generosità $e_i$ ] (è Giorgio)
a person of whom we appreciate the great generosity (is Giorgio)

(iv) NP in subject position

a. ?Giorgio $[_{PP:i}$ di cui] $[[_{NP}$ l'onestà $e_i$ ] è, credo, nota a tutti. . .
Giorgio of whom honesty is I believe known to everybody

b. Giorgio, $[_{PP:i}$ di cui] è nota $[_{NP}$ l'onestà $e_i$ ],. . .
Giorgio of whom is known the honesty

According to Cinque, the marginality of (iv.a) results from an external factor. When the subject NP is postposed, as in (iv.b), the extraction is fully grammatical. The constructions in (i)-(iv) show that more is involved in accounting for possible extractions of *wh*-phrases out of NP than what is predicted by the Subjacency Condition alone. (See Cinque 1980 for further details and analysis.) These examples show that the motivation for the parametric analysis of Subjacency in terms of CP may be limited to the facts concerning *wh*-clauses.

19. The terms "English" and "Italian" refer to idiolects of these languages—i.e., to the speech of individuals considered as unique linguistic patterns. Thus, it is possible that some idiolect of English manifests Italian-type bounding properties or that some idiolect of Italian manifests English-type bounding properties.

20. The relation between the *wh*-phrase and its two traces can be conceptualized as a **chain** (i)—that is, as three elements linked together.

(i) [*what*$_i$, e$_i$', e$_i$]

The trace in SPEC-CP is given as *e*$_i$' to distinguish it from the trace in complement object position. If each link of the chain satisfies the Subjacency Condition, then the chain satisfies the condition. If any link of the chain fails to satisfy the Subjacency Condition, then the chain is ill formed. The two links of (i), [*what*$_i$, e$_i$'] and [e$_i$', e$_i$], satisfy the Subjacency Condition, as noted in the text.

21. This is a preliminary formulation of the principle, which will be developed further in later chapters. See the bibliographical remarks at the end of the chapter for more discussion.

22. As formulated, the ECP raises questions about the status of traces in subject position [NP;IP] and SPEC-CP. Answers to these questions must be put aside until a more detailed analysis of the structure of IP and CP has been developed in chapters 4, 5, and 6.

23. However, there have been proposals for including PP as a bounding category (see Baltin 1978b and Van Riemsdijk 1978 for details). If PP is taken to be a bounding category, then (100) would violate the Subjacency Condition. This analysis creates problems for simple cases of *wh*-movement (e.g., (96b)) and therefore will not be considered further here.

24. This perspective on transformations has been the dominant view for over a decade. It has been instantiated in the formulation of a single movement transformation, Move α, which moves constituents from one position in a phrase marker to another. In actuality, "Move α" is an abbreviation for two distinct elementary transformational operations: substitute α for β (102) and adjoin α to β. See appendix B for further discussion.

25. As formulated, the Superiority Condition is too strong since it rules out the class of acceptable sentences illustrated in the following (b)-examples:

(i) a. which students read which books
b. which books did which students read

(ii) a. whose students read which books
b. which books did whose students read

(iii) a. which students read whose books
b. whose books did which students read

Given that the Superiority violations in (i.b), (ii.b), and (iii.b) are well formed sentences, the Superiority Condition needs to be reformulated. It is not clear how this is to be accomplished—so far an account that distinguishes (103b) and

(104b) from (i.b) remains an unsolved problem. For some discussion, see Pesetsky 1987.

26. For a detailed discussion of the history of island constraints, see Newmeyer 1986. For additional discussion, see Van Riemsdijk and Williams 1986 and Grosu 1981.

27. Chomsky (1973:fn. 55) notes that movement of the *wh*-NP out of the PP in SPEC-CP (or COMP in his earlier terminology), as indicated in the ill-formed (110) in the text, could be construed as a violation of the A-over-A Principle, where the PP in CP is interpreted as a feature complex [*wh*, PP]. "This observation is redundant, however, since the rules of interpretation to be given will in any event block interpretation of sentences with dangling prepositions in COMP" (pp. 140-141). These rules of interpretation involve the binding relation between a *wh*-phrase and its trace. This point will be discussed further in chapter 8.

28. It is not clear that this would also hold if we allowed adjunction to the head of a phrasal projection. Given that a lexical item instantiates a head under the feature analysis of categories (as discussed in chapter 2), it is not clear how such an adjunction would operate. I leave this as an open question.

**Chapter 4**

1. This is in contrast to the transformations discussed previously, where there was almost no interaction between the different rules. The one exception was the case where *Wh*-Movement could apply to an NP containing a relative clause before the relative clause was extraposed (i.e., adjoined to VP). Given the discussion in appendix B of chapter 3, *Wh*-Movement and CP-Extraposition could have applied in either order.

2. The distinction between present and past tense is taken to be syntactic—that is, one that accounts for the differences in the syntactic forms of sentences. Whether there is also a semantic (or interpretive) significance to this distinction as applied across the full class of auxiliaries is left open. Perhaps not. It is not obvious, for example, how *would* is to be analyzed as the semantic past tense of *will* in all cases. In (4a.i) the event described takes place in the past and so a case can be made that *would* should be interpreted as the semantic past tense of *will*. In a sentence like *Bernie would work on his Yugoslavia project on if you were to pay him $50*, where the event is hypothetical, *would* does not appear to translate as the past tense of *will*. For further discussion of the interpretation of tenses, see Hornstein 1990.

3. Designating *will* as the present tense form of the modal rather than the infinitive form is motivated in part by the fact that modals, in contrast to the other two auxiliary forms, cannot occur in infinitival clause constructions (i.e., sentential constructions where the infinitive form of the leftmost auxiliary or verb is preceded by *to*).

(i) a. *John expects Bill to will leave by 4 p.m. today
 b. John expects Bill to have left by 4 p.m. today
 c. John expects Bill to be leaving by 4 p.m. today

If *have* and *be* in (i) are the infinitive forms of the perfective and progressive auxiliaries, then (i.a) indicates that the morphological paradigm for the modal we have given as *will/would* (henceforth WILL) does not contain a "no tense" form. This also holds for the other modal auxiliaries (e.g., CAN, MAY, and SHALL).

4. In chapter 2, categorial features were expressed with capital letters, following the standard convention in the literature. In this chapter and throughout the remainder of this text categorial features will be expressed in lower case letters. The reason for the change is that under the multiple feature analysis of categories, the equivalence between a single feature and a category disappears. In this instance, [+v] encompasses auxiliary verbs (perfective aspect, progressive aspect, and the modals) as well as main verbs. Categorially, these four classes must be kept distinct, for obvious reasons.

5. This condition was first proposed, though in a slightly different form, in Lasnik 1981a. The main difference between Lasnik's analysis and the one developed here is that Lasnik formulates the rule of Affix Hopping as an adjunction operation, whereas we are assuming that it involves substitution.

6. It should be noted at this point that the movement of affixes does not appear to be a general phenomenon. For example, nonverbal affixes like the plural affix on nouns or the comparative and superlative affixes on adjectives are never subject to movement operations. If we assume that affixes are designated in terms of features, then verbal affixes that undergo Affix Hopping would be analyzed as [+affix, -n], in contrast to nominal and adjectival affixes (which are presumably [+affix, +n]). However, given our assumptions about the form of the Affix Hopping rule and the base-generated verbal string, this distinction need not be made explicit in the analysis that follows.

7. Nothing further will be said here regarding the feature [-finite]. In the remainder of this chapter we will concentrate on the syntax of finite clauses. The analysis of infinitivals is discussed in chapter 5 and following.

8. Since the aspectual auxiliaries have fixed forms—in contrast to modals, which allow for some choice among lexical items—we may suppose that the forms [HAVE + EN] and [BE + ING] are base generated as grammatical formatives and are therefore not subject to lexical insertion. These auxiliaries will be distinguished from modals via a feature [±modal] and also from each other via a feature [±perfective]. The motivation for these feature distinctions will become clear when we deal with the details of the transformational analysis in section 4.5.

9. In previous analyses (e.g., Chomsky and Lasnik 1977) the absence of complementizers in embedded clauses resulted from deletion in CP. Under the assumption that complementizers optionally undergo lexical insertion, such deletions seem to be unnecessary. A question also arises concerning the variable in term 3 of (30). It is obvious that this operation must be clause-bounded; that is, it cannot involve an auxiliary of one IP and a C that is not adjacent to that IP. We might imagine that the Subjacency Condition holds for verb movement. This will block long-distance movements. However, Subjacency alone does not account for the impossibility of successive cyclic movements of the auxiliary from C to C. How such movements are prohibited remains to be determined.

10. Three historical notes: (i) In early transformational grammar the output of the base component was called *deep structure* and the output of the transformational component was called *surface structure.* (ii) In the earliest models of transformational grammar lexical insertion was done by phrase structure rule. (iii) Prior to 1974 what we are calling S-structure did not involve traces.

11. An alternative position, that D-structure is the unique level for semantic interpretation, was first proposed in Katz and Postal 1964, and developed during the late 1960s and early 1970s under a model of grammar known as **generative semantics**. Also see Chomsky 1965 for some discussion of this position.

Under this hypothesis, we could avoid complicating the auxiliary rules with respect to the negative *not* by postulating an abstract D-structure marker NEG that obligatorily triggers the insertion of *not* by a transformation. Note that the same strategy would have to be applied in the case of interrogatives, given that the interpretation of an indicative and its corresponding interrogative must be distinguished. One disadvantage to such proposals is that they necessitate marking rules as optional or obligatory—thereby requiring a less constrained theory of transformations than we have been assuming.

The alternative position, that D-structure alone is insufficient to determine the semantic interpretation of all sentences, was pursued under the designation **interpretive semantics**. Proponents argued that certain facts about the scope of quantifiers and negation (among others) supported the view that S-structure was relevant to interpretation. See Jackendoff 1972 for some discussion.

If D-structure is not the unique level for semantic interpretation, then there is no need to tag interrogative or negative sentences with abstract D-structure markers that act as triggers for certain obligatory transformations. Under this model, the affirmative/negative and indicative/interrogative distinctions are established at S-structure. Thus SAI and Negative Insertion do not affect the semantic interpretation of sentences in this model because it does not exist prior to S-structure.

12. When a negative c-commands a quantifier, the quantifier is said to be in the **scope** of the negative. The scope of an operator "includes whatever is dominated by the constituent immediately dominating it" (Harman 1972:32). This applies generally to all logical operators in syntactic structure.

13. Given this adjunction operation, Postulate I of appendix B, chapter 3 (only maximal projections may be adjunction sites) must be revised as follows:

Postulate I (revised)
Only maximal projections or nonphrasal categories may be adjunction sites.

To this we might add the following:

Postulate II
Only a maximal phrasal projection or a nonphrasal element may be moved by adjunction or substitution.

As revised, Postulate I now allows [+aux] to be an adjunction site for *Not*-Contraction; and Postulate II allows *not* (a nonphrasal element) to be moved via adjunction. With Postulates I and II as formulated above, it would be possible for an adjunction operation to adjoin a maximal projection to a lexical head, or conversely, to adjoin a head to a maximal projection. Thus, we might further restrict the possibilities for movement rules by imposing some sort of compatibility condition on adjunctions (similar to the Nondistinctness Condition on substitutions) such that movement by adjunction may only involve equivalent categories—thus, maximal projections may only adjoin to maximal projections and heads may only adjoin to heads. The exact formulation of the postulates and such ancillary conditions as may be required is an open empirical question.

14. Note that Aux Raising will not create a context in which *Do*-Support would apply improperly since the empty aux position will be marked [+aspect] and therefore be distinct from *do*, which is [-aspect].

15. Lasnik notes that (74) is a slight modification of the Elsewhere Condition proposed by Kiparsky 1973:94.

**Chapter 5**

1. Recall that this is necessary given that the analysis of pronominal genitives like *her* as in *her theory*. To prevent *'s*-Insertion from applying to pronominal NPs, it was necessary to invoke a prohibition against multiply Case-marked NPs. Since the pronoun is already inherently marked for genitive Case, the *'s* Case marking cannot be added to the pronoun's maximal phrasal projection. If we extend this analysis to pronouns in other NP positions, then presumably they are also not subject to Case marking per se.

2. There is an alternative analysis under which Case assignment always involves Case marking. Suppose that pronouns are treated like nonpronominal Ns and therefore are not marked for Case in their lexical entries. Under this analysis, the lexical entries for pronouns would be a set of features minus a Case feature. Hence, the lexical entries for pronouns would not be associated with a phonological representation in the lexicon. A pronoun would receive a phonetic realization only after it was specified for Case—which would not happen until after the pronoun (i.e., the set of features minus Case) was marked for Case in the syntax. In the case of *'s*-Insertion, the *'s* would have to be incorporated in the feature matrix for the pronoun; otherwise, the pronoun could not be phonetically realized and the *'s* would violate the DAC as formulated in chapter 4. Whether this is a better analysis than the one given in the text remains to be determined.

3. There remains a question about adjacency with respect to nominative Case assignment. In sentences like *John already owns two copies of that book* the subject NP is not adjacent to the AGR element in Infl that assigns nominative Case. We could say that nominative Case is nonetheless assigned under adjacency at underlying structure and then the adverb is moved between the subject and verb. But if this is possible, then we may not have a Case-theoretic explanation for the deviance of **John read quickly the book* where the adverb separates the object NP from its Case assigner V. The deviance of such examples would then have to be accounted for by an analysis of adverb movements that prohibits placing an adverb between a verb and its object.

4. In contrast to this analysis of infinitival IP, we would want to say that finite IP is somehow projected from a head with lexical features (e.g. ±n, ±v) for reasons that will become clear in section 5.2.2.

5. In some earlier treatments (e.g., Chomsky and Lasnik 1977; Lasnik and Freidin 1981) the *for*-complementizer was subject to a deletion rule. Thus, it was possible that *for* could assign Case and then delete—a possibility that had to be blocked to prevent the derivation of examples like (32) where the *wh*-phrase has been Case marked by *for*, which has subsequently deleted.

6. Although SPEC-head agreement accounts for examples like (35a) and (36a), it does not explain why a *wh*-phrase cannot occur in the same CP that takes as [+Q] complementizer.

(i) a. *it is unclear [$_{CP}$ who$_i$ whether [$_{IP}$ PRO to believe e$_i$]]
b. *it is unclear [$_{CP}$ who$_i$ whether [$_{IP}$ anyone believed e$_i$]]

In earlier treatments (see note 5) such constructions were ruled out by a filter prohibiting a "doubly filled COMP" (under the analysis that there was a phrasal category COMP that contained only the *wh*-phrase and the complementizer):

(ii) **Doubly Filled COMP Filter**
*[$_{COMP}$ $\alpha$ $\beta$]
where $\alpha$ and $\beta$ are lexical.

However, this analysis is no longer viable since there is no category that contains only the *wh*-phrase and the complementizer as constituents.

7. Earlier analyses assumed the deletion analysis and with it the model of grammar illustrated in figure (i).

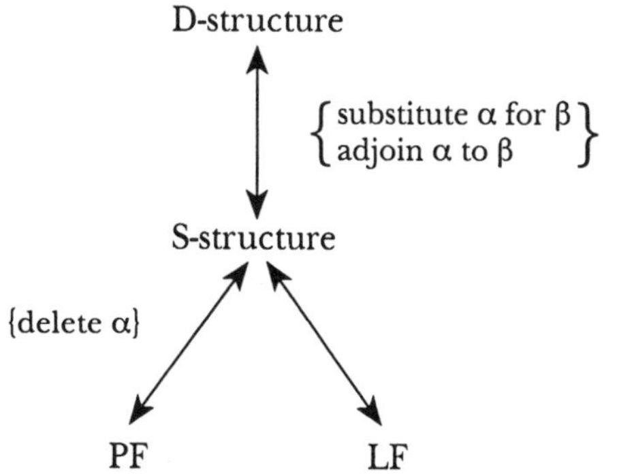


**Figure i.**

PF (for "phonetic form") is a level of syntactic representation distinct from D- and S-structure which interfaces with the articulatory/acoustic properties of sentences. The mapping from S-structure to PF involves the deletion operation, contraction rules, phonological rules, and perhaps other operations (e.g., Case Assignment, as in Lasnik and Freidin 1981). This gives essentially Chomsky and

Lasnik's (1977) model of grammar where S-structure maps onto two different levels of representation, PF and LF (for "logical form").

Under this model there are four levels of syntactic representation—each presumably associated with its particular set of well-formedness conditions (filters). For example, the *For-To* Filter would apply at PF. If, however, the *for*-complementizer is optionally inserted and never deleted, then the filter could just as well apply at S-structure and the role that a level of PF plays in the syntax is called into question.

One consequence of this model is that the derivation from D-structure to LF is deletion-free. Thus, the noncompounding of elementary operations with the deletion elementary now follows from the organization of the grammar.

8. The fact that the null NP moves CP-to-CP in these examples (to avoid a Subjacency violation) suggests that this null NP is actually a null *wh*-phrase and that its traces are essentially *wh*-traces.

9. This is a fairly standard assumption in most of the current literature (see Chomsky 1986a). Alternatively, we could limit the definition of "barrier to government" to only maximal phrasal projections of lexical heads. Thus, finite IP would always be a barrier, whereas infinitival IP would never be a barrier. CP would be a barrier just in case it contained a lexical complementizer. If the adjacency requirement for Case ignores empty categories, then CP-deletion will be unnecessary and both Subjacency and the Case Filter can apply at S-structure. The details of this suggestion need to be filled in. See Van Riemsdijk and Williams 1986:292f. for further discussion of the "transparency" of CP with respect to government.

10. Notice that if CP-deletion applied to a finite clause complement, the verb taking the complement could not govern the subject of the complement since finite IP would be a barrier to government.

11. (58a) does not have the interpretation of (58b-c) where *unusual* is being predicated of an event—that is, the interpretation corresponding to the structure (58b).

12. See Freidin 1975b for a discussion of passive participles as adjectives and Wasow 1977 for a critique of this position.

13. It should be noted that this property appears to hold across languages with certain qualifications. See section 5.3 for some discussion of this phenomenon in Russian and Icelandic.

14. The trace in object position is a way of representing that the surface syntactic subject *they* bears the same logical relation to the verb *arrested* as the grammatical function object in the corresponding active sentence *The police arrested them.*

15. Why (61b.i) is ill formed, in contrast to (61a.i), remains to be explained. (61b.i) would be excluded if the passive participle of *want* did not allow CP-deletion. Then (61b.i) would violate the ECP. But this is a mere stipulation and further suggests that the lexical properties of verbs and their corresponding passive predicates can be different. This opens the way for a lot of variation between the syntactic behavior of a verb and its corresponding passive predicate. In general this does not seem to be the case, but compare the following examples:

(i) a. $John_i$ is said $[_{IP}\ e_i$ to be a brilliant student]
b. *they said (for) John to be a brilliant student

The active form of the verb *say* does not allow an infinitival complement, but its corresponding passive form is a CP-deletion predicate.

16. Something more must be said about how Case is assigned to subjects of infinitival complements of predicate adjectives (e.g., (56)). The difference between the passive cases in (61) and the predicate adjective cases in (56) remains to be explained.

17. In Russian NPs, the modifiers of N (e.g., Det and Adj) are morphologically marked with the same Case as the noun they modify. This phenomenon will be discussed in detail later in the text.

18. Whether *dovolen* in these examples should be analyzed as an adjective or a verb is a topic of debate. See Babby 1973 for discussion.

19. When Q is configurationally Case marked genitive (e.g., as an adnominal genitive), N* is also marked genitive. Of course, the end result cannot be distinguished from constructions where the whole NP is lexically Case marked genitive.

20. See Babby 1987 for a detailed analysis of this construction, and Pesetsky 1982a for a different analysis.

21. There is an extensive literature on the subjecthood of sentence-initial lexically Case-marked NPs in Icelandic. See Cole et. al. 1980, Zaenen, Maling, and Thráinsson 1985, and Sigurðsson 1989 for extensive discussion.

22. The facts concerning Icelandic passives are actually more complicated. For some discussion, see Zaenan, Maling, and Thráinsson 1985, Sigurðsson 1989, and Freidin and Sprouse 1991.

**Chapter 6**

1. Note that we are assuming here that control PRO and noncontrol PRO are syntactically identical.

2. Recall that PRO in Icelandic can be Case-marked (see (78) in chapter 5), so we do not want to prohibit Case-marked PRO generally. The Case-marked PRO we discussed for Icelandic was, however, not Case-licensed.

3. Although this analysis works for *believe*-type verbs, it is not sufficient for predicates where CP-deletion is optional. Consider the distribution of noncontrol PRO in the infinitival complements of predicate adjectives.

(i) a. $[_{IP}$ it is unlikely $[_{CP}$ for $[_{IP}$John to write a book in a month]]]
b. $[_{IP}John_i$ is unlikely $[_{IP}\ e_i$ to write a book in a month]]
c. *$[_{IP}$ it is unlikely $[_{IP}$ PRO to write a book in a month]]]
d. *$[_{IP}$ it is unlikely $[_{CP}$ C $[_{IP}$ PRO to write a book in a month]]]

(i.a) shows that *unlikely* takes a full CP infinitival complement, and (i.b) establishes that CP-deletion must be possible so that the subject trace of the complement satisfies the ECP (compare (7b) in the text). Although (i.c) is ruled out by the constraint that PRO cannot occur in a Case-licensed position, nothing so far rules out the analysis (i.d), since it does not violate this constraint. Nonetheless, (i.d) is not a well-formed sentence of English—in contrast to (7c), which has the same structure.

4. The qualification "from CP" in (13b) is necessary at this point since we need to exclude binding between subjects of finite clauses, as in (i).

(i) *Jill$_i$ was expected [$_{IP}$ e$_i$ had recommended Sam]

The trace is locally bound, though not lexically governed since finite IP is a barrier to government in the analysis presented here. See section 6.3.1.2 for further discussion.

5. Under an alternative analysis proposed for (11) (see Chomsky 1986a), the *wh*-phrase remains in situ at the level of representation relevant to the ECP. Thus, it could be that the *wh*-phrase moves at LF but not at S-structure. The lack of movement could be ensured by a prohibition against "vacuous movement" (movement that has no effect on the linear order of a sentence). Note that this would have to apply globally to prevent movement of both the subject and an auxiliary into CP (e.g., *who$_i$ has$_j$ e$_i$ e$_j$ seen John*) since there would be derivations of these structures for which neither movement was "string vacuous" in the relevant sense.

6. See Lasnik and Saito 1984 for discussion of why an intermediate trace in CP must be subject to the ECP.

7. Chomsky and Lasnik 1977 proposed the filter in (i), prohibiting structures containing a *that*-complementizer followed by a trace.

(i) ***that*-Trace Filter**
*[*that* - e$_i$]

Since (i) covers only these constructions, it is less general than a constraint like the ECP. Furthermore, there are exceptions to (i) with respect to relative clause and cleft constructions (see section 6.1) that require a more complicated formulation of the filter (see Chomsky and Lasnik 1977 and Chomsky 1980 for discussion). See also Pesetsky 1982b for discussion of complementizer-trace phenomena across languages.

8. Chomsky (1986a) offers a further proposal for an ECP account of the *that*-trace effect. He suggests that antecedent government be subject to a **Minimality Condition** whereby a category $\alpha$ cannot govern a category $\beta$ when a category $\gamma$ governs $\beta$ and is structurally closer to $\beta$ than $\alpha$. Note that this analysis of government differs significantly from the one developed here. Nonetheless, the following sketch of Chomsky's proposal should be intelligible.

To illustrate with the *that*-trace violation in (11a): since the complementizer *that* is a governor that is closer to the subject trace than the trace in SPEC-CP, antecedent government by the trace in CP is blocked by the Minimality Condition—hence, the subject trace yields an ECP violation, assuming that the complementizer does not count as a lexical governor of the subject trace. Note too that if the Minimality Condition blocks antecedent government between a subject and the local CP, then there is a danger that it will block antecedent government between a trace in CP and its binder in a local CP.

If this analysis is viable, then it also accounts for all "doubly filled COMP" violations (see chapter 5, note 6) with respect to subject trace. Thus, the set of violations *$[_{CP}$ who$_i$ {that, for, whether} $[_{IP}$ e$_i$... ]] all reduce to ECP violations via blocking of antecedent government under the Minimality Condition. This does not account for the other "doubly filled COMP" violations not involving an adjacent subject trace. These would have to be handled in other ways, which perhaps might be redundant with respect to the ECP cases.

For discussion of potential problems with an ECP analysis of the *that*-trace effects, see Lasnik and Saito 1984.

9. Chomsky and Lasnik's (1977) analysis did this by stipulating the exceptions in an "unless" clause as part of the *that*-Trace Filter. In subsequent attempts to derive the effects of the filter with the ECP, it is often the case that whatever rules out complementation structures also rules out the single clause relatives. Consider, for example, the analysis sketched in note 8.

10. In some analyses, it is assumed that the relative pronoun is moved into CP and then deleted, with the result that its index is assigned to the complementizer. The analysis is referred to as **COMP Indexing**.

The mechanism of COMP Indexing has been used to argue that the ECP holds at LF. The argument concerns an account of Superiority effects (see section 3.3) with respect to LF representations where *Wh*-Movement applies again after S-structure. The basic idea is that the Superiority Condition violation in (i) and the well-formed sentence in (ii) have the LF representations (iii) and (iv), respectively, which are derived at LF via *Wh*-Movement and COMP Indexing.

(i) *what did who see

(ii) who saw what

(iii) $[_{CP}$ [who$_i$ what$_j$]$_j$ did$_k$ $[_{IP}$ e$_i$ $[_{I*}$ e$_k$ see e$_j$]]]

(iv) $[_{CP}$ [what$_j$ who$_i$]$_i$ did$_k$ $[_{IP}$ e$_i$ $[_{I*}$ e$_k$ see e$_j$]]]

Under this analysis, $e_i$ in (iii), which is not properly governed, violates the ECP, whereas $e_i$ in (iv), which is antecedent-governed by the coindexed *wh*-phrase complex, does not. $e_j$ in both examples satisfies the ECP by being lexically governed by the verb *see*. Since the index of the *wh*-phrase in SPEC-CP is fixed at S-structure, the LF movement of a *wh*-phrase out of subject position in a finite clause will automatically create an ECP violation, whereas *wh*-movement out of a lexically governed position does not.

Like the Superiority Condition, this ECP account would also rule out well-formed examples such as *Which books did which students read?*, as discussed in chapter 3. (See Lasnik and Saito 1984 for further discussion of problems with the ECP account of Superiority.)

Though we will leave it at this point, this argument for the LF analysis of the ECP merits closer consideration. For such an analysis that extends the ECP to adjunct traces (as opposed to traces in grammatical function positions) see Lasnik and Saito 1984.

11. Cleft sentences may also be constructed with a PP instead of an NP, as in *It was to Mary that John sent the book*.

12. It is important to note here that the complementizer for non-interrogative sentential complements, *at*, is distinct from the complementizer for relative clauses, which is always *som*.

13. See chapter 5, note 7 for remarks on where deletions might be organized in a grammar. Under that model, this analysis requires that the ECP be a filter on PF representations. In note 10, we looked at an argument that the ECP applies at LF. Does this provide counterevidence to the proposal regarding pro-drop languages or is it possible that the ECP applies at both levels of representation?

14. We cannot use the less complicated example (i) to illustrate why we need additional constraints on trace binding because it violates the Case Uniqueness Principle.

(i) *[$_{IP}$ John$_i$ likes e$_i$]

*John* in (i) would be marked nominative in its S-structure position and also objective via inheritance from its trace in object position.

15. Alternatively, it could be hypothesized that this argument function is assigned to the head of an NP—for example, to *criticism* in (31f)—and not the maximal phrasal projections of N-heads. The choice between these alternatives is not crucial at this point. We will return to it later.

16. A single θ-role can of course be assigned to a conjunction of NPs and hence spread to each conjunct. Thus, in (i) both *police* and *FBI* have the θ-role of *arrest* associated with the subject position in an active sentence, and similarly for the object of the passive *by*-phrase in (ii).

(i) the police and the FBI arrested John

(ii) John was arrested by the police and the FBI

17. This principle was first suggested in Freidin 1975b:fn. 20 to account for the fact that a passive *by*-phrase cannot occur with the active form of a verb. Additional motivation came from motional predicates like *give*. There are two syntactic configurations in which an NP can be assigned the θ-role Goal: either as the indirect object of a double object construction or as the object of the preposition to. Suppose that the phrase structure rules of the grammar generate a V-NP-NP-PP construction and that lexical insertion yields the following ill-formed sentence.

(i) *Adam gave Bernie a present to Barbie

If the verb *give* can assign the θ-role Goal to only one NP, then either *Bernie* or *Barbie* will not be assigned a θ-role (see below in the text for how this situation is to be dealt with). Alternatively, if the representation of (i) assigns the θ-role Goal to both NPs, then (i) violates Unique Assignment.

18. Semantically null lexical NPs (e.g., existential *there*, as in (i.a), and nonreferential (or pleonastic) *it*, as in (i.b)) can appear in nonthematic positions.

(i) a. there is growing support for linguistics at Princeton
b. it was reported that Smith was traveling under an alias

Existential *there*, like nonreferential *it*, also occurs as the subject of a passive construction.

(ii) a. there was reported to be increasing interest in linguistics at Princeton.
b. [$_{IP}$ there$_i$ was reported [$_{IP}$ e$_i$ to be [$_{NP:i}$ increasing interest in linguistics]] at Princeton]

(ii.b) is the S-structure representation of (ii.a). This provides stronger evidence than (40) that the subject position in a passive construction is a nonthematic position. As Howard Lasnik (personal communication) points out, the fact that (40) is ill formed shows only that the subject position in a passive and the object of the *by*-phrase in the same construction cannot both be thematic. For detailed discussion of the syntax of pleonastic elements, see Emonds 1976, Milsark 1977, Stowell 1978, Davis 1984a, and Williams 1984.

19. Otherwise, a lexical argument could be base-generated in a nonthematic position and then moved to a thematic position at S-structure. As far as linguists have determined to date, trace binding with this property—where the trace is in a nonthematic position and its lexical antecedent is in a thematic position—does not occur. Consider (i):

(i) *[$_{IP}$ John$_i$ reported [$_{IP}$ e$_i$ to be likely [$_{CP}$ that Bill will win the race]]]

By hypothesis, *John* has moved from the nonthematic subject position of *be likely* to the thematic subject position of *reported*. Note that the related example (ii), where the pleonastic *it* has replaced the trace, is well formed, as is (iii), where movement starts from a thematic position in the most deeply embedded IP and moves successive cyclically to nonthematic positions.

(ii) [$_{IP}$ John$_i$ reported [$_{IP}$ it to be likely [$_{CP}$ that Bill will win the race]]]
(iii) [$_{IP}$ John$_i$ is reported [$_{IP}$ e$_i$ to be likely [$_{IP}$ e$_i$ to win the race]]]

Here too Case theory overlaps with Functional Relatedness (see exercise 6.7). (Case Uniqueness also accounts for (i) since John will be marked nominative in its main clause subject position and also objective via inheritance from its trace, which is governed by the matrix verb *reported* (as required by the ECP).)

20. One of the earliest proposals regarding extraction out of finite clauses was called the **Tensed-S Condition** (see Chomsky 1973), which prohibited movement out of tensed clauses. To distinguish between NP-movement and *wh*-movement, it was necessary to stipulate that a node COMP in a structure [$_{S'}$ COMP S] (where S' corresponds to our CP and COMP is a category containing what are now called SPEC-CP and C) served as an "escape hatch" for movements with respect to the Tensed-S Condition.

21. The original proposal for this condition was the **Specified Subject Condition** (see Chomsky 1973), which prohibited extraction over a "specified" subject. The exact characterization of "specified" for that version of the condition was somewhat complicated, for reasons that need not concern us here. As we will see, all subjects (including empty subjects) in fact count as "specified subjects."

22. Both examples violate the Case Uniqueness Principle since the matrix

subjects *John* in (57a.i) and *a unicorn* in (57a.ii) will be assigned Case in their S-structure positions and via inheritance from their respective traces. We could eliminate this by turning the main clauses into infinitivals and embedding the result as the complement of a CP-deletion predicate adjective. The resulting monstrosity would not violate Case Uniqueness.

(i) *it is likely [$_{IP}$ John$_i$ to be expected [$_{CP}$ for [$_{IP}$ Mary to like e$_i$]]

23. Note that (57b.ii) also violates the Case Filter since *Mary*, as the object of a passive participle, will not be marked for Case. Whether there is independent empirical motivation for the claim that PRO subjects create binding domains remains to be established. As there appears to be no empirical evidence against the claim, we will assume that the most general statement—"domain of subject" is correct (but see chapter 7).

24. Positions that can be directly assigned θ-roles are A-positions; therefore, an object position or the subject position in an active sentence is an A-position. This designation applies generally to all such positions, even in cases where a particular verb (e.g., *seem*) does not assign any θ-role to its subject.

25. Another way to derive the deviant sentence *John was reported had recommended Mary* involves movement through an embedded CP, as illustrated in (i).

(i) *John$_i$ was reported [$_{CP}$ e$_i$ [$_{IP}$ e$_i$ had recommended Mary]]

This binding between *John* and the trace in CP does not violate the Proper Binding Condition. Instead, the example involves CP-to-NP movement in violation of the requirement for CP-to-CP movement. In chapter 8 we will look at an account of examples like (i) as another kind of binding violation.

26. This explanation also applies to (60c.i), so we cannot use the example to establish unequivocally that the ECP holds for Portuguese. The paradigm in (60) is compatible with a proper binding analysis; however, (60b) also violates Case Uniqueness, under the assumption that the matrix subject *eles* is doubly marked for nominative Case by AGR in the infinitival complement and also by AGR in the matrix IP.

27. A clitic pronoun is a type of pronoun that cannot occur in a grammatical function position and therefore usually occurs in front of a verb, as in (61b.i) or as a suffix of a verb, as in the following Spanish examples (from Perlmutter 1971:75):

(i) a. quería seguir gritándomelo
he-wanted to-continue shouting=to-me=it
'he wanted to continue shouting it to me'
b. quería seguirmelo gritando
he-wanted to-continue=to-me=it shouting
'he wanted to continue shouting it to me'

Note that the clitics in (i.a-b) can also occur in front of the matrix finite verb, as shown in (ii).

(ii) me lo quería seguir gritando

to-me it he-wanted to-continue shouting
'he wanted to continue shouting it to me"

28. That it is assigned follows from the part of the θ-Criterion that states that each θ-role of a predicate must be assigned.

29. The syntactic analysis of alternations like (63b-c) remains an open question. For example, are (63b-c) transformationally related? If so, what is the D-structure position of the embedded CP? What is the matrix clause structure for (63c)? For discussion of alternative analyses, see Emonds 1972, 1976, Koster 1978b, and Baltin 1978a.

30. This is always true of traces, but not always true of PRO, which can occur without any antecedent (so-called noncontrol PRO), as in (i).

(i) it is impossible [PRO to revise a book manuscript in a week]

31. Saying that PRO cannot be lexically governed, however, may not be sufficient to account for all the facts concerning the distribution of PRO. In particular, the prohibition against lexically governed PRO does not exclude the possibility of its occurring in the subject of finite clauses, as in (i), unless we assume that the copula *be* (in Infl?) can lexically govern the subject position in IP.

(i) *John$_i$ believes [$_{CP}$ that [$_{IP}$ PRO$_i$ is happy]]

Otherwise, something else must account for (i).

32. Note that *likely* is used in (74b) rather than *difficult* so that the subject trace will not also violate the ECP. The predicate adjective *difficult* does not allow CP-deletion, as shown in (i).

(i) *John is difficult to shave himself

33. Although the binding of PRO by the main clause subject is obligatory in (74a), this is due to the presence of the reflexive pronoun *himself*, and not to some lexical property of the adjective *difficult* or the matrix verb *found*. In (i), where the reflexive is replaced with a name (e.g., *Bill*), *John* need not be interpreted as the controller of PRO.

(i) after the accident John found [$_{CP}$ that [$_{IP}$ it was difficult [$_{CP}$ [$_{IP}$ PRO to shave Bill]]]]

Although the preferred interpretation of (i) might be the anaphoric one, it is still possible to interpret (i) as containing an instance of noncontrol PRO. In general, obligatory control structures (where an infinitival complement must have a PRO subject and that subject is always interpreted as anaphoric on a particular argument (e.g., subject or object) of a c-commanding verb) involve a verb and its complement (see (71) above). As far as I know, there are no languages with verbs that impose obligatory control between their subject or object and a noncomplement PRO. That is, we do not find obligatory control relationships where a controller binds a PRO across an intervening subject.

34. The CED accounts for the impossibility of extracting an interrogative *wh*-phrase from a subject NP of a finite clause in Italian. Such extractions are

not covered by the formulation of Subjacency motivated in section 3.2.3. For discussion of the CED, see Davis 1984b, Browning 1987, and Chomsky 1986a (where the CED is reduced to a formulation of Subjacency).

## Chapter 7

1. Given that reference is an expression-to-world relation whereas anaphora is a expression-to-expression relation (see Neale 1990), let us try to avoid talking about reference in defining the notion "antecedence." Following Neale 1990, let us say that β is the *antecedent* of α where α is anaphoric on β. "Roughly, we can say that an expression α is *anaphoric* on an expression β if and only if (*i*) the semantical value of α [its denotation—RF] is determined, at least in part, by the semantical value of β, and (*ii*) β is not a constituent of α" (p. 167). Thus, it is more accurate to say that some linguistic expression is *anaphoric on* some other linguistic expression (which is its antecedent).

2. The following examples show that an anaphor may take a pronoun as an antecedent.

(i) a. $he_i$ believes [$_{IP}$ $himself_i$ to be clever]
 b. $they_i$ considered [$_{IP}$ each $other_i$ to be responsible for the accident]

3. Recall that the standard definition for c-command is as follows:

A category α c-commands a category β iff the first branching category that dominates α dominates β and neither α nor β dominates the other.

The proviso regarding c-command and binding distinguishes the following cases:

(i) a. $Mary_i$ believes [$_{CP}$ that $she_i$ is clever]
 b. each $woman_i$ believes [$_{CP}$ that $she_i$ is clever]

(ii) a. when $Mary_i$ won an award, [$_{IP}$ $she_i$ was delighted]
 b. *when each $woman_i$ won an award, [$_{IP}$ $she_i$ was delighted]

In (i.a-b) the pronoun is c-commanded by *Mary* and the quantificational phrase *each woman*, but in (ii.a-b) the pronoun is not c-commanded by either NP. In (i.b) the quantificational phrase can function as an antecedent to the pronoun, but not in (ii.b). Thus, (i.b) can have the interpretation (iii), but (ii.b) cannot have the interpretation (iv).

(iii) (for each woman *x*) [*x* believes [that *x* is clever]]

(iv) (for each woman *x*) [[when *x* won an award] [*x* was delighted]]

On the basis of this distinction, we will assume that only when a pronoun is c-commanded by an antecedent is it bound. The pronoun in (ii.a) is not bound even though it has an antecedent.

4. The same pattern holds for binding of an object in a PP complement.

(i) a. *$we_i$ expect [$_{CP}$ (that) [$_{IP}$ Mary will send a letter [$_{PP}$ to each $other_i$]]]
 b. *$we_i$ expect [$_{IP}$ Mary to send a letter [$_{PP}$ to each $other_i$]]

Therefore, in what follows only the object of the verb cases will be cited under the assumption that what holds for them also holds for the PP object constructions. In this section the reciprocal *each other* is used as an example of an anaphor. Unless otherwise noted, corresponding examples using reflexive pronouns can also be constructed.

5. With the definition of c-command in note 3 it is not absolutely clear whether a subject is in its own c-command domain. If a category does not dominate itself, then it could c-command itself given this definition. Rather than pursue this truly arcane question any further, we will assume that c-command can only hold between two categories that are in a linear precedence relation and that no category is in a linear precedence relation with itself.

6. See Chomsky's discussion on page 209f, which contains some additional assumptions that will not be discussed here.

7. The similarity between this condition and the one for NP-trace developed in section 6.3.1.1 will be discussed in section 8.3.2.

8. The SPEC-NP position is designated as a subject based on the correspondence between certain nominal constructions and sentences, as illustrated in (1).

(i) a. they reviewed three new movies
 b. their review of three new movies

There is also a correspondence between the passive sentence construction and a nominal, as illustrated in (ii).

(i) a. three new movies were reviewed by them
 b. a review of three new movies by them

Assuming that only an underlying syntactic subject can occur as the object of a passive *by*-phrase, we conclude that the third person plural pronoun in the nomimal construction is a syntactic subject when it occurs in front of the head noun.

9. For an alternative characterization of the notion "accessible SUBJECT" see Chomsky 1981:211f. The approach is not without empirical problems; see Freidin 1986:fn. 14 for an example.

10. Some speakers may not find the (ii)-examples fully acceptable. The point is that they are more acceptable than one would expect if pleonastic NPs were equivalent to nonpleonastic NPs for determining binding domains.

11. For the remainder of this chapter and the next, I will use the term "c-command" generically to stand for whatever the appropriate command relation is. For English we have seen some evidence for choosing m-command as the correct command relation. In the languages discussed in sections 7.1.2.1-7.1.2.3 we will not cover the syntax of the clause in such detail. A propos the terms "c-command" and "m-command," see Chomsky 1981:sec. 3.2.1 for a proposal to redefine c-command in terms of m-command.

12. Rappaport notes that whether reflexive binding in Russian is actually subject-oriented is a complicated issue. See his footnote 5 for references.

13. Presumably subject-oriented binding for reflexives holds only within a clause, but not across a clause boundary.

14. However, there are examples in Icelandic where bound PRO does not block reflexive binding by an antecedent outside the infinitival clause.

(i) a. Jón$_i$ leyfði mér$_j$ [$_{CP}$ að PRO$_j$ raka sig$_i$]
'John allowed me to shave himself'

b. Jón$_i$ skipaði mér$_j$ [$_{CP}$ að PRO$_j$ raka sig$_i$]
'John ordered me to shave himself'

The difference between (39) and the examples in (i) is that in (39) PRO is bound by a subject whereas in (i) it is bound by an object. Given that reflexive binding in Icelandic appears to be subject-oriented, it may be that only subject-bound PRO in these examples counts as a bound SUBJECT. The issue is complicated—see Maling 1986 for discussion.

15. This is a controversial issue (see Hong 1985 and Koster 1982).

16. Given the striking correspondence between the IP-paradigms for anaphor binding and pronoun binding cited above in (56)-(57), it might appear that the domain statement for Principle B is identical to that of Principle A and thus that bound pronouns are impossible just where anaphors are possible. It was this correspondence that motivated earlier analyses (e.g., Chomsky 1981) in which the domain statements of Principles A and B were taken to be identical. As we will see, the facts concerning the NP-paradigm indicate a different conclusion.

17. We will postpone discussing accessibility until we have discussed the NP-paradigm for pronouns because the facts concerning this paradigm bear crucially on the question of accessibility for pronoun binding.

18. The following examples show that "any subject" includes the subject of NP.

(i) a. John$_i$ doesn't read [$_{NP}$ Mary's books about him$_i$]
b. *Mary doesn't read [$_{NP}$John's$_i$ books about him$_i$]

19. Some speakers find (61a) on the anaphoric reading to be unacceptable.

20. The example in (61a) seems unexceptional. However some linguists have questioned the grammaticality of a related example (i) (see, for example, Chomsky 1982:fn. 24).

(i) ?*John$_i$ reads [$_{NP}$ books about him$_i$]

Just how the binding domain varies among speakers is unclear. It seems that the addition of negation improves acceptability. Similar judgments appear to hold for the pair *like* and *dislike*. As observed in Lasnik and Uriagereka 1988, though examples like (i) (and their example (30b) on page 37: *?John$_i$ saw pictures of him$_i$*) may be somewhat deviant, they seem substantially better than the standard Principle B violations like (56a) and (57a.ii) in the text.

21. Therefore, the issue of accessibility of AGR (or Infl) for pronoun binding never arises, as it did with anaphors.

22. In contrast to the questionable status of (61a) and similar examples involving simple sentence cases, the grammaticality of (63a-b) is unexceptional.

23. The notions "θ-domain" and "domain of subject" are conceptually connected in that a subject marks the periphery of a θ-domain. A θ-domain is what Chomsky 1986b designates as a "complete functional complex."

24. For discussion of alternative proposals, see Freidin 1986 and the works cited there.

25. Therefore, in a construction involving an NP that contains two conjoined NPs and binds a pronoun (as in (i)), the two conjuncts would not be considered as split antecedents.

(i) $[_{NP}$ Bernie and Adam] thought that they would leave in an hour

In such cases, the two conjuncts are in the same grammatical function position and share the same θ-role.

26. (70b) seems less felicitous than (70c). Substituting *clue in* for *tell* improves the acceptability with the binding relation in (70b).

(i) $\text{Adam}_i$ clued $\text{Bernie}_j$ in about $\text{himself}_j$

27. For further discussion on the analysis of split antecedence and the indexing of pronouns, see the appendix in Lasnik 1989a.

28. The notion of coreference used here is that of "intended coreference," not "actual coreference." For some discussion of potential difficulties with the notion "intended reference," see Higginbotham 1980a and Heim 1982.

29. An alternative solution to the problem of indexing is to construct a second index for NPs that will allow us to express the relation of disjoint reference. Indeed, Chomsky (1980b) has proposed that NPs have two distinct indices, a referential index consisting of a single integer, and an anaphoric index consisting of a set of integers. The anaphoric index of an NP is constructed from the set of c-commanding referential indices. Thus, *They like him* and *He likes them* would have the indexed representations given in (i).

(i) a. $\text{they}_{(i,\{\emptyset\})}$ like $\text{him}_{(j,\{i\})}$
b. $\text{he}_{(i,\{\emptyset\})}$ likes $\text{them}_{(j,\{i\})}$

The index (j, {i}) indicates that an NP with the referential index *j* must be disjoint in reference from an NP with the referential index *i*. Intersecting reference (both partial and complete) between a pronoun and a c-commanding NP would be possible only if the anaphoric index of the pronoun did not contain the referential index of the NP.

See Chomsky 1980b and Freidin and Lasnik 1981 for discussion of this approach, and Chomsky 1981 for some criticism. An extremely lucid discussion of the issue of indexing vis-à-vis binding theory is given in Lasnik 1981b.

**Chapter 8**

1. For further discussion see section 8.1.2 and Lasnik 1989b.

2. Note that if a copy of an R-expression is substituted for the epithet, a grammatical sentence also results—thereby providing further evidence that the

matrix subject does not c-command the subject position in the subordinate clause.

3. For a concrete analysis, let us assume that the fronted CP forms an adjunction structure with IP.

(i) $[_{\wedge IP}$ CP $[_{IP}$ NP was slicing onions]]

One piece of evidence for this is the fact that such constructions can occur as embedded clauses following an overt complementizer, as in (ii).

(ii) Mary remembered that when John cut his finger, he was slicing onions.

4. Some of the earliest work on pronominal coreference in generative grammar assumed that linear precedence as well as some notion of command was required. See Langacker 1966, Jackendoff 1972, and Lasnik 1976 for some important discussion. The problem with including linear precedence in the statement of binding conditions is that most (if not all) of the facts follow from c-command given the facts about branching direction in phrase structure. This position is discussed in Reinhart 1976, 1981.

5. Lasnik's formulation differs from the one given in (18). His proposal is that an R-expression is free *in its governing category*. The term "governing category" is defined as follows: $\beta$ is a *governing category* for $\alpha$ if and only if $\beta$ is the minimal category containing $\alpha$, a governor of $\alpha$, and a SUBJECT accessible to $\alpha$.

6. In support of this notion of hierarchy, Lasnik notes that in Japanese and Korean an anaphor cannot bind a pronoun. The fact that this is possible in some languages (e.g., English) suggests that cuts on this hierarchy will differ from language to language. Presumably a native English speaker knows that there is no cut between pronouns and anaphors on the basis of positive evidence.

7. In this case, the formulation of Principle C given in (6), rather than the two subparts discussed in section 8.1. Since the remainder of this chapter deals exclusively with English, we will retain the formulation of Principle C given in (6), which covers both subparts. Note, though, that the examples discussed in this section are specifically violations of Principle C'.

8. S'-structure, a level of representation that differs minimally from S-structure only in that certain CP brackets have been deleted (as discussed in chapter 5) will not be considered separately.

9. Note that a sentence corresponding to (27a) is also deviant (Howard Lasnik, personal communication).

(i) *$[_{IP}$ it seems to $her_i$ $[_{CP}$ that $[_{IP}$ $Jill_i$ was happy]]]

This cannot be a Principle C violation however since the pronoun does not c-command (or m-command) the R-expression it is coindexed with. (See section 8.1.1 for other examples.) Nonetheless, however we account for (i), (27b) violates Principle B and shows that certain Principle B violations result from NP-movement and therefore are not manifested until S-structure.

10. This analysis is not without problems—see Higginbotham 1983 for some discussion. An alternative to the LF analysis has been suggested in Van Riemsdijk and Williams 1981. This proposal involves postulating an interme-

diate level of representation between D- and S-structure called **NP-structure** that indicates the results of NP-movement but (crucially) not the results of *wh*-movement. Like the other proposals in this domain, the NP-structure analysis also runs into empirical problems, as we will see in the discussion of (40)-(42) in the text.

11. The same points can be made with structures using a pair of R-expressions. The pronoun is used here to bind the R-expression to avoid any oddness that results from repeating names in the same sentence.

12. Moreover, the sentence (i) is perfectly acceptable—in contrast to the corresponding example for pronouns mentioned in note 9 and repeated below as (ii).

(i) $[_{IP}$ it seemed to $John_i$ $[_{CP}$ that $[_{IP}$ $he_i$ was happy]]]

(ii) *$[_{IP}$ it seems to $her_i$ $[_{CP}$ that $[_{IP}$ $Jill_i$ was happy]]]

This again seems to be a linear order effect, not a binding effect. However, the following example is not deviant at all (Howard Lasnik, personal communication):

(ii) $[_{IP}$ it seems to $[_{NP}$ $her_i$ mother] $[_{CP}$ that $[_{IP}$ $Jill_i$ was happy]]]

Note further that if we substitute the name for the pronoun in (i), the result (iii) is only slightly odd in contrast to the perfectly acceptable (i).

(iv) ?$[_{IP}$ it seemed to $John_i$ $[_{CP}$ that $[_{IP}$ $John_i$ was happy]]]

Still, compared to the completely unacceptable (ii), (iv) seems relatively well formed.

13. (40) also presents a difficult problem for the NP-structure model of Van Riemsdijk and Williams mentioned in note 10.

14. Under this analysis, the LF representation of (40c) would be something along the lines of (i).

(i) (for which $x$ such that $[_{CP}$ that $John_k$ revised $x$], $x$ = a report ) did $[_{IP}$ $he_k$ $e_j$ submit $x$]

In this representation, the relative clause modifies the variable. To derive the representation on which the binding principles apply, we replace the variable in IP by the phrase it represents—in this case *a report.*

15. The LF representation of (42) would include the nominal complement *that John was a genius* as part of the specification of the variable. Thus, the representation would be derived from something like (i).

(i) (for which $x$, $x$ = a report $[_{CP}$ that $John_k$ was a genius]) did $[_{IP}$ $he_k$ $e_j$ submit $x$]

The LF reconstruction results when the variable in IP is interpreted as the phrase it represents—in this case *a report that John was a genius.* In the relative clause case (e.g. (44)) the variable is given as "x = a report" which is modified by the relative clause. This difference accounts for the difference in LF reconstruction effects.

For discussion of the issues concerning LF representations, see Williams 1986, 1988 and May 1988, as well as the works cited therein.

Along the same line, note that Principle C must apply to structures prior to the rule of Quantifier Raising (QR).

(i) *he$_i$ liked [$_{NP}$ every motet that Bach$_i$ wrote]

Since QR will adjoin the quantified NP to IP, the R-expression *Bach* will not be bound in the resulting structure. Thus, the Principle C effects for relative clauses moved by *Wh*-Movement and QR differ. This indicates that the Principle C holds at a level of representation following reconstruction at LF, but prior to QR.

16. Although it is generally true that traces created by NP- or *wh*-movement are bound in the structures in which they occur, it is not true that the trace left by extraposition is ever bound (see section 6.3.1).

17. This analysis is due to May 1979. For further discussion of May's analysis and the binding-theoretic account of crossover phenomena, see Freidin and Lasnik 1981.

18. For further discussion of crossover phenomena, see appendix A.

19. The fact that *wh*-trace is subject to a principle of binding theory raises the question of whether binding theory can be extended to other empty categories. As discussed in appendix B, such extensions to NP-trace and PRO are problematic.

20. For discussion of how Subjacency might relate to government, see Kayne 1983 and Chomsky 1986a. For discussion of the notion of locality in syntax, see Koster 1978a and Culicover and Wilkins 1984.

21. This distinction comes from Wasow 1979.

22. The formulation is from Chomsky 1976. The designation "Leftness Condition" is due to Higginbotham 1980b, which contains some important critical discussion.

23. The paradigms for *wh*-trace and quantified NP are taken from Higginbotham 1980b. It should be noted that Higginbotham marks the (iii)-examples as "???" whereas I have marked them as ill formed on a par with the (iv)-examples.

24. The LF representations of (57c) and (58c) are as follows:

(i) (for which $x$, $x$ = a person) [$_{IP}$ [$_{NP}$ his$_i$ mother] love $x_i$]

(ii) ($\forall x$, $x$ = a boy) [$_{IP}$ [$_{NP}$ his$_i$ mother] love $x_i$]

25. Unlike strong crossover, where the same analysis holds for interrogative and relative pronouns, weak crossover does not hold for the corresponding relative pronoun cases. Consider the following pair of sentences.

(i) a. the boy who his mother rejected had no place to go
b. the boy whose mother he rejected had no place to go

The weak crossover case (i.a) allows two interpretations; the strong crossover case (i.b) allows only one.

26. The overlap is, however, only partial. As illustrated in note 25, relative clauses do not show weak crossover effects. Thus, the Leftness Condition analysis would require that the trace of a relative pronoun is not analyzed as a variable at LF. This conclusion would then leave us with no explanation for the relative clause facts with respect to strong crossover.

27. It should be noted that the term "crossover" comes from an earlier stage in the development of generative syntax when research was focused on the behavior of rules, rather than on the representations they produce.

28. See Lasnik 1985 for further discussion of illicit movement constructions that appear to slip through loopholes in the binding theory.

29. (72) is structurally equivalent to example (12) in Lasnik 1985), given below as (i).

(i) *John$_i$ is believed [(that) [he$_i$ is proud e$_i$]]
(cf. it is believed that John is proud of himself)

That is, (i) does not have the interpretation of the italicized sentence.

30. The fact that PRO must be bound by *John* in (76) is not required by either the predicate adjective *easy* or the matrix verb *know*, as illustrated in (i).

(i) a. it isn't easy [$_{CP}$ C [$_{IP}$ PRO to shave in the dark]]
b. John$_i$ knows [$_{CP}$ that [$_{IP}$ it isn't easy [$_{CP}$ C [$_{IP}$ PRO$_j$ to outmaneuver him$_i$ on a committee]]]]

In (i.a) there is no antecedent for PRO. In (i.b) the matrix subject *John* cannot be the antecedent of PRO since it is bound to the pronoun *him*. If it were bound to PRO, then PRO would also bind the pronoun, in violation of Principle B. That PRO must be bound by the matrix subject in (76) is required by the lexical anaphor *himself*. Although PRO structurally binds the anaphor in its binding domain, it appears that the antecedent of the anaphor must bear all the f-features (i.e., number, person, and gender) that the anaphor has inherently. Presumably PRO has no inherent $\phi$-features and must get them via binding to a lexical antecedent.

31. Assuming that *expect* allows optional CP-deletion (in contrast to *believe*, which requires obligatory CP-deletion with infinitival complements), the representation in (75a) is ill formed; however, the sentence would be allowed with the representation (i) where CP-deletion has not applied.

(i) we$_i$ expect [$_{CP}$ C [$_{IP}$ PRO$_i$ to see Mary at the meeting]]

Taking CP to be a barrier to government, PRO is not lexically governed.

An alternative solution would be to say that PRO cannot be lexically governed by its minimal governor (i.e., subject to the Minimality Condition discussed in chapter 6, note 8). Under the X-bar analysis of clauses we have adopted, PRO in (75a) would be governed by nonfinite Infl (instantiated as the grammatical formative *to*). Assuming that the maximal phrasal projection of a nonlexical head does not constitute a barrier to government, then PRO would also be governed by the matrix V. However, its minimal governor would be nonlexical and so (75a) would not violate the modified prohibition against lexically governed PRO. Note that this alternative no longer accounts for the fact that *believe*-type verbs cannot take an infinitival complement with a PRO subject (see the discussion in section 5.2.2). Although this result renders the alternative less attractive than the CP-deletion analysis, notice that something more has to be said about the bound PRO constructions in order to exclude the possibility of unbound PRO. The exclusion of unbound PRO for *expect*-type verbs (and others, such as *try*) would probably extend automatically to *believe.* Then if *believe* simply precludes bound PRO as a lexical property, we no longer need the CP-deletion analysis to account for the fact that *believe* cannot occur with an infinitival complement that has a PRO subject.

32. See Freidin 1986 and Koster 1987 for some critical discussion. Williams 1980 presents a different approach to the analysis of PRO binding.

# References


Abraham, W., ed. (1983). *On the formal syntax of the Westgermania.* John Benjamins, Amsterdam.

Adams, M. (1984). Multiple interrogatives in Italian. *The Linguistic Review* 4, 1–27.

Akmajian, A. (1975). More evidence for an NP cycle. *Linguistic Inquiry* 6, 115–129.

Akmajian, A., S. Steele, and T. Wasow (1979). The category AUX in Universal Grammar. *Linguistic Inquiry* 10, 1–64.

Anderson, S. (1986). The typology of anaphoric dependencies: Icelandic (and other) reflexives. In Hellan and Christensen 1986.

Anderson, S., and P. Kiparsky, eds. (1973). *A festschrift for Morris Halle.* Holt, Rinehart and Winston, New York.

Andrews, A. (1976). The VP complement in modern Icelandic. In *Proceedings of the sixth annual meeting, NELS.* Department of Linguistics, Harvard University, Cambridge, Massachusetts.

Andrews, A. (1982). The representation of case in modern Icelandic (1982). In Bresnan 1982.

Aoun, J. (1985). *A grammar of anaphora.* MIT Press, Cambridge, Massachusetts.

Aoun, J., N. Hornstein, D. Lightfoot, and A. Weinberg (1987). Two types of locality. *Linguistic Inquiry* 18, 537–577.

Aoun, J., and D. Sportiche (1982). On the formal theory of government. *The Linguistic Review* 2, 211–236.

Babby, L. (1973). The deep structure of adjectives and participles in Russian. *Language* 49, 349–360.

Babby, L. (1980a). *Existential sentences and negation in Russian.* Karoma, Ann Arbor.

Babby, L. (1980b). The syntax of surface Case marking. In *Cornell working papers in linguistics* 1. Department of Modern Languages and Linguistics, Cornell University, Ithaca, New York.

Babby, L. (1987). Case, prequantifiers, and discontinuous agreement in Russian. *Natural Language and Linguistic Theory* 5, 91–138.

Baker, C. L. (1979). Syntactic theory and the projection problem. *Linguistic Inquiry* 10, 533–581.

Baker, C. L., and J. McCarthy, eds. (1981). *The logical problem of language acquisition.* MIT Press, Cambridge, Massachusetts.

Baltin, M. (1978a). Toward a theory of movement rules. Doctoral dissertation, MIT. [Published by Garland, New York, 1985.]

Baltin, M. (1978b). PP as bounding node. In *Proceedings of the eighth annual meeting, NELS.* Department of Linguistics, University of Massachusetts, Amherst.

Baltin, M. (1981). Strict bounding. In Baker and McCarthy 1981.

Baltin, M. (1982). A landing site theory for movement rules. *Linguistic Inquiry* 13, 1–38.

Baltin, M., and A. Kroch, eds. (1989). *Alternative conceptions of phrase structure.* University of Chicago Press, Chicago, Illinois.

Belletti, A., L. Brandi, and L. Rizzi, eds. (1981). *Theory of markedness in generative grammar: Proceedings of the 1979 GLOW conference.* Scuola Normale Superiore di Pisa, Pisa.

Besten, H. den (1983). On the interaction of root transformations and lexical deletive rules. In Abraham 1983.

Blake, B. (1990). *Relational grammar.* Routledge, London.

Bouchard, D. (1984). *On the content of empty categories.* Foris, Dordrecht.

Bresnan, J. (1971). Sentence stress and syntactic transformations. *Language* 47, 257–281.

Bresnan, J., ed. (1982). *The mental representation of grammatical relations.* MIT Press, Cambridge, Massachusetts.

Brody, M. (1984). On contextual definitions and the role of chains. *Linguistic Inquiry* 15, 355–380.

Browning, M. A. (1987). ECP ≠ CED. *Linguistic Inquiry* 20, 481–491.

Browning, M. A. (1991). Bounding conditions on representation. *Linguistic Inquiry* 22, 541–562.

Browning, M. A. (forthcoming). Comments on "relativized minimality." [To appear in the proceedings of the 2nd Princeton Workshop on Comparative Grammar.]

Burzio, L. (forthcoming). The role of antecedent in anaphoric relations. [To appear in the proceedings of the 2nd Princeton Workshop on Comparative Grammar.]

Chomsky, N. (1957). *Syntactic structures.* Mouton, The Hague.

Chomsky, N. (1963). Formal properties of grammars. In Luce, Bush, and Galanter 1963.

Chomsky, N. (1965). *Aspects of the theory of syntax.* MIT Press, Cambridge, Massachusetts.

Chomsky, N. (1966). *Cartesian linguistics.* Harper and Row, New York.

Chomsky, N. (1970). Remarks on nominalizations. In Jacobs and Rosenbaum 1970. [Reprinted in Chomsky 1972c.]

Chomsky, N. (1972a). *Language and mind.* Enlarged edition. Harcourt Brace Jovanovich, New York.

Chomsky, N. (1972b). Some empirical issues in the theory of transformational grammar. In Peters 1972. [Reprinted in Chomsky 1972c.]

Chomsky, N. (1972c). *Studies on semantics in generative grammar.* Mouton, The Hague.

Chomsky, N. (1973). Conditions on transformations. In Anderson and Kiparsky 1973. [Reprinted in Chomsky 1977b.]

Chomsky, N. (1975a). *Reflections on language.* Pantheon, New York.

Chomsky, N. (1975b). *The logical structure of linguistic theory*, Plenum Press, New York. [Also published by University of Chicago Press, Chicago, Illinois, 1985.] [Manuscript written 1955–1956.]

Chomsky, N. (1976). Conditions on rules of grammar. *Linguistic Analysis* 2, 303–351. [Reprinted in Chomsky 1977b.]

Chomsky, N. (1977a). On wh-movement. In Culicover, Wasow and Akmajian 1977.

Chomsky, N. (1977b). *Essays on form and interpretation.* North-Holland, New York.

Chomsky, N. (1980a). *Rules and representations.* Columbia University Press, New York.

Chomsky, N. (1980b). On binding. *Linguistic Inquiry* 11, 1–46. [Reprinted in Heny 1981.]

Chomsky, N. (1981). *Lectures on government and binding.* Foris, Dordrecht.

Chomsky, N. (1982). *Some concepts and consequences of the theory of government and binding.* MIT Press, Cambridge, Massachusetts.

Chomsky, N. (1986a). *Barriers.* MIT Press, Cambridge, Massachusetts.

Chomsky, N. (1986b). *Knowledge of language: Its nature, origin, and use.* Praeger, New York.

Chomsky, N. (1991). Some notes on the economy of derivation and representation. In Freidin 1991.

Chomsky, N., and H. Lasnik (1977). Filters and control. *Linguistic Inquiry* 8, 425–504.

Cinque, G. (1980). On extraction from NP in Italian. *Journal of Italian Linguistics* 5, 47–99.

Cole, P., W. Harbert, G. Hermon, and S. Sridhar (1980). On the acquisition of subjecthood. *Language* 56, 719–743.

Comrie, B. (1981). *Language universals and linguistic typology: Syntax and morphology.* University of Chicago Press, Chicago, Illinois.

Culicover, P. (1976). A constraint on coreferentiality. *Foundations of Language* 14, 109–118.

Culicover, P., T. Wasow, and A. Akmajian, eds. (1977). *Formal syntax.* Academic Press, New York.

Culicover, P., and W. Wilkins (1984). *Locality in linguistic theory.* Academic Press, Orlando, Florida.

Davidson, D., and G. Harman, eds. (1972). *Semantics of natural language.* Reidel, Dordrecht.

Davis, L. J. (1984a). Arguments and expletives. Doctoral dissertation, University of Connecticut, Storrs.

Davis, L. J. (1984b). Entailments of the CED. In *Cornell working papers in linguistics* 6. Department of Modern Languages and Linguistics, Cornell University, Ithaca, New York.

Emonds, J. (1970). Root and stucture preserving transformations. Doctoral dissertation, MIT.

Emonds, J. (1972). A reformulation of certain syntactic transformations. In Peters 1972.

Emonds, J. (1976). *A transformational approach to English syntax: Root, structure preserving, and local transformations.* Academic Press, New York.

Emonds, J. (1978). The verbal complex V'–V in French. *Linguistic Inquiry* 9, 151–175.

Emonds, J. (1985). *A unified theory of syntactic categories.* Foris, Dordrecht.

Feynman, R. (1965). *The character of physical law.* MIT Press, Cambridge, Massachusetts.

Fiengo, R. (1974). Semantic conditions on surface structure. Doctoral dissertation, MIT.

Fiengo, R. (1977). On trace theory. *Linguistic Inquiry* 8, 35–61.

Fodor, J., and J. Katz, eds. (1964). *The structure of language: Readings in the philosophy of language.* Prentice-Hall, Englewood Cliffs, New Jersey.

Freidin, R. (1975a). Review of Jackendoff 1972 in *Language* 51, 189–205.

Freidin, R. (1975b). The analysis of passives. *Language* 51, 384–405.

Freidin, R. (1978a). Review of Emonds 1976 in *Language* 54, 407–416.

Freidin, R. (1978b). Cyclicity and the theory of grammar. *Linguistic Inquiry* 9, 519–549.

Freidin, R. (1983). X-bar theory and the analysis of English infinitivals. *Linguistic Inquiry* 14, 713–722.

Freidin, R. (1986). Fundamental issues in the theory of binding. In Lust 1986.

Freidin, R., ed. (1991). *Principles and parameters in comparative grammar.* MIT Press, Cambridge, Massachusetts.

Freidin, R., and L. Babby (1984). On the interaction of lexical and structural properties: Case structure in Russian. In *Cornell working papers in linguistics* 6. Department of Modern Languages and Linguistics, Cornell University, Ithaca, New York.

Freidin, R., and W. Harbert (1983). On the fine structure of the binding theory: Principle A and reciprocals. In *Proceedings of the thirteenth annual meeting, NELS.* Department of Linguistics, University of Quebec at Montreal.

Freidin, R., and H. Lasnik (1981). Disjoint reference and *wh*-trace. *Linguistic Inquiry* 12, 39–53. [Reprinted in Lasnik 1989b.]

Freidin, R., and A. C. Quicoli (1989). Zero stimulation for parameter setting. *Behavioral and Brain Sciences* 12, 338–339.

Freidin, R., and R. A. Sprouse (1991). Lexical case phenomena. In Freidin 1991.

George L., and J. Kornfilt (1981). Finiteness and boundedness in Turkish. In Heny 1981.

Greenberg, J. (1963). *Universals of language.* MIT Press, Cambridge, Massachusetts.

Grimshaw, J. (1990). *Argument structure.* MIT Press, Cambridge, Massachusetts.

Grosu, A. (1981). *Approaches to island phenomena.* North-Holland, New York.

Gruber, J. (1965). Studies in lexical relations. Doctoral dissertation, MIT.

Gruber, J. (1976). *Lexical structures in syntax and semantics.* North-Holland, New York. [Includes Gruber 1965.]

Haegeman, L. (1991) *Introduction to government and binding theory.* Basil Blackwell, Oxford, England.

Harman, G. (1972). Deep structure as logical form. In Davidson and Harman 1972.

Hasegawa, K. (1968). The passive construction in English. *Language* 44, 230–243.

Heim, I. (1982). The semantics of definite and indefinite noun phrases. Doctoral dissertation, University of Massachusetts, Amherst.

Hellan, L., and K., Christensen, eds. (1986). *Topics in Scandanavian syntax.* Reidel, Dordrecht.

Heny, F., ed. (1981). *Binding and filtering.* MIT Press, Cambridge, Massachusetts.

Heny F., and B. Richards, eds. (1983). *Linguistic categories: Auxiliaries and related puzzles.* 2 vols. Reidel, Dordrecht.

Higginbotham, J. (1980a). Anaphora and GB: Some preliminary remarks. In *Proceedings of the tenth annual meeting, NELS.* Department of Linguistics, University of Ottawa.

Higginbotham, J. (1980b). Pronouns and bound variables. *Linguistic Inquiry* 11, 679–708.

Higginbotham, J. (1983). Logical form, binding, and nominals. *Linguistic Inquiry* 14, 395–420.

Hong, S. (1985). A and Ā-binding in Korean and English. Doctoral dissertation, University of Connecticut, Storrs.

Hornstein, N. (1991). *As time goes by: Tense and Universal Grammar.* MIT Press, Cambridge, Massachusetts.

Hornstein, N., and D. Lightfoot, eds. (1981). *Explanation in linguistics: The logical problem of language acquisition.* Longman, London.

Horrocks, G. (1987). *Generative grammar.* Longman, London.

Huang. C.-T. J. (1982). Logical relations in Chinese and the theory of grammar. Doctoral dissertation, MIT.

Huang, C.-T. J. (1989). PRO-drop in Chinese: A generalized control theory. In Jaeggli and Safir 1989.

Hust, J., and M. Brame (1976). Jackendoff on interpretive semantics. *Linguistic Analysis* 2, 243–277.

Jackendoff, R. (1972). *Semantic interpretation in generative grammar.* MIT Press, Cambridge, Massachusetts.

Jackendoff, R. (1977). *X–bar syntax: A study of phrase structure.* MIT Press, Cambridge, Massachusetts.

Jackendoff, R. (1990). *Semantic structures.* MIT Press, Cambridge, Massachusetts.

Jacobs, R., and P. Rosenbaum, eds. (1970). *Readings in English transformational grammar.* Ginn, Waltham, Massachusetts.

Jacobson, P. (1977). The syntax of crossing coreference sentences. Doctoral dissertation, University of California at Berkeley. [Published by Garland, New York, 1980.]

Jaeggli, O., and K. Safir, eds. (1989). *The null subject parameter.* Kluwer, Dordrecht.

Katz, J., and P. Postal (1964). *An integrated theory of linguistic descriptions.* MIT Press, Cambridge, Massachusetts.

Kayne, R. (1975). *French syntax: The transformational cycle.* MIT Press, Cambridge, Massachusetts.

Kayne, R. (1980). Extensions of binding and case-marking. *Linguistic Inquiry* 11, 75–96. [Reprinted in Kayne 1983b.]

Kayne, R. (1983a). Connectedness. *Linguistic Inquiry* 14, 223–249. [Reprinted in Kayne 1983b.]

Kayne, R. (1983b). *Connectedness and binary branching.* Foris, Dordrecht.

Kayne, R., and J. Y. Pollock (1978). Stylistic inversion, successive cyclicity, and move NP in French. *Linguistic Inquiry* 9, 595–621.

Keyser, S. J., ed. (1978). *Recent transformational studies in European languages.* MIT Press, Cambridge, Massachusetts.

Kimball, J., ed. (1974). *Syntax and semantics,* vol. 4. Academic Press, New York.

Kiparsky, P. (1973). Elsewhere in phonology. In Anderson and Kiparsky 1973.

Klima, E. (1964). Negation in English. In Fodor and Katz 1964.

Koopman, H., and D. Sportiche (1982). Variables and the Bijection Principle. *The Linguistic Review* 2, 135–170.

Koster, J. (1978a). *Locality principles in syntax.* Foris, Dordrecht.

Koster, J. (1978b). Why subject sentences don't exist. In Keyser 1978.

Koster, J. (1982). Counteropacity in Korean and Japanese. In *Tilburg papers in language and literature* 13. Tilburg University, Holland.

Koster, J. (1987). *Domains and dynasties: The radical autonomy of syntax.* Foris, Dordrecht.

Koster, J. and E. Reuland (1991). *Long-distance anaphora.* Cambridge University Press, Cambridge.

Kroch, A., and A. Joshi (1986). Analyzing extraposition in a tree-adjoining grammar. In *Papers on tree adjoining grammar: The linguistic relevance of TAG.* vol. 2, Department of Computer and Information Science, University of Pennsylvania.

Kupin, J. (1978). A motivated alternative to phrase markers. *Linguistic Inquiry* 9, 303–308.

Langacker, R. (1966). Pronominalization and the chain of command. In Reibel and Schane 1966.

Lasnik, H. (1976). Remarks on coreference. *Linguistic Analysis* 2, 1–22. [Reprinted in Lasnik 1989.]

Lasnik, H. (1981a). Restricting the theory of transformations: A case study. In Hornstein and Lightfoot 1981. [Reprinted in Lasnik 1990.]

Lasnik, H. (1981b). On two recent treatments of disjoint reference. *Journal of Linguistic Research* 1, 48–58. [Reprinted in Lasnik 1989b.]

Lasnik, H. (1985). Illicit NP movement: locality conditions on chains? *Linguistic Inquiry* 16, 481–490. [Reprinted in Lasnik 1989b.]

Lasnik, H. (1989a). On the necessity of binding conditions. In Lasnik 1989b. [Also in Freidin 1991.]

Lasnik, H. (1989b). *Essays on anaphora.* Kluwer, Dordrecht.

Lasnik, H. (1990). *Essays on restrictiveness and learnability.* Kluwer, Dordrecht.

Lasnik, H., and R. Freidin (1981). Core grammar, case theory, and markedness. In Belletti, Brandi, and Rizzi 1981. [Reprinted in Lasnik 1990.]

Lasnik, H., and J. Kupin (1977). A restrictive theory of transformational grammar. *Theoretical Linguistics* 4, 173–196. [Reprinted in Lasnik 1990.]

Lasnik, H., and M. Saito (1984). On the nature of proper government. *Linguistic Inquiry* 15, 235–289. [Reprinted in Lasnik 1990.]

Lasnik, H., and M. Saito (1992). *Move α.* MIT Press, Cambridge, Massachusetts.

Lasnik, H., and T. Stowell (1991). Weakest crossover. *Linguistic Inquiry* 22.4.

Lasnik, H., and J. Uriagereka (1988). A course in GB syntax: Lectures on binding and empty categories. MIT Press, Cambridge, Massachusetts.

Lightfoot, D. (1982). *The language lottery: Toward a biology of grammars.* MIT Press, Cambridge, Massachusetts.

Luce, D., R. Bush, and E. Galanter, eds. (1963). *Handbook of mathematical psychology*, vol. 2. Wiley, New York.

Lust, B., ed. (1986). *Studies in the acquisition of anaphora: Defining the constraints.* Reidel, Dordrecht.

Maling, J. (1986). Clause-bounded reflexives in modern Icelandic. In Hellan & Christensen 1986. [Reprinted in Maling and Zaenen 1990.]

Maling, J., and A. Zaenen, eds. (1990). *Syntax and semantics*, vol. 24, *Modern Icelandic syntax.* Academic Press, New York.

Manzini, M. R. (1983). On control and control theory. *Linguistic Inquiry* 14, 421–446.

May, R. (1979). Must COMP-to-COMP movement be stipulated? *Linguistic Inquiry* 10, 719–725.

May, R. (1988). Ambiguities of quantification and *wh:* A reply to Williams. *Linguistic Inquiry* 19, 118–135.

Milsark, G. (1977). Towards an explanation of certain peculiarities of the existential construction in English. *Linguistic Analysis* 3, 1–29.

Montague, R. (1974). *Formal philosophy: Selected papers of Richard Montague.* Yale University Press, New Haven, Connecticut. [Edited and with an introduction by R. Thomason.]

Muysken, P., and H. C. van Riemsdijk, eds. (1986). *Features and projections.* Foris, Dordrecht.

Neale, S. (1990). *Descriptions.* MIT Press, Cambridge, Massachusetts.

Newmeyer, F. (1983). *Grammatical theory, its limits and its possibilities.* University of Chicago Press, Chicago, Illinois.

Newmeyer, F. (1986). *Linguistic theory in America.* 2nd ed. Academic Press, Orlando, Florida.

Nordgård, T. (1986). *Som* and word order. *Working papers in linguistics* 3. Department of Linguistics, University of Trondheim, Norway.

Partee, B., A. ter Meulen, and R. Wall (1990). *Mathematical methods in linguistics.* Kluwer, Dordrecht.

Perlmutter, D. (1971). *Deep and surface structure constraints in syntax.* Holt, Rinehart and Winston, New York.

Pesetsky, D. (1982a). Paths and categories. Doctoral dissertation, MIT.

Pesetsky, D. (1982b). Complementizer-trace phenomena and the Nominative Island Constraint. *The Linguistic Review* 1, 297–343.

Pesetsky, D. (1987). *Wh*-in-situ: Movement and unselective binding. In Reuland and ter Meulen 1987.

Peters, S., ed. (1972a). *Goals of linguistic theory.* Prentice-Hall, Englewood Cliffs, New Jersey.

Peters, S. (1972b). The projection problem. In Peters 1972a.

Pica, P. (1987). On the nature of the reflexivization cycle. In *Proceedings of the seventeenth annual meeting, NELS.* Department of Linguistics, University of Massachusetts, Amherst.

Pollock, J. Y. (1989). Verb movement, Universal Grammar, and the structure of IP. *Linguistic Inquiry* 20, 365–424.

Postal, P. (1971). *Crossover phenomena.* Holt, Rinehart and Winston, New York.

Quicoli, A. C. (1976a). Conditions on clitic-movement in Portuguese. *Linguistic Analysis* 2, 199–223.

Quicoli, A. C. (1976b). Conditions on quantifier movement in French. *Linguistic Inquiry* 7, 583–607.

Quicoli, A. C. (1987). Inflection and parametric variation: Portuguese vs. Spanish. [To appear in the proceedings of the 2nd Princeton Workshop on Comparative Grammar.]

Rappaport, G. (1986). On anaphor binding in Russian. *Natural Language and Linguistic Theory* 4, 97–120.

Ravin, Y. (1990). *Lexical semantics without thematic roles.* Oxford University Press, Oxford, England.

Reibel, D., and S. Schane, eds. (1966). *Modern studies in English.* Prentice-Hall, Englewood Cliffs, New Jersey.

Reuland, E., and A. ter Meulen, eds. (1987). *The representation of (in)definiteness.* MIT Press, Cambridge, Massachusetts.

Reinhart, T. (1976). The syntactic domain of anaphora. Doctoral dissertation, MIT.

Reinhart, T. (1981). Definite NP anaphora and c-command domains. *Linguistic Inquiry* 12, 605–635.

Reinhart, T. (1983). *Anaphora and semantic interpretation.* Croom Helm, London.

Reinhart, T., and E. Reuland (1991). Anaphoric territories. In Koster and Reuland 1991.

Riemsdijk, H. C. van (1978). *A case study in syntactic markedness: The binding nature of prepositional phrases.* Foris, Dordrecht.

Riemsdijk, H. C. van, and E. S. Williams (1981). NP–structure. *The Linguistic Review* 1, 171–217.

Riemsdijk, H. C. van, and E. S. Williams (1986). *Introduction to the theory of grammar.* MIT Press, Cambridge, Massachusetts.

Rizzi, L. (1980). Violations of the *Wh*-Island Constraint in Italian and the Subjacency Condition. *Journal of Italian Linguistics* 5, 157–195. [Reprinted in Rizzi 1982.]

Rizzi, L. (1982). *Issues in Italian syntax.* Foris, Dordrecht.

Rizzi, L. (1990). Relativized minimality. MIT Press, Cambridge, Massachusetts

Robins, R. H. (1966). The development of the word class system of the European grammatical tradition. *Foundations of Language* 2, 3–19.

Robins, R. H. (1979). *A short history of linguistics.* 2nd edition. Longman, London.

Roeper, T., and E. S. Williams, eds. (1987). *Parameter setting.* Reidel, Dordrecht.

Ross, J. R. (1967). Constraints on variables in syntax. Doctoral dissertation, MIT.

Ross, J. R. (1986). *Infinite syntax!,* Ablex, Norwood, New Jersey. [Published version of Ross 1967.]

Rouveret, A., and J.-R. Vergnaud (1980). Specifying reference to the subject: French causatives and conditions on representations. *Linguistic Inquiry* 11, 97–202.

Russell, B. (1931). *The scientific outlook.* Norton, New York.

Safir, K. (1984). Multiple variable binding. *Linguistic Inquiry* 15, 663–689.

Sells, P. (1985). *Lectures on contemporary syntactic theories: An introduction to government-binding theory, generalized phrase structure grammar, and lexical-functional grammar.* Center for the Study of Language and Information, Stanford University, Stanford, California.

Sigurðsson, H. (1989). Verbal syntax and case in Icelandic. Doctoral dissertation, University of Lund.

Sportiche, D. (1981). On bounding nodes in French. *The Linguistic Review* 1, 219–246.

Steele, S. et. al. (1981). *An encyclopedia of AUX: A study in cross-linguistic equivalence.* MIT Press, Cambridge, Massachusetts.

Stowell, T. (1978). What was there before there was there. *Proceedings of the fourteenth annual meeting, CLS.* Chicago Lingusitics Society, University of Chicago.

Stowell, T. (1983). Subjects across categories. *The Linguistic Review* 2, 285–312.

Stuurman, F. (1985). *Phrase structure theory in generative grammar.* Foris, Dordrecht.

Taraldsen, K. T. (1981). The theoretical interpretation of a class of marked extractions. In Belletti, Brandi, and Rizzi 1981.

Taraldsen, K. T. (1986). *Som* and binding theory. In Hellan and Christensen 1986.

Thráinsson, H. (1979). *On complementation in Icelandic.* Garland Publishers, New York.

Thráinsson, H. (1990). A semantic reflexive in Icelandic. In Maling and Zaenen 1990.

Torrego, E. (1984). On inversion in Spanish and some of its effects. *Linguistic Inquiry* 15, 103–129.

Vergnaud, J.-R. (1985). *Dépendances et niveaux de représentation en syntaxe.* John Benjamins, Amsterdam.

Wall, R. (1972). *Introduction to mathematical linguistics.* Prentice-Hall, Englewood Cliffs, New Jersey.

Wasow, T. (1979). Transformations and the lexicon. In Culicover, Wasow, and Akmajian 1977.

Wasow, T. (1979). *Anaphora in generative grammar.* E. Story-Scientia, Ghent. [Revised version of Anaphoric relations in English, Doctoral dissertation, MIT, 1972.]

Williams, E. S. (1974). Small clauses in English. In Kimball 1974.

Williams, E. S. (1980). Predication. *Linguistic Inquiry* 11, 203–238.

Williams, E. S. (1984). *There*-insertion. *Linguistic Inquiry* 15, 131–153.

Williams, E. S. (1986). A reassignment of the functions of LF. *Linguistic Inquiry* 17, 265–299.

Williams, E. S. (1988). Is LF distinct from S-structure?: A reply to May. *Linguistic Inquiry* 19, 161–168.

Zaenen, A., J. Maling, and H. Thráinsson (1985). Case and Grammatical Functions: The Icelandic passive. *Natural Language and Linguistic Theory* 3, 441–483.

# Index

Boldface type indicates either a reformulation of a rule or principle, or the original formulation of a condition where the page on which it occurs is not the first referenced. Normally, a concept, rule, or principle of grammar is defined or formulated on the first page referenced.